The Princeton Reader

The Princeton Reader

Contemporary Essays by Writers and Journalists at Princeton University

Edited by John McPhee and Carol Rigolot

PRINCETON UNIVERSITY PRESS ■ PRINCETON AND OXFORD

Published by Princeton University Press,
41 William Street, Princeton, New Jersey 08540

In the United Kingdom:
Princeton University Press,
6 Oxford Street, Woodstock, Oxfordshire OX20 1TW

press.princeton.edu

Library of Congress Cataloging-in-Publication Data

The Princeton reader : contemporary essays by writers and journalists at Princeton
University / edited by John McPhee and Carol Rigolot.
     p.   cm.
  Includes index.
  ISBN 978-0-691-14307-1 (hardcover : alk. paper) — ISBN 978-0-691-14308-8
(pbk. : alk. paper)   1. Journalism—United States.   2. Reportage literature,
American.   3. American essays.   I. McPhee, John, 1931–   II. Rigolot,
Carol.   III. Princeton University.
  PN4726.P76   2010
  814'.708—dc22   2010021600

British Library Cataloging-in-Publication Data is available

This book has been composed in Berkeley with Univers display

Printed on acid-free paper. ∞

Printed in the United States of America

10 9 8 7 6 5 4 3 2 1

This book is dedicated to the extraordinary writers who have taught at Princeton University since the beginning of the journalism seminars in 1964 and to our generous benefactors:

Edwin F. Ferris, Princeton Class of 1899, former *New York Herald* journalist and owner and founding editor of the *Scranton Times*, whose bequest in 1957 established the Ferris Professorship in Journalism.

Harold W. McGraw, Jr., Princeton Class of 1940, chief executive of McGraw-Hill from 1975 to 1983, who endowed the McGraw Seminars in recognition of the importance of writing in all disciplines.

Joyce Michaelson, who created the Robbins Professorship in 2000 with a gift from the E. Franklin Robbins Trust, in honor of her late husband, William G. Michaelson, Princeton Class of 1959, and their daughter, Robin L. Michaelson, Princeton Class of 1989.

CONTENTS

PREFACE

JOHN MC PHEE

In 1964, Princeton University was offered a bequest from Edwin Ferris, an alumnus whose intent was to establish a professorship in journalism. The conditions were that if Princeton did not accept the funds, they were to go to the Society of the Home for Friendless Women and Children of the City of Scranton. With a touch of ethical pause, I have long pondered this dichotomy. A decade ago, I mentioned it in the preface to this anthology's twentieth-century predecessor, and also recollected that the chair of Princeton's English Department—called in for consultation, in 1964—had not been similarly burdened with ambiguity. He said, in so many words, that journalism would enter the university's curriculum over his dead body. However, when he was told the size of the bequest, he quickened. Journalistic nonfiction writing—in those years, in most colleges and universities—as yet had no standing or vogue. The beginnings of such courses at Princeton were tentative, experimental, and modest.

For many years, they were presented under the rubric Humanistic Studies and were taught at first, spring and fall, by one visiting professor. In the mid-seventies, the number of courses increased to two—one in the fall semester (Humanistic Studies 447, "Politics and the Press") and one in the spring semester (Humanistic Studies 440, "The Literature of Fact"). Soon, the annual number of teachers and courses grew to three, four, and more as their popularity with students proved durable and the money grew in bull markets. In 1984, meanwhile, McGraw-Hill's publisher Harold McGraw, Jr., also a Princeton alumnus, endowed an essentially identical professorship, augmenting the already burgeoning number of writing courses taught by visiting professors from ever more varied journalistic fields.

At the end of the twentieth century, fifty-eight journalists who had taught at Princeton contributed self-selected examples of their work to this anthology's ancestral volume. In the year of its publication, a third professorship, funded by the E. Franklin Robbins Trust, was created by Joyce Michaelson in honor of her late husband, William Michaelson, Princeton Class of 1959, and their daughter Robin Michaelson, Class of '89, who had studied in the Ferris program. The numbers crescendo continued until there were as many as ten visiting journalists teaching courses in a single academic year.

In all, seventy-five writers have taught Ferris, McGraw, or Robbins courses during the first decade of the twenty-first century. Their contributions are the contents of this book. They came to teach at Princeton not only from the *Washington Post*, the *New York Times*, the *Los Angeles Times*, the *Times* of London, the *Chicago Tribune*, the *Boston Globe*, and *USA Today*, but also from the *Hong Kong Standard*, the Palestinian Institute for Media Studies, and South African Public

Broadcasting. They came from CNN, ABC, NBC, and NPR. They came from the Internet and its colony the blogosphere. They came from *Sports Illustrated*, *Time, Newsweek, New York*, and the *New Yorker*. *Rolling Stone*. They included a producer, a biographer, and a freelance cultural critic. A documentary filmmaker. A medical doctor. Collectively, they had written a hundred and forty-four books. Ten of these twenty-first-century professors returned to Princeton to teach journalism courses in which—or in something very close to which—they once had been students.

All the courses these people taught were absolutely idiosyncratic, in the sense that they reflected the absorptions, passions, commitments, and experience of the visiting professors and not a curricular template laid down by a committee. Much the same are the contents and semirandom structure of this book, which includes memoirs and profiles, pieces on science, pieces on the environment, war correspondence. The book is actually a verbal and informational feast, ranging from a hotel in Sweden made of ice to extraterrestrial aliens and something called the Achenblog, from a tragedy on Lake Minnetonka to arson in Philadelphia, from positional plagiocephaly to the use of hypnosis in the case of a missing child, and from a felon in college football to the pot of gold that is cyberpornography ("Find a website that is in the black and, chances are, its business and content are distinctly blue"). Not to mention Iraq, Afghanistan, Serbia, Indonesia, and many other places and topics.

Nearly all the visiting writers come for a single semester. Within this history, I am a grandfather in more ways than one, having joined the Ferris program when Jimmy Carter was governor of Georgia. All through the years, I have told incoming Ferris, McGraw, and Robbins professors that I would be happy to offer suggestions to help them plan their courses. They thanked me politely and did their own thing.

I would be exceptionally remiss if I did not add here a comment about my coeditor, Carol Rigolot, executive director of Princeton's Council of the Humanities, whose efforts have made my own "co" seem very small, indeed. She helped the authors select the pieces and shepherded them through to their final form. She gave the book its freewheeling, loosely associational, unpigeonholed structure.

And we both thank Beate Witzler, who worked with the writers and with numerous publications to obtain permission to reprint all these pieces. We are grateful to her, to the authors, and to the publishers for making this book possible.

The Princeton Reader

Joel Achenbach is a writer and columnist for the *Washington Post* as well as the author of six books and the Achenblog, which can be found at http://blog.washingtonpost.com/achenblog. This piece is drawn from *Captured by Aliens: The Search for Life and Truth in a Very Large Universe* (Simon and Schuster, 1999).

Aliens

"Anomalistics" is the study of things outside the accepted reality of mainstream science, and as an enterprise, it's a big gamble. It wagers on dark horses, stuff like telepathy, telekinesis, near-death experiences, reincarnation, past-life recall, astral projection, UFOs, the Bermuda Triangle, Bigfoot, Atlantis, interdimensional travel, the "Mars Effect," and the Loch Ness Monster. The payoff on one of these dark horses, should it turn out to be "true," would be phenomenal. For the anomalistic community, there are numerous historical precedents that provide inspiration. Giant squids were supposedly a figment of the imagination of drunken sailors, and then they turned out to be real. And what about meteorites? Mainstream scientists in the eighteenth century refused to believe that rocks could fall from the sky. Such a thing simply *could not be*. Yet it was so. Andy Knoll, a paleobiologist at Harvard and a leading thinker in exobiology circles, told me, "Ninety-nine times out of a hundred, things outside the canonical envelope are wrong. But the hundredth is Copernicus."

On June 24, 1947, amateur pilot Kenneth Arnold saw nine mysterious "disks" flying at otherworldly speed across the Cascade Mountains near Mount Rainier. He assumed they were secret U.S. military planes. His radio report to ground control incited reporters to go to the airport and question him. Arnold told the reporters the objects moved "like a saucer skipping across the water." He was describing their motion, not their shape. But the headline writers took the story from there and boldly declared that Arnold had seen "flying saucers." Two years later, Major Donald Keyhoe, a retired Marine, published an article in the inaptly named *True* magazine in which he established the standard narrative of alien visitation and government cover-up. He expanded the article into a book, *Flying Saucers Are Real*, and a publishing phenomenon was born.

The aliens in those saucers proved, like their science-fiction counterparts, remarkably adaptable to modern civilization. No amount of skepticism and debunking could erase them as a cultural presence. The UFO narrative managed to grow, mutate, and expand far beyond the initial phenomenon of mysterious disks and flashing lights. The lore began to include elements of direct contact, and then abduction, and then breeding experiments. The aliens who had been invisible inside their flying saucers began, by the 1970s, to take on physical form: spindly, hairless bodies trucking around a head the size of a watermelon, the biological warehouse of a phenomenal brain. They were not little green men (that's just science fiction!) but rather had gray skin. Their lidless, black, almond-shaped eyes were pools of darkness in which no emotion could be discerned. In the alien bestiary, the Grays were joined by Tall Nordics, a humanoid species; by Reptilians; and by a smattering of Praying Mantis creatures.

The emergence of these entities was unconstrained by the rejection of the belief system by the mainstream. It didn't matter that Carl Sagan and his fellow astronomers said the evidence for such aliens was uniformly unimpressive. Nor did it matter that the Air Force, in investigations code-named Sign, Grudge, and Blue Book, spent twenty-two years reaching the conclusion that the aliens didn't exist. They could not be so easily vanquished. For many ordinary people, the existence of alien visitors seemed by far the most plausible explanation for the strange things happening in the skies. Many of the "official" explanations were hard to swallow. The scientists claimed that people were sometimes seeing nothing more than a weather balloon, or the planet Venus, or a meteor, or "swamp gas." Clearly, the scientists had a dim view of the intelligence of the average human being. The scientists were essentially saying that everyone who saw a UFO was some kind of moron. Swamp gas! Now that was a stretcher. People didn't know what swamp gas was, exactly, but they knew for certain that they'd never mistake such a thing for a spaceship full of aliens.

If NASA's Henry Harris and his intellectual compatriots were correct, the scientific establishment in the second half of the twentieth century managed to miss the biggest story of all time. The same people who had discovered the structure of the DNA molecule, found subatomic constituents of matter and energy, and photographed craters on the far side of the moon had somehow—amazingly—failed to detect entire fleets of alien starships buzzing around the American West and even in the airspace above Washington, D.C. Carl Sagan and Frank Drake were listening to Andromeda when, if they'd had any sense, they would have been tuning in military radio traffic around Area 51 in Nevada. The true believers have a sense that this can't and won't go on much longer, this collusion of ignorance and outright deception. There is much talk of the "Disclosure." The government has been setting up the big event. The Mars rock? It's all part of the plan, the plan to prepare the public for the shattering news. Many people remember what the Brookings Institution wrote in 1962: that the public might be extremely disturbed by an announcement that intelligent life has been found beyond the Earth and that primitive civilizations often collapse when they come into contact with technologically more advanced civilizations. It all makes sense in the larger context. Of course the government wouldn't reveal the truth about aliens. People would freak. The Disclosure is a long-term project. People are getting warmed up for it. *Close Encounters of the Third Kind* and *E.T.* were just part of the plan.

The UFO enigma can be viewed as an astrosociopolitical issue of great complexity or, more simply, as a question of human psychology. Why do some people construct their worldviews around ideas that other people find ludicrous? Where's the fault line? It's not intelligence or social class. It's not as if poor, fat, Velveeta-eating people believe in aliens and rich, thin, Brie-eating people don't. Socioeconomic and educational status don't seem to be factors of great import. Geography is probably one of the few factors that have an influence. Aliens seem to be more prevalent in the West, and in California they're simply taken for granted, more strange guests at the cocktail party. There are also more aliens in America than in most other nations. In a country like India, the aliens never show up on the radar.

If there is one thing that reliably separates believers from nonbelievers, it is probably the attitude toward intellectual authorities—toward the "reality police." To believe in aliens requires a rejection of official wisdom. It requires that we believe that the individuals in power, and particularly the gatekeepers of scientific knowledge—Carl Sagan, Dan Goldin, and the American Astronomical Society—are either wittingly or through ignorance telling us a story that simply isn't true. Old-guard leftists, feminists, right-wing conservatives, and gun-toting militia members can all be found in UFO circles. They all think they're being lied to, and they're probably right in certain cases. Suspicion is a powerful motivator. When we lose trust in authority, we lose trust in every aspect of it, every assertion, every alleged fact. Out for a dime, out for a dollar.

"Trust no one" is a mantra on *The X-Files*. It's a perfect philosophy for the Age of Bad Information. There has never been a time when a lie could be so professionally produced. Even the charlatans have graduate degrees from the Institute of Advanced Charlatanry. Got a dumb idea? Start a Web site! On the Internet, the extraterrestrial issue is legendarily the second most popular topic, after sex (though I must quickly admit that this is one of those classic Internet factoids that emerge from the digital universe unsourced, their origins a mystery). The new electronic medium is perfect for the transmission of a diffuse UFO mythology in which there is no central governing narrative but, rather, an abundance of theories and anecdotes and half-baked eyewitness accounts and assorted poppycock (undergirded by balderdash). A person can get online and jump from one paranormal site to another, from the writings of a serious ufologist to those of a pure lunatic, endlessly skipping through an infinite network of intrigue. The anarchy of the alien mythology is one thing that makes it so enchanting.

The writers and producers of *The X-Files* understood this perfectly—for years, millions of people watched the painfully gradual unfolding of a vast government conspiracy to cover up some kind of alien-related agenda. The show began in 1993, just as the alien theme was hitting its cultural stride. Creator Chris Carter used the space-alien theme sparingly, and in fact the actual showing of an alien was initially taboo. One of the chief writers in the early years, Glen Morgan, remembers Carter saying, "The minute you see an alien, this show's over."

Instead there were hints and clues about the alien presence and the government cover-up. The show had a "Mythology," as Carter called it. It was a shaggy-dog story—there were always new twists and turns, and no resolution in sight. Gradually, the rule against showing aliens succumbed to creative pressures, and by the time Carter made the first *X-Files* feature film, there was no more playing peekaboo. The Mythology hardened into a fixed narrative: the aliens, it turned out, had cut a deal with evil white men who ran a secret global government, sort of like the Trilateral Commission. The evil white men were going to infect the entire population of the Earth with a virus that would turn humans into slaves of the aliens, in exchange for the aliens' not wiping us out completely, but in fact the aliens had lied to the evil white men and were using the virus to gestate new aliens in the guts of humans. (At least, that's what I think I was seeing up there on the big screen. Plot clarity did not seem to be the movie's paramount aspiration.) The plot is oddly familiar, because it's essentially just a dramatization of what people have been saying in recent years on the fringe of the UFO movement. An alien presence, a breeding program, a massive cover-up—this is virtually plagiarism from a real-life mythology.

The X-Files was spookier when it didn't tell you what was going on. The movie violated the first rule of anomalies: it's what you *don't* know that's really interesting. One day in 1997, I visited *The X-Files'* set in Vancouver to interview Gillian Anderson, the actress who plays Scully. She had just won an Emmy for best actress in a TV drama, and amid her congratulatory flowers, she was engaged in damage control, having failed to thank any of her colleagues in her acceptance speech. She'd already thanked them, she said, when she won a Golden Globe, but that, unfortunately, wasn't as prominent an event. At the Emmys, she'd thanked only her family. This made for some tension on the set in the days afterward, and she'd taken the step of putting an ad in the trade papers to make up for her gaffe.

Gradually, we got around to talking about aliens. On the show, Anderson plays a skeptic, an FBI agent with a medical degree, an entirely rational person who is loath to believe in alien abductions, psychic power, or anything supernatural. Her character follows the rules and teachings of mainstream science. But "Dana Scully" is a purely fictitious entity. The real person, Gillian Anderson, is like millions of other people: She believes that aliens have come to Earth and that there is a government conspiracy to keep the public ignorant.

"It would shock the hell out of me if the government had never been involved in a UFO cover-up and if there were not life on other planets," she said, conflating two distinct issues (which I interject not to be nasty to Anderson, but because everyone does it, almost reflexively). The government, she said, wants to be in total control of people's lives and does not want them to know that there are beings, creatures, more powerful than humans. The government doesn't want people to be scared. This was the Brookings report, filtered through many channels.

"The concept of other beings being ultimately more powerful than us human beings places the public in a state of fear. And once the public's in a state of fear, the government no longer has the same kind of control."

I asked her why aliens would cross interstellar space to visit Earth and then spend so much time hiding, skulking around in the desert, whispering in little kids' ears, abducting people, and so on.

"Because that is how we have created them," she said. "I mean, I think that we have subconsciously created the kind of alien beings that we believe there are. And that they operate, vibrate—this is going to make me sound like a complete nut—they vibrate on a different energy level than we do, and they are adaptable to our beliefs."

She was just an actress in a trailer, extemporizing, but she was also speaking for millions of people. She was a medium for powerful cultural beliefs, one of which, an extremely alluring one, is that we don't merely detect the nature of reality, we create it. Our beliefs have direct physical consequences. We *make things happen*. Postmodernism has met the self-help movement. The postmodernist professor at an elite university might say that reality is whatever we decide it is—but even that statement would be hedged by the admission that we don't literally change reality. The postmodernist simply believes that reality isn't a fixed, immutable, objectively real system that is external to our minds. To a New Ager, there truly is something real out there, and we are tapping into it, and altering it, in a continual interactive process. The subjective and the objective are the same thing. The working of our minds, the workings of the universe—no longer are these separate matters.

At least that's how I interpret what's going on—one man's subjective take on an alleged trend in a universe with no absolute truth. Talk about vaporous! Talk about something you can't sink your teeth into. (If you spend enough time thinking about this stuff, you suddenly want to go out and grow some corn or build a barn, to do anything at all that has the superficial appeal of being tangible.)

Gillian Anderson paused after her attempt to explain the different energy levels.

"I'm speaking as I think," she said.

She meant that she hadn't really thought it all the way through, she was still developing her cosmology.

"Given my belief systems," she said, "this is what follows my thought processes."

Later I spoke with David Duchovny, who plays Agent Fox Mulder. He lived next door to me when we were freshmen in college, a factoid—a conversational nugget—that will serve as hard currency throughout the world for the rest of my life. The young Duchovny was alarmingly brilliant for such a good-looking guy. Shortly after the start of school, he showed me a paper he'd written in high school on *The Waste Land*, and it was unlike anything I'd ever seen before, a confident and fresh analysis of a much-analyzed classic, by someone who wasn't even old enough to buy a beer. He went on to Yale graduate school and could easily have become a tenured Ivy League professor in a musty English department instead of settling for being a millionaire superstar with countless adoring fans and a glamorous wife. What a waste.

I gave him a ride home, and we talked about the alien idea. On his TV show, "Mulder" is the conspiracy theorist, like the real-life Gillian Anderson. The real-life Duchovny is a skeptic, like "Dana Scully." He gave me his concise thesis about why so many people are attracted to the conspiracy theories of *The X-Files*: "At the base of it, it gives a very easy answer. Which is that there's bad guys out there, they're all-powerful, and they're making your life miserable. It's the Oliver Stone answer. There's a reason bad things happen to good people. We show why. It's not random. We're more religious than *Touched by an Angel*."

Evan Thomas is editor at large and former Washington bureau chief for *Newsweek*. He has written 6 books and more than 100 cover stories on national and international news. Both of these pieces appeared in *Newsweek*. The first, written with Peter Annin and Steve Rhodes, appeared on October 27, 1997. The essay about American myths, written with Andrew Romano, was published on August 7, 2006.

Baby Jessica Grows Up

The little girl in the well survived, but her rescuers lost their way.

The tree they planted by the well where she almost died a decade ago has long since withered, and the flower bed is now a dirt patch. But the oil painting still hangs in the civic center: Baby Jessica, the golden-haired angel, held aloft by her rescuers. A TRIUMPH OF THE HUMAN SPIRIT, says the plaque on the wall, and it was. On October 16, 1987, as the world watched, the dusty, hard-luck town of Midland, Texas, came together to rescue a little girl trapped in a dark hole far below the ground. What came later was less uplifting. The parents bitterly divorced. Addicted to sudden fame, tempted by money, the town split apart over a made-for-TV movie. The man who actually pulled Jessica to safety killed himself. Ten years later, the story of Baby Jessica seems like a Frank Capra movie in reverse: first the redemption, then the fall. It is a morality tale that is not lost on the ordinary people who were made instant heroes—and came to rue their celebrity.

At the time, the people of Midland had no way of knowing that they were actors in a larger drama about the national zeitgeist—America in 1987 was coming out of the cold war and entering a confessional age that transforms domestic traumas into popular obsessions. Wisely, Jessica's parents chose to keep their daughter away from the spotlight and to allow her to grow up as a normal little girl. Now in sixth grade at a private school, she gets As and Bs, likes country music, is sweet on a boy and plays with her three cats and two kittens. The adults around her, however, were swept up in a whirlwind that they recall today with bewilderment and shame.

Jessica McClure was almost one and a half when she fell down an eight-inch-wide well in her aunt's backyard. Her mother had gone inside—just for a moment—to answer the phone. For 58 hours, nearly 100 rescue workers labored to get her out, drilling a shaft 29 feet down and 5 feet across. Diamond-tipped drill bits snapped on the bedrock; the progress was slowed when the drillers, exhausted, broke down and sobbed because they could hear the little girl, still alive, singing nursery rhymes and crying for her mother. While she was being pulled free, inch by inch, by a paramedic using K-Y lubricating jelly,

3.1 million people were watching live on CNN—at the time, the largest audience ever to watch the cable news service. (According to polls by the Pew Charitable Trust, Jessica's rescue is the only news event about an individual that has rivaled Princess Diana's death in public interest.) "Everybody in America became godfathers and godmothers of Jessica while this was going on," President Reagan told her parents, Cissy and Chip McClure, over the phone. She was invited to throw out the first pitch for the Texas Rangers and serve as grand marshal for the National Independence Day Parade.

The euphoria began to wear off shortly after the Hollywood producers arrived in town. They offered people involved in the rescue thousands of dollars for permission to tell their story. A committee of rescuers formed to entertain their bids. Then a second committee of different rescuers formed to hear other proposals. Each insisted that they were trying to tell the true story and accused the other of being greedy.

Then the rumors started up about Jessica's parents. Cissy, it was whispered, was getting uppity, refusing to wait in line at Denny's because, she announced, "I'm Jessica's mother." Chip and Cissy had supposedly bought a Mercedes and a Rolls-Royce with the donations that had poured in. (Actually, they bought a Thunderbird and a new pickup truck—and set up a lucrative trust for Jessica; it's now reportedly worth about $700,000.) Married at 16, the pair might have split anyway, but their divorce was messy.

Fame also addled two of the most prominent rescuers. During the rescue, Andy Glasscock, now a police sergeant, spent nearly three days lying on the ground by the well, trying to keep up Jessica's spirits with gentle chatter. ("What does a kitty do?" he asked. "Meow," came the distant whimper.) Soon he was jetting to Hollywood and neglecting his own family. He thanks his wife for forcing him into marriage counseling—and saving him from the fate of his co-worker Robert O'Donnell.

Prone to claustrophobia, O'Donnell was not the most obvious choice to take on the task of extricating Baby Jessica from the pipe where she was stuck, 22 feet below the ground. But he was tall and thin, the right shape for wedging into the rocky tunnel drilled into the well just below her resting place. O'Donnell later compared the experience to lying in a grave. When, spent in every way, he finally surfaced from the hole that October evening, he heard church bells ringing all over town. He was soon asked to appear on *Oprah* and judge the G.I. Joe American Heroes contest. He became intoxicated with fame. Could *People* magazine, he asked, help him with his autobiography? Then the migraine headaches began coming every day. He began popping pills. His wife kicked him out, and he lost his job when he began passing out from heavy doses of sedatives. Living alone at his mother's, he would read his scrapbook, inscribed by his mother-in-law with the words MY HERO, and hurl it angrily across the room. "This is what ruined my life," he swore. "I never want to see it again." When terrorists blew up the federal building in Oklahoma City in 1995, he longed to go help in the rescue—but, jobless, he didn't have bus fare. He shot himself a few days later.

Jessica's mother still has nightmares. She hears the drills pounding and her daughter's cries, and she wakes up in a cold sweat. Jessica, however, seems quite happy; she lives with her mother, who has remarried, and she visits her dad on the weekends. As a little girl, she would cry out "No!" and "Don't!" in her sleep, and she will always have a spidery scar on her forehead from skin grafts, and the trace of a limp from losing a little toe. But she says she has no actual memory of falling down the well or being rescued. Asked by a visiting reporter from the *Ladies' Home Journal* recently whether she wanted to look at clippings about her accident, she wrinkled her nose and replied, "Nah." Neighbors say she appears quite normal.

That is consolation to retired fire chief James Roberts, who helped supervise the rescue. "I'm ashamed of the way we all acted," he told *Newsweek* last week. "But you know, for all the talk, all the problems, we have a healthy little 11-year-old girl running around here, and there isn't anyone who can take that away from us."

When the Cameras Stopped

The McClures: Just 16 when they had Jessica, the McClures blamed their 1990 divorce on their youth rather than the intensity of the spotlight. Both Chip, a sales representative, and Cissy, a homemaker, have since remarried. Both still live near Midland.

Steve Forbes: The paramedic who carried Jessica out of the tunnel managed to avoid the limelight—and the town's infighting. He still works for the Midland Fire Department.

Robert O'Donnell: The paramedic who eased the little girl out of the well succumbed to the pressures of sudden fame. He committed suicide in 1995.

Andy Glasscock: The detective had the heartbreaking job of talking to the 18-month-old, getting her to sing and stay awake during the 58-hour ordeal. Afterward, he became depressed and nearly wrecked his marriage; now he's a Midland patrol sergeant.

Jessica: The 11-year-old has no memory of the accident, and says of the scars on her leg and forehead, "I'm proud of them. I have them because I survived."

History: How American Myths Are Made

Nations need a good story line to learn how to cope with their tragedies.

The story of workaday men and women rising to greatness is one of America's most cherished myths. As a term, myth is much misunderstood; hearing it, many people take the word to mean "lie," when in fact a myth is a story, a narrative, that explains individual and national realities—how a person or a country came to be, why certain things happen in the course of a life or of history, and what fate may have in store for us. Myths are a peculiar hybrid of truth and falsehood, resentments and ambitions, dreams and dread. We all have personal myths running through our heads, and some chapters would withstand fact checking while others would fail miserably.

Nations are the same way. In America, the underlying faith is that in a truly free and democratic society, every man and woman has the potential to realize greatness, that freedom and openness liberate and ennoble ordinary citizens to do extraordinary things. The Triumph of the Common Man is a myth deeply rooted in American culture, and unlike some popular myths, it is true enough. Tom Hanks may have played a fictional character in *Saving Private Ryan*—the small-town American called to arms—but World War II was won by a million citizen soldiers very much like him.

There is, unfortunately, another, less admirable myth that Americans concoct to explain crises and disasters. It is rooted in the paranoid streak that runs through pop culture, the conspiracy theories that blame some sinister (and usually make-believe) Other for whatever went wrong. In 1950, many frightened Americans wanted to know: how could Russia have gotten the bomb so soon after America won World War II? There had to be traitors among us, railed Senator Joe McCarthy and other conspiracists as they tore up the country looking for communists under every bed.

One might expect Hollywood's Oliver Stone to drum up a conspiracy theory to explain 9/11. He is, after all, known as the director of a movie, *JFK*, that essentially accuses Lyndon Johnson, the CIA and the Joint Chiefs of Staff of killing President Kennedy. That Stone did not go to the dark side to explain the attacks of September 11 tells us something about the American sensibility toward that day. True, Stone was under pressure from the studio not to make the story political or conspiratorial. It is also true, though, that public-opinion surveys show that many Americans (42 percent in a recent Zogby poll) believe the government must be covering up something about 9/11, and many blame President Bush for using the attacks to justify invading Iraq. Scaremongers on the Internet and Michael Moore's entertaining but outlandish *Fahrenheit 9/11* have fueled popular suspicions of devious plots.

Nonetheless, 9/11 has become a kind of sacred day in American life. Stone's movie *World Trade Center* will stand as a civic elegy, a statement that the events of 9/11, and the memories of the nearly 3,000 people who died that day, should not be degraded or sullied by politics or the fevered imaginings of people who see tragedy and assume scheming and betrayal.

All nations need myths to understand crises that shock, the wars and riots, assassinations and natural disasters that wrench history. The myth of the Triumph of the Common Man was born in the first battle of the American Revolution, when farmers and tradesmen made their stand against British redcoats at Lexington and Concord in April 1775. These minutemen were our first citizen soldiers, and their example still inspires. "In our mind's eye we see a scattering of individual militiamen crouched behind low granite walls, banging away at a disciplined mass of British regulars," writes historian David Hackett Fischer. "We celebrate the spontaneity of the event, and the autonomy of the Americans who took part in it. As a writer put it in the 19th century, 'Everyone appeared to be his own commander.' "

Myths evolve as circumstances and needs change. The Founders at first portrayed Lexington and Concord as an unprovoked attack on innocents; "Bloody Butchery, by the British," proclaimed a printed broadside of the time, illustrated with 40 small coffins. The propagandists were trying to stir up sympathy for the rebellion and a desire for revenge. Only a later generation of popularizers, who wanted to inspire a young democracy, stressed the bold resistance of the minutemen who "fired the shot heard round the world."

The fantasists of the American South after the Civil War had to justify not just defeat but the elimination of a way of life. Thus was born the "Lost Cause," the dreamy fiction that chivalrous "gentlemen officers" had fallen to forces of greater number but weaker character, and that rapacious "damn Yankees" and carpetbaggers had been exploiting the South ever since. The real cause of the Civil War—slavery—was swept into the shadows. The Lost Cause was used to justify the evils of Jim Crow and perpetuate the myth of white supremacy.

World War II remains the greatest of American myths. (In an old *New Yorker* cartoon, a glassy-eyed man leans toward the bartender and says, "I remember the Second World War. That's the one that kind of flickers on the screen, right?") President Franklin D. Roosevelt did not hesitate to play to the desire for revenge in his address to Congress after the Japanese surprise attack on Pearl Harbor. "Yesterday, December 7, 1941, a day which will live in world history," the president dictated to a secretary. Looking over the resulting draft, he crossed out "world history" and wrote "infamy" instead. With a flick of his pen, FDR switched from the cool judgment of history to a personal attack on the character of the Japanese people. They were soon portrayed as monkeys, snakes, insects—villainous vermin to be exterminated. Hollywood signed on. In *Air Force* (1943), a grinning Japanese guns down an American pilot who has parachuted and is floating helplessly in the air.

But the moviemakers more often venerated Everyman as they rallied the country to the soldiers' cause. The standard trope became the polyglot platoon—the wise-guy from Brooklyn, the Midwest farmer, the hillbilly, the rich kid—all fighting for their buddies and their moms and apple pie against the fascist beast. Even when postwar books and movies grew more nuanced and worldly, often edged with bitter satire, the basic myth persisted: that the sons of American democracy had triumphed over tyranny.

Vietnam was a lot harder to explain. Hollywood initially packaged it as the Good War, Part Two, with John Wayne's gung-ho potboiler *The Green Berets* (1968). The film was panned by critics and picketed by antiwar protesters. Later, better movies, including Stone's overwrought but masterful *Platoon* (1986), captured the alienation of the soldiers and the futility of the war. But Vietnam remains troublesome in the American psyche; it's as if we cannot reconcile the war with our mythic (and heroic) self-image.

September 11 could have been equally vexing. What is there to celebrate in the slaughter of nearly 3,000 innocent civilians? Early attempts to canonize George Bush as a take-charge commander in chief, as in the hokey made-for-TV production *DC 9/11: Time of Crisis*, were mostly embarrassing. But there were real heroes on 9/11, and not just the firemen and cops who died trying to rescue their fellow citizens. Although some critics have contended that the quasi documentary *United 93* (2006, directed by Paul Greengrass) is a little too raw for the families of the dead, the film shows in graphic, gripping detail how a group of ordinary passengers on an airplane could, as they faced the enormity of their fate, marshal themselves to overwhelm trained killers and terrorists. That these modern-day minutemen perished in the effort just makes their story more affecting.

United 93 offers a gritty, convincing reality. So, too, does Stone's *World Trade Center*. Stone's movie will live on in the national consciousness, not just as a skillful exercise in movie making, but also as tribute to a profound national faith in the courage and steadfastness of common men and women. The greatest of myths are the ones that ring true.

Nancy Gibbs is an essayist and executive editor at *Time* magazine. A longer version of this article, which was written in the twenty-four hours after the World Trade Center attacks, appeared on September 14, 2001, and won the National Magazine Award that year.

If You Want To Humble an Empire

If you want to humble an empire, it makes sense to maim its cathedrals. They are symbols of its faith, and when they crumple and burn, it tells us we are not so powerful and we can't be safe. The Twin Towers of the World Trade Center, planted at the base of Manhattan Island with the Statue of Liberty as their sentry, and the Pentagon, a squat, concrete fort on the banks of the Potomac, are the sanctuaries of money and power that our enemies may imagine define us. But that assumes our faith rests on what we can buy and build, and that has never been America's true God.

On a normal day, we value heroism because it is uncommon. On September 11, we valued heroism because it was everywhere. The firefighters kept climbing the stairs of the tallest buildings in town, even as the steel moaned and the cracks spread in zippers through the walls, to get to the people trapped in the sky. We don't know yet how many of them died, but once we know, as Mayor Rudy Giuliani said, "it will be more than we can bear." That sentiment was played out in miniature in the streets, where fleeing victims pulled the wounded to safety, and at every hospital, where the lines to give blood looped round and round the block. At the medical-supply companies, which sent supplies without being asked. At Verizon, where a worker threw on a New York Fire Department jacket to go save people. And then again and again all across the country, as people checked on those they loved to find out if they were safe and then looked for some way to help.

This was the bloodiest attack on American soil since the Civil War, a modern Antietam played out in real time, on fast-forward, and not with soldiers but with secretaries, security guards, lawyers, bankers, janitors. It was strange that a day of war was a day we stood still. We couldn't move—that must have been the whole idea—so we had no choice but to watch. Every city cataloged its targets; residents looked at their skylines, wondering whether they would be different in the morning. The Sears Tower in Chicago was evacuated, as were colleges and museums. Disney World shut down, and Major League Baseball canceled its games, and nuclear power plants went to top security status; the Hoover Dam and the Mall of America shut down, and Independence Hall in Philadelphia, and Mount Rushmore. It was as though someone had taken a huge brush and painted a bull's-eye around every place Americans gather, every icon we revere, every service we depend on, and vowed to take them out or shut them down, or force us to do it ourselves.

Terror works like a musical composition, so many instruments, all in tune, playing perfectly together to create their desired effect. Sorrow and horror, and fear. The first plane is just to get our attention. Then, once we are transfixed, the second plane comes and repeats the theme until the blinding coda of smoke and debris crumbles on top of the rescue workers who have gone in to try to save anyone who survived the opening movements. And we watch, speechless, as the sirens, like some awful choir, hour after hour let you know that it is not over yet, wait, there's more.

It was, of course, a perfect day, 70 degrees and flawless skies, perfect for a nervous pilot who has stolen a huge jet and intends to turn it into a missile. It was a Boeing 767 from Boston, American Airlines Flight 11, bound for Los Angeles with 81 passengers, that first got the attention of air traffic controllers. The plane took off at 7:59 a.m. and headed west, over the Adirondacks, before taking a sudden turn south and diving down toward the heart of New York City. Meanwhile, American Flight 77 had left Dulles; United Flight 175 had left Boston at 7:58; and United Flight 93 had left Newark three minutes later, bound for San Francisco. All climbed into beautiful clear skies, all four planes on transcontinental flights, plump with fuel, ripe to explode. "They couldn't carry anything—other than an atom bomb—that could be as bad as what they were flying," observed a veteran investigator.

The first plane hit the World Trade Center's north tower at 8:45, ripping through the building's skin and setting its upper floors ablaze. People thought it was a sonic boom, or a construction accident, or freak lightning on a lovely fall day; at worst, a horrible airline accident, a plane losing altitude, out of control, a pilot trying to ditch in the river and missing. But as the gruesome rains came—bits of plane, a tire, office furniture, glass, a hand, a leg, whole bodies, began falling all around—people in the streets all stopped and looked, and fell silent. As the smoke rose, the ash rained gently down, along with a whole lost flock of paper shuffling down from the sky to the street below, edges charred, plane tickets and account statements and bills and reports and volumes and volumes of unfinished business floating down to earth.

Almost instantly, a distant wail of sirens came from all directions, even as people poured from the building, even as a second plane bore down on lower Manhattan. Louis Garcia was among the first medics on the scene. "There were people running over to us burnt from head to toe. Their hair was burned off. There were compound fractures, arms and legs sticking out of the skin. One guy had no hair left on his head." Of the six patients in his first ambulance run, two died on the way to St. Vincent's Hospital.

The survivors of the first plot to bring down the Twin Towers, the botched attempt in 1993 that left six dead, had a great advantage over their colleagues. When the first explosion came, they knew to get out. Others were paralyzed by the noise, confused by the instructions. Consultant Andy Perry still had the reflexes. He grabbed his pal Nathan Shields from his office, and they began to run down 46 flights. With each passing floor more and more people joined the flow down the steps. The lights stayed on, but the lower stairs were filled with water from burst pipes and sprinklers. "Everyone watch your step," people called out. "Be careful!" The smell of jet fuel suffused the building. Hallways collapsed, flames shot out of a men's room. By the time they reached the lobby, they just wanted to get out—but the streets didn't look any safer. "It was chaos out there," Shields says. "Finally we ran for it." They raced into the street in time to see the second plane bearing down. Even as they ran away, there were still people standing around in the lobby waiting to be told what to do. "There were no emergency announcements—it just happened so quickly nobody knew what was going on," says Perry. "This guy we were talking to saw at least 12 people jumping out of [the tower] because of the fires. He was standing next to a guy who got hit by shrapnel and was immediately killed." Workers tore off their shirts to make bandages and tourniquets for the wounded; others used bits of clothing as masks to help them breathe. Whole stretches of street were slick with blood, and up and down the avenues you could hear the screams of people plunging from the burning tower. People watched in horror as a man tried to shimmy down the outside of the tower. He made it about three floors before flipping backward to the ground.

Architect Bob Shelton had his foot in a cast; he'd broken it falling off a curb two weeks earlier. He heard the explosion of the first plane hitting the north tower from his 56th-floor office in the south tower. As he made his way down the stairwell, his building came under attack as well. "You could hear the building cracking. It sounded like when you have a bunch of spaghetti, and you break it in half to boil it." Shelton knew that what he was hearing was bad. "It was structural failure," Shelton says. "Once a building like that is off center, that's it." "There was no panic," he says of his escape down the stairs. "We were working as a team, helping everyone along the way. Someone carried my crutches, and I supported myself on the railing."

Gilbert Richard Ramirez works for BlueCross BlueShield on the 20th floor of the north tower. After the explosion, he ran to the windows and saw the debris falling, and sheets of white building material, and then something else. "There was a body. It looked like a man's body, a full-size man." The features were indistinguishable as it fell: the body was black, apparently charred. Someone pulled an emergency alarm switch, but nothing happened. Someone else broke into the emergency phone, but it was dead. People began to say their prayers.

"Relax, we're going to get out of here," Ramirez said. "I was telling them, 'Breathe, breathe, Christ is on our side, we're gonna get out of here.'" He prodded everyone out the door, herding stragglers. It was an eerie walk down the smoky stairs, a path to safety that ran through the suffering. They saw people who had been badly burned. Their skin, he says, "was like a grayish color, and it was like dripping, or peeling, like the skin was peeling off their body." One woman was screaming. "She said she lost her friend, her friend went out the window, a gust sucked her out." As they descended, they were passed by fire-fighters and rescue workers, panting, pushing their way up the stairs in their heavy boots and gear. "At least 50 of them must have passed us," says Ramirez. "I told them, 'Do a good job.'" He pauses. "I saw those guys one time, but they're not gonna be there again." When he got outside to the street, there were bodies scattered on the ground, and then another came plummeting, and another. "Every time I looked up at the building, somebody was jumping from it. Like from 107, Windows on the World. There was one, and then another one. I couldn't understand their jumping. I guess they couldn't see any hope."

The terror triggered other reactions besides heroism. Robert Falcon worked in the parking garage at the towers: "When the blast shook it went dark and we all went down, and I had a flashlight and everyone was screaming at me. People were ripping my shirt to try and get to my flashlight, and they were crushing me. The whole crowd was on top of me wanting the flashlight."

Michael Otten, an assistant vice president at Mizuho Capital Markets, was headed down the stairs around the 46th floor when the announcement came over the loudspeakers that the south tower was secure, people could go back to their desks or leave the building. He proceeded to the 44th floor, an elevator-transfer floor. One elevator loaded up and headed down, then came back empty, so he and a crowd of others piled in. One man's backpack kept the doors from closing. The seconds ticked by. "We wanted to say something, but the worst thing you can do is go against each other, and just as I thought it was going to close, it was about 9:00, 9:03, whenever it was that the second plane crashed into the building. The walls of the elevator caved in; they fell on a couple people." Otten and others groped through the dust to find a stairway, but the doors were locked. Finally they found a clearer passage, found a stairway they could get into, and fled down to the street.

Even as people streamed down the stairs, the cracks were appearing in the walls as the building shuddered and cringed. Steam pipes burst, and at one point an elevator door burst open and a man fell out, half burned alive, his skin hanging off. People dragged him out of the elevator and helped get him out of the building to the doctors below. "If I had listened to the announcement," says survivor Joan Feldman, "I'd be dead right now."

Felipe Oyola and his wife Adianes did listen to the announcement. When Oyola heard the first explosion in his office on the 81st floor of the south tower, he raced down to the 78th floor to find her. They met at the elevator bank; she was terrified. But when the announcement came over the loudspeaker that the tower was safe, they both went back to work. Oyola was back on 81 when the second plane arrived. "As soon as I went upstairs, I looked out the window, and I see falling debris and people. Then the office was on top of me. I managed to escape, and I've been looking for my wife ever since."

United Flight 175 left Boston at 7:58 a.m., headed to Los Angeles. When it passed the Massachusetts-Connecticut border, it made a 30-degree turn, and then an even sharper turn, and swooped down on Manhattan, between the buildings, to impale the south tower at 9:06. This plane seemed to hit lower and harder; maybe that's because by now every camera in the city was trained on the towers, and the crowds in the street, refugees from the first explosion, were there to see it. Desks and chairs and people were sucked out the windows and rained down on the streets below. Men and women, cops and firefighters, watched and wept. As fire and debris fell, cars blew up; the air smelled of smoke and concrete, that smell that spits out of jackhammers chewing up pavement. You could taste the air more easily than you could breathe it.

P.S. 89 is an elementary school just up the street; most of the families live and work in the financial district, and when bedlam broke, mothers and fathers ran toward the school, sweat pouring off them, frantic to get to their kids. Some people who didn't know whether their spouses had survived met up at school, because both parents went straight to the kids. "I just wanted to find my kids and my wife and get the hell off this island," said one father. And together they walked, he and his wife and young son and daughter, 60 blocks or so up to Grand Central and safety.

The first crash had changed everything; the second changed it again. Anyone who thought the first was an accident now knew better. This was not some awful, isolated episode, not Oklahoma City, not even the first World Trade Center bombing. Now this felt like a war, and the system responded accordingly; the emergency plans came out of the drawers and clicked one by one into place. The city buckled, the traffic stopped, the bridges and tunnels were shut down at 9:35 as warnings tumbled one after another; the Empire State Building was evacuated, and the Metropolitan Museum of Art, the United Nations. First the New York airports were closed, then Washington's, and then the whole country was grounded for the first time in history.

With reporting by the staff of *Time* magazine.

Jim Dwyer has spent most of his professional life writing about New York as a reporter, columnist, and author. In May 2001, he joined the staff of the *New York Times*, where these two pieces first appeared. After the attacks of September 11, 2001, he wrote a series, entitled "Objects," made up of short articles about small things connected with life, death, and memory. "Fighting for Life" was the first article in the series, published on October 9, 2001. The other story, from January 16, 2009, describes the bitterly cold afternoon when a U.S. Airways flight lost power and landed in the Hudson River. Everyone onboard survived.

Fighting for Life 50 Floors Up, with One Tool and Ingenuity

Now memories orbit around small things. None of the other window washers liked his old green bucket, but Jan Demczur, who worked inside 1 World Trade Center, found its rectangular mouth perfect for dipping and wetting his squeegee in one motion. So on the morning of the 11th, as he waited at the 44th-floor sky lobby to connect with elevators for higher floors, bucket and squeegee dangled from the end of his arm.

The time was 8:46 a.m. With five other men—Shivam Iyer, John Paczkowski, George Phoenix, Colin Richardson and Al Smith—Mr. Demczur boarded car 69-A, an express elevator that stopped on floors 67 through 74. The car rose, but before it reached its first landing, "We felt a muted thud," Mr. Iyer said. "The building shook. The elevator swung from side to side, like a pendulum." Then it plunged. In the car, someone punched an emergency-stop button. At that moment, No. 1 World Trade Center had entered the final 102 minutes of its existence. No one knew the clock was running, least of all the men trapped inside car 69-A; they were as cut off 500 feet in the sky as if they had been trapped 500 feet underwater.

They did not know their lives would depend on a simple tool. After 10 minutes, a live voice delivered a blunt message over the intercom. There had been an explosion. Then the intercom went silent. Smoke seeped into the elevator cabin. One man cursed skyscrapers. Mr. Phoenix, the tallest, a Port Authority engineer, poked for a ceiling hatch. Others pried apart the car doors, propping them open with the long wooden handle of Mr. Demczur's squeegee. There was no exit. They faced a wall, stenciled with the number 50. That particular elevator bank did not serve the 50th floor, so there was no need for an opening. To escape, they would have to make one themselves.

Mr. Demczur felt the wall. Sheetrock. Having worked in construction in his early days as a Polish immigrant, he knew that it could be cut with a sharp knife. No one had a knife. From his bucket, Mr. Demczur drew his squeegee. He slid its metal edge against the wall, back and forth, over and over. He was

spelled by the other men. Against the smoke, they breathed through handker-
chiefs dampened in a container of milk Mr. Phoenix had just bought. Sheetrock comes in panels about one inch thick, Mr. Demczur recalled. They cut an
inch, then two inches. Mr. Demczur's hand ached. As he carved into the third
panel, his hand shook, he fumbled the squeegee and it dropped down the
shaft. He had one tool left: a short metal squeegee handle. They carried on,
with fists, feet and handle, cutting an irregular rectangle about 12 by 18 inches.
Finally, they hit a layer of white tiles. A bathroom. They broke the tiles. One by
one, the men squirmed through the opening, headfirst, sideways, popping
onto the floor near a sink. Mr. Demczur turned back. "I said, 'Pass my bucket
out,'" he recalled.

By then, about 9:30, the 50th floor was already deserted, except for firefighters, astonished to see the six men emerge. "I think it was Engine Company 5,"
Mr. Iyer said. "They hustled us to the staircase." On the excruciating single-file
descent through the smoke, someone teased Mr. Demczur about bringing his
bucket. "The company might not order me another one," he replied. At the
15th floor, Mr. Iyer said: "We heard a thunderous, metallic roar. I thought
our lives had surely ended then." The south tower was collapsing. It was 9:59.
Mr. Demczur dropped his bucket. The firefighters shouted to hurry.

At 23 minutes past 10, they burst onto the street, ran for phones, sipped
oxygen and, five minutes later, fled as the north tower collapsed. Their escape
had taken 95 of the 102 minutes. "It took up to one and a half minutes to clear
each floor, longer at the lower levels," said Mr. Iyer, an engineer with the Port
Authority. "If the elevator had stopped at the 60th floor, instead of the 50th, we
would have been five minutes too late. And that man with the squeegee. He
was like our guardian angel."

Since that day, Mr. Demczur has stayed home with his wife and children. He
has pieced together the faces of the missing with the men and women he knew
in the stations of his old life: the security guard at the Japanese bank on the
93rd floor, who used to let him in at 6:30; the people at Carr Futures on 92;
the head of the Port Authority. Their faces keep him awake at night, he says.
His hands, the one that held the squeegee and the other that carried the bucket,
shake with absence.

U.S. Airways Flight 1549: Old Hands on the River Didn't Have to Be Told What to Do

Around 3:30 on Thursday afternoon, Captain Carl Lucas fired up the engines
on the *Athenia*, a high-speed catamaran ferry docked at a pier in Weehawken,
N.J., getting ready for the evening commuters on the Hudson River. The first

wave would start in half an hour. Then he spotted a plane in the water. "We just threw off the lines and went out there," said Captain Lucas, 34.

At the same pier, Captain John Winiarski, 52, and a deckhand, Frank Il-luzzi, 62, were onboard the catamaran *Admiral Richard E. Bennis*. They noticed the *Athenia* speeding away. "We seen them scurrying out into the river, so we turned around and saw the plane in the river," Captain Winiarski said. "We made a beeline."

And so it went: a flotilla of rescuers, created by people who caught glimpses of something going wrong and did not have to be told to help. The *Athenia*, the *Admiral Bennis* and 12 other boats—all operated or chartered by New York Waterway—picked 135 people out of the river. The crews stopped their work and changed the world. "You don't look nowhere," said Cosmo Mezzina, 62, a deckhand on the ferry *Governor Thomas H. Kean*. "You don't look right or left. You just look right in front of you, just to save, to rescue those people."

One of the ferry captains, Manuel Liba, ticked off the strokes of fortune: the pilot brought the plane down smoothly, the Hudson was calm, it was daylight and it was 45 minutes before the evening rush on the river. There was more than luck. On a bitter, frigid afternoon, the plane had come down minutes from people who regularly practice helping.

The first ferry to reach it was the *Thomas Jefferson*, which pulled out of Pier 79 on the Hudson River at 39th Street in Manhattan. "As we turned around, we noticed the plane in the water," said Vincent Lombardi, captain of the *Thomas Jefferson*. "We thought it was an odd-looking vessel." He radioed the Coast Guard, then headed for the plane. On a Coast Guard video, the *Thomas Jefferson* can be seen arriving at 3:34 p.m., about four or five minutes after the plane hit the water. Other videos show more ferries nestled around the jet, drifting alongside as it was pulled south by the current.

"I've been on the water since I was 2 years old," said Brittany Catanzaro, 20, the captain of the *Thomas Kean* and a ferry pilot for five months. "I pulled out of Pier 79, I looked for any kind of southbound traffic, and I saw the plane there." "It was hard to stay next to it, but you practice that by throwing life rings in the water and trying to stay alongside them. One of the people got on board, turned around and hugged my deckhand. We're just working as if we're training and drilling."

Each of the captains hailed the ferry deckhands—as well as a ticket agent and a bus driver—for hoisting people from the water. The last person to leave a life raft was Chesley B. Sullenberger III, the captain of the U.S. Airways flight. He climbed aboard the *Athenia* after everyone else had been lifted to safety. "Very calm," Captain Lucas reported. "He had a metal clipboard with the passenger manifest. He came up into the wheelhouse, and we tried to organize a count of who was recovered from the water. I asked him if he thought there was anyone left on the plane. He said no, that he had checked twice himself."

Muscle memory had steadied people in the currents of a disaster and the strong tides of the Hudson: an airline pilot remembering his metal clipboard, and ferry pilots who never moved out of reach of the bobbing airplane. "You train so much, you don't have to think about it," Captain Lucas said. "I didn't have to give any orders to the crew." And by Friday, another kind of memory began to take hold. "We were getting the boat ready, and we saw the plane going down," said Captain Liba, 52, who pilots the ferry *Moira Smith*. "We called management; we said, 'We got to go.' We just took off for the airplane. Right away, the doors flew out from the plane, and people came out. It's like a dream. I still can't believe it."

Marilyn W. Thompson is a national editor at the *Washington Post* and a former editor of the *Lexington (KY) Herald-Leader*. She is the author or coauthor of four books. This is an excerpt from *The Killer Strain: Anthrax and a Government Exposed* (HarperCollins, 2003), which was reprinted in *U.S. News and World Report* on May 18, 2003.

Anthrax

When a series of letters packed with anthrax spread terror along the East Coast in late 2001, the FBI turned to the 42,000-member American Society for Microbiology, asking scientists to seek out clues that might lead to the arrest of the bioterrorist. The bureau also turned to one microbiologist in particular, John Ezzell, then head of the special-pathogens division at the U.S. Army Medical Research Institute of Infectious Diseases (USAMRIID) at Fort Detrick, Maryland, to help them understand this deadly bacterium. Here we learn what happened when Ezzell confronted "The Face of Satan," the most refined anthrax he had ever seen.

John Ezzell stood by the guarded entrance to USAMRIID, waiting for the FBI to arrive with the evidence, as he had so many other times during the anthrax scares. Ezzell and his team knew that this package, coming straight from Capitol Hill, would focus the eyes of the world on his Special Pathogens Sample Test Laboratory. He did not consider its danger until later, when he opened the envelope and out burst a spore powder so pure that it evaporated in midair.

An intern in the office of Senate Majority Leader Thomas Daschle, a South Dakota Democrat, had cut open the envelope around 9:45 that Monday morning, October 15. The FBI promptly called Ezzell to alert him that they were sending the evidence from Daschle's office for testing. A few hours later, the FBI team pulled into Fort Detrick's gates, bearing sealed containers and layers of Ziploc bags. The containers held the rapid assays that had tested positive at the Senate site, though the Centers for Disease Control and Prevention had cautioned that the scientific accuracy of these tests had not been absolutely established.

Ezzell's team would have to do the next level of analysis. The most authoritative analysis required cultures that took 14 hours to process. Ezzell and his team began work under a safety hood. Wearing a mask and gloves, Ezzell had confidence in his own protection. He had been vaccinated so many times that he considered himself virtually anthrax-proof.

First, the team dealt with the sealed canisters, the assays wet with chemicals taken from the crime scene. They removed the contents and drained off some of the liquid to use for further testing. Their concern heightened when they began examining the envelope and its contents. They had all been trained to conduct risk analysis on suspicious packages and envelopes and to take extra precautions if they found anything even slightly alarming. The powdery material packed inside was shifting with movement. He told the team that for added protection they would step up laboratory safeguards before opening the letter and its inner layers of packaging.

The Ziploc bags were placed in a secure isolation chamber, known as an air lock, located outside the lab. An FBI agent guarded the bags until Ezzell and his colleagues could get inside. Ezzell removed his street clothes and pulled on green surgical scrubs. To access the lab, he had to pass through another security checkpoint by punching his personal ID number into a keypad. Once inside, he changed into lab shoes and made his way over to the biological safety cabinet. The FBI agent watched through a window.

Ezzell thoroughly cleaned the cabinet, rinsing it with bleach and distilled water. He could see the fine powder dispersed inside the plastic bags and knew that his cabinet could become contaminated unless he took special precautions. He lined its bottom with a layer of bleach-soaked paper towels to keep the spores under control.

Wearing multiple layers of latex gloves covered by sleeve protectors, Ezzell propped up the envelope against the back of the cabinet, forming a kind of artist's easel that would allow him to photograph the full image. He moved back to focus the camera. That was when he noticed it: the bleach had wicked up through the dry panels. The bottom of the envelope had become smudged with bleach solution.

"Oh my God, what have I done?" Ezzell thought. Worried that he might have tainted the evidence but unable to undo the damage, he carried on. He began slowly removing the letter from its envelope. As he worked, he noticed a bit of white powder tucked into one of the letter's folds. Almost as soon as he saw it, the powder dispersed, spreading invisibly through the safety cabinet.

Even though he had been studying anthrax for years, Ezzell had never actually seen the bacterium in its weaponized form. This was a powder so virulent that normal laboratory rules did not apply. "After all these years of looking, here it is," he thought. "This is the real thing."

Ezzell kept his fear suppressed, determined to finish the job carefully. He finished pulling the letter out, then coaxed the powder back into its Ziploc bag. The letter went into a sterile baggie, and he sealed the envelope in another one. Then he wrapped both in plastic bags that had been decontaminated with bleach solution. Ezzell took the sterile bags to the lab's glass window so FBI agent Darin Steele could photograph them. The images he snapped were seen around the globe.

To protect himself, Ezzell started antibiotics to guard against infection. He also took another precaution. He mixed a solution of diluted bleach and, bracing himself, took a deep snort. The pain that surged through his sinuses almost knocked him to the ground, but he could not stand the thought of carrying anthrax spores in his nostrils.

That night, a friend who worked for the CIA woke Ezzell from a deep sleep: His assessment—that this was indeed "weaponized" anthrax—had been passed on to the president of the United States.

After opening the Daschle envelope, Ezzell would bolt awake in the middle of the night, worrying about what would happen if anthrax powder made its way into American households. This stuff was coming through the mail, he told himself. Everyone was vulnerable. What could the average person do to protect himself? It was well documented in the scientific literature that two hours of exposure to dry heat at 320 degrees Fahrenheit would kill spores. Ezzell, an accomplished cook, set his kitchen oven to 320. He inserted an assortment of daily mail—sealed envelopes of various sizes and types, plastic-encased magazines—and waited two hours.

Voila! The stamps were still firmly in place and the envelopes sealed, though the plastic windows showed slight shrinkage. Glossy magazines had a slightly burned appearance but were readable. Over the next few days, he perfected the technique. It worked much better if the batch of mail was placed inside a turkey-basting bag or foil container. A careful person could take the bag to the mailbox, dump the contents inside, secure with a twist-tie, and easily pop it into the oven.

Finally, after testing the oven technique in his lab, Ezzell sat down and wrote a paper called "Procedure for Killing Bacillus Anthracis Spores in Mail." He wrote: "While there may be opportunities for fine-tuning the process, the advantages of this approach are that the process is low-tech, immediately available, and can be performed in residences or offices. It is based on firm scientific data with respect to temperature and time required for killing Bacillus anthracis spores and with respect to initial experiments which have shown that spores from Senator Daschle's office are killed well within the two-hour heating period." He added this disclaimer: "The author assumes no responsibility for loss of plastic items (including credit cards), fires, odors or other damage."

Ezzell began distributing the guide to friends and fellow worshipers at his Methodist church. Someone posted it on the Internet. He was amused that, after a lifetime of scientific endeavor, studying the fine points of an obscure and mystifying bacterium, this would be his most practical contribution to the common good. Like a chef in a Betty Crocker cook-off, he had created the homemaker's guide to baking anthrax, sealed in the U.S. mail.

Walt Bogdanich is an assistant editor for the investigations desk of the *New York Times*. Previously, he was an investigative producer for *60 Minutes* and ABC News and an investigative reporter for the *Wall Street Journal* in New York and Washington. He is the winner of three Pulitzer Prizes. This article appeared in the *New York Times* on October 1, 2007.

The Everyman Who Exposed Tainted Toothpaste

Eduardo Arias hardly fits the profile of someone capable of humbling one of the world's most formidable economic powers. A 51-year-old Kuna Indian, Mr. Arias grew up on a reservation, paddling dugout canoes near his home on one of the San Blas islands off Panama's Caribbean coast. He now lives in a small apartment above a food stand in Panama, the nation's capital, also known as Panama City.

But one Saturday morning in May, Eduardo Arias did something that would reverberate across six continents. He read the label on a 59-cent tube of toothpaste. On it were two words that had been overlooked by government inspectors and health authorities in dozens of countries: diethylene glycol, the same sweet-tasting, poisonous ingredient in antifreeze that had been mixed into cold syrup here, killing or disabling at least 138 Panamanians last year.

Mr. Arias reported his discovery, setting off a worldwide hunt for tainted toothpaste that turned out to be manufactured in China. Health alerts have now been issued in 34 countries, from Vietnam to Kenya, from Tonga in the Pacific to the Turks and Caicos Islands in the Caribbean. Canada found 24 contaminated brands, and New Zealand found 16. Japan had 20 million tubes. Officials in the United States unwittingly gave the toothpaste to prisoners, the mentally disabled and troubled youths. Hospitals gave it to the sick, while high-end hotels gave it to the wealthy.

People around the world had been putting an ingredient of antifreeze in their mouths, and until Panama blew the whistle, no one seemed to know it. The toothpaste scare helped galvanize global concerns about the quality of China's exports in general, prompting the government there to promise to reform how food, medicine and consumer products are regulated. And other countries are re-examining how well they monitor imported products.

Lost in this swirl of activity was the identity of the person who started it all—Mr. Arias. Until the *New York Times* tracked him down with the help of the Panama City mayor's office, his name had not been known, even to some people working on the case. "We haven't been able to find him," said Julio César Laffaurie, the Panamanian prosecutor pursuing the case of the contaminated toothpaste. In looking back over events of the past year, Dr. Jorge Motta, director of the Gorgas Memorial Institute, a prominent research center in Panama City, said he was grateful that some good had come from the national trauma brought on by the toxic cough syrup. "The whole questioning about Chinese goods began in Panama with our deaths," he said, putting a twist on an old Chinese saying by adding, "A little butterfly in Panama beat her wings and created a storm in China."

Mr. Arias, who lives alone and does not own a car, went to buy blank CDs on May 5 at Vendela, a discount store where he had heard prices were so low that street vendors bought supplies there. Stepping into the store, a large display of toothpaste caught his eye. "Without touching the tube, the letters were big enough for me to read: diethylene glycol," Mr. Arias said. A year ago, those words would have meant nothing to him. "Nobody had ever heard of this stuff," Mr. Arias said. But a steady drumbeat of news about poison cough syrup had engraved the words in his mind. "It was inconceivable to me that a known toxic substance that killed all these people could be openly on sale and that people would go on about their business calmly, selling and buying this stuff," said Mr. Arias, who has a midlevel government job reviewing environmental reports.

Mr. Arias thought about alerting the store clerk but figured nothing would come of it. Instead, he bought a tube with the plan of turning it over to the health authorities. It was not easy. Since government offices were closed on the weekend, he said, he used a vacation day on Monday to walk the tube to the nearest Health Ministry office. But that office refused to accept it, directing him to a second health center. Mr. Arias walked there and found himself in a crowded office. "It's always filled with people who are seeking medical attention," he said. The clerk there directed him to another section of the building, where he spoke to another official. "I said, look, here is this toothpaste I bought on the pedestrian mall," he said he told the official, "and it says right here—it's got diethylene glycol." The official told him he needed to take the toothpaste to a third health center, this one much farther away. "I said, wait, wait, do I have to walk all the way over there?" he recalled. "Can't I give it to you and make the complaint here?" At this point, Mr. Arias said he was given a form to fill out. He left wondering what if anything would come of his complaint.

Mr. Arias got his answer three days later when the nation's top health official, Dr. Camilo Alleyne, announced that toothpaste containing diethylene glycol had been found by an unidentified shopper in Panama City. The news set off alarms. In 2006, the government had mistakenly mixed mislabeled diethylene glycol into 260,000 bottles of cold medicine, and Panama was still coping with its aftermath. The day before Dr. Alleyne's announcement, a front-page newspaper article here reported the finding by the *Times* that the diethylene glycol in the cold medicine had come from a Chinese company not certified to sell pharmaceutical ingredients, and that it had been sold under a false label.

Over the years, counterfeiters have used diethylene glycol as a cheap substitute for its more expensive chemical cousin, glycerin, a common ingredient in medicine, food and household products. Could the suspect toothpaste have come from China as well, investigators wanted to know? And how did it enter the country unnoticed? "Under no circumstances were we ever going to let another incident such as happened last year happen again," said Eric Conte, a top drug official at the Panamanian Health Ministry. The label did not list its origin. "There was stuff in English, how to brush your teeth, and there was a list of ingredients," Mr. Conte said. Markings suggested that it came from Germany, but the authorities were skeptical. "We had a good idea where it came from," said Reynaldo Lee, director of the national food-protection agency. He suspected China, and shipping records proved him right.

The toothpaste had entered Panama through the Colón Free Trade Zone on the Atlantic side of the Panama Canal. One of the world's biggest free zones, with 30,000 workers and 2,500 businesses, it is a place where billions of dollars in goods are unloaded, stored and either sold or reshipped free of tariffs. From there, 5,000 to 6,000 tubes slipped into the Panamanian market, without proper certification, mixed in with animal products, investigators said. A much larger number of tubes were reshipped from the free zone to other Latin American countries.

But it was not until the United States disclosed on June 1 that tainted tubes had penetrated its borders that the hunt intensified, a task that grew more difficult when investigators discovered that some contaminated toothpaste did not list diethylene glycol on the label. Even two well-known brands, Colgate and Sensodyne, got caught up in the sweep when counterfeiters were found to be selling toothpaste with antifreeze under their names. Some fake Colgate tubes also contained potentially harmful bacteria, according to a statement from Health Canada, the national health agency. "Consumers should seal the tube and put the tube in a sealed bag," Canadian officials advised. Investigators told the *Times* that both counterfeit brands came from China.

As the complaints mounted, China's government defended legitimate manufacturers that used diethylene glycol as a thickening agent in toothpaste, saying it had caused no health problems among Chinese consumers. Officials outside China took a different view. "They should apologize to the world, and not say that it is not dangerous," said Dora Akunyili, who runs the National Agency for Food and Drug Administration and Control in Nigeria. "This is ridiculous."

Like Panama, Nigeria had had its own lethal encounter with diethylene glycol: dozens of children died in 1990 from medicine that also contained the poison. In laboratory tests, Canadian authorities found diethylene glycol concentrations of nearly 14 percent in Chinese toothpaste—about twice the level of poison detected in the deadly Panamanian cough syrup. "While toothpaste is not meant to be swallowed, it is often swallowed by young children," Health Canada warned. Action against Chinese toothpaste is continuing. In late September 2007, Brunei and Australia announced bans on toothpaste containing unacceptable levels of diethylene glycol.

As reports from around the world mounted, Chinese officials showed they were not immune to the criticism. When the makers of Sensodyne tracked counterfeit toothpaste through the Dubai Free Trade Zone to a factory in Zhejiang Province, in China, regulators there shut it down, a spokesman for Sensodyne said. The government also closed the chemical company that made the poison used in the toxic Panamanian cough syrup.

And in July, China ordered its manufacturers to stop using diethylene glycol in toothpaste. The decision generated news coverage around the world. The name Eduardo Arias was nowhere to be found. He did not seem to mind. "At least I contributed something," he said.

R. M. Koster contributed reporting from Panama.

Alexander Wolff is a senior writer at *Sports Illustrated* and the author of *Big Game, Small World: A Basketball Adventure.* As a student of Ferris professor Robert Massie in 1977, he decided to become a history major and began to appreciate the power of historical narrative, like this retelling of the 1972 massacre at the Munich Olympics for *Sports Illustrated* (August 26, 2002). Thirty years later, the hostage drama that left eleven Israeli Olympians dead seems even more chilling and offers grim reminders to today's security experts.

When the Terror Began

For a citizen of a country manacled to its past, Dr. Georg Sieber had a remarkable knack for seeing the future. In the months leading up to the 1972 Olympic Games in Munich, West German organizers asked Sieber, then a 39-year-old police psychologist, to "tabletop" the event, as security experts call the exercise of sketching out worst-case scenarios. Sieber looks a bit like the writer Tom Clancy, and the crises he limned drew from every element of the airport novelist's genre: kidnappers and hostages, superpower patrons and smuggled arms, hijacked jets and remote-controlled bombs. Studying the most ruthless groups of that era, from the Irish Republican Army and the Palestine Liberation Organization to the Basque separatist group ETA and West Germany's own Baader-Meinhof Gang, he came up with 26 cases, each imagined in apocalyptic detail. Most of Sieber's scenarios focused on the Olympic Village, the Games' symbolic global community; one that did not—a jet hired by a Swedish right-wing group crashes into an Olympic Stadium filled with people—foreshadowed a September day in another city many years later.

But on September 5, 1972, at the Munich Olympics, history would not wait. It hastened to crib from one of Sieber's scenarios virtually horror for horror. The psychologist had submitted to organizers Situation 21, which comprised the following particulars: At 5:00 one morning, a dozen armed Palestinians would scale the perimeter fence of the Village. They would invade the building that housed the Israeli delegation, kill a hostage or two ("To enforce discipline," Sieber says today), then demand the release of prisoners held in Israeli jails and a plane to fly to some Arab capital. Even if the Palestinians failed to liberate their comrades, Sieber predicted, they would "turn the Games into a political demonstration" and would be "prepared to die. . . . On no account can they be expected to surrender."

To Sieber, every terrorist organization has an MO that makes it a kind of text to be read. With the Black September faction of the PLO, he hardly had to read between the lines. "I was simply trying to answer the question, If they were to do it, how would they do it?" Sieber says, in his house in the Nymphenburg district of Munich, the Bavarian capital.

There was only one problem with Sieber's "situations." To guard against them, organizers would have to scrap plans to stage the Games they had been planning for years—a sporting jubilee to repudiate the last Olympics on German soil, the 1936 Nazi Games in Berlin. The Munich Olympics were to be "the Carefree Games." There would be no place for barbed wire, troops or police bristling with sidearms. Why, at an Olympic test event at Munich's Dante Stadium in 1971, when police deployed nothing more menacing than German shepherds, foreign journalists had teed off on the organizers, accusing them of forgetting that Dachau lay only 12 miles away. *Nein*, the organizers came to agree: whereas Berlin had been festooned with swastikas and totalitarian red, Munich would feature a one-worldish logo and pastel bunting. Whereas Hitler's Olympics had opened and closed with cannon salutes and the Führer himself presiding, these would showcase a new, forward-looking Germany, fired with the idealism pervading the world at the time. Security personnel, called Olys, were to be sparse and inconspicuous, prepared for little more than ticket fraud and drunkenness. They would wear turquoise blazers and, during the day, carry nothing but walkie-talkies.

The organizers asked Sieber whether he might get back to them with less-frightful scenarios—threats better scaled to the Games they intended to stage.

Thirty years later, Sieber recalls all this with neither bitterness nor any apparent sense of vindication. He betrays only the clinical detachment characteristic of his profession. "The American psychologist Lionel Festinger developed the theory of cognitive dissonance," he says. "If you have two propositions in conflict, it's human nature to disregard one of them."

With security tossed aside, the Olympics became one big party. Mimes, jugglers, bands and Waldi, the dachshund mascot, gamboled through the Village, while uncredentialed interlopers slipped easily past its gates. After late-night runs to the Hofbrauhaus, why would virile young athletes bother to detour to an official entrance when they could scale a chain-link fence only 6 feet high? The Olys learned to look the other way. A police inspector supervising security in the Village eventually cut back nighttime patrols because, as he put it, "at night nothing happens." Early in the Games, when several hundred young Maoist demonstrators congregated on a hill in the Olympic Park, guards dispersed them by distributing candy. Indeed, in a storeroom in the Olympic Stadium, police kept bouquets of flowers in case of another such incident. Hans-Jochen Vogel, who as mayor had led Munich's campaign to land the Games, today recalls the prevailing atmosphere: "People stood on the small hills that had been carved out of the rubble from the war. They could see into some of the venues without a ticket. And then this fifth of September happened. Nobody foresaw such an attack."

Nobody except Sieber. To be sure, he turned out to have been slightly off. Black September commandos climbed the fence about 50 minutes earlier than envisioned in Situation 21. To gain entry to the Israelis' ground-floor apartment at 31 Connollystrasse, they did not, as Sieber had imagined, have to ignite a blasting compound, because they were able to jimmy the door open. But the rest of his details—from the commandos' demands for a prisoner exchange and an airliner; to the eventual change of venue from the Village; even to the two Israelis killed in the first moments of the takeover—played out with a spooky accuracy. By the early hours of the next day, nine more Israelis were dead, along with five of the terrorists and a Munich policeman, after an oafish rescue attempt at a military airfield in the suburb of Fürstenfeldbruck.

Following indignant words from the paladins of the Olympic movement, after a little mournful Beethoven, the Games of Munich went on. It's an article of faith that The Games Must Go On. For the 30 years since, the Olympics—indeed, all sports events of any great scale—have carried on, even if permanently altered by the awareness that terrorists could again strike.

To revisit the Munich attack is to go slack jawed at the official lassitude and incompetence, and to realize how much has changed. But today the Munich attack is irrelevant in a sense, for terrorists are unlikely to try to duplicate it. In the cat-and-mouse world of terrorism and counterterrorism, the bad guys strive for audacity, as only the unthinkable will both confound security planners and achieve what terrorists truly hope for, which is to galvanize the attention of the world. So organizers think and think in order to close that window of vulnerability. For the Summer Games in Sydney, they tabletopped 800 scenarios, even as they girded for that unthinkable 801st.

Details about the massacre in Munich have dribbled out since 1972, slowly at first and then, over the past decade, in a rush. These accounts, most self-serving and some maddeningly incomplete and contradictory, nonetheless reveal how a kind of perfect storm gathered over the Munich Olympics, a confluence of determination and naiveté.

It turns out that Georg Sieber envisioned the events of September 5 even before Black September had planned them. The plot wasn't hatched until July 15, when Abu Daoud and Abu Iyad joined another Black September leader, Abu Mohammed, at a café in Rome's Piazza della Rotonda. Leafing through an Arabic newspaper, they spotted a report that the IOC had failed even to respond to two requests from the Palestinian Youth Federation that Palestine be permitted to take to Munich an Olympic team of its own. "If they refuse to let us participate, why shouldn't we penetrate the Games in our own way?" Abu Mohammed asked. They conceived their plan.

On August 24, two days before the opening ceremonies, Abu Iyad flew from Algiers to Frankfurt via Paris with a male and a female associate and five identical Samsonite suitcases as checked luggage. As Abu Daoud watched through plate glass outside the baggage claim, customs officials picked out one of the five bags and popped it open. They saw nothing but lingerie. The female associate looked on indignantly, which may explain why the other four bags went uninspected. Taking a separate taxi, Abu Daoud met Abu Iyad and his colleagues at a hotel in downtown Frankfurt, where they consolidated the contents of the five suitcases—six Kalashnikovs and two submachine guns, plus rounds of ammunition—into two bags.

In the meantime, six junior Palestinians—mostly *shabab*, "young guys," culled from refugee campus in Lebanon—were training in Libya, with an emphasis on hand-to-hand combat and jumping high walls.

Abu Daoud says he told the eight fedayeen to exercise restraint: "The operation for which you've been chosen is essentially a political one . . . to defend yourselves. Nonetheless, only fire if you truly can't do otherwise. . . . It's not a matter of liquidating your enemies, but seizing them as prisoners for future exchanges. The grenades are for later, to impress your German negotiating partners and defend yourselves to the death."

To which his associate added, "From now on, consider yourself dead. As killed in action for the Palestinian cause."

Yossef Gutfreund apparently heard the rattling of the door at the threshold of the ground-floor duplex apartment the other Israelis called the Big Wheels' Inn because it housed senior members of the delegation. When the door cracked open in the darkness, he could make out the barrels of several weapons. He threw his 290 pounds against the door and shouted a warning: "Danger, guys! Terrorists!"

The commandos herded their captives to the second floor of that first duplex apartment. At 5:08 a.m., a half hour before dawn would break over the Village, two sheets of paper fluttered down from the balcony and into the hands of a policeman. The communiqué listed the names of 234 prisoners held in Israeli jails and, in a gesture to win the sympathy of radical Europeans, those of Andreas Baader and Ulrike Meinhof, Germany's most notorious urban guerrillas. If the lot weren't released by 9 a.m., a hostage would be executed. "One each hour," a terrorist told the policeman. "And we'll throw their bodies into the street."

At 8:15 a.m., an equestrian event, the grand prix in dressage, went off as scheduled.

The terrorists pushed back their deadline twice more, to 3 p.m., then to 5, knowing that each postponement only redoubled the TV audience. "The demand to free our imprisoned brothers had only symbolic value," one of them would say later. "The only aim of the action was to scare the world public during their 'happy Olympic Games' and make them aware of the fate of the Palestinians."

Shortly before 5 p.m., the terrorists made a new demand. They wanted a jet to fly them and their captives to Cairo. The Germans saw a potential opening. If the crisis relocated, there would be buses and helicopters and planes, embarkations and disembarkations, the agora of an airport tarmac—perhaps an opportunity to draw a bead on the fedayeen.

Just before midnight, the armored-personnel carriers finally arrived to bear down on the helicopters. Only here did the hostages lose their lives, to judge by what can be pieced together from portions of a long-suppressed Bavarian prosecutor's office report. A terrorist strafed the four hostages inside one helicopter. Then he sprang to the ground, wheeled and flung a grenade back into the cockpit before being shot dead as he fled. Weightlifter David Berger would be the last hostage to die. He had taken two nonlethal bullets in his lower extremities, only to perish of smoke inhalation. The last shot, fired at about 12:30 a.m., ended nearly three hours of an operation that, as an official involved later put it, "was condemned to fail from the beginning."

Even as the shootout continued at the airport, a rumor had cruelly mutated into fact. At 11 p.m., Conrad Ahlers, a spokesman for the West German federal government, told reporters that all the hostages had been liberated. The wire services sent this misinformation around the world, and Israeli newspapers hit the streets on September 6, repeating it in banner headlines. Even Golda Meir went to bed believing the Germans had freed the nine captives.

On the morning of the 6th, the grim truth became known. "Until today, we always thought of Dachau as being near Munich," said Israeli interior minister Josef Burg. "From now on, unfortunately, we'll say that Munich is near Dachau."

Willi Daume, the president of the Munich organizing committee, at first wanted the remainder of the Games called off, but IOC chairman Avery Brundage and others talked him out of it. "I too questioned the decision to continue," says Vogel, the former mayor of Munich, "but over time I came to believe that we couldn't let the Olympics come to a halt from the hand of terrorism."

So, after a memorial service on September 6, the Carefree Games resumed. Many of the 80,000 people who filled the Olympic Stadium for West Germany's soccer match with Hungary carried noisemakers and waved flags, while authorities did nothing to intervene in the name of decorum. Yet when several spectators unfurled a banner reading "17 DEAD, ALREADY FORGOTTEN?" security sprang into action. Officials seized the sign and expelled the offenders from the grounds.

Today, most of the apartment block at 31 Connollystrasse is filled with middle-class Germans going about the banal business of living. Well-tended flowers spill from windowsills. A young girl prances off with her bicycle. A memorial plaque by the main doorway is in temporary storage, but it will return in the spring, after renovations are complete on the pedestrian-only street.

If you know what went on there, however, the scene hints at the sinister. The plastic tape of the construction cordon suggests the crime scene the spot once was. Chain-link fencing is a reminder of what the Black Septembrists scaled to steal into the Village. On the side of the building, faded graffiti evokes the ferment of another time, of shouted slogans and violent means.

The entryway and apartment where Moshe Weinberg and Yossef Romano were murdered now belong to a Max Planck Institute, a scientific think tank.

A sign reads PLEASE RESPECT THE PRIVACY OF OUR GUESTS. "Of course we all know what happened," one of the three residents, all Russian scientists on contract with the institute, recently told a stranger who knocked on his door anyway, "but none of us knows exactly where the guys were murdered. We don't want to know. If we knew, it would make it very hard to live here."

Sieber has never again worked with an organizing committee for a sporting event. "It's nothing but frustration," he says. "The officials aren't able to develop a tradition because everyone is a rookie. Nine out of 10 aren't paid—they're volunteers—and the paid professional can't lead them. If you're not a professional, you incur no risk, take no responsibility. This disaster in Munich, it was a horror trip, the whole thing, a chain of catastrophes large and small. Who paid? O.K., the German government paid, but of those individuals who were responsible, no one paid. We can't change the past. But more important, we're not learning for the future, because nothing's really different."

In fact, Munich changed forever how the Olympics are conducted. Athletes at the 1980 Winter Games in Lake Placid, New York, stayed in a Village built to be so secure that it was eventually converted into a prison. Later that year, in Moscow, the Soviets X-rayed every piece of incoming luggage at the airport and deployed 240,000 militiamen to show they meant business. Though the USSR's boycott of the 1984 Olympics in Los Angeles was surely payback to the U.S. for passing up those Moscow Games, the Soviets claimed they stayed home because of inadequate security, even as the LA Olympics introduced such gadgets as a remote-controlled robot that could examine suspicious objects. Sixteen years ago the IOC began to collect and share information related to security, and in 1997 formally established a "transfer of knowledge" program so Olympic know-how—from the food tasters for athletes in Seoul to the palm-print recognition technology in Atlanta—could be passed from one organizing committee to the next.

Sieber is out of the business of tabletopping the Olympics and refuses to talk specifically about Athens. But he brings up one of his 30-year-old scenarios. The Basque separatist group ETA is "very patient," Sieber says, his imagination as vivid as ever. "They pick out a man they want to kill. They send one of their operatives, disguised as a worker, to the construction site for his new home and plant a bomb. For several years they do nothing. Then one morning, perhaps after he is married, with a family, they detonate it by radio. He finds himself up in the sky."

Don Yaeger provided additional reporting for this article.

Michael Dobbs is a former *Washington Post* reporter turned Cold War historian. His *One Minute to Midnight: Kennedy, Khrushchev, and Castro on the Brink of Nuclear War* (Knopf, 2008) was designated one of the five best nonfiction books that year by the *Washington Post*. This text is excerpted from *Saboteurs: The Nazi Raid on America* (Knopf, 2004).

Saboteurs: The Nazi Raid on America

Looking at a map of the territory he controlled, Hitler had every reason to feel at the peak of his power in the spring of 1942. The failed artist and retired corporal had become the unchallenged master of much of the Old World, from the Caucasus Mountains to the English Channel, from the fjords of Norway to the deserts of North Africa. He saw himself as the "greatest German ever," the more than worthy successor of Bismarck and Frederick the Great. He had more than avenged the humiliations heaped on Germany after World War I. Through a mixture of bullying, bluff, and blitzkrieg, his armies had sliced through supposedly impregnable defenses in Czechoslovakia, Poland, the Balkans, Belgium, the Netherlands, France, and finally Russia. His plan for the annihilation of the Jewish race—a long-held dream—was well under way.

But the Führer was astute enough to understand that the propaganda accounts of an almost unbroken succession of military triumphs did not tell the whole story. Problems were surfacing that threatened the very foundations of the Third Reich and his own ability to hold on to absolute power. On the western edge of Europe, Great Britain remained a stubborn holdout, refusing to recognize the New Order that Hitler had established for the rest of the continent. In the east, on the Russian front, the German juggernaut had ground to a halt in the depths of the Russian winter after a series of sweeping advances the previous summer.

In the meantime, on the other side of the Atlantic, America was dramatically increasing the production of iron, aluminum, and steel, the first step to churning out the tanks, airplanes, and submarines needed to win the war. At the end of 1940, President Franklin D. Roosevelt had held out a vision of America as "the great arsenal of democracy," using its "industrial genius" to "produce more ships, more guns, more planes, more of everything." But Hitler had a scheme that, if put into effect, would wreak havoc on America's ability to make war. The plan was known as Operation Pastorius.

June 13, morning
Six months after Pearl Harbor, foreign-inspired terrorism was low on the list of concerns of ordinary Americans. Even though German U-boats were known to be off the East Coast, the idea of Nazi saboteurs looming ashore to wreak havoc behind American lines seemed far-fetched, even ludicrous.

Enemy sabotage missions were the stuff of Hollywood movies rather than daily newspaper headlines.

For most Americans, the war in Europe and Asia was still a long way away. American boys might be dying in places like Corregidor and Bataan, but there was still a quality of innocence about domestic life. People had grown accustomed to the protection afforded by two great oceans: the American homeland seemed an oasis of peace and relative prosperity, somehow insulated from the murderous passions afflicting the rest of the world. Saks Fifth Avenue was still advertising its semiannual clearance sale; Irving Berlin was still performing on Broadway; Joe DiMaggio was still hitting home runs in Yankee Stadium.

The sense of American invulnerability was reflected in the low priority placed on homeland security. The defenses set up along the eastern seaboard in the immediate aftermath of America's entry into the war were "scanty and improvised," in the words of the army's official history. They were strengthened somewhat in April as a result of the growing U-boat menace and intelligence reports that the Germans might be trying to land saboteurs along the coast. But there were many glaring holes, caused in large part by bureaucratic turf fights between the agencies responsible for homeland defense.

If there was one person in Washington who took the threat of internal subversion very seriously, it was President Roosevelt. As assistant secretary of the navy during World War I, Roosevelt had been responsible for naval intelligence, and he constantly suspected the Germans of plotting attacks against American military installations. Some of these suspected plots were the figment of his own hyperactive imagination and lifelong fascination with the cloak-and-dagger, but others were real enough. In July 1916, saboteurs blew up a huge ammunition depot on Black Tom Island in New York Harbor opposite the Statue of Liberty, killing seven people and destroying two million pounds of munitions intended for Allied forces in Europe. It was the greatest explosion in the history of New York City, and could be heard in Philadelphia, nearly a hundred miles away. Thousands of heavy plate-glass windows fell out of skyscrapers and office buildings in Manhattan and Brooklyn, and pieces of shrapnel landed as far away as Governors Island. Six months later, in January 1917, the roar of exploding munitions again shook New York City, this time from a fire in a shell assembly plant near Kingsland, New Jersey. Responsibility for the Black Tom and Kingsland explosions—which took place at a time when the United States was still officially neutral—was eventually traced to the German secret service. Among those implicated in the plot was Franz von Papen, a former German military attaché in Washington and future mentor to Adolf Hitler. It seemed reasonable to conclude that the Germans would try something similar in World War II.

Roosevelt's suspicions were piqued by an intelligence report dated March 15, 1942, from the U.S. embassy in Switzerland, warning that German submarines were transporting groups of "two or three agents at a time" to the north and central coasts of America. The report cited a trusted source who had just returned from the German port of Kiel, where he met with the relatives of U-boat men.

Agents carry communications and very valuable explosives . . . They are very familiar with area where they will work and very amply supplied with dollar bills obtained in Sweden and Switzerland. During darkness submarines proceed very near inshore (some commanders related having seen glare New York skyline), whence member submarine crew takes them ashore in hard rubber boats with outboard motors. Well developed plan prescribes that, at moment ordered, agents and accomplices in America will commence simultaneously everywhere on continent a wave of sabotage and terror, chief purpose of which is to cause United States military authorities to keep greatest possible number of troops on home front, reducing thereby to minimum number sent abroad.

The report was discussed by the Joint Chiefs of Staff on March 30 and passed on to the intelligence agencies "for appropriate action."

On the night of Saturday, June 13, Seaman Second Class John C. Cullen was assigned the midnight patrol east from Amagansett Lifeboat Station. He had been walking for about fifteen minutes, and had covered just under half a mile, when he spotted a group of three men holding a dark object in the surf, silhouetted against the misty sea. It was rare to run into anyone at this time of night: under the blackout regulations, everybody not in uniform was meant to be off the beach.

"Who are you?" Cullen yelled. He shined his flashlight in the direction of the strangers, but it was of little use in the fog, so he turned it off.

One of the men came toward him, shouting out a question.

"Coast Guard?"

"Yes. Who are you?"

"Fishermen. From East Hampton. We were trying to get to Montauk Point, but our boat ran aground. We're waiting for the sunrise."

"What do you mean, East Hampton and Montauk Point?" said Cullen, surprised that the fishermen would run aground less than five miles from their starting point and fifteen miles from their destination. Logically, they should have been farther out to sea. "Do you know where you are?"

The stranger acted cagey. "I don't believe I know where we landed. You should know."

"You're in Amagansett. That's my station over there," the coastguardsman replied, gesturing back over his head through the mist. "Why don't you come up to the station, and stay there for the night?"

The other man hesitated a little before murmuring, "All right." They walked together a few steps in the direction of the lifeboat station. Then the stranger changed his mind.

"I'm not going with you."

"Why not?"

Another hesitation.

"I have no identification card, and no permit to fish."

"That's all right. You better come along "

"No, I won't go."

Cullen made a motion to grab the stranger's arm. "You have to come."

Although the stranger spoke fluent English, he seemed strangely out of place. He didn't look much like a fisherman. He was wearing a red woolen sweater with a zipper up the front, a gray mechanic's coat, gray-green dungarees, white socks, tennis shoes, and a dark brown fedora hat. His pants, Cullen noticed, were dripping wet. The stranger seemed anxious to distract Cullen's attention from his two companions. Rather than submit to the coastguardsman's authority, he abruptly changed the subject.

"Now listen, how old are you, son?"

"Twenty-one."

"You have a mother?"

"Yes."

"A father?"

"Yes."

"Look, I wouldn't want to kill you. You don't know what this is all about."

The stranger reached into the left pocket of his pants and pulled out a tobacco pouch with a thick wad of bills.

"Forget about this and I will give you some money and you can have a good time."

"I don't want your money."

Another man appeared out of the fog, from somewhere higher up the beach, wearing only a dripping bathing suit and a chain with some medallions around his neck. He was dragging a canvas bag, which was also wet, through the sand. "Clamshells," said the man in the fedora hat by way of explanation. "We've been clamming."

The newcomer began saying something in a language that Cullen could not understand but that sounded vaguely like the German he had heard in war movies. The use of the foreign language seemed to upset the man in the fedora. He immediately put his hand over the other man's mouth, ordering him, in English, to shut up and "get back to the other guys." He then took Cullen's arm, saying, "Come over here."

After a few steps, the stranger produced more money from the tobacco pouch, shoving what he said was three hundred dollars into Cullen's hands. By now, Cullen was very worried. His life had been threatened, and he was outnumbered at least four to one.

"Take a good look at my face," said the stranger, removing his hat and coming closer. "Look in my eyes."

The stranger's eyes were dark brown, almost black. He was thin, and seemed to be about five feet six inches tall. He had unusually long arms, a large hooked nose, and prominent ears. His most noteworthy feature, apart from a thin, elongated face, was a streak of silvery gray that went through the middle of his combed-back black hair.

"Look in my eyes," the stranger repeated. "Would you recognize me if you saw me again?"

"No sir, I never saw you before."

"You might see me in East Hampton some time. Would you know me?"

"No, I never saw you before in my life."

"You might hear from me again. My name is George John Davis. What's your name, boy?"

It had been a bizarre conversation, and Cullen was not about to reveal his real name.

"Frank Collins, sir," he mumbled.

With that, he backed away from the strangers, clutching the bills in his hand. The man in the fedora seemed willing to let him go, even though he and his companions could easily have overpowered him. Once Cullen reached the safety of the fog, he ran for his life.

It took Cullen no more than five minutes to run back to the lifeboat station. Most of his fellow coastguardsmen had gone to sleep; he woke them with shouts of "There are Germans on the beach" and "Let's go."

Cullen found a pack of German cigarettes near the spot where he had had his bizarre encounter with the man in the fedora. As dawn was breaking, other coastguardsmen followed some tracks along the beach to the top of the dunes, where they discovered a freshly turned mound of sand. Poking around with a stick, they felt something hard. In a few minutes they came across four wooden crates bound with marlin twine that could be used as a handle. Barnes pried open the crate with a bayonet and discovered a hermetically sealed tin container.

A short distance away, in another newly dug hole, the coastguardsmen found a canvas seabag and two trench shovels. A pair of light blue bathing trunks was lying on the sand, along with a belt and a shirt.

To avoid being seen, the saboteurs kept behind a hedgerow. "Filthy and wet and as stained as anyone could have been going through water and wet grass," they cleaned themselves up as best they could. The real name of the man who had identified himself as George Davis was George Dasch. He got rid of his wet clothes—swimming trunks, tennis shoes, tattered shirt, and a pair of socks—by throwing them into a hedge opposite the railroad station. At six, Dasch noticed smoke coming out of the station chimney, suggesting that the stationmaster was up and about. Examining the railway timetable, he noted that the first train of the morning—an express from Montauk to Jamaica, in

Queens—was due at 6:59 A.M. Dasch feigned nonchalance as he asked for four one-way tickets to Jamaica.

"We were going fishing, but it's a nasty foggy morning, and I guess we will go back home," he told the stationmaster, Ira Baker.

They were the only passengers to board the train at Amagansett. Soon afterward, Baker discovered some wet clothes in the station hedge. Thinking nothing of it, he threw the items into the incinerator.

A small team of experts assembled by the FBI examined the sabotage materials retrieved by the Coast Guard from Amagansett Beach. They laid out the contents of the wooden crates and seabag on the floor of the basement shooting range of the federal courthouse in downtown Manhattan, and began tagging every single explosive device and item of clothing. Cursing the Coast Guard for ripping open the boxes so unmethodically, they drew up their own meticulous inventory:

1. Two small bags marked "C. Heinrich Anton Dusburg Reibanzünder" 6.1939, containing ten fuse lighters, pull wire
2. One small paper bag containing five fuse lighters
3. Twenty-five electric blasting caps, .30 caliber
4. Fifty electric match heads contained in small brass tabular adapters
5. Fifteen wooden box containers, approximately 2 × 3 inches, apparently containing five detonators each with threaded ends

And so on down the list of seventy-three different items, ending with "coil of detonating fuse approximately 82' in length." Assistant FBI director Eugene J. Connelley, assigned by J. Edgar Hoover to head the investigation, described the haul as the "most impressive" array of sabotage equipment he had ever seen. Whoever put it together must have had access to some extraordinary resources.

The FBI scientists were led by Donald Parsons, an eight-year bureau veteran and one of the top explosives experts in the country. As he picked up each item, he marveled at its sophisticated construction. He conducted a series of tests on the explosive devices, checking the fuses against a stopwatch and firing bullets into the yellow blocks of TNT to test their explosive velocity. It did not take him long to conclude that there was enough material in the boxes to do millions of dollars' worth of damage to the American war industry.

Serge Schmemann, the editorial page editor of the *International Herald Tribune,* has been a correspondent for the Associated Press in Johannesburg and for the *New York Times* in Moscow, Bonn, Jerusalem, and New York. He won a Pulitzer Prize in 1991 for his coverage of the reunification of Germany. What follows is the beginning of his book *When the Wall Came Down: The Berlin Wall and the Fall of Soviet Communism* (New York Times Books, 2006).

A Knock on the Door

November 9, 1989. A chilly evening in West Berlin. I was in my hotel room, writing furiously on my laptop. The stories were breaking fast. The Communist government in East Germany was in crisis. All through the autumn, East Germans had been fleeing their country in droves through Hungary and Czechoslovakia. Even greater numbers had been holding regular marches in East German cities, demanding reform. The government's authority was crumbling. Every day there were new changes, new announcements, new surprises.

I had just returned from a press conference in East Berlin at which the Communist leaders had announced new travel regulations for East Germans who wanted to visit the West. That was big news: up to then, the majority of East Germans, like most Eastern Europeans, had been prevented from leaving the East. It was a good story, probably page one, so when somebody knocked on the door around midnight, I was annoyed. It was my assistant from East Berlin, Victor Homola.

"I'm busy, Victor," I barked. "Grab something from the minibar and wait."

"But, Serge . . ."

"Not now! Not now . . ."

Then it struck me: Victor? He was an East German! He wasn't allowed to cross into the West; he'd never even *been* to the West. "Victor! What on earth are you doing here?"

"That's what I'm trying to tell you, Serge! The wall is down!"

That began one of the most exciting stories I've covered as a foreign correspondent: the fall of the Berlin Wall. For many, the event has come to represent the end of forty years in which Eastern Europe was held captive by the Soviet Union. But it was not only a political story. It was also an intensely human story, about people rising up to break down a wall that had kept them brutally apart—a wall that had divided Germany, and all of Europe, into a free and democratic West and an East that lived under dictatorship.

It was about people choosing freedom.

I grabbed my West German assistant, Tom Seibert, and with Victor we jumped into a taxi. The streets near the Berlin Wall were quickly filling with celebrating Germans, and the police were trying to divert traffic. The taxi driver, a big woman with a bigger voice, was yelling out the window, *"Ich habe hier drei Pressefritzen!"*—"I have three press guys here!"—and the police waved us through. We drove right up to the most important stretch of the wall—the spot where it passed by the Brandenburg Gate, once the very center of Berlin.

The Berlin Wall was a frightening sight, a twelve-foot-high concrete barrier that divided one of the major cities of Europe right in half. It did more than that—since West Berlin was deep inside East Germany, the wall actually ran all around it, creating a large urban island of the free, democratic, and brightly lit West right inside the tightly controlled Communist-ruled East. The worlds inside and outside the wall were completely different—within its wall, West Berlin looked like any large Western city. Shiny Mercedes and BMW sedans cruised the neon-lit Kudamm—the grand Kurfürstendamm boulevard; store windows displayed the latest in fashions; restaurants and nightclubs were open late into the night. West Berlin had theaters, museums, a university, skyscrapers, two airports, a lake, rivers, canals, parks, even a zoo. West Berliners could easily go to West Germany, or anywhere else in Western Europe, so they felt free and secure inside their walled-in island.

On the East German side of the wall, large blocks of anonymous apartment buildings loomed. There were far fewer shops, and everything seemed grayer and poorer. The East Germans heated their buildings with poor-quality coal, so everything was covered with soot. Still, parts of East Berlin had retained the old-fashioned charm of a central European city, recalling old black-and-white spy movies.

In fact, life in East Berlin was better than in Moscow and many other Eastern European cities. But the East Germans were always aware of the bright lights in the Western island in their midst. West Germany deliberately aimed radio and television signals eastward, so it was easy for most East Germans to receive them. East German teenagers were more savvy about what was happening in the West than teenagers in other parts of Eastern Europe—and because of that they were much more frustrated. Though it was West Berlin that was encircled, many East German children grew up thinking the wall was around *them*.

The wall itself reflected the difference between the two governments it divided—from the eastern side, it was like a prison wall, with watchtowers and glaring lights; from the west, or from inside, it was covered with bright and ever-changing graffiti.

Before Berlin was divided, the Brandenburg Gate had been the city's most famous landmark. Now, the gate was actually part of the Berlin Wall. The main wall ran past it on the west side, while police barriers on the east formed a no-man's-land around it. For decades, trying to cross that no-man's-land had meant possible death or imprisonment for East Germans.

Now, joyful East Berliners were scaling the barriers and running to the wall. On our side, West Germans were climbing up on top of the wall and reaching down to haul up their eastern cousins. An observation platform on the western side, built so visitors could look at the Brandenburg Gate, was full of dancing people.

"The wall is gone! The wall is gone!" people chanted. As we watched, more and more East Germans poured over, and more and more West Germans gathered to greet them with tears and champagne. For thirty years, these people had dreamed of the day when they could be together again. Tom, a university student from Bonn who was my interpreter and assistant in West Germany, was seized by the excitement and started climbing up the wall to join the party.

I grabbed him by the foot and yelled, "Not tonight! Tonight we work. Tomorrow we celebrate!" And work we did. It was close to five a.m. when we finished filing the stories. The historic front page of the next day's *New York Times* had my story with a picture across the whole page of people dancing in front of the Brandenburg Gate. Over it, the huge headline read: "EAST GERMANY OPENS FRONTIER TO THE WEST FOR EMIGRATION OR VISITS; THOUSANDS CROSS."

In the popular German tabloid *B.Z.,* a headline screamed, *"Die Mauer ist Weg! Berlin ist wieder Berlin!"*—"The Wall Is Gone! Berlin Is Again Berlin!"

Rose Tang is a former CNN producer, senior writer for *The Standard* in Hong Kong, and radio reporter-announcer for the Australian Broadcasting Corporation. Surviving the Tiananmen Massacre prompted her to become a journalist. This piece is part of a memoir she is writing about China.

Tiananmen Massacre

It started with curiosity. In 1989, I was a freshman at the Beijing Foreign Languages Institute. It was April 22. A usual sunny Saturday. I was shopping with my roommates. We heard that students had been marching to Tiananmen Square following the death of the former general secretary of Chinese Communist Party, Hu Yaobang, a week earlier, so we strolled over to see whether there were any rallies.

In front of the Great Hall of the People, rows of police in green uniforms locked hands to form human walls in front of the protesters. On top of the steps, three students, kneeling side by side, holding a scroll above their heads, reminded me of petitioners in ancient times pleading before the emperor.

"Dialogue, dialogue! Li Peng, come out!" they shouted for the premier.

I did not know the students' agenda or want to. My father, who had been jailed for eleven years for having questioned Mao Zedong in his personal diaries, always said, "Stay away from politics, it's very dangerous." I was never interested in politics, dangerous or not.

In the next few days, more students took to the streets. Many universities started boycotting classes. Our university already had a bad reputation as a party school, indifferent to national affairs. But one day a few students blocked entrances to classroom buildings, so naturally all classes were suspended indefinitely.

The square was a red, white, and black sea of flags, banners, makeshift tents, and people. The word "democracy" figured on nearly all the banners and slogans that people shouted. I had never heard the word "democracy" by itself, detached from expressions like "proletarian democratic dictatorship" from our textbooks. "What is democracy?" I asked around. No one could answer.

Demonstrations escalated to hunger strikes. Placards announced how many hours the students had been fasting. I joined picket lines, but had second thoughts about becoming a hunger striker—I loved eating. Cokes and mineral water, cakes and bread, were abundant everyday, provided by our university or donated. It was a free party. Standing in the blazing sun was no fun, though. I lost my voice from shouting, "We want democracy. Down with corruption! Down with Li Peng!"

Our job on picket lines was to keep onlookers and foreigners away from the hunger strike areas. We stretched bedsheets on bamboo poles to make shelters for hunger strikers; we locked our hands to form human walls. "This is our internal affair," we told foreign journalists. I tore a piece of red flag to make a headband and decorated it with signatures of fellow protesters. A headband was a protester's license. Wearing mine, I could hitchhike on any vehicle.

Every day, more and more people came to the square: workers, peasants, artists, academics, journalists, even monks. My hairdresser, who had shaved the back of my head in the shape of Marilyn Monroe's lips, recognized my hair and was proud of me. The square was our utopia. Students from other cities streamed in. During the day, we shouted slogans and marched. At night, we danced by campfires. Romances budded. Pop songs circulated around the square. My favorite was "Follow Our Senses":

> Follow our senses.
> Grasp the hand of dreams.
> Our steps are getting lighter and merrier . . .
> My heart feels as free as wind.
> Suddenly I find a completely new me.

Martial law was declared on May 20. A dozen students from my university were carried back to campus after being brutally beaten by the police. Outraged, I went to the gate of Zhongnanhai, near the square, where top party leaders worked. The area was packed. After hours of shouting, most students lost their voices. Since I was the loudest, I was given a bullhorn to lead the crowd. Facing hundreds of protesters, with the soldiers as backdrop, I felt like a revolutionary hero. With my headband drenched in sweat, I jumped up and down in a red shirt and white jeans. I led the mob in shouting slogans and delivered speeches about democracy and corruption, though I still knew nothing about democracy or corruption.

I conducted "The Internationale" with a romantic pop beat:

> Arise! Slaves suffering from hunger and cold.
> Arise! Those from all over the world in hardships.
> Our blood is boiling.
> We will fight for the truth.

Not all days were euphoric. The hunger strike was going nowhere. The square, smelling of sweat and rotten food, was littered with garbage. In between marches and rallies, we lazed about on piles of banners. Every morning, student announcers urged us on loud speakers to get up and tidy up our tents.

I ran into Wang Qiong, a freshman I had met at the rally in front of Zhongnanhai. He looked distressed and related infights among student leaders. I returned to campus. Classes were still boycotted, but the library was open. I looked in vain for books on democracy. Cultural Revolution–style big-character posters covered bulletin boards. I put up my poster urging a rewrite of the constitution. As schoolmates gathered and commented on my "masterpiece," I realized I had barely studied the constitution.

I spent afternoons playing tennis with political supervisor Liu, whose job was to monitor and guide students' political thoughts. He said some students had complained about my drinking beer and smoking cigarettes in the canteen. Why, I argued, is it okay for male students to do the same? Liu smiled and said nothing.

Then it was June 3, another balmy sunny Saturday afternoon, another tennis game. The campus was filled with the racket of trucks. Several students ran past the sports ground, shouting, "They are smashing military trucks!" Tennis racket in hand, I rushed to the scene, but the smashing job had already been done by other students. I released air from tires, a trick I had mastered as a child. I climbed on the trucks and begged the soldiers to retreat. The troops, jammed like sardines in the back of the trucks, were silent, their faces innocent and frightened. Probably younger than we. They avoided eye contact.

My boyfriend, Guang, cycled by. He had just visited the square. "There aren't enough students in the square. They need backup. A lot of military trucks and tanks are going in!" he said. "It's time to become a revolutionary hero!" I thought. "I'd rather be ashes than dust," a line from Jack London, my childhood hero.

Our schoolbooks were full of stories about how young Communist martyrs were killed by the Kuomintang or Japanese troops. I had seen revolutions only in the movies but dreamed of being part of one. I regretted being too young to become a Red Guard before the Cultural Revolution ended.

The sun was setting. "Something big will happen tonight," I thought as I put on a black jacket and black jeans for camouflage. I wrote my last wishes in a short letter and asked a roommate to pass it on to Guang if I did not return the next morning. I removed a Uighur dagger from my suitcase, a gift from a friend that I had never intended to use. With the dagger in my jeans pocket, I hopped on my red Flying Deer bicycle and sneaked through a side gate, avoiding the main doors, where professors were preventing students from going out.

Entering the square, I couldn't believe my eyes. It was so peaceful! People holding paper fans were strolling as on any summer evening. Children were running around; street hawkers were selling snacks; students were hanging around as usual. In my university's tent, a pile of bamboo sticks looked like wimpy weapons, so we searched for real ones. With two empty beer bottles in each hand, I felt like a warrior clutching hand grenades. We had been trained—throwing model hand grenades was a staple of our elementary school physical education classes. I bought eggs from a food vendor. A few people slurping wontons pointed their chopsticks at him: "These students are defending our Tiananmen with their lives. How could you charge them money?" I pleaded for them to leave the square. No one budged.

Just before midnight, a burning tank, chased by rock-throwing crowds, rattled into the square and bulldozed roadblocks in front of the Great Hall of the People. A few thousand students sat in front of the monument. A speaker declared the establishment of the University of Democracy. Then some speakers urged us to fight to the very end; others made equally impassioned pleas for us to leave.

We were told to disarm. I surrendered the beer bottles but kept the dagger. We distributed wet towels in case of tear gas. Hearing sounds of firecrackers exploding in the distance, we cheered: "It's like the Spring Festival." But soon bullets whizzed over our heads. "Must be rubber bullets, they would not dare kill us!" we laughed. A few minutes later, sparks bounced off the monument, and we realized they were real bullets. Wounded students were carried into the square. A young woman held up a bloodstained white shirt and told us of the killings outside the square.

It was still a party for us in the square. Taiwanese singer Hou Dejian, who had been on a hunger strike, led us in singing "Descendants of the Dragon": "Giant dragon, giant dragon, you open your eyes . . ."

My schoolmate Zhao was writing passionately on a poncho he had made from a white bedsheet. "I'm writing revolutionary rock 'n' roll," he said.

Student leader Chai Ling stood on a box and shouted with a quavering voice, "My fellow students! It's time to die for revolution. We're like a group of ants on top of a hill. There's a big fire below us. The only way to get out is to unite and form a big ant ball. We roll down the hill, the ants outside the ball will die but the ants inside will survive and carry on our revolution!" "So you will live, and we will die?!" I yelled at her. I'd rather die as a hero, not an ant.

Then it was a long quiet wait. All lights in the square were switched off. The silhouette of Tiananmen looked like a giant dark stage backdrop lit by burning tanks. A high-pitched female voice warned through loudspeakers from the Great Hall of the People that counterrevolutionary riots had begun, and urged us to leave or be responsible for whatever happened to us. Suddenly, droves of soldiers scuttled out like ants from under the hall. I ran back to the monument to alert other students, fearing I was going to be shot in the back. But no one was after me.

All the lights were turned on at the same time, followed by the deafening noise of tanks thundering toward us from three directions like green monsters. Time was frozen. Everything was in slow motion. We gasped at the tumbling of our Goddess of Democracy. The tanks neared, crushing the tents. Soldiers carrying enormous sticks emerged from behind the tanks and surrounded us. "This is real military action. Just like the movies!" we yelled. A group of soldiers dashed onto the stairs of the monument, shot the loud speakers, and aimed at us. Their bayonets shone in the bright lights. I felt a sharp pain thrusting in my chest. After a brief standoff, Hou Dejian announced that he had persuaded a captain to let us leave peacefully. We walked slowly toward a narrow pathway between the tanks at the southeastern corner of the square. My mind was blank. A girl in front of me sobbed.

Soon the soldiers started to bludgeon us. With my feet lifted from the ground, I was pushed and pulled, carried by the stampede. Amid screams and thuds, my chest was squeezed, my glasses smashed. I could see only blurry streetlights above the black silhouettes of people around me. I suddenly regretted coming to the square and wished there were a God. "I don't want to die, please, I beg you. God, please let me live," I mumbled, and gasped for air.

I trampled over a few bodies, not knowing whether they were dead or alive. I was dragged along by the mob that was moving like a huge ball of ants. I tumbled to the ground. A soldier kicked me and wielded his enormous wooden stick, but the stick only grazed my head as he loudly abused me. I scrambled back to the "ant ball," but was pushed against a tank. I climbed up the tank and crawled over the tread. The tank's turret lid was open. A soldier was aiming his gun at the crowd. He did not turn his head as I crawled past him and jumped off the other side. Shivering, I staggered past more tanks and soldiers. I was finally on my way out of the square.

Zhao, the revolutionary rock 'n' roller, was wiping his bleeding head with the white poncho of music scores. "I lost my Nike shoes," he moaned and headed back to the square. Nike shoes were very expensive and were a status symbol. I realized I was barefoot too. A few minutes later, Zhao returned, smiling, with his Nike shoes dangling around his neck.

It was dawn. We found more students from our university. Some had bleeding heads or feet. The square was cordoned off by tanks. A few large puffs of smoke rose. "They're burning corpses," said a bystander.

The sky was gray, like a heavy sheet of lead. It started to drizzle. "Even the sky is crying," I thought. We heard gunshots in the distance as we walked slowly in narrow lanes among traditional courtyards. Locals came out and gave us shoes. A weeping student joined us. Holding a small pair of bloodstained glasses with two bullet holes, he described how a twelve-year-old girl had been shot by troops near Mao's mausoleum. She had been taking a stroll with her five-year-old sister.

Two students and I volunteered to return to campus for help. Along the way, we saw burning trucks and tanks piled along the Avenue of Eternal Peace. Hours later we arrived. The university dispatched an ambulance. We drove through the outskirts of Beijing to avoid troops, but they were everywhere, even in the wheat fields. It was a full-on military campaign. For the first time since the movement began, more than forty days before, I cried, not sure whether my friends were still alive. We were relieved to find them hiding in a courtyard.

That night, a few students were still missing. I borrowed a roll of black sheets and sewed armbands at a professor's home. We planned a memorial service, but canceled it at the last minute when we heard rumors about troops marching onto campuses. Instead, we stood outside the dormitories and listened to the BBC.

My father called the next day. I had not contacted my parents since the movement began because I did not want them to nag me out of it. "I knew you would be there that night," he said. "I am so proud of you! I'm so glad our family has contributed to democracy."

I received a call from a student at the University of Science and Technology. His roommate, Wang Qiong, had been shot. I slammed down the phone and howled, "Why did they have to kill him? Why? Why? Why?!" Wang had visited me only a few days before, blushing constantly as we chatted in my dormitory. He was nineteen.

I went to the Fuxing Hospital to look for Wang's body. All major intersections were guarded by troops. I was barred from the morgue. In the wards, gauze-bound patients were moaning. An outspoken man in a plaster cast showed me a tiny piece of metal. "They took it out of my thigh. The doctors couldn't find any whole bullets. The troops must have used shrapnel." He had been wounded while watching television at home on the Avenue of Eternal Peace, where troops were shooting indiscriminately.

My classmates returned home. I burned the armbands and lists of protesters' names, hid my dagger and headband under the bed, and waited for the war. Political supervisor Liu was surprised to see me. Apparently, university security guards had banged on my dorm door one afternoon and concluded no one was there. Universities were ordered to hand over student leaders to the police. My habit of sleeping late had come in handy: I was so deeply asleep that I did not wake up to be arrested. The guards grabbed someone else.

Many nights I was awakened by gunshots and tanks rumbling in the distance. I cried in the dark. I was confused, scared, sad, angry. I missed my dead friend Wang. I did not know whether other friends were dead or injured. I wanted to do something, but I did not know what. I hoped martial law would soon be lifted so I could retrieve my bicycle.

War never came. The fall semester started in September, with a compulsory assignment for every student: a 3,000-word essay confessing and criticizing our behavior and vowing to stand by the party. We copied each other's notes. The professors did not seem to mind the plagiarism.

Martial law was finally lifted in January. On a freezing night, I took a bus to the square. It was empty except for a few armed soldiers patrolling. Water trucks were sprinkling the ground. I walked around and around, trying to find proof of my memories.

There were no bloodstains or bullet holes. Not a single trace of what had happened during that late spring and early summer. The protesters, red flags, white banners, burning tanks, troops, my Flying Deer bicycle: where had they gone? All I could see was the clean wet concrete glittering in the streetlights. "The Internationale," "Follow My Senses," the screams, the roaring tanks, the loudspeakers: where had they gone? All I could hear was the sound of sprinkling water. More than forty days of joy, tears, and blood had been washed away.

Jill Abramson, the managing editor for news at the *New York Times* and a former Washington bureau chief, is the coauthor, with Jane Mayer, of *Strange Justice: The Selling of Clarence Thomas* (Houghton Mifflin, 1994). This piece appeared in the *New York Times* on September 20, 2008, soon before the demolition of the old Yankee Stadium.

Finding Respite from Worries

In 1929, my Uncle Philly, who worked the stadium snack bars as a lifelong employee of the concessionaire Harry M. Stevens, arranged for my mother, then 12, to have her picture taken with the Babe. That was the beginning of his taking "the chickens," his raft of nieces and nephews from my mother's generation and mine, to the ballpark. Philly, who was unmarried, spent Yankees seasons at the ballpark and winters at the track in Hialeah Park, and had the perfect life. But he could never remember our names, which is why he called each of us "Chicken."

In the summer of 1962, I was about to be sent to sleep-away camp in Maine, for the first time, while my mother was hospitalized with spinal meningitis. I was an understandably worried girl. Philly kindly took my mind off my troubles by taking me with him to the park. He'd tip one of the ushers to watch me while he tended to the beer and dogs. That was the summer I learned how to stop worrying.

Looking out at that monster gorgeous field, studying the program, I learned that the darkest hour could come, only to be brightened by the crack of a bat. So brooding and worrying on behalf of my team didn't make any difference. I gazed at Bobby Richardson, the boyishly handsome second baseman, knowing that I was destined to marry him. How bad could life be? (Many decades later, I met Richardson when he was a no longer boyish and running, unsuccessfully, for Congress. I kept my long-ago fantasy to myself.) My mother recovered in time to visit me at camp later that summer.

At other worried points in my life, I found that I could relax immediately once I was in my seat at the park. (The first hot dog and beer help, too.) When Uncle Philly died, I was working out of state, and I hadn't been to a game in years. He left one of those wills only a bachelor of modest means leaves: very specific endowments to the remaining chickens. I got his collection of silver dollars and his autographed Yankees pictures, a trove that included heartfelt messages from many of the biggest stars, including two from Joe DiMaggio. There is even one that is simply signed by Ruth and Gehrig on Lou Gehrig Day. It hangs near the photo of that 12-year-old girl with Band-Aids on her knees, in an almost new Yankee Stadium, next to the man who built the house that won't be there anymore.

Babe Ruth and Jill Abramson's mother, Dovie, 1929. Photo courtesy of Jill Abramson.

John Seabrook has been a staff writer at the *New Yorker* since 1993. His most recent book is *Flash of Genius, and Other True Stories of Invention* (St. Martin's Griffin 2008). This evocation of his father appeared in the *New Yorker* on March 16, 1998.

My Father's Closet

When I think about my father's long and eventful life, my mind's eye fills up with his silhouette at different times over the years, as defined by his beautifully tailored Savile Row suits. I see the closet where his suits hang. Viewed from his dressing room, my father's closet appeared to be the ordinary, well-appointed closet of a successful businessman. It wasn't until you stuck your head inside that you became aware of a much larger collection of suits, hanging on a motorized apparatus, the kind you'd see at a dry cleaner's, extending up through the ceiling of the second floor and looming into the attic, which was filled with a lifetime of his clothes.

As with most bespoke suits, each jacket had the exact day, month, and year it was ordered marked on the inside pocket. You could stand in the doorway, press a button, and watch as the history of my father, in the form of suits from all the different eras of his life, moved slowly past. Drape suits, lounge suits, and sack suits, in worsted, serge, and gabardine; white linen suits for Palm Beach and Jamaica before the invention of air-conditioning; Glen plaids and knee-length loden coats for brisk Princeton-Harvard football games and a raccoon coat for Princeton-Dartmouth, which was later in the season. Suits for a variety of business occasions, from wowing prospective underwriters with a new offering (flashy pinstripes) to mollifying angry shareholders whose stock was diluted by the offering (humble sharkskin). Then, as the life-is-clothes approach succeeded at the office, suits for increasingly rarefied social events, from weddings at eleven and open-casket "viewings" at seven, to christenings, confirmations, and commencements, culminating in the outfits needed for four-in-hand driving, in which four horses are harnessed to a carriage—a sport that presents one with a daunting range of wardrobe challenges, determined by what time of day the driving event is taking place, whether it's in the country or in town, whether one is a spectator or a participant, or a member or a guest of the club putting it on. Three-quarter-length cutaway coats, striped trousers, fancy waistcoats, top hats: his four-in-hand outfits were the part of his closet that verged on pure costume.

In a nearby closet were his shirts, made by Sulka or Lesserson or Turnbull & Asser; another closet contained a silken waterfall of neckties of every imaginable hue; still another held shoe racks, starting at the bottom with canvas-and-leather newmarket boots and then rising in layers of elegance through brown ankle-high turf shoes, reversed-calf quarter brogues, medallion toe-capped shoes with thick crêpe soles, and black wingtips with curved vamp borders, to the patent-leather dancing pumps at the top.

When he wasn't dressed up, my father was either in pajamas (sensible cotton pajamas like the ones Jimmy Stewart wears in *Rear Window*) or naked. He was often naked. He embarrassed not a few of my friends by insisting on swimming naked in the pool when they were using it. But his nakedness was also a form of clothes, in the sense that it was a spectacle. Dressing without regard to clothes at all, occupying that great middle ground between dressed and undressed—dressing just to be warm or comfortable, which is the way most people wear clothes—didn't seem to make sense to him.

My father's closet was his inheritance from his father. Not the clothes themselves, but the belief that a custom-made English suit, worn properly, was a powerful engine of advancement within the establishment. Without his clothes, my grandfather was an uneducated man who had spent his early years in the dirt, more or less. (The expression "dirt farmer" is still used sardonically by farmers in South Jersey to describe their profession: when you're out all day in that loamy clay and sand, you begin to feel as though the dirt itself were your product.) But, dressed in his Savile Row suits, my grandfather was a man of substance, taste, grace.

My father was more of a fashion innovator. He was the Duke of Edinburgh as played by Douglas Fairbanks, Jr. The cut of the clothes was still that of the sensible establishmentarian, but within those controlled contours you'd get flashes of purple and pink in the widespread-collared shirts, polka dots in the ties, and a green chalk stripe of imagination in the suits, signifying the American tycoon. In his youth he experimented with elements of both the Brooks Brothers style, which he encountered as an undergraduate at Princeton, and his father's Edward, Prince of Wales look, hitting upon his own synthesis around 1950: double-breasted, high-waisted suits with wide lapels, snug in the body but with deep vents in the back.

The gaga-in-my-toga sixties, which threw men's fashion toward the more relaxed, anything-goes mentality that prevails in our time, burst against my father's solid shoulders of English wool and receded, leaving but one very interesting trace behind. This was a blue velvet Nehru smoking jacket, decorated with light-blue-and-navy flower-and-ivy psychedelia, and matched with midnight-blue velvet pants. It was made by Blades of London, and dated April 25, 1968, a period when the Nehru was enjoying a brief vogue among the men my father aspired to dress like, thanks mainly to Lord Snowdon's wearing a Nehru-style dinner jacket in a famous photograph in the sixties. I had never seen my father wear the outfit, but there it hung, among all the sober garments in his closet, a sign that somewhere inside the businessman was an artist.

The attic portion of my father's closet was for me the most alluring part of the house. It had a beauty born of the obsessive pursuit of perfection. Other men wore clothes easily and well, and took good care of them, but my father cared about his wardrobe to a degree that might have alarmed some of the men whose style he emulated, had they set foot in this room. However, while a great imagination was evidently at work in here, my father's closet was also oppressive: the chalk lines and pinstripes and windowpane checks had a kind of suffocating effect on me. It became important for me to believe that these were the iron bars through which I would have to squeeze in the struggle for my own authority. My father's ways of making me into the man he wanted me to be were so subtle that they were often hard to notice, much less resist; clothes, however, were a patch of open ground on which I would engage him.

In an early photograph of my brother and me, we're dressed according to my father's Little Lord Fauntleroy ideals, in blue or gray serge short pants, with matching woolen blazers and woolen caps. I look miserable. Somewhere just out of the frame of the picture, Miss Mann, our scary English nanny, lurks.

In the fullness of time—I'm twelve—my father escorts me to Brooks Brothers and buys me my first No. 1 Sack Suit, exclaiming approvingly as I emerge from the fitting room, "John, you look exactly like an investment banker!" Five years later, he takes me to have my first suit of evening clothes made, at Hall Brothers in Oxford; still later I go with him to A-Man Hing Cheong, his Hong Kong tailor, to be "measured up" for a few "country" suits (a Glen plaid and a windowpane check) and, presumably, many others in the future. ("Big men can wear bolder plaids and more details without appearing to be fairies," Dad once advised me.)

My visit to the tailor turns out to be a rite of some kind of passage. "Which side?" he asks; he speaks a bit of English. He is kneeling in front of me, pointing at my crotch and waggling his forefinger back and forth.

"He wants to know which side you wear your pecker on," my father says.

"Yeh yeh, ha ha ha, yar peck-ah!"

In short order, I am on my way to acquiring a fabulous closet of my own. And yet all is not well with the little lord. Without intending to, exactly, he manages to rip the silk lining in the beautiful camel's-hair coat, lose buttons off a Brooks suit, tear the seams around the pockets of the evening clothes. Inside my scrubbed and Etonian exterior there seems to be a dirt farmer struggling to get out.

"You're so *hard* on your clothes," my mother would say, and she was right. My boyhood closet was a riot of passive-aggressive behavior exhibited toward innocent garments. Beautiful slacks were bunched up on hangers, never hung along the pleat line. I always forgot to pull out the pocket flaps of my jackets, so that the next time I wore them they'd be full of creases. Shirts had fallen off their hangers and were lying on the floor, with shoes chucked into a pile on top of them. The shoes themselves were a mess—the leather, once soaked, was now flaking off, and the backs had all been crushed by my bad habit of cramming my feet into the shoes while they were still tied.

My brother, on the other hand, seemed effortlessly to acquire my father's ability with clothes. His closet was like an Eagle Scout's version of my father's. Mine was the Anticloset.

When it became clear that I was going to be more or less my father's shape and size, there was rejoicing in my parents' household. Naturally, my father was pleased. He had never spent much time with me as a boy, being so busy providing all the amazing advantages that we enjoyed. We never threw a ball together, or went camping—he didn't have the clothes for it. But in the art of dressing for success, he would gladly be my adviser and my friend.

My mother was also pleased. Having grown up with little money, she could never reconcile herself to her husband's clothing purchases (a Huntsman suit today costs more than three thousand dollars), to the point where my father had to smuggle new clothes into the house. Now, at least, his reckless extravagance would have a practical outcome: I would never have to buy any clothes of my own. I could just start wearing my father's, beginning with the earliest items in his wardrobe and working my way along the endless mechanical circle.

Not long after I moved to my first apartment in New York, my father took me to his New York tailor, Bernard Weatherill, to have a couple of his old suits refitted on me. The shop was upstairs on a midtown street—just a nameplate on a wall you'd pass every day in the city without giving it a second glance. The man who measured me up was an elderly white-haired Englishman, whose slightly stooped posture seemed like an unparsable synthesis of class-based deference and the physical toll of years of bending down to measure the bodies of young gentlemen like me. His tremendous discretion seemed to suck all the oxygen out of the air.

The jackets fitted almost perfectly. A little big in the body, but the length in the sleeves was beautiful. My father and the tailor beamed with pleasure. The pants, however, needed taking in; the tailor asked me to "stand naturally" as he marked them up. But for some strange reason I had suddenly forgotten how to stand naturally. It was as if I'd lost the concept of posture.

"Why are you standing like that?" my father said. "Knock it off."

During most of the eighties, these suits hung among my so-called wardrobe like a landing party that had set up a base camp in my closet from which to launch an assault on the rest of my life. Can clothes be a form of destiny? My father had made no secret of his wishes for my career: an investment banker or, failing that (since I seemed to enjoy writing), an investment analyst. These were the clothes for the job.

Among these suits was an inky blue-black drape suit, double-breasted, with three closely bunched parallel rows of silvery dot stripes, the groups of three about half an inch apart. The peaked lapels extended to the bottom buttons of the jacket, while the cuffed pants had a deep pleat near the fly buttons and a shallower pleat two inches farther out, which was immediately echoed by the almost hidden slash of the pocket. The date inside the jacket pocket said "9/21/61," although in style it was fifties—a suit that Burt Lancaster could have worn in *Sweet Smell of Success*. My father was forty-four when he had the suit made and was just starting out on a new career, having been fired from his previous one. He had a new wife and a new family: I was two then, and my little brother, Bruce, had just been born. It was not, perhaps, the best time to order yet another custom-made suit. But if Dad felt at all uncertain about his new responsibilities, or about the future and his title to it, his doubts were not expressed in these dot stripes. It was a highly confident suit.

I wore this suit to certain precrash eighties evenings. I was aware of an authority—when I wasn't attempting to undermine it with irony—that I didn't feel in *my* clothes. Men followed the suit with their eyes as I walked through a restaurant. Women wanted to put their hands on the fabric. Worn properly, a suit like this was clearly capable of incredible things. Perhaps it could attract some of the money, beauty, and power that were in the air in the mideighties in New York—guys I had been in college with a few years earlier were making two million dollars a year selling mortgage-backed securities—and redirect that energy into me.

My own choice of a career for myself, writing, did not require much in the way of clothes. (Part of the reason I was first drawn to writing as a profession was that it appeared possible almost never to wear a necktie.) But as I had success at my work, performed in T-shirt and jeans, something unexpected happened. On receiving payment for a writing project, I could think of nothing I wanted more to do with it than spend it on clothes. I may have rebelled against my father's closet, but the fetish for clothes appeared to be deeply implanted in me.

With my check in my pocket, I'd set out for the bank, and then for Barneys, at Seventh Avenue and Seventeenth Street. My behavior on entering the store was eccentric. I appeared calm, standing there pensively fingering some fabric, but inside my head a fashion psychopath was at work. Three hundred dollars for a pair of pants! Then again, they're asking two hundred and thirty for a shirt. And pants are a more major item than a shirt, so in a way, three hundred is cheap for pants. Thus did I gradually reduce the price through rationalization until I heard myself saying, "O.K., I'll take them." Signing the receipt felt like the moment after an accident, when you can't believe it's happened. Then, to prove that it wasn't that bad to spend three hundred dollars for a pair of pants, I'd go into another part of the store and spend two hundred and ninety dollars for a merino wool turtleneck.

I was drawn to the most expensive brands. Only a famous label had the talismanic power to ward off the Savile Row succubus that lived in my father's clothes. To my father, the whole concept of designer labels in men's fashion was ridiculous, another triumph of the marketers. What did these swishy women's dressmakers know about making clothes for a man? Ralph Lauren has made a fortune imbuing his brand with images of people like my father, but my father would never, ever wear Ralph Lauren.

The first time I wore an expensive Italian suit I had bought with my own money, an Ermenegildo Zegna, was to meet my father at "21" for lunch. He arrived at the restaurant first, and as I walked in, I saw that his attention was instantly riveted on the boxy, ventless, close-to-the-hips silhouette of my jacket. P. G. Wodehouse, describing the reaction of Jeeves upon spotting his master wearing a scarlet cummerbund with his evening clothes, wrote that "Jeeves shied like a startled mustang." My father, watching this Italian garment moving toward him around the checked tablecloths, reacted similarly. He recovered in time to greet me cordially; then, plucking the lapel of the Zegna between his thumb and forefinger, he looked at the label.

"Hmp," he said softly. That was all: "Hmp." It was the sound of a world ending.

I have only a few of my father's suits left—I am slowly de-accessioning them to friends my size who have jobs that require suits. But I have hung on to a few items I feel strongly nostalgic about. The prize of my collection is the blue velvet Nehru smoking jacket. I began wearing it at Christmas, more or less as a joke, but each year I look for more excuses to put it on. Last Halloween, I went to a party as Austin Powers, but somewhere in the course of the evening, the role I was playing blended in with a natural predilection for the costume until I wasn't wearing the blue Nehru in the spirit of Halloween anymore. I was wearing it in earnest.

Elizabeth Kendall is a writer and journalist specializing in arts and culture, and a professor in the Literary Studies program at Eugene Lang College of the New School. In this piece from *Vogue* (April 2008), she recalls the moment—and the Marimekko dress—that changed her life forever.

A Backward Glance

It is a little painful to remember myself in the first gathering of college freshmen, in the fall of 1965, in the faded genteel living room of a Radcliffe dorm. The other girls, in drapey clothes, offered limp hands and languid smiles. I, midwestern in wraparound skirt and shirt, all but pounced on my new classmates, quoting them back their middle names—Claire Adriana Nivola!—memorized from the photos in the freshman handbook. By the end of that year, I myself had become languid, or a facsimile of it—and that's a little painful to remember, too. I tried to speak in a bored breathy voice. I wore slingback heels to the library and a little tweed skirt suit smoothed inside by a severe Lycra girdle. That, I thought, was how you attracted a Harvard grad student. After all, I had been schooled by my mother to believe that my body's whole task in life was to avoid doing something shameful: never to bulge out of clothes, reveal underwear straps or leg hair, get too hungry, restless, or joyful. My body was not to be trusted.

Fortunately, a wave of new thinking was rolling in from the West Coast, a slow wave that would come to be called the sixties. My first taste of it came at the beginning of sophomore year, when a girl from California appeared on the front steps of my dorm, wearing a sky blue coat and a straw boater. I'd heard about Robin Von Breton from older girls. She'd taken a year off to work in L.A. for Charles and Ray Eames. She was a poet. But the jolt of this sky blue coat (coats then were gray, black, brown) on this blonde earnest person, and the hat out of a Victorian novel—this sense of a costume that pleased her alone—was unlike anything I had ever seen. We proceeded inside together. She took off the coat. She was wearing a trim tent-shaped dress of stiff canvas, imprinted with huge red strawberries on a field of yellow.

There are moments that are watersheds in one's life—when a vast structure of assumptions shifts, opens, tumbles. Robin wasn't trying to look like an adornment to a Harvard man. She was a young woman whose every move proclaimed originality. And it wasn't just a pose. Her poems were clean and natural (although turquoise, from a turquoise typewriter ribbon). Robert Lowell had let her into his seminar. But the most potent of Robin's traits, to a dazzled me, was the boldness that had led to that dress. Actually, she had several such dresses, all with different patterns. "You don't know about Marimekko?" she said.

I did know vaguely about the small fabric company in faraway Finland, the source of these geometrically shaped canvas dresses with the wild patterns.

They had become all the rage in fashion magazines. *Vogue's* pictorial had been positively sylvan: Marimekko-clad Finnish models posed on old wooden docks, among lakeside reeds, in forests. But I hadn't known about the store right here in Cambridge, on elegant Brattle Street, which was called Design Research, or D.R.

Did I dare go there? My allowance was whatever my mother could squeeze out of the household budget (and I had five younger brothers and sisters and a father who sometimes gambled on the commodity market). But one sunny day I rode my bike to the old white-brick row house with the stark, bright interior. Upstairs, in their own pink-and-white selling space, were the dresses, ranged on blond wood hangers. I can see myself, dark hair parted in the middle, wearing a trim navy skirt and white blouse, staring at these dresses, which were anything but well behaved. Each one was saying something like "Rejoice!" in a language of huge fruits, psychedelic stripes, flower explosions.

I was waitressing then at the faculty club. I stopped buying books; I saved all my tips. After a few months, I went back to get "my" dress. It was a stiff canvas sheath with a mandarin collar whose top half featured plum-colored sea urchins swimming in a sea of rust, with rust sea urchins on plum on the bottom. I put it on, right in the store. I can still remember the feel of that canvas—so clean and crisp. I can feel again the relief of my body set free—the dress's geometry required no girdle.

The Marimekko didn't unleash the erotic me—that would come later. It stood for something even bigger than eros. When I think of the dress, I see myself in motion: racing to class, whizzing on my bike, in animated conversation about Edith Wharton (ignored then by Harvard) with a beautiful graduate-student teacher, Ann Douglas, who became my thesis adviser. It was as if the Marimekko dress emboldened me to write the thesis about women writers—and by extension, to dare to be a writer myself. I, who'd assumed (as my mother did) that under my faux suaveness lurked the inevitable marriage to a boy back in St. Louis, the ferrying of children to the country club, the volunteer work.

On a trip home, I gave the dress to my mother. Why? Because another girl in the dorm had given me her cast-off Marimekko, with its brazen black-and-white stripes. I could be generous—or rather defiant: "Here, Mom, in one dress, are all the things you said I couldn't be, yet somehow wanted me to be—a creature of pleasure, boldness, devil-may-care-ness." But my mother loved the Marimekko. She'd already broken out of her own young-matron mold, it turned out, to become a passionate civil rights worker. She'd become bright like the dress, which she wore to meetings and rallies. She wrote to thank me in a new tone of voice—not as a mother but as a confidante.

Little did I know how short a time we would have to enjoy our new status. A few months later I flew home for spring break. As a surprise, she'd booked a beach cabin in Alabama for a family vacation. We set off in the car in the rain, she and I and four younger siblings; my father would join us later. As we headed south on Highway 61, the rain got heavier. I'd just replaced her as driver. A truck roared past, flooding the windshield. I braked hard; we smashed a low bridge; I blacked out. The kids in the back slammed knees, elbows, heads. In the passenger seat, my mother broke her neck.

I remember a rural hospital; bandages and wheelchairs; the nurse with the country twang who told me my mother was dead; my uncle shepherding in my shattered father—they'd flown down in a small plane. The rest of us, except for cuts and bruises, miraculously weren't injured—but how would we ever recover? We flew back through clouds and rain to find our driveway suddenly full of cars; our house full of neighbors putting casseroles on the dining-room table. At the funeral, packed with people, the plain pine coffin stood alone on the altar steps.

I stayed home a week more as aunts, grandparents, friends, and strangers passed through our living room, bestowing tearful hugs. I walked around in a daze, not sure, suddenly, of anything. When it came time to go back to college, I felt it as a relief. Packing on the eve of my departure, I went alone to her closet, which already smelled of neglect. In a row of somber dresses, the plum-and-rust Marimekko stood out. I put it in my suitcase.

From then on, I would wear it for both of us.

John McPhee, a *New Yorker* staff writer since 1965, won the Pulitzer Prize for General Nonfiction in 1999. He has been Ferris Professor of Journalism at Princeton since 1975. *Silk Parachute* is the title piece of his twenty-eighth book (Farrar, Straus and Giroux, 2010).

Silk Parachute

When your mother is ninety-nine years old, you have so many memories of her that they tend to overlap, intermingle, and blur. It is extremely difficult to single out one or two, impossible to remember any that exemplify the whole.

It has been alleged that when I was in college she heard that I had stayed up all night playing poker and wrote me a letter that used the word "shame" forty-two times. I do not recall this.

I do not recall being pulled out of my college room and into the church next door.

It has been alleged that on December 24, 1936, when I was five years old, she sent me to my room at or close to seven p.m. for using four-letter words while trimming the Christmas tree. I do not recall that.

The assertion is absolutely false that when I came home from high school with an A-minus, she demanded an explanation for the minus.

It has been alleged that she spoiled me with protectionism because I was the youngest child and therefore the most vulnerable to attack from overhead—an assertion that I cannot confirm or confute, except to say that facts don't lie.

We lived only a few blocks from the elementary school and routinely ate lunch at home. It is reported that the following dialogue and ensuing action occurred on January 22, 1941:

"Eat your sandwich."

"I don't want to eat my sandwich."

"I made that sandwich, and you are going to eat it, Mister Man. You filled yourself up on penny candy on the way home, and now you're not hungry."

"I'm late. I have to go. I'll eat the sandwich on the way back to school."

"Promise?"

"Promise."

Allegedly, I went up the street with the sandwich in my hand and buried it in a snowbank in front of Dr. Wright's house. My mother, holding back the curtain in the window of the side door, was watching. She came out in the bitter cold, wearing only a light dress, ran to the snowbank, dug out the sandwich, chased me up Nassau Street, and rammed the sandwich down my throat, snow and all. I do not recall any detail of that story. I believe it to be total fabrication.

There was the case of the missing Cracker Jack at Lindel's corner store. Flimsy evidence pointed to Mrs. McPhee's smallest child. It has been averred that she laid the guilt on with the following words: "'Like mother like son' is a

saying so true, the world will judge largely of mother by you." It has been asserted that she immediately repeated that proverb three times, and also recited
it on other occasions too numerous to count. I have absolutely no recollection
of her saying that about the Cracker Jack or any other controlled substance.

We have now covered everything even faintly unsavory that has been reported about this person in ninety-nine years, and even those items are a collection of rumors, half-truths, prevarications, false allegations, inaccuracies,
innuendoes, and canards.

This is the mother who—when Alfred Knopf wrote her twenty-two-year-old
son a letter saying, "The readers' reports in the case of your manuscript would
not be very helpful, and I think might discourage you completely"—said,
"Don't listen to Alfred Knopf. Who does Alfred Knopf think he is, anyway?
Someone should go in there and k-nock his block off." To the best of my recollection, that is what she said.

I also recall her taking me, on or about March 8, my birthday, to the theatre
in New York every year, beginning in childhood. I remember those journeys as
if they were today. I remember *A Connecticut Yankee*. Wednesday March 8,
1944. Evidently, my father had written for the tickets, because she and I sat in
the last row of the second balcony. Mother knew what to do about that. She
gave me for my birthday an elegant spyglass, sufficient in power to bring the
Connecticut Yankee back from Vermont. I sat there watching the play through
my telescope, drawing as many guffaws from the surrounding audience as the
comedy on the stage.

On one of those theatre days—when I was eleven or twelve—I asked her
whether we could start for the city early and go out to LaGuardia Field to see the
comings and goings of airplanes. The temperature was well below the freeze
point and the March winds so blustery that the wind-chill factor was forty below
zero. Or seemed to be. My mother figured out how to take the subway to a stop
in Jackson Heights and a bus from there—a feat I am unable to duplicate to this
day. At LaGuardia, she accompanied me to the observation deck and stood there
in the icy wind for at least an hour, maybe two, while I, spellbound, watched the
DC-3s coming in on final, their wings flapping in the gusts. When we at last left
the observation deck, we went downstairs into the terminal, where she brought
me what appeared to be a black rubber ball but on closer inspection was a pair
of hollow hemispheres hinged on one side and folded together. They contained
a silk parachute. Opposite the hinge, each hemisphere had a small nib. A piece
of string wrapped round and round the two nibs kept the ball closed. If you
threw it high into the air, the string unwound and the parachute blossomed. If
you sent it up with a tennis racket, you could put it into the clouds. Not until
the development of the ten-megabyte hard disk would the world ever know
such a fabulous toy. Folded just so, the parachute never failed. Always, it floated
back to you—silkily, beautifully—to start over and float back again. Even if you
abused it, whacked it really hard—gracefully, lightly, it floated back to you.

Peter Godwin was raised in Zimbabwe, studied at Cambridge and Oxford, and became a foreign correspondent for the *Sunday Times* of London and the BBC, reporting from more than sixty-five countries. Since moving to New York, he has written for many publications and has published four books, the latest of which is *The Fear: Robert Mugabe and the Martydom of Zimbabwe*. The following two passages, also set in Zimbabwe, are excerpted from *When a Crocodile Eats the Sun: A Memoir of Africa* (Little, Brown, 2007).

The Road Block

I drive home up Enterprise Road to see whether they have any fuel yet at the Chisipite service station, as my gauge is on red. The streetlights are dark because of the power cut. Ahead, I see the glowing tip of a pedestrian's cigarette, and I slow up a little and move into the centre of the road to avoid a huge pothole. Suddenly men with guns loom. It's a police roadblock. I slam on my brakes. I should have anticipated it; tomorrow is another in a series of less and less effective opposition strikes, and the police always cordon off the city the day before a strike to stop the opposition moving its supporters around.

Two armed policemen are standing in the middle of the road, across which they have dragged a couple of logs. There are no warning signs, and the policemen themselves wear no reflective armbands or vests. The roadblock is all but invisible, save for the red glow of their cigarettes.

A baby-faced sergeant leans into my window and exhales a beery plume of smoke into the car.

"You should be stopping further back," he says crossly.

"Your roadblock is very hard to see," I smile.

He ignores me. "License," he says thickly.

I explain that I don't actually have it on me but I'm happy to go and get it, happy for him to escort me if necessary. His interest is piqued: there is a potential for baksheesh here.

"If you no have license, then you have to wait over there until our shift is finished, and then you must go to the police station with me." He pauses for effect. "You have broken the law," he says magisterially. "You will have to pay a fine."

"According to the law," I say genially, "I only have to produce my license at a police station within twenty-four hours of having been so requested."

He looks momentarily disconcerted and then reverts to his script. "Where is your license?" And we do another round. And this time he warns me that I will have to spend the entire night "in the prison cells."

"OK," I say giving up. "Where would you like me to wait?"

He looks confused again. Our roadblock duet is discordant. I am supposed to be in a hurry, offer a bribe, and be allowed on my way. But no, I am a freak. A white man with time on his hands.

Annoyed now, he motions me to park at the side of the road. I sit there for a few minutes in the inky dark under a tree. Then a bus wheezes up. According to its route window, it is coming in from the tribal area north of Mount Darwin. The policemen order everyone off the bus and instruct the conductors to hand down the mountain of goods on the roof rack. Down it all comes: wicker cages of chickens, bicycles, dozens of red-and-white-striped jute bags, a hobbled goat, furniture, firewood. The contraband the police are most interested in is maize meal, the local staple. The government still insists on a monopoly of grain sales. To transport more than five kilograms of it constitutes the crime of black marketeering.

The country is on the verge of a famine, and the UN has warned Mugabe that half the country's twelve million people are now in danger of starvation. But he has spurned offers of more international food aid, saying, "Why do they want to choke us with their food? We have enough." And one of his most senior ministers, Didymus Mutasa, on hearing of the UN famine projection, implied that such a die-off, at least in opposition areas, was actually desirable. "We would be better off with only six million people, with our own people, who supported the liberation struggle," he was reported as saying. "We don't want these extra people."

The policemen confiscate several bags and put them on their growing pile of loot at the side of the road. An old lady my mother's age pleads with them. She has come all the way from the Zambezi Valley to bring this small burlap bag of meal to her son, "a young boy just like you," she says, "but he is without a job, he has nothing to eat." The sergeant does not want to be stripped of his badges of office and humanized. He knows that she doesn't have enough for a bribe, so the corn meal itself will be his bounty.

She is determined not to cry, but two tears well over onto her long lined cheeks. This is not shop-bought maize meal. This is from corn that she has tended from the beginning, that she has ploughed and seeded and watered as tiny, tender lime-green shoots, and hoed and weeded and harvested and dried and shucked and carried for miles to a grinding mill and paid to have it ground there into powdered meal and carried back home on her head and loaded onto this bus. It has evaded drought and birds and locusts and rats and antelopes and elephants. And just a few miles and a few minutes from its intended beneficiary, it has been wrenched away from her. This is what this young policeman is casually stealing tonight, all these months and months of work by this old lady. But he is unmoved by her earnest entreaties.

I should sit quietly in my car. I know this woman is beyond my help. But if I don't at least *try*, I will hate myself for it. I will lie awake during New York nights remembering this moment, the look on her face.

I open my door and walk over. "Sergeant?"

He starts at my voice. "Back! Back inside your car!" he says.

"Please, Sergeant, it's such a small bag of mealie-meal, please can you let her take it? I can give you *bonsela* . . . " I reach for my wallet. For this I can break my father's ban on bribes.

"*Wena, mukiwa!* You, white man!" he says, furiously fumbling with the press stud of his holster. Realizing how badly I have misread the situation, I start to retreat, my arms out, palms forward, placating. Over his shoulder, I can see the passengers on the bus, which is repacked and ready to go, are agog. The sergeant has managed to pull out his pistol now and he's waving it at me. "This is not your business. Do not interfere with police matters," he screams.

The bus conductor is fearful of getting caught up in crossfire, and he calls down urgently to the old lady that they are leaving and she must board now or be left behind. So she limps over to the door and hauls herself up on the chipped metal rail, shaking her head in disgust that it has come to this. That young boys, young enough to be her grandsons, would steal the food she has worked for a whole season to grow. As she reaches the top of the stairs, she half turns and looks down at me as I stand there with my hands up, facing the fulminating sergeant. She inclines her head slightly and raises a hand, bestowing on me her acknowledgment. And then she turns and is gone. The conductor hops in after her, bangs on the side, and the bus revs up and accelerates away in a great black belch of diesel fumes.

The sergeant frog-marches me to my car. If I come out again, he says, he will shoot me "for resisting arrest," and he slams my door shut.

I need to call Mum and tell her not to wait up for me. I dial the number on her cell phone, which I have borrowed. It rings and rings and the answer message kicks in just as she picks up.

"Hello? Hello?" says Mum.

"This is 490947," says Dad, in his deliberately enunciated voice.

We wait for him to finish his outgoing message, and then I tell her that the Worswicks' supper is running late and she should go to bed.

I sit there in the dark, incarcerated in my car, until finally, as the sun rises, the policemen drag the branches off the road and pack up their roadblock. The sergeant saunters over to me. "I'm going off shift now," he says. "I'm too busy to be bothered with you. Go," and he cocks his head in dismissal.

"Thank you so much, Sergeant," I say with a smile he recognizes as false.

"Ah, just *voetsak*," he says. It's an Afrikaans expletive. Like "fuck off," only worse.

Burning My Father

My father is now more than an hour late. We sit on a mossy stone bench under a giant fig tree, waiting for him. We have finished the little Chinese thermos of coffee that my mother prepared, and the sandwiches.

Tapera looks up. The motion pleats the base of his shaven skull into an accordion of glistening brown flesh.

"At last," he says. "He is arrived."

The car, long and low and sinister, glides slowly towards us, only the black roof visible above the reef of elephant grass. It passes us and then backs up into position.

Keith jumps out of the passenger side.

"Sorry we're late," he says. "We were stopped at a police roadblock up on Rotten Row, they wanted to check inside, can you believe it?"

He hands me a clipboard. "Sign here and here."

The driver reaches down to unlatch the tailgate. It opens with a gentle hydraulic sigh. Inside is a steel coffin. Together we slide it out and carry it over to the concrete steps. Keith unlatches the lid to reveal a body, tightly bound in a white linen winding sheet.

"Why don't you take the top," he says.

I ease one hand under the back of my father's head and my other arm under his shoulders and I give him a last little hug. He is cool and surprisingly soft to my touch. The others arrange themselves along his body and on Keith's count, we lift it out of the coffin.

We shuffle up the concrete stairs that lead to the top of the iron crib. We have woven fresh green branches through its black bars. And on top of the tiers of logs inside it, we have placed a thick bed of pine needles, and garnished it with fragrant pine shavings. Upon this bed we lay my father down.

Gently, Tapera lifts Dad's head to place a small eucalyptus log under his neck, as a pillow. As he does so the shroud peeps open at a fold and I get a sudden, shocking glimpse of my father's face. His jaw, grizzled with salt-and-pepper stubble; the little dents on his nose where his glasses rested; his moustache, slightly shaggy and unkempt now; the lines of his brow relaxed at last in death. And then, as his head settles back, the shroud stretches shut again, and he is gone.

Tapera is staggering up the steps with a heavy musasa log. He places it on top of the body.

"Huuuh." My father exhales one last loud breath with the weight of it.

"It is necessary," Tapera says quietly, "to hold the body down in case . . ." He pauses to think if there is a way to say this delicately. "In case, if it explodes because of the build-up of the gases." He looks unhappily at the ground. "It happens sometimes, you know."

Keith slides the empty coffin back into the hearse and drives away down the track, where it is soon swallowed up again by the green gullet of grass.

The old black gravedigger, Robert, has his hand in front of me now. His palm is yellow, and barnacled with calluses. He is offering me a small Bic lighter made of fluorescent blue plastic.

"It is traditional for the son to light the fire," says Tapera, and he nods me forward.

I stroke my father's brow gently through the shroud, kiss his forehead. Then I flick the lighter. It fires up on my third trembling attempt, and I walk slowly around the base of the trolley, setting the kindling alight. It crackles and pops as the flames take hold and shiver up the tower of logs to lick at the linen shroud. Quickly, before the cloth burns away to reveal the scorched flesh beneath, Tapera hands me a long metal T-bar and instructs me to place it against the back of the trolley, while he does the same next to me. We both heave at it. For a moment the trolley remains stuck on its rusty rails. Then it groans into motion and squeaks slowly toward the jaws of the old red-brick kiln a few yards away.

"Sorry it's so difficult," says Tapera, breathing heavily with the effort. "The wheel bearings are shot."

The flaming pyre enters the kiln and lurches to a rest against the buffers. Robert the gravedigger clangs shut the cast-iron doors and pulls down the heavy latch to lock them.

We all squint up into the brilliant blue sky to see if the fire is drawing. A plume of milky smoke flows up from the chimney stack, up through the green and red canopy of the overhanging flame tree.

"She is a good fire," says Tapera. "She burns well."

Paula Span, a veteran *Washington Post* reporter, now freelances and teaches at the Columbia University Graduate School of Journalism. Her book *When the Time Comes* (Grand Central) came out in 2009. This piece appeared in the *Washington Post* on September 25, 2005.

A Moving Experience

It was a fairly simple real estate transaction, as these things go: price set and met. Nice young buyers all lined up, mortgage approval in hand. Attorneys but no Realtors and, thus, no open houses or other stressful shenanigans. So why did selling the house feel as if I were aboard a scary thrill ride without a safety strap? Why was it hard to sleep? Why was my Weight Watchers group leader, of all people, cautioning me to put some of those shed pounds back on?

Maybe the answer is that there are no simple real estate transactions, not really. But I think the likelier explanation is the doorjamb. Our kitchen was painted yellow and white. On one doorpost, we'd marked our daughter's height since the month we moved in, an ascending column of inked notations. Emma, pint size at 3, leggy at 8. Emma growing past the mark labeled "Mommy." (When Mommy is 5-foot-1, this is not such a big deal, but we made a fuss anyway.) Then that big jump at 14, after spinal surgery left her suddenly two inches taller. The record grew spottier from there, teenagers being less inclined to stand against a door while a parent musses their hair with a ruler, but continued past high school graduation to her college commencement.

She'd just turned 23 when Jon and I decided that we'd really like to let someone else come up with $15,000 for that overdue new roof. "Gutter cleaning" and "housing bubble" had become two of our least favorite phrases. It was time to sell.

"A doorjamb is easy to replace," friends advised when I confided that the undertaking was making me teary, angst-y, overwhelmed by the lengthening lists and notes in my red spiral notebook labeled HOUSE. "You can just pick up a doorjamb at Home Depot and take the old one with you."

But I didn't really want to transport the thing to our new apartment. The idea of what we were leaving, not the chunk of wood or even the house itself, was the achey part. We were walking away from the place where Jon and I had raised our child and grown into middle age, the only house Em could recall, the repository of 20 years' worth of history and memory and a staggering amount of stuff that had once seemed important. We were selling the family home.

Leaving it proved more than a daunting amount of work; it packed an emotional wallop. At times, with the family scattered, the old house emptying and the new apartment mostly an idea, I couldn't figure out where home was. At others, something unexpected happened, the start of that role reversal that will probably culminate at an assisted living facility in another 20 years: the child who'd depended on us for so long became an ally and helper, the one assuring me it would all be okay.

It was a comfy old house, a clapboard colonial built around 1920. From the first, we liked the big oaks that shaded the front porch, the stained-glass window on the stairway landing, the yard we could fence for kid and dogs. So what if there were no doors on the garage and the kitchen needed a major upgrade? It felt like home. We painted and puttered, fenced the yard, set up our home offices with these newfangled things called computers. We swapped our daughter's crib for a big-girl bed.

Even the junk had associations. That border of hot pink palm trees that the buyer will no doubt strip from the bedroom wall? It's what Emma, at 7, thought cool. The black trunk in the basement that no one had used for years? She took it to sleepaway camp in Vermont, along with the adjacent backpack that no one had used for years, either.

Year after year, we'd celebrated holidays and birthdays, hosted sleepovers, acquired a succession of gerbils and cats, retrievers and border collies. I kept, out of dopey sentimentality, some of their collars and name tags. The house took better care of us (just two frozen pipes in two decades; not a bad record) than we took of it, however. Drained financially by career shifts and college bills, plus the purchase of a rural retreat a few hours away, we never really embarked on major renovations. Next year, we told ourselves, concentrating meanwhile on repairing things that might invite lawsuits, such as rotting front steps. After a while, we stopped saying next year. Jon wanted to spend more time on the farm in upstate New York; Emma had moved into the city; I was often alone in too much house that was growing too dilapidated. Time to pay off the mortgage(s) and move on.

That friends of friends wanted to buy the house, even before we'd listed it for sale, proved both a godsend and a reason for panic. We were lucky to have a deal so quickly. We were lucky simply to have a house to sell in this seller's market. But we also had just 90 days to get the place in shape, pass various inspections and dispose of its contents. Someone had to comb through the drawers full of financial papers, the shelves of vinyl records, the unoccupied childhood bedroom that still contained a lifetime of books, a chiffon prom gown and a tribe of dusty stuffed animals. Since this was all happening faster than expected, and my husband needed to stay upstate with his flock of very pregnant sheep (it's a long story), the someone was mostly me.

Faced with an attic and a basement stuffed with detritus—cracked Play-Doh sculptures of yore, stacks of statements from banks that no longer exist, a veritable graveyard of aged, semifunctional computers—I sold and donated and tossed what I could, then located A Guy With a Truck to haul the rest away. It ultimately cost me more to get rid of what I didn't want than to move what

I did. I also hired—see how American capitalism can rise to any occasion?—a company specializing in destruction. Health insurance claims, 401(k) updates—virtually all documents more than a few years old, I discovered, contain Social Security numbers. We've all heard too much about identity theft to feel easy putting sacks of such papers out in trash bags, but buying a shredder and feeding it canceled checks for hours on end was an equally unappealing prospect.

Enter Shred-it. "I'm calling to discuss your shredding needs," said the manager who returned my phone call. For a mere $95, someone in an official-looking uniform would make a house call with a shredder aboard his truck. Much larger and speedier than the home-office variety, it would chew through mountains of paper right on the spot.

So it did, in just 10 minutes, and Mr. Shred-it handed me a certificate attesting that my paperwork was now confetti. I don't know how legally significant it was, but it made me feel better.

But some jobs can't be farmed out. Those piles of photographs, way too many to stuff into albums, lots of them duplicates or just lousy shots—only I could whittle them down to a manageable boxful. So I sat and sorted for most of a day, remembering Cape Cod vacations, and puppies we'd raised and later mourned, and the Halloween that Emma went trick-or-treating as Barbara Bush. It was a tough day.

Women get this. I was surprised to discover that selling a house and moving are, as a sociologist might say, "gendered" activities. With a few exceptions, notably my husband, men offered their congratulations and then immediately wanted to know how much we'd sold the house for. Men: real estate transaction. Women: psychological milestone. It was women who looked concerned, who said things like "That must be so difficult emotionally" and "How's Emma taking it? This must be hard for her." It feels petty to want sympathy during this process—you are, after all, about to receive quite a large check for your pains—but, well, it *is* difficult emotionally.

And coming out on the train to purge her room of childhood tokens and treasures *was* something of a wrench for Emma. Two years past college, she was launched, but not fully fledged. She accepted with equanimity the possibility that on overnight visits—increasingly rare these days, anyway—she might have to bed down on a sleep sofa. Still, when I found a flat with a spare room just big enough for her single bed, a rag rug and a bookshelf, she was relieved. If she were between jobs or apartments and had to come "home" again, she could, though not to the home she remembered.

Meanwhile, she had a lot to throw away, too. One evening, as I sat in my office filling bags with old newspapers, she discarded CDs (the Gin Blossoms and Counting Crows had become embarrassing) while boxing up an eclectic assortment of Nirvana and Aretha Franklin, and many books by P. G. Wodehouse and Berkeley Breathed. Aside from one lop-eared white rabbit, she ditched the stuffed animals. Then she lugged everything to the staging area for the Guy With a Truck and came to see how I was faring. Not only did she gracefully handle her own sense of loss, she propped me up as well.

"Let me know when you schedule the move," Emma had said when we first told her our plans. "I'll take a few days off work and come help." Sure, we agreed, not really paying much attention. But she made a point of regularly reminding us. "This is really nice of you," I said, when she arrived to spend the last two nights in the old house, then the first in the new apartment. "Thanks, sweetie." "Are you kidding?" She was practically insulted. "Think how many times you and Dad did this for me. Every fall when I went to school. Every spring when school was over. The first sublet in New York. The second sublet in New York. I could do this 20 times and never make it up to you." "Don't forget every summer at camp," I added, because I didn't want her to see me choking up. I was doing that a fair amount.

Appreciation is not what you expect from a kid; it's what you expect from a grown-up. When did she gain so much perspective? I'd expected mostly her companionship through a fraught few days, but what I got in addition was tangible assistance. Not only did Em play a last game of Scrabble with me in the old kitchen the dreary night before the move, when everything was in boxes, including the TV and the lampshades. She also shuttled items to the new place, dashed to the supermarket to stock the fridge, drove us to the movies when we were in need of comic relief. After a while, exhausted from three months of decision making, I merely started doing what she told me. Should we take this poster? What about that CD player? And then, once the boxes had been moved—she unpacked half of them—where should we stow the candlesticks?

It was a comfort to have her around, especially when we took a final walk through the old house after the cleaning crew had finished, just to say good-bye. The rooms looked denuded and sad. The garage still lacked doors, the kitchen with its inked doorjamb still needed major renovation, and it was probably a good thing that its new owners would have the means and energy to do the place justice. Yet in my mind's eye, I still saw us there, Jon and I and our little girl. Now that girl, much taller than Mommy, put a protective arm around my shoulders as I cried a bit, then locked the door.

It took a few weeks to overcome the impulse to drive to the old address, not the new one a few blocks away. When the first housefly of spring entered the apartment, I had to stop and think: Had I brought the swatter? And if I had, where the hell had I stashed it? For a while, I felt as though I were house-sitting for a friend with similar taste, in a place that was pleasant enough but wasn't home. The truth is, we will never have a family home again, not in the classic sense. It's a thought that takes some getting used to. But the house will shelter another family, which has already installed a swing set in the yard. And we are awfully fortunate to have two comfortable places to live, one urban and one rural. As the strangeness of the whole experience wears off, I'm coming to feel at ease in both of them.

We're lucky, too, to have this kid, who still needs our help and counsel but is increasingly able to supply some of her own. With luck, she won't need to be making decisions for us for many years, but it's reassuring to know that if we need her to, she can. Something subtle in our relationship has shifted. Not everything, though. A few weeks after the move, the last of the boxes barely out for recycling, Em called to say that she was ready to leave the apartment she'd been sharing with four roommates and had found a tiny studio of her own. There was so much to do; she was feeling so stressed. Would I come help her move? And what could I say?

Julia Keller of the *Chicago Tribune* won the 2005 Pulitzer Prize for Feature Writing for her series about a deadly tornado in Utica, Illinois. She is the author of *Mr. Gatling's Terrible Marvel: The Gun That Changed Everything and the Misunderstood Genius Who Invented It* (Viking 2008) and a novel, *Back Home* (Egmont, 2009). This article appeared in the *Chicago Tribune* on March 13, 2003.

The Lure of the Frozen Lake

They were good-looking kids with just a hint of mischief in their eyes. Not troublemakers, no sir, but not meek little rule-followers, either. Evan Wilson and Jackie Fricke liked to have fun. They liked adventure. And they liked the ice. But then again, everybody around here likes the ice. Everybody in the communities edging the 132-mile shoreline of Lake Minnetonka, just west of Minneapolis, seems drawn to the vast frozen slab. The iced-over lake is a playground, a hangout, a thoroughfare, a shortcut, a second home. A way of life. "You grow up with it," says John Powers, who was raised here and now sells real estate in the area. "I have an 8-year-old, and he really wants to go out on the ice. For him, it's as natural as breathing. I can see it in his eyes."

There was no reason, then, why Wilson and Fricke, 16 and 17, shouldn't have headed for Lake Minnetonka on the night of Tuesday, January 21, in Wilson's red 1992 Acura Legend. No reason why they shouldn't have driven a few miles from their neighborhood to the shore and then right out onto the lake, which is really a system of some 31 interlocking waterways that can freeze all the way across. People did it all the time. Always have. Still do.

In northern states with prolonged low temperatures and lots of lakes and ponds, going out on the ice is commonplace. "They build whole cities out there," says Jim Rice, who owns a coffeehouse in Deephaven, a small town along Lake Minnetonka, marveling at the fishermen whose huts freckle the ice all winter. Around the communities of fish houses are ice skaters, ice golfers, sledders, snowmobilers and the many people who race cars across the slippery glaze. Going out on the frozen lake is routine. It's no big deal.

But even if the excursion seemed ordinary to Wilson and Fricke and to everybody they knew, it wasn't. Not, that is, in the winter of 2003. "No one has ever seen a year like the one we've had," says Lt. Brian Johnson of the water patrol unit of the Hennepin County sheriff's office, which oversees the 22.2 square miles of Lake Minnetonka. "Even the old-timers haven't seen this." A paucity of snow, unseasonably warm weather and other factors about which scientists still are arguing have combined to make the icy lakes fickle and perilous. Although this is not the deadliest season ever on Minnesota's lakes (22 perished in the winter of 1982–83), there has been a remarkable number of near misses this winter, and 10 people have died after falling through the ice—fishermen, snowmobilers, drivers.

Two of them were Wilson and Fricke. The car was some 300 yards from shore on the lake's eastern side when it went under. Friends say the two were heading for Big Island Regional Park, a campground in the middle of the lake. The area in which the car sank—where the water is 12 to 30 feet deep—typically is safe for driving in winter, Johnson reports. Experts recommend that ice be 8 to 12 inches thick before a car is driven on it—for a truck or van, the thickness should be 12 to 15 inches—and in January on Lake Minnetonka, that's usually no problem, he adds. Ice fishermen routinely plow roads on the ice, leading to what are called "fish houses." Tire tracks are clearly visible from shore. For him and others who live and work around the lake, Johnson says, driving on the ice "is just like driving down the road."

But the ice must have been thinner that night, thinner than anybody knew, plunging the startled teenagers into the frigid lake. Fricke made it out of the water, but died of hypothermia a hundred yards from shore. She was found the next morning by a contractor who spotted her from the site of a house he was building near the water's edge. Wilson, who drowned, was pulled from the lake later that afternoon.

Amid the grief and incredulity that accompany sudden death, especially the deaths of people so young, slowly grows another emotion: a kind of hushed awe. A mystery about why ice-topped water draws us inexorably toward it—in reality if we live close to it, in our dreams if we don't. Frozen lakes, Powers says, are "exciting and enticing." They are more than just wide patches of ice. "There's a sense of power in being able to walk where two months earlier, you wouldn't dream of it. I walked across a lake once and stood in the center of it, just looking around," he recalls. "It's there—and then it disappears" when the warmer temperatures of approaching spring transform the lake yet again. But while they can, he and his son, Ori, go sledding on the ice, he says.

Bud Larsen, an outdoors columnist who lives in Moyie Springs, Idaho, some 30 miles from the Canadian border, says, "It's the sense of the unknown, the thrill of taking a risk. And it's the sheer beauty of a field of ice." Indeed, there is something solemn and hypnotic about a frozen lake. People can just sit and look at it for hours. It's a magnet for contemplation. "You conjure up all kinds of visions," Larsen says. "You think, 'What's going on in there?' It's awesome."

A frozen lake is more than a meteorological phenomenon. It's a crucial element in our internal visual landscape, a relic of a kind of lost wildness in our lives. When Franz Kafka defined literature as "the ax for the frozen sea within us," he didn't choose the metaphor lightly; a frozen body of water is an instantly recognizable symbol of mysterious depths, of the hinted-at and longed-for but ultimately unknowable. There is an enchantment that clings to frozen lakes, a sense of suspended time. A frozen lake is like a held breath: it can't last forever—it doesn't even last very long, relative to the rest of the year—but before it is released, it seems filled with possibility.

One of those possibilities, of course, is disaster. For all its polished, pristine beauty, a frozen lake can be a deathtrap—more so this year than any other time in recent memory. Frozen lakes in several states have been behaving strangely, and nobody really knows why. A mysterious hole in the ice in North Long Lake near Brainerd, Minnesota, made national news, including a front-page story in the *Wall Street Journal*. By early January, five Wisconsin residents—two on snowmobiles, two in a truck and one ice-skating—had fallen through ice-covered water and drowned in separate accidents. And in southern Maine, four snowmobilers went through the ice of a frozen lake in January; two drowned.

Fluctuating temperatures that weaken ice were cited, as well, for the relocation of this year's Iditarod sled dog race from Anchorage to Nome, Alaska. The competition shifted 360 miles north so that the dogs wouldn't fall through thin ice. Some scientists believe heavy rains have left a backlog of warm groundwater that's been seeping into normally frigid lake waters, impeding ice formation. Name your theory and some expert has espoused it, says Johnson, who adds, "I don't think you'll find anybody who can explain the big open water areas. Bottom line is, we've had a series of mild winters and little snow cover. Not a good year for ice." As a rule, Johnson says, he never tells anyone that it is absolutely safe to walk or drive on the ice. But it isn't illegal, and even in the wake of the spate of ice-related tragedies, authorities haven't forbidden ice travel or posted signs. It's as popular as ever. "For every person you ask," Johnson reports, "you'll get a different reason why. Some like the serenity and beauty. Some are fanatical ice fishermen. The kids just like to slide around on it."

Perhaps it's that very juxtaposition—serenity rubbing up against potential peril—that makes frozen lakes especially alluring. The forbidden and the familiar. The calm and the catastrophic. Duane Rioux, a writer and ice fisherman in Waterville, Maine, believes the accessibility of frozen lakes is what makes them special. "Most people can't afford to go fishing during the summertime because they can't afford to buy a boat. Ice fishing lets you take the whole family out for the day. Snowmobilers love the ice because it's flat, it's wide open—and you can go a long way."

A frozen lake is a "living thing," Larsen says, and like all living things, it communicates with those who know how to listen to it. The sounds emitted by a frozen lake are weirdly memorable. Ice cracks, yes, but it does more than that too. It sends forth a deep, plangent note, like a muffled sonic boom. "The first time I heard it," says Larsen, who writes an outdoors column for www .ruralnorthwest.com, "I was ice fishing. I looked up at the sky and asked my buddy if a storm was coming. The ice is shifting and adjusting—it sounds just like an earthquake." Experienced outdoorsmen such as Larsen have rules for traversing the ice: they make sure the surface is level ("Low spots means cracks with water seeping up through compacted snow," he says) and clear ("Cloudy ice means compacted snow, and it has only half the weight-bearing ability of solid ice").

But as any expert will tell you, no ice is totally safe—a fact that provides those who frequent frozen lakes a chilly little frisson of excitement. Mark Wilson needs no reminders about the enthrallment of frozen lakes. He grew up in North Dakota, moved to Minneapolis to attend dental school in 1974 and stayed here to raise his children: Brian, 26; Alex, 18; and Ian, 13. And Evan, who was 16. "You don't know how you should feel," Wilson says. "There's no way to prepare for this."

On his right wrist, Wilson wears a silver charm bracelet that was taken from his son's body, a present from Jackie Fricke. Each charm had a special meaning: chef's hat (Evan wanted to be a professional chef); palm tree (Evan and his father had spent the Christmas holidays in Florida); lizard (Evan had a pet lizard). "I spent a lot of time with him," says Wilson. "He was a fun-loving kid." And, Wilson believes, a brave one: he is sure that his son helped Fricke try to survive. "They probably had time in the water to decide what to do. They planned their escape," he says, with quiet matter-of-factness. "They struggled. They did everything they could." He hasn't been to the lake since his son and Fricke died, says Wilson. "I don't want to go there."

Others, though, go quite a bit. The spot where Fricke's body was found is marked by a makeshift shrine, with flowers and messages. He didn't know Evan was going to the lake that night, Wilson says, but it wouldn't have mattered even if he had. It wasn't the sort of activity parents think of warning their kids about. Everybody does it. Audra Dittmer, 19, agrees. She didn't know Evan and Jackie, but she knows plenty of kids who ice fish and drive on the ice throughout the winter. She's done it herself. She'd do it again. "If you know the lake, you know which parts are safe," she says. "But the weather's been up and down for the past few years." Mia Rice, 24, who works in her father's coffeehouse near Lake Minnetonka, says that when you grow up here, you don't think twice about sledding, fishing, walking or driving on the ice. Yet she has four friends who have gone through the ice this year while aboard snowmobiles. They weren't injured, but they got the scare of their lives, she says.

Nobody seems to stay scared long, however. The frozen lake's pull is too powerful, its spell too strong—and always has been, says David Nitz, 61, who lives in Wayzata, another small town along Lake Minnetonka. The semiretired building contractor recalls that on the same day Wilson and Fricke died— 42 years earlier—he, too, almost perished on the ice. "It's a coincidence, but what a strange coincidence," says Nitz. He and a girlfriend were driving on the lake at night in 1961. "All of the sudden, the front of the car started going down. I looked at her and said, 'Uh-oh.' I got out and was in the water paddling. The car was pointing down at a 45 degree angle—the engine is heavy, and the trunk floats because it's got air in it—and I reached back in and pulled her out."

The car's head- and taillights stayed on, Nitz recalls, and their illumination of the icy water was eerily disconcerting. Somehow—he's not sure how—they hoisted themselves out of the lake and rolled to more solid ice. "You don't feel the cold water. You don't feel a thing. It's all instinct." And another instinct, perhaps equally strong, is the one that sends us out to explore a frozen lake in the first place, Nitz says. He's driven on the lake repeatedly since his ordeal.

A frozen lake is gorgeous one moment, deadly the next. The ice can be mesmerizing but dangerous, a blankness upon which we project our anxieties and fantasies, a nifty site for winter sports. And a graveyard. Ice is—and then isn't. The ice looks as if it will last forever, but never does. The ice, then, is like a memory—perhaps like a memory of a 16-year-old's smile. Memories seem permanent, but in the fullness of time, in the endless turnover of seasons and climates and eras, all things change, and the ice that seemed massive and menacing and inviolable yesterday is, today, a harmless-looking pocket of water, a shifting liquid ghost of the solid body that was.

Michael Vitez, recipient of a Pulitzer Prize in 1997, has been a staff writer at the *Philadelphia Inquirer* for twenty-five years. These are two of his favorite stories. They were published in the *Inquirer* on February 13, 1998, and March 19, 2000.

True Love Is Made of This

Fifty-five years ago, Jim Way went to the library to borrow a book on telescopes. "I borrowed the librarian instead," he says. It was London. The war was on. Things happened fast. A few weeks later, she wrote him a note and signed it: "Yours as long as you wish, Wynne." "It was the wish that endured," he says.

Tomorrow, as he has done nearly every day for nine years now, Jim Way will drive the five miles to a nursing home to spoon-feed lunch—pureed chicken, spinach and applesauce—to his beloved librarian, his valentine of 53 years, a woman who hasn't recognized him, and barely uttered a word, in six years.

His wife is one of two million Americans with Alzheimer's disease. Jim, 81, cared for Wynne, 79, for eight years in their Drexel Hill home before moving her to Saunders House, a long-term care facility next to Lankenau Hospital in Wynnewood. He relented only when he could no longer lift her out of bed himself, when she'd wander outside in her pajamas the moment he went to the bathroom. "It was impossible," he said. "I had to wash her. I even had to wipe her bottom. I'd put her to bed. Before I was out of the room, she was out of bed, falling over."

He arrives every morning at 11:30. Coming to see his wife is anything but a burden. As he walked in on Wednesday, carrying old, beautiful pictures of Wynne, he explained, "I enjoy coming. I look forward to seeing her." He spread the photographs out on a table in the lobby. "I'm still crazy about her even though she . . ." His voice trailed off.

For the first four years, Jim never took a day off. He'd come seven days a week, feeding her lunch and dinner. "We had a really tough time getting him to do anything but this," said his son, Geoffrey, who visits with his father here on Monday nights. Now Jim will take two weeks off a year, one to return to London, one to visit a warm beach in winter for a few days with his sister and cousin. He also faithfully rides his exercise bike, walks the malls in winter and reads voraciously. And every Thursday now, he spends the day at the Philadelphia Art Museum, attending lectures (yesterday's was on Van Eyck) and then lunching with his old colleagues from Wanamaker's, where he rose from floor sweeper to merchandise manager, traveling the world buying merchandise, and always taking along his wife.

On Wednesdays, Wynne gets her hair done in the beauty salon at Saunders House. At noon, Jim greeted his bride. His voice was sweet, soft. "Hello, Dear . . . Wynnie . . . Wynnie . . ." He pulled her chair into the elevator. "Come on,

Sweetie," he said. He gently touched her cheeks, then lifted her jaw, trying to get her attention, to let her know he was here. This woman whose children insist she could once spell anything and who was so robust she could out-wrestle her oldest son—now a black belt in karate—until he was 15, a woman who always had perfect hair and perfect nails, sat in a geriatric recliner, be-neath an afghan blanket, pink slippers on her feet, her blue eyes still soft and clear. Her mouth hung open. Her face was red with a rash, a reaction to a medi-cine. She looked at her husband, but her expression was as blank as the eleva-tor wall. She was silent.

The doors opened on the second floor, and down the long hall he pushed her, greeting all the nurses and staff, of whom he is so fond. "Every lunch, every dinner, you can kind of set your watch by him," said Pam Kamariotis, the registered nurse on the floor. "He's so dedicated. He will sneak kisses. What he does is incredibly uncommon. Just a really nice thing to see."

Jim pushed the recliner past his wife's room, which he fills with stuffed ani-mals and flowers and photographs of their three children and seven grandchil-dren, just in case, somewhere inside her diseased brain, she recollects these things that were once so dear and familiar. He pushed on to the solarium at the end of the hall to feed her lunch. "This thing gets heavier and heavier," he says. Jim is a small man, 138 pounds, who suffers from osteoporosis and only this winter—after a bout of shingles impaired his vision—gave up night driving and his dinnertime visits this time of year.

A tray of food is waiting. He puts a long paper bib over her head that covers her chest and lap. He grabs a handful of napkins. He stands beside her and begins to spoon-feed her at 10 minutes after noon, mixing the chicken with the applesauce and putting a little lemon water ice on the tip of the spoon. "The lemon makes her pucker and helps her swallow," he says. He spoons it back in as it keeps falling out of her mouth, down her chin, over and over. He spoons it in, scraping it back up her chin, or off her bib, back into her mouth. So gentle and faithful. "Come on, Sweetie." He kisses her and cuddles her, even when she's covered with glop. He is happy to kiss her. Delighted to have the chance. "Maybe I didn't do enough of it when she was home," he says.

He carries two poems in his wallet, poems about the endurance of love. The final line of the second poem reads: "over time and grief prevail recollections—all she is."

She starts to choke. He gingerly wipes her mouth. They keep a suction pump in her room now for emergencies, a recent development. "They say the smile is the last thing to go," he says. "We've already decided—no tubes." After the pu-reed solids, he cleans her up, carries away the dishes and dirty napkins, and turns to glasses of apple juice and iced tea. He puts on a new bib and, spoon by spoon, feeds her the liquids, both the consistency of honey. Anything thinner or thicker and she will choke. At 1:13 he puts down the spoon. One hour and three minutes. He cleans her up again. Kisses and cuddles her. Then he sits beside her, quietly, and holds her hand. After a few more minutes, he wheels her back to her room, where he leaves her in the recliner. A nursing assistant will change her and put her to bed. He puts on his cap and zips his jacket and heads home to Drexel Hill.

The Greatest Penn Success Story

When Dan Harrell applied to the University of Pennsylvania at age 46, he was asked to take a composition class to prove he was Ivy League material. The first assignment: write about a favorite place. The young woman on his left chose Paris in the spring; the one on his right, the slopes of Aspen. "I've never been out of Southwest Philly," Harrell recalled, "and I'm thinking I'm in trouble." He decided his favorite place was the john. "Do you know there are 50 different names for it?" he said. "It's a great place to check out the horses for the next race. Your boss can't find you there. I wrote four pages, and I got an A."

On May 22, after 10 years as a part-time student, Harrell will receive his bachelor's degree. He will graduate surrounded by people who revere him as a Penn institution—not only because of his academic achievement at age 56, but because of the love he lavishes on a fabled floor and the students who play on it. Harrell is custodian of the Palestra.

Once a day, sometimes twice, he mops the hardwood in one of the most celebrated arenas in college hoops. He has spent, in sum, an eternity on one knee, scraping gum. And when he does his job right, the floor sings to him with the squeak of sneakers. With a toilet brush in one hand, cleanser in the other, he scours the locker rooms. Not once in his eight years there, he brags, "has there been a case of athlete's foot."

Dan Harrell also is a custodian in the larger sense of the word. He looks out for the athletes, scribbles notes of support, gives them rides and good-luck charms, asks about their grandmothers, advises them on classes to take—and, through his pursuit of a dream, inspires them. "I think he's the greatest Penn success story," said Cynthia Johnson Crowley, who played basketball at Penn in 1952 and has since been a fixture at the Palestra. "There isn't anything he won't do to make your life better. And in return, it all comes back." Fran Dunphy, the men's coach, calls him "kind of a hero of mine."

On graduation day, Harrell will dye his six-foot-wide dust mop red and blue, Penn's colors. He will tape photographs of his mother, father, and brother Frankie, all of them gone now, to the back of the mop, and march with it down Locust Walk to collect his diploma. "The mop," he said, "represents where I'm from."

At 4:55 a.m. on a March Tuesday, the day of the big Penn-Princeton double-header, Dan Harrell parked his 1980 Caprice Classic with the rusted roof right at the Palestra's back door, the best spot in the lot. Inside, everything was dark. The only sound was Big Daddy Graham talking sports on all-night radio. "I leave it on for the spirits," Harrell said. The Palestra opened in 1927; some believe that ghosts of former players and fans reside there. "I've seen them plenty of times," he insisted. "Their faces are misty, and they remain in view only long enough so you know they're there." Harrell, 6-foot-1 and a husky 240 pounds, went about collecting his supplies. He carried a boom box to the scorer's table at midcourt and popped in a CD of Irish tenors. The same lullabies his mother sang when he was a toddler filled the arena. Championship banners hung from the rafters. Dawn filtered through the skylights. The spirits retreated to the shadows.

Harrell grabbed his dust mop and started sweeping. He lives just three blocks from the rowhouse where he grew up, near 67th and Elmwood. His six daughters are sweet on him, but joke that he does not take his work home with him. "He's never picked up a towel, taken out the trash, cut the lawn, or even picked up the remote," said his third-eldest, Debbie Cianci. "He has the remote handed to him." "But," added his wife, Regina, "the Palestra sparkles."

After graduating from West Catholic High School in 1961, Harrell went to the mail room at General Electric. "In those days, maybe only one kid in 10 went to college," he said. He worked at GE 20 years, moving up to marketing. But in 1981, everyone in his office was laid off. He dug ditches for a plumber, processed support payments for family court, and tended bar. "I was down, drinking too much," he said. "I had to get a goal." In the late '80s, he found work at the Wharton School—in housekeeping—and soon moved to the Palestra. To Harrell, who had been going to Big Five games there since he was a kid, it felt like home. He learned that, as a university employee, he could enroll for free in the College of General Studies, providing he qualified. Penn also would pay part of his daughters' tuition. That is how he put Melissa and Jackie, his fourth and fifth, through Penn State. "I owe this place a lot," he said.

After he graduates, Harrell wants to keep working at Penn. His youngest daughter is a high school junior; the tuition benefit could be a big help. He might continue as the Palestra custodian, but, he said, "I think I have a lot more to offer." He talks about working in Penn community relations, in neighborhoods he has known since childhood. He talks, as well, about sports facilities management. "I think a natural for him is to be in teaching or counseling or mentoring," Dunphy said. "He's got a doctorate in life." Curtis Brown, the equipment manager, said that his close friend "eventually wants to be athletic director. I think he'd like to start in operations and work his way up. Nothing wrong with dreaming."

By 10 a.m., Harrell's forehead was pasted with sweat, and his gray Pennsylvania Athletics XXL T-shirt soaked. He put on another CD, thirteen versions of

"Danny Boy." He waxed poetic: "When you get the floors clean, and you come in here, it's like it was the first time when you'd walk into Connie Mack Stadium and see that sea of green grass—a beauty-ful thing." The floors done, he headed for the locker rooms with a handful of envelopes. Inside each was a jade shamrock key ring, bought the night before in South Philly, and a hand-written note. He tucked them in the lockers of the seniors on the men's and women's teams, for whom this would be the last home game. Harrell has a locker, too, filled with books and papers—the sign of a man with a 3.19 GPA.

Most days, he finishes at the Palestra by 1:30, then showers and goes to class or the library. He writes his papers in Catholic-school longhand and hands off to his daughters to type them. On game days, he is back at 4:30, and rarely leaves before midnight. In the last decade, he has studied Russian history and the American West, anthropology and even Swahili, though he dropped that. To fulfill the language requirement, he studied sign language—useful for a man who is deaf in one ear. Some of his favorite courses have been with anthropology professor Melvyn Hammarberg, who inspired him to major in American Civilization. Harrell thrives in the classroom, Hammarberg said, and brings his life experience with him. For a class on the American Indian, he wrote a paper on the Lenape's version of football. For a class on modern American cultural values, he observed the dynamics of the Penn women's volleyball team. For another, he studied how West Philadelphia real estate agents adapted to a changing population.

"One of the things I got from going to Penn," Harrell said, "was a better understanding of what happened to my own city. It was white flight based on fear and ignorance. Nobody really knew each other." This semester, he is doing an independent-study project—on boxball. Of all the street games he played growing up, boxball was his passion. His project, he said, will celebrate the freedom children once had to create their own games and rules. Since 1961, he has tried to preserve that culture, and his neighborhood, by coaching football at parish schools. Two weeks ago, he became the first inductee to a new hall of fame established by graduates of St. Barnabas School, his alma mater. He wore a blue suit and tie. His wife, who works at a shoe store, bought him Italian loafers—his first shoes without laces.

The same night, Penn was playing Yale at the Palestra. Before the induction, he dropped in to check the floor. In suit, tie and fancy loafers, he bent and scraped some gum. "If you are a good person, you're in with Dan," said Julie Soriero, the former Penn women's coach. "If you are a little shady, you're out. He likes to be around good people. And in return, he's a good person to all those he cares about." Matt Langel, a senior guard, found the proof of that in his locker that Tuesday afternoon. When he walked out on the floor for a warm-up, the first thing he did was thank Dan for the shamrock and the note and hug him. Next in line was senior forward Frank Brown. "Dan is such an example of perseverance," Brown said. "He's like another coach to us."

At 5:30, the women's game began. Harrell was too busy working to catch much of it. Yet at the end, he was posted by the locker room, slapping five to the women as they ran in. Soon the Palestra was mobbed for the men's game. In the front row was Karim Sadak, a senior who took Group Dynamics 240 at Wharton with Harrell.

"You walking with me at graduation, right?" Harrell yelled. "Absolutely," Sadak replied.

With Harrell out of earshot, he confided, "I learned as much from him as I did from the professor in that class. He showed me how to interact with people, to treat people with respect. . . . He made the classroom a nicer place."

With a minute left, and Penn ahead by 70–48, Harrell worked his way up to the Penn bench, where Michael Koller was getting ready to go in. Koller, a senior, had played on the junior varsity this season. Because this was the last game, Dunphy let him dress with the varsity and, with Penn so far ahead, let him play the last minute. With 34 seconds left, Koller drove to the basket and was fouled. He went to the free-throw line with a chance to score his first-ever varsity points. The crowd roared for him. He missed the first foul shot. He hit the second. Harrell stabbed the air with such glee that his feet left the ground. When a time-out was called, Koller came to the bench. Harrell kissed him on the cheek. "Hold on," Koller screamed. "This is what did it!" Koller rolled down the waistband of his shorts. Pinned to the inside was a shamrock from Dan Harrell.

Peter Applebome writes the "Our Towns" column for the *New York Times*. His course was about finding revealing stories—important, touching, goofy, whatever—in everyday life. Here are two of his. They appeared in the *Times* on March 27, 2007, and May 25, 1991.

A Pit Bull Who Provided Lessons in Loyalty and Unfailing Love

In the pecking order of man and beast, there was no lower rung than the one shared by Randy Vargas and Foxy on the streets of Hoboken. He was 46 and homeless, regular work like that fondly remembered machine-shop job long in the past. She was a member of dogdom's least fashionable demographic, a 10-year-old brindled pit bull, compact as a pickup truck, ears askew, two-tone face, white neck, the rest an arbitrary mix of light and dark.

And yet in this city increasingly defined by creatures who drew the long straw—winners in real estate and on Wall Street, sleek goldens, pampered Yorkies, fashionable puggles and doodles—there was something transcendent in their bond.

Maybe in a world of opaque relationships, theirs was a lesson in clarity, like a parable from the Bible. He had rescued her back when she was homeless and abused, a scared runty thing living with homeless men who had no use for her. She in turn gave him purpose and companionship and love.

Maybe it was how the relationship brought out the best in both. It brought him to life and into the world, as much a part of Hoboken street life as any young comer with his black Lab. And it made her a creature of eternal sweetness, unfailingly friendly to people and animals, tail wagging at the merest glance, a pit bull in name but not metaphor.

So if you spent any time in Hoboken, the odds are pretty good you would have seen the two of them, sleeping in front of SS. Peter and Paul Parish Center, visiting the Hoboken Animal Hospital, walking down the street—the dog keeping perfect pace with him, dressed in winter in raffish layers of sweatshirts and T-shirts plucked from the St. Mary's Hospital Thrift Store, she keeping perfect pace with him.

Cheryl Lamoreaux remembered seeing Mr. Vargas resting on a condo's shaded concrete steps on a sweltering August weekend day, flat on his back with Foxy in the same position one step below. It was the perfect image of man and dog, she said, and added, "This really was a dog with a deep soul."

Everyone who knew them said the same thing: Mr. Vargas cared for the dog better than for himself. "If it was the dead of winter, the dog would get all the blankets, he'd get the sidewalk with nothing on it," said Robin Murphy, a groomer at the Hoboken Animal Hospital. "If it was raining, he'd put the umbrella up for the dog before he'd put it up for himself."

But there's not much margin for error at the bottom rung. Once this winter, he was arrested, accused of making threatening remarks to women. The case was dismissed, and friends say it should never have gone that far. But Ms. Murphy had to rescue Foxy from the pound in Newark, where she could have been euthanized.

It all ended so fast, people still can't explain it. Aside from a dog run, she had seldom been seen off the leash, but on the morning of March 19 in the park, she was. She saw a dog she knew across Hudson Street, dashed across to say hello and was hit by a white pickup that stopped briefly and then sped off.

He held the dog, blood spurting from her mouth, and waved at passing cars, but none stopped. So he carried her 60 pounds, feeling the broken bones in his hand, as far as he could, then put her down and ran to the animal hospital for help. But it was too late.

People come by every day, some fighting back tears, to leave donations, more than $900 so far. Some come from people who knew them, most from people who felt like they did. Alone they might have been invisible. Together, they were impossible to miss.

In different ways, they're still around. Her picture is in some store windows, wearing a gray sweatshirt with a red T-shirt under it, gazing to the right like a sentry, a wondrous study in essence of dog with a touch of human thrown in. Since the accident Mr. Vargas has had good days and bad ones, sometimes being up and around, sometimes, like the other day, looking groggy and defeated under his red comforter on the street. "I feel," he told a friend, "like I have a hole in my soul."

At the animal hospital they're buying a pendant to hold some of her ashes that he can wear around his neck. Friends check on him regularly, bring him food, talk of finally getting him a place to live. There's talk of getting him a new dog when he's ready, which surely isn't now. "It's like most relationships," he said from under the red blanket. "You have to wait for the right time."

A Sign: It's Jesus, or a Lunch Bargain

A lot has happened here since Joyce Simpson saw the face of Jesus in the forkful of spaghetti on the Pizza Hut billboard near Coleman Watley's Jiffy-Lube.

Ms. Simpson has decided to stay in the church choir rather than try to sing professionally. Mr. Watley's business, normally hamstrung by an unfortunately placed highway median divider, has miraculously soared. Throughout Atlanta, people have taken to peering at other Pizza Hut billboards: where some indeed see Jesus, others make out bearded singers like Willie Nelson, Jim Morrison or John Lennon, and most see a clump of orange spaghetti flecked with oregano.

It all has something to do with either the power of faith, man's search for the miraculous in the numbing void of modern life, or the ability of people to see what they want in almost anything.

The saga began with an effort by Pizza Hut to increase its lunch business by lowering the price of spaghetti and pan pizza. The promotion, done only in Atlanta, included about 70 billboards, half for pizza and half for spaghetti.

Nothing strayed far from the realm of normal commerce until Ms. Simpson, a 41-year-old fashion designer, bodybuilder and mother of two teenagers, stopped at a Texaco service station on Memorial Drive in northeast Atlanta. She said she was lost in thought over whether to leave her church and do some secular singing, and asked the Lord for a sign.

This is how she described what happened. "The Holy Spirit, which for non-Christians is basically that small, still voice, inside of you, the Holy Spirit simply said, 'Look up.' I looked up, and as soon as I looked up, I lost my breath. I simply lost my breath. . . . I saw the Michelangelo version of Christ. I saw the crown of thorns. I saw the deep-set eyes. I saw the nose, the mustache. I saw just the total vision of Christ."

She took her daughter, India, and her cousin Gloria to see the billboard, and they saw Jesus, too. It took her neighbor the sheriff 45 minutes, but he finally saw it, too.

Ms. Simpson called the *Atlanta Constitution* to tell them what she saw, and it turned out that dozens of motorists, some of whom did U-turns to take a longer look, saw the same thing, too. Local publicity brought out hundreds of others.

The Memorial Drive billboard already has come down as part of a regularly scheduled rotation, replaced by a recruiting billboard reading "The Few. The Proud. The Marines." But all across town now, the remaining Pizza Hut billboards have been undergoing a cultlike scrutiny.

Many are skeptical. "I guess you could make it whatever you wanted to make it," said Donna Carmichael, who stopped at an Amoco service station near a billboard south of downtown Atlanta. "If you wanted a religious experience, you could probably have one, but you really would have to be in some kind of state of mind to look up and see that, riding by, on a billboard. I didn't know before that Pizza Hut sold spaghetti."

Some are helpful. "O.K., see where it says, 'Outdoor Systems,'" a deliveryman instructed some employees at the East Point Housing Authority studying the billboard near them. "See where the 'S' is? Right under it, there's a little brown spot. It looks like the forehead of a man with his cheeks and a nose there. You can see it looks kind of like the face of a man in it, with maybe a beard or something and a whole lot of hair hanging off side of his head and something in his hair above his forehead."

Some are convinced. "It was very easy for me to see," said Danny Harrison, a customer at the Amoco station. "Of course I believe in miracles anyway, so I didn't find it that unusual. The miracle was that people declared it as being the face of Jesus instead of just any old face."

Some are merely hungry. "I'm Italian, man, full blooded," said Jerry Padovano, who works at the Aamco transmission shop. "I'm hungry all the time. When I see spaghetti, I'm ready to eat."

A Pizza Hut spokesman, Jeff Moody, said that unless it appeared that the billboards offended people, they would be left up until scheduled to come down.

Ms. Simpson said she is still exhilarated. "The really touching thing is I live in Stone Mountain, which is the Ku Klux Klan capital of America," she said, "but the most important thing is that I saw black people and white people hugging and praying together, and people were on their knees praying together. I guess the world just needed a miracle, and it's something that's so simple, just to ask and you get. It's that kind of simple."

Melvin R. McCray retired from ABC News on April 10, 2009, after twenty-eight years. He continues to teach at the Columbia University Graduate School of Journalism. McCray has produced several documentaries for Princeton, including *Looking Back: Reflections of Black Princeton Alumni*; *Carl Fields: Mentor, Teacher, Friend*; and *Coming Back and Looking Forward: A Princeton University Conference for Black Princeton Alumni*. After interviewing more than one hundred African American Princeton alumni, he found John Favors, Class of '72, aka Bhakti-Thirtha Swami, to be among the most fascinating. Their paths crossed so many times—at restaurants, gas stations, and rallies, and while just walking down the street—that McCray began to feel their meetings were more than serendipitous. This profile appeared in the *Princeton Alumni Weekly* on February 9, 1983.

The Two Lives of John Favors '72: A Political Activist Becomes a Monk in the Hare Krishna Movement

I saw John Favors for the first time in the fall of 1970, at the introductory meeting of Princeton's Association of Black Collegians. As ABC's president, he delivered an impassioned speech on the role of blacks at Princeton. Though only five feet nine inches, he was an imposing figure in his leopard-print dashiki and matching fez-like hat, with walking stick, pipe, bushy afro, and full beard. At that time he called himself Toshombe Abdul, and he spoke with the force and dynamism of Malcolm X.

Favors reminded us that we were products of the black community and argued that blacks were now being admitted to Ivy League universities mainly because of the demonstrations and riots of the '60s. He insisted that those struggles gave us a responsibility to return to the community and help rebuild it. His audience of 200 black students, mostly freshmen, was enthralled by his charismatic delivery, and filled McCosh 50 with thunderous applause.

I barely recognized Favors when I ran into him nine years later at a vegetarian restaurant in New York City. His face and scalp were clean-shaven, and he was dressed in an orange robe-like garment. He held a cloth pouch in one hand and a long cloth-covered staff in the other. Much to my surprise, John Favors, alias Toshombe Abdul, had become Bhakti-Tirtha Swami of the Hare Krishna movement. He had set aside the politics of the revolution and adopted the life of a monk in what is formally known as the International Society for Krishna Consciousness (ISKCON).

My curiosity aroused, I questioned him at length about this metamorphosis. My first impression was of a man who had swung from one tangent to the other with no consistency of purpose, his joining the Hare Krishnas being just the latest in a series of dramatic personality changes. But as our conversation progressed, I realized that this was not the case. There was, in fact, an inner constancy that had guided his transition from revolutionary to spiritualist. His was a story of evolution rather than abrupt transformation.

Favors was born in Cleveland, Ohio, in February 1950, the youngest of six children in what he describes as "an impoverished but deeply religious family." The combination prompted him to adopt "a very humanitarian, socialistic posture." As a teenager, he was active in local politics. He tutored in neighborhood centers, and at the age of fourteen he became president of the Southern Christian Leadership Conference's Midwest student division.

After graduating from Cleveland's East Technical High School, Favors received a scholarship to attend the Hawken Academy for an additional year of college preparation. By the time he arrived at Princeton in 1968, he had developed an enthusiasm for intellectual inquiry and a desire to improve the material circumstances of his fellow human beings in general and blacks in particular. "Because I had seen so much poverty," he says, "I was interested in doing something for myself and others."

During the turbulent late '60s and early '70s, Princeton saw its share of civil disobedience. In May 1968, the Princeton chapter of Students for a Democratic Society demonstrated at the Institute for Defense Analysis, insisting that the university sever all ties with the Department of Defense think tank. In the spring of 1969, black students barricaded themselves in the New South building, protesting the university's investment in companies doing business in South Africa. A newly formed Third World Coalition, composed of black, Latino, Asian American, and American Indian students, occupied Firestone Library in March 1971 to press their demand for increased minority enrollment. During this period, activist Angela Davis and Black Panther Party chairman Huey Newton addressed large audiences at Princeton.

Favors joined the Student Nonviolent Coordinating Committee, the Black Panther Party, and other activist groups. He developed an ideology that stressed his African roots, and he began traveling extensively in black-nationalist and socialist circles in the United States and abroad. It was during this time that he adopted the name Toshombe Abdul.

Some of the groups Favors became involved with advocated violent tactics to achieve their goals. "It wasn't that I was a violent or irrational person," he says. "But I was committed to thinking that violence was necessary to make people live better. I still felt that I was concerned for people in a humanitarian way—in that sense I felt no contradiction."

Eventually, Favors became disenchanted with political activism, feeling that it was bringing little or no progress. "I traveled to a few other countries and saw how so many revolutionary leaders who had good intentions became exploitative once they got into power. Sometimes they were more exploitative than the previous regime. I saw racism and class struggles and started to realize that it's not just one political paradigm versus another that is going to bring man equanimity, peace of mind, and a more just order."

He concluded that other approaches must be tried to attack such seemingly insoluble problems as the depletion of natural resources, the widening gap between rich and poor, the threat of nuclear war, and man's inhumanity to man. "If you put a very exploitative man in a socialist environment," Favors decided, "he's still going to find some way to exploit. What we really need is for man to have a change of consciousness." So Favors, a psychology major, began doing research on hypnosis, mental telepathy, clairvoyance, and dreams. He also studied the writings of Plato, Aristotle, Emerson, Thoreau, and Schopenhauer on sense perception, consciousness, and the nature of reality.

Favors turned next to Eastern religions, attracted by their emphasis on expansion of consciousness and purification of the senses as well as their ideal of service to God and man. He started reading the Vedas and the Bhagavad Gita, the scriptures of Hinduism, and was intrigued by what he called their "scientific" approach to the mastery of life. He wondered whether these mystical philosophies could succeed where political action had failed in bringing about a more just world order.

While still at Princeton, he undertook formal lessons with Sri Chinmoy, Swami Satchidananda, and other Indian gurus who related Hindu philosophy to the Western world. Favors continued his political activism at the same time that he began pursuing these spiritual inquiries: "I would leave a Black Panther rally or an ABC meeting and go to New York and study meditation for a couple of days with some swamis."

The conflicting demands of his double life came to a head at graduation, in June 1972. He was awarded a scholarship to attend the University of Tanzania, where he could become more directly involved in Third World political and social activities. "But I wasn't sure whether I really wanted to continue working in politics," he says, "or whether I wanted to become more contemplative and introspective." He put off this decision by taking a job in the office of New Jersey public defender Stanley Van Ness, where he worked on penal-reform projects, while also taking lessons in Vedic philosophy at the Hare Krishna temple in New York City. "It gave me a chance to scrutinize the different polarities in myself, the political and the spiritual."

Favors believed that Hare Krishna devotees were following the original Vedic teachings more closely than any other sect, but he was not yet convinced that he wanted to commit himself to a totally spiritual life, nor was he sure the Hare Krishnas would be the right choice for him. "The first time I saw a Hare Krishna," he says, "was up in Harvard Square at a football game. It was very cold, and a group of them were standing on the corner chanting. I looked at them and thought, 'This is the epitome of absurdity.' I presumed they were rich white students just out looking for some different kind of drug or alternate experience. But when I passed by again two hours later, they were still on the corner chanting in the cold. I knew then there was something extraordinary about them. Years later I was shocked to find that those people ringing cymbals and playing drums in the street possessed an intense philosophy about God."

Though Favors was doing quite well financially, and felt his job directing prison programs was an important one, he still was dissatisfied. After working with Van Ness for a year, he decided to leave. "He knew I was a little unusual," Favors says, "because I would go to parties and never drink or eat meat. I told him that I was becoming a member of a religious organization and that we had a school in Dallas where I was being called to do some teaching. It was an unusual situation. Just overnight I knew I had to leave. I knew at that point my whole life was going to change. I gave away all my possessions. I took a razor and shaved my head. The next morning I got on a plane and went to Dallas."

Americans have come to know the Hare Krishnas by their street chanting, airport bookselling, and portrayal in the media as a religious cult. It is not generally known that they are an international organization with several thousand members supported by centers in many of the world's major cities. Even less is known about their religious beliefs, based on the 5,000-year-old Vedas, which teach the worship of one supreme God and many of the same concepts presented in the Ten Commandments. The name Krishna means "all-attractive one," and is used to describe the supreme qualities of God. The chant—"Hare Krishna, Hare Krishna, Krishna Krishna, Hare Hare / Hare Rama, Hare Rama, Rama Rama, Hare Hare"—is a prayer that means, "O Lord, please engage me in Your service."

The religion of the Hare Krishnas is basically the same as the Hinduism practiced by 600 million Indians. The notable difference is that the Krishnas follow the Vedic interpretations of A. C. Bhaktivedanta Swami Prabhupada, who founded the Hare Krishna movement to spread Krishna consciousness to the English-speaking world. He arrived in America in 1965 at the age of sixty-nine and began teaching that the Vedas specify the Hare Krishna mantra as the most effective method of spiritual realization in this age. The chant, therefore, is at the core of the sect's religious practices. Not all followers of Vedic scripture give such prominence to this particular mantra over other Vedic chants, however.

The negative reaction of most Americans to this religious doctrine was understandable, given the country's deep-rooted cultural biases against such beliefs, dress, and behavior. Many parents and the religious community as a whole remain alarmed at the proliferation of cultlike religious organizations that attract large numbers of young persons. Favors's decision to join the Hare Krishnas was received with chagrin by most of his family, friends, and classmates.

At first, he taught academic courses in the ISKCON school in Dallas. Later he was assigned to the organization's Bhaktivedanta Book Trust, the largest publisher of books on Hindu philosophy and religion in the world. Its primary function is to print and distribute more than seventy volumes of translations of and commentaries on the Vedic scriptures by Swami Prabhupada. In fact, with more than sixty million volumes distributed, ISKCON derives most of its income from the sale of these books.

For his first seven years in the organization, Favors undertook a rigorous study of Indian philosophy and Sanskrit literature. Meanwhile, he was moving up rapidly in the ISKCON hierarchy. "I was sort of taken under the wings of the leading swamis," he says.

Then, in 1979, Favors became a sannyas, which means renunciate, or monk. He was one of two black swamis in the Vaishnava order and one of two-dozen leaders directing the work of the Hare Krishna movement. At that time, he was renamed Bhakti-Tirtha Swami, which means "one in whom others can take shelter." Not all Hare Krishnas are encouraged to become monks; in fact, most marry and raise families. Even within the hierarchy, priesthood is a radical step. "I've been celibate for ten years," he notes. "One may ask how it is that a young man who is at his prime, when sexual tendencies are very active, could take to such a lifestyle. But obviously enjoyment must be there. When you are developing a higher taste, then it becomes easy to give up something else."

For the last four years, he has been directing ISKCON's Urban Spiritual Development Committee (USDC). In keeping with his desire to serve blacks and poor people, USDC provides what Favors describes as humanitarian, social welfare, and spiritual programs in the United States and Africa—especially in Kenya, Nigeria, Ghana, Zimbabwe, and Zambia. "Sometimes you have a missionary group or a spiritual group with good intentions, but no expertise to execute necessary programs," he says. "At other times, you have some well-ordered development programs but they lack humanism. At USDC we are bringing both elements together."

Favors has received enthusiastic support from the Africans he has met, which he attributes to his spiritual posture. "Once you are out of America," he says, "there is a whole different mood of how a spiritualist is treated. In America people may say, 'Look at this weird guy.' But in Africa they know immediately that my dress indicates a very high priest. I can meet with ambassadors, chiefs, princes, and I can get funds just based on the programs and the posture that I represent." Backing up his words is the fact that most of the land ISKCON operates on in Africa has been donated by governmental or private sources.

Some of Favors's classmates might question the validity of spreading a religious philosophy from India among Africans. Why should Krishna consciousness be any more relevant than indigenous African religions or, for that matter, the Western religious doctrines that are taught there? According to Favors, the Vedic religion has been acceptable to the Africans he has encountered because of its similarity to their own. "The principles we follow are not much different from what a spiritualist in Ghana or a person in the Yoruba tribe would follow: the same hierarchy, the same concepts of life after death, and the same knowledge of psychic centers.

"Africans feel that Vedic teachings clarify beliefs they have long held. Our contribution is a scientific explanation of phenomena they have accepted for centuries without understanding. Rather than propose a change of culture, as the Christian missionaries did, Krishna consciousness suggests that people simply add an understanding of the scientific process of devotional service, as described in the Bhagavad Gita."

Favors feels that African culture is being eroded by influences from the West and that the Vedic religious philosophy can strengthen native practices. "I am trying to get Africans to realize what great teachings they have—teachings that deal with man's relationship to man in a very pure way. But Africa and all of the Third World is becoming more and more Western in consciousness, so we are telling them, 'Don't take this materialism as a priority.'"

Favors acknowledges that his role in Africa is similar to that of the missionaries who have come before him. "Christian missionaries often go to some impoverished place and start a farm or a school," he says. "They are doing it for basic humanitarian reasons, but they are also thinking that they are going to convert a few people. Missionaries have ulterior motives, and I think we should be honest and let people know that we are teaching religion as well."

Encouraged by the warm reception he has received in Africa, Favors is planning a number of major projects, including hospitals, more schools, and expanded food-distribution systems. He is actively recruiting people to run these programs from both inside and outside the Hare Krishna organization. He is also seeking nonvoting status for the USDC at the United Nations so that support for his humanitarian projects can be sought in the international community.

Looking back on his experience at Princeton, Favors says, "It was the best thing that ever happened to me because it helped me to understand some of the illusions of the material world. The educational experience I had was fair in that it allowed you a certain amount of freedom and creative thinking. My experience at Princeton helped me to see that I didn't want to be a materialist. As I move from country to country, I see that some of the planners, organizers, and dynamic politicians were trained at Princeton. I think it is a good sign that Princeton has been able to produce such interested and concerned persons to engage in service for the whole of mankind. I'd like to stress that we should carry on the spirit of Princeton in the nation's service, and in the world's service."

Melvin McCray and John Favors last met in 2005, just months before Favors's death. Although he was battling cancer, his inner fire and passion to serve humanity were undiminished.

Barbara Demick has reported from Seoul, Jerusalem, Cairo, Sarajevo, and Berlin, first for the *Philadelphia Inquirer* and later for the *Los Angeles Times*. She is currently the *Times'* Beijing bureau chief. She wrote this piece about Albanian virgins during her first stint as a foreign correspondent, covering Eastern Europe, and it is still one of her favorites. She had heard old tales of the Albanian women who spent their lives masquerading as men—Alice Munro had even written a short story called "The Albanian Virgin"—but the assumption was that they had died out. She rented a four-wheel drive in Tirana and drove up to the mountains with a translator, who thought it was a wild-goose chase. It took them less than a day to find Sema Brahimi, who is featured in this story, which appeared in the *Philadelphia Inquirer* on July 1, 1996.

In Albania, a Girl Who Became a Man

Sema Brahimi was 14 years old when she decided to become a man. It was a sacrifice dictated by the harsh circumstances in which her family found itself living. Sema's father had died, leaving his hapless widow, four daughters and a baby son to cope on their own. In these pitiless mountains choked with rock and brush, it was unthinkable to run a household without a man in charge. Sema volunteered to take on the job. She cropped her hair short and donned trousers. She went to work in the fields. She changed her name from Sema to its masculine equivalent, Selman, and her mother and sisters began referring to her with the pronouns "he" and "him." "I've lived my whole life as a man. I've got the habits of a man. . . . If anybody has a problem with it, I've got my gun to deal with them," said Selman Brahimi, now 55, with a blustery gesture to the back pocket of her baggy gray trousers.

Perhaps more remarkable than Brahimi's permutation of gender is that nobody does have a problem with it. The men in the village accept Selman as a man among equals. In this deeply conservative culture, in which the responsibilities and customs of men and women are sharply delineated, Brahimi's decision to become a man is regarded as part of a centuries-old, noble tradition.

In a 1909 book about Albania, the British travel writer Edith Durham described the tradition of the "Albanian virgins"—women who took an oath never to marry in order to fill a void left by a dearth of males. The folklore of northern Albania and bordering Montenegro is rich with heroic accounts of these avowed virgins, who sometimes became fierce warriors or village chieftains.

Until recently, when Albania was reopened to outsiders after a half century of Stalinist communism, it was widely believed that the tradition had died out. Its survival into the modern era can be attributed to the extreme isolation of mountainous villages such as Lepurosh, which are terra incognita even for most Albanians.

This is about as far off the beaten track as you can roam on the European continent. The terrain of the Dinaric Alps is so rugged and inhospitable that they are nicknamed the "Accursed Mountains." The poor soil supports few crops, and from afar the mountains, with their thin tufts of vegetation and rock, appear to be covered with a patchy skin disease. Albanians fled from Ottoman invaders into these foreboding hills in the fifteenth century, and the ensuing tragedies of Albanian history provided little incentive for them to come down from their remote perches. To reach Lepurosh, you drive 70 miles north on a potholed asphalt road from the capital of Tirana. Then you turn east into the hills to bump along a stony path that is barely passable by four-wheel drive and more prudently traveled by mule.

The village itself (population 300) has not a single telephone, automobile or house with indoor plumbing. The women wear traditional attire of long skirts, aprons and white head scarves. The Brahimis live in a sun-bleached stone house overlooking the fields of tobacco, cucumbers, tomatoes and onions from which the family ekes out a hardscrabble existence. Selman Brahimi was born in this house in 1940, the youngest of four daughters. The older girls already were married or engaged, their brother still a baby, when their father died. Selman gradually assumed responsibility for tending to the fields and for making the arduous, three-hour trip to the nearest city by mule when it was time to sell crops.

"The idea came as the result of necessity. There was nobody to take care of the men's work," said Selman, recalling her remarkable life as she rolled a cigarette with homegrown tobacco. "Until I was 18 to 20, I had proposals of marriage. My brother was old enough to work and my mother said that I should follow the fate of my sisters and get married. But once something is decided you can't undo it, and I already thought of myself as a man."

As the head of the household, Brahimi took responsibility for selecting a wife for her brother. She wore a suit and tie at his wedding, assuming the role of father of the groom. In keeping with village tradition, she learned to play musical instruments reserved for men, the flutelike *fyell* and a stringed instrument known as the *lahute*. "I've had to work very hard to earn bread for the family and to be honest and correct in my relations with others," she said. "But no, I never regret the decision. I've not had a bad life as a man."

Although she has the petite stature of a woman, Brahimi has a wry, masculine smile, displaying gold-capped teeth through a crooked grin. She happily acknowledges that her life is far easier today than before. Her brother, Elez, has four sons—two of whom work abroad, sending money back to the family, and two who work the fields. She now spends much of her time smoking and drinking the brandy known as raki with the men of the village. Elez Brahimi's wife, Hasije, does all the housework and looks at the woman to whom she refers as her brother-in-law with just a hint of envy. "There is no doubt that the woman's life is tougher. I have to do everything—the laundry, the cleaning up, the cooking for six men."

Selman Brahimi is the first and only avowed virgin in Lepurosh, which is entirely Muslim. The tradition is more common among Albanian Catholics. But villagers do not seem in the least perturbed. "He respects all the rules and always conducts himself properly," said 70-year-old Dyl Dylholli, one of the village elders; Elez said nonchalantly, "I consider Selman to be my brother."

As far as the Albanian government is concerned, Selman is still a woman by the name of Sema. She never has made any effort to legally change her gender, since that would have obliged her to serve in the military. But Selman notes that it doesn't matter much, since her special status is recognized under a centuries-old body of law that prevails in the region.

The Kanun of Lek, named for a fifteenth-century Albanian hero, Lek Dukagjini, is the unofficial bible of northern Albania. Paperback copies can be purchased in kiosks and are found in many homes. The Kanun lays down formal rules of etiquette for family and village life. Women can be beaten or chained if they disobey their husbands, and they have no property or inheritance rights whatsoever. "A woman is a sack, made to endure" is how one article of the Kanun is titled. Under the strictures of Kanun law, the only escape from this dismal fate is to vow virginity and assume the life of a man.

The British anthropologist Antonia Young, who was the first to discover that avowed virgins still were living in the postcommunist era, has attributed the custom to three factors. First, the women might be avoiding arranged marriages with unwanted suitors. Second, they had no brothers to carry on family traditions. Third, they might be replacing males who were killed in war or in the relentless blood feuds and vendettas that have characterized rural life in northern Albania for centuries. It is unclear how many Albanian virgins are still alive—in part because many villages are accessible only on foot, and are seldom, if ever, visited by outsiders. Journalists, aid workers, and anthropologists have identified at least four such women, but the number is likely much larger.

The tradition also would seem to come in many permutations—not all of them involving virginity in the technical sense.

Hasan Xhaferaj, 60, tells how his mother, Sugare, transformed herself into a man after his father was killed in a fire in 1941. The woman was 28 at the time and eight months pregnant with her fourth child. Having no brothers or grown sons to run the family, she assumed the role of a man. "She had to work as a man. She wore man's clothes to show that she was not available for marriage. The other men addressed her as a man—she was equal to everybody—and we kids called her father," said Xhaferaj, who still lives with her in a remote village called Uji i Shenjte (Sacred Water) on the Kir River.

Sugare, who is now 78, resumed wearing women's clothing only four years ago, her son said.

As Albania reopens to foreign travel and influences, and modern mores intrude into this traditional culture, the custom of the avowed virgin seems destined for extinction. If for no other reason, women are able to take a more active role in society and commerce without going to the extreme of donning men's clothing.

In Lepurosh, the Brahimis acquired a television set two years ago—bought with money sent by the relatives abroad. With less work to do on the farm, Selman avidly watches broadcasts from Italy, only 135 miles away, with bewilderment at the career women depicted on screen. "The society here is very male. Women are not used to having liberties," she said thoughtfully. "I don't believe in immorality or lewdness, but for a woman to have some independence, it is completely right. Up to a point."

The North Korean Film Festival: No Stars, No Swag, but What a Crowd!

The reclusive society's film event is like no other. No paparazzi, no cellphones, and the foreign attendees are sequestered on an island. This account is excerpted from the Los Angeles Times, *October 11, 2008.*

You know you're not in Cannes when the all-female marching band, wearing white go-go boots, belts out communist anthems at the opening ceremony. This is a film festival like none other in the world. There are no movie stars, no paparazzi, hardly any press. No studio executives doing deals on their BlackBerrys—cellphones and other wireless devices are banned in North Korea.

For that matter, so are most movies. North Korea is the closest thing the world has to a hermetically sealed society. There is no Internet. Radios and televisions are welded to government stations. Yet every two years since 1987, North Korea has opened its doors, and its screens, just enough to host the Pyongyang International Film Festival.

Back in the days when North Korea had allies, it was called the "Film Festival of Non-Aligned and Other Developing Countries." Now that the government in Pyongyang has few real friends, it accepts entries from countries that are at least not overtly hostile.

Hollywood need not apply. "It is practically the only occasion where North Koreans can see foreign films," said Uwe Schmelter, who heads the Japan office of the Goethe Institute, the German cultural organization that supplied Germany's films to the festival.

The film festival is thought to have been the brainchild of North Korean leader Kim Jong Il, who spent much of his youth obsessed with movies, and is believed to have a personal library of 20,000 titles. As the band played on for last month's opening ceremony, an unlikely mingling of Communist Party apparatchiks and European filmmakers filed up a long ramp past a row of Korean movie posters at the Pyongyang International Cinema, a poured-concrete structure with a spiral design that must have looked very modernistic in the 1980s.

Although the sun was still high over the capital on the unseasonably warm afternoon, most people wore black, the North Korean cadres buttoned into stiff business suits with the obligatory badges of founding father Kim Il Sung on their lapels, the European men in jeans. Adding a little glamour, a few of the visiting women wore diaphanous sleeveless outfits, their blond hair cascading over bared shoulders, a curious sight in a country where people are not expected to show arms, knees or midriffs. The culture clash is such that the festival organizers keep the foreign attendees and the North Koreans apart. Like other visitors in Pyongyang, the filmgoers were escorted at all times by official guides, better known as minders. Foreigners were lodged in the Yanggakdo Hotel on an island in the middle of the Taedong River, which runs through town—a further disincentive to anyone who might want to wander off into the city. (Visitors to Pyongyang call the hotel "Alcatraz.") Without any opportunities to explore, foreigners spent evenings on the hotel's forty-seventh floor in a revolving restaurant that no longer revolves, with green carpeting that looks as though it was stripped from a miniature-golf course. "You can't just go up to people and have a little chat about film," said Anke Redl, who works for a German film distributor based in Beijing.

This year, 110 films from 46 nations were screened, among them China, Russia, Germany, Sweden, Britain, Egypt and Iran. Although most films aren't overtly propagandistic, there is a strong preference for themes emphasizing family values, loyalty, the temptations of money. *The Tender Heart*, a little-known Chinese film that opened the 10-day festival, is about a small boy searching for the mother who abandoned him and his father in search of riches in the city. Because there was no budget for subtitles, the film had a Korean-language voice-over with an adult actress reading the boy's histrionic dialogue. Several members of the audience walked out in disgust before the film was over. But things picked up from there. A Chinese war film, *Assembly*, by acclaimed director Feng Xiaogang and a big hit last year in China, won the grand prize at the closing ceremony.

Screenings of two British films, *Atonement* and *Elizabeth I: The Golden Age*, were so crowded that guards had to bar the doors to prevent gate-crashers. Two years ago, a mob overpowered security to get into a sold-out showing of a Swedish vampire film. "I've seen them beating down the doors," said Henrik Nydqvist, a Swedish producer who has attended the festival three times since 2004. He says filmmakers like to attend Pyongyang's festival despite the limited deal-making opportunities because of the passion of the crowds: "Their emotional responses are very direct and natural. They don't anticipate the endings of the film. This is something you can't see in Europe, and it is very refreshing."

The Ministry of Culture, which oversees the festival, pays for filmmakers to attend. Most come from European countries that have diplomatic relations with

North Korea; others come from China. Tickets are usually distributed through workplaces and universities, often through the ruling Workers' Party, but many end up being resold by scalpers. "Going to the film festival is very popular. Kids of high party officials get tickets that they resell to others at the university," said Zhu Sung-ha, a 34-year-old graduate of Pyongyang's Kim Il Sung University, who defected to South Korea in 2001. He said North Korean students view the festival as a chance not only to see foreign films, but also to glimpse the outside world. "They want to see the reality of developed countries," Zhu said. "The North Korean government doesn't really want people to see it, so they show a lot of films from Third World countries like Iran and Egypt."

One of the underlying myths of this country is that people are lucky to be born North Korean. ("We have nothing to envy in this world" goes a popular slogan.) So the government doesn't want the people salivating over the cars, cell phones or kitchen appliances that show up in movies. Festival organizers get around that by favoring historical dramas that won't invite North Koreans to compare their lifestyles with those of the people depicted in the films. As Culture Minister Kang Nung Su said at the opening ceremony, film must not "harm the sound mind of the people." Still, participating countries have tried over the years to send films that would raise the public consciousness. There have been films about German reunification (a sore subject for a regime that fears being swallowed up by wealthier South Korea) and a film about Auschwitz, also touchy given the analogies to North Korea's labor camps for political undesirables.

This year, the festival screened the Austrian-German production *The Counterfeiters*, a curious choice given the evidence that North Korea is a major counterfeiter of U.S. currency. "We try to see how far we can go," said the Goethe Institute's Schmelter. "We are surprised and grateful. We have never gotten a no for a German film." This year, the festival had only one new North Korean movie, *The Kites Flying in the Sky*, about a woman who cares for orphans. It was not well received, with foreign viewers dismissing it as syrupy and propagandistic. Two years ago, the North Korean film *A Schoolgirl's Diary* was a surprising success at the festival and went on to Cannes.

North Korea's film industry was once surprisingly robust, nurtured by the personal interest of Kim Jong Il. In the 1970s and '80s, while being groomed to succeed his father, Kim oversaw the country's film studios and arranged the kidnapping of a South Korean actress and her director husband to help him make movies. He also wrote a book, *On the Art of Cinema*, on how movies can be used to instill correct thinking. But Kim hasn't been to the studios in more than two years—whether because of ill health, as many reports claim, or lack of interest is unclear. "Kim Jong Il is very busy, leading the party and the revolution," Choi said. He said 10 to 12 movies were filmed at the studios each year, but other North Korean officials say the number is much lower and that lack of funding has crippled the country's film industry.

Another problem they are reluctant to discuss: despite the ban on foreign films, cheap pirated DVDs from China are smuggled across the border and screened illegally in the privacy of people's homes. Among the most popular, say North Korean defectors, is *Titanic*, in part because of a mystical belief that the ship's sinking was related to the birth the same day, April 15, 1912, of Kim Il Sung. Other favorites are South Korean soap operas, Chinese kung fu movies— and pornography from any nation.

Bob Mondello has written arts criticism for National Public Radio since 1984 and, beginning a decade earlier, for publications and broadcast outlets including WJLA-TV, WETA-TV, the *Washington Post*, and *Washington City Paper*. This piece aired on NPR's *All Things Considered* on January 16, 2009.

Title Inflation: How Hollywood Watches Our Wallets

It started with a dumb joke as world economies spun out of control, and Hollywood handed the Oscar for Best Picture to *Slumdog Millionaire*. I was looking at my 401(k) and seeing desolation, emptiness, a parched landscape, and mumbling to myself about how my Fistful of Dollars was becoming a Fistful of Dimes.

Maybe I should have invested overseas so I'd at least have a fistful of euros, which led me to wonder what Clint Eastwood's fistful of 1964 dollars would be worth now. So I checked with the Bureau of Labor Statistics. Each 1964 dollar would now have the buying power of almost $7. Well, you know where that took me. The Six-Million-Dollar Man of 1974 would cost $25 million to build now. Those romance-starved secretaries who threw Three Coins in the Fountain? They'd have to throw two-dozen coins today. And while diamonds are still a girl's best friend, about the only other commodity holding its value is the precious metal that 007 worked so hard to protect from Goldfinger. Imagine Shirley Bassey trying to belt a song called "Platinumfinger"? Just wouldn't sing.

As I kept looking at movie titles, I stopped turning Pennies into Nickels from Heaven and started thinking about what the titles meant to audiences back then. The first money title I could find was from the days of storefront nickelodeons, an 1897 half-minute short called *Scrambling for Pennies*, a title perfect for audiences who'd recently survived the Panic of 1893.

For a couple of decades after that, silent films often had titles like *His Last Dollar* and *The Five Dollar Baby*. But in the 1920s, the stock market zoomed, and Hollywood sent titles zooming, too. *Million Dollar Mystery*, for instance, though there were also *Her Fatal Millions*, *Vanishing Millions*, and *Melting Millions*, as if screenwriters could see the stock-market crash coming. And sure enough, after 1929, you start getting titles like *Dollar Dizzy*, *Too Many Millions*, and *Million Dollar Swindle* as well as a whole set of down-and-out titles like *The Nickel Nurser* and *A Dime a Dance*.

Now, let's note that what I'm doing here is the world's least scientific survey. I haven't gone back to watch these pictures to see what they're about, but their titles do say something about the public's moody relationship with money. There are about 100 titles containing the words "million dollar," for instance. And while there are a few from every decade, they tend to cluster when times are good, as do other phrases.

Take the title *Money Talks*. In 1997 it was attached to a flick starring Chris Tucker as a small-time con man. *Money Talks* had long been a popular title. There had been films called *Money Talks* in the '20s, '30s, '40s, and '50s. But, intriguingly, the title fell out of fashion during the mid-1970s, when the U.S. was experiencing high interest rates and inflation. In other words, when people thought money kind of didn't talk, *Money Talks* didn't strike producers as a good title. Those same inflationary years instead brought titles like *Take the Money and Run* and *Billion Dollar Bubble*. (Also, *Tango and Cash*, but I don't think that means much.)

So what's the trend going to be from here? Well, Hollywood seems optimistic. Nicole Kidman recently bought the rights to 1953's *How to Marry a Millionaire*, apparently because she wants to play the Marilyn Monroe part:

> *Ms. Marilyn Monroe:* (As Pola Debevoise) Do you know who I'd like to marry?
> *Ms. Betty Grable:* (As Loco Dempsey) Who?
> *Ms. Monroe:* (As Pola Debevoise) Rockefeller.
> *Ms. Grable:* (As Loco Dempsey) Which one?
> *Ms. Monroe:* (As Pola Debevoise) I don't care.

For the record, to match Marilyn's catch from 1953, Nicole Kidman will need to marry a millionaire worth at least $8 million.

Below, the list that inspired today's essay: a noncomprehensive survey of money-movie titles through the years, drawn from the exhaustive database at IMDb.com.

1910s
His Last Dollar (1911); *The Mighty Dollar* (1912); *The Hundred Dollar Elopement* (1913); *The Five-Hundred Dollar Kiss* (1914); *Room & Board: A Dollar-and-a-Half* (1915); *Thousand Dollar Husband* (1916); *The Pawnshop* (1916); *The Almighty Dollar* (1916).

1920s
The Great Nickel Robbery (1920); *The Ten Thousand Dollar Trail* (1921); *The Dollar-a-Year Man* (1921); *The Five Dollar Baby* (1922); *Her Fatal Millions* (1923); *Greed* (1924); *Million Dollar Derby* (1926); *God Gave Me 20 Cents* (1926); *Vanishing Millions* (1926); *Million Dollar Mystery* (1927); *Melting Millions* (1927); *Million Dollar Collar* (1929; Rin Tin Tin).

1930s
Dollar Dizzy (1930); *Quick Millions* (1931); *Million Dollar Swindle* (1931); *Million Dollar Legs* (1932; W. C. Fields); *Too Many Millions* (1934); *Ten Dollar Raise* (1935); *Pennies From Heaven* (1936); *Million Dollar Racket* (1937); *A Dime a Dance* (1937); *Million Dollar Legs* (1939; Betty Grable).

1940s

Dancing on a Dime (1940); *Million Dollar Baby* (1941); *A Good Time for a Dime* (1941); *Million Dollar Kid* (1944); *Gents Without Cents* (1944); *Ten Cents a Dance* (1945).

1950s

Million Dollar Mermaid (1952); *Two Cents Worth of Hope* (1952); *How to Marry a Millionaire* (1953); *Three Coins in the Fountain* (1954); *Million Dollar Movie* (1954; TV); *Working Dollars* (1956).

1960s

It's Only Money (1962); *Goldfinger* (1964); *The Pawnbroker* (1964); *A Fistful of Dollars* (1964); *For a Few Dollars More* (1965); *Five Thousand Dollars on One Ace* (1965); *How to Steal A Million* (1966); *For One Thousand Dollars Per Day* (1966); *Ten Thousand Dollars for a Massacre* (1967); *Take the Money and Run* (1969).

1970s

Dollars to Die For (1970); *Diamonds Are Forever* (1971); *A Barrel Full of Dollars* (1971); *Nickel Queen* (1971); *The Six Million Dollar Man* (1974; TV); *The Nickel Ride* (1974); *Brother Can You Spare A Dime* (1975); *Billion Dollar Bubble* (1976); *Twelve and a Half Cents* (1977).

1980s

Pennies From Heaven (1981); *Silver Spoons* (1982); *Come Back to the Five and Dime, Jimmy Dean, Jimmy Dean* (1982); *Brewster's Millions* (1985, also 1914, 1921, 1935, 1945); *The Color of Money* (1986); *I Love Dollars* (1986); *The Money Pit* (1986); *Tango & Cash* (1989).

1990s

Other People's Money (1991); *Nickel and Dime* (1992); *For a Few Lousy Dollars* (1996); *Forty Thousand Dollars* (1996); *Six Dollars a Minute* (1997); *Six Dollars and One Sense* (1997); *Money Talks* (1997; also 1914, 1919, 1921, 1926, 1932, 1940, 1951, 1972, 1990).

2000s

Million Dollar Hotel (2000); *Million Dollar Baby* (2004); *The Trouble With Money* (2006); *King of Kong: A Fistful of Quarters* (2007); *Mad Money* (2008); *Slumdog Millionaire* (2008).

Juliet Eilperin is the national environmental reporter at the *Washington Post*, where she has worked since 1998. Her job has taken her diving with sharks in the Caribbean and the Pacific, crawling on her hands and knees in the caves of Tennessee searching for rare insects, and trekking in both the Canadian and Swedish Arctic. This piece, adapted from a story published in the *Washington Post Magazine* on February 24, 2008, explores the virtues of experiencing the extreme cold in an unusual hotel in Jukkasjarvi, Sweden.

Ice Accommodations

"It's a dry cold," Swedish foreign ministry officer Gabriella Augustsson tried to reassure me as we made our way through the Stockholm airport. *A dry cold.* The phrase was eerily reminiscent of that hairy chestnut "a dry heat," which people use to try to convince you it doesn't matter when the mercury regularly climbs well above 100 degrees Fahrenheit in some region of the world. Augustsson and I, along with a freelance writer named Eric Roston, were heading to the Ice Hotel to learn how an exceptionally pure river can produce one of the most visually arresting construction projects on Earth.

Made entirely from blocks of ice and packed snow, the Ice Hotel combines the best elements of highly stylized interior design with one of nature's most basic elements, water. Swedish officials view it as a sort of national treasure because it fits neatly into the government's project of educating people around the world about how clean water is essential for a healthy environment. And since 1992, the Ice Hotel has attracted 100,000 guests from around the globe to an unforgiving landscape during the chilliest time of the year. A replica of it has been featured in a James Bond film as well as in high-end-fashion ad campaigns, and its rooms are booked for months in advance.

There was only one problem: I don't like the cold. I can trot out an array of reasonable explanations. I have poor circulation, I'm pretty skinny, and my skin becomes reddened and chafed once the temperature begins to dip. Some of my friends and family members were skeptical of my plans to travel in the dead of winter to the Arctic. Just a few days before my departure, my physical therapist looked at me with concern and said, "You know, you probably have 5 percent body fat, at most." My mother was even more protective once I confessed the day before leaving that I had developed a severe cold. "You can't go to the Arctic with a cold," she insisted.

As the national environmental reporter for the *Washington Post*, I spend a great deal of time thinking about what it means that Earth is warming. Each week, new scientific studies chart how glaciers around the globe are melting, sea ice cover is shrinking and animals are migrating northward in search of cooler habitats. I have interviewed Inuit leaders about how climate changes are eroding their traditional way of life, and spoken to public health experts about how shifting precipitation patterns and temperatures could affect the spread of famine and disease across Africa and Asia.

Over the past couple of years, as it becomes increasingly clear that the northernmost regions of the globe are becoming less frigid, I began pondering the intrinsic value of cold. Climate-change contrarians like to speak of new shipping lines through the Northwest Passage, lower heating bills and humankind's ability to stave off rising sea levels through dikes and other technological innovations. But what would it be like to visit a place of bitter iciness that faces the risk of losing that cold altogether? Only one place would satisfy my curiosity: the village whose townspeople have turned freezing into an asset.

By the time my companion, Eric, and I were seated on a Scandinavian Airlines plane headed for the northern town of Kiruna, I peered out the window and saw a sticker for a university located not far from our ultimate destination, the tiny village of Jukkasjarvi. "First Choice Scandinavia—Great ideas grow better below zero." Clipped exchanges Eric and I had with each other underscored our joint sense of trepidation. As the plane took off from Stockholm, he turned to me and remarked, "There's no going back." I nodded. As our aircraft approached the ground 90 minutes later, Eric peered out at row upon row of snow-covered pine trees. "It looks pretty white out there," he observed. "Yup," I said. We made our way out of the plane onto the snow-covered tarmac. While it was only 1:30 in the afternoon, the sun was beginning to set. But as I scurried inside the airport I felt . . . *a dry cold*. It was crisp, and chilly, but it wasn't the kind of wet, oppressive cold that seeps into your bones during Washington's worst winter moments.

Joined by Ice Hotel spokeswoman Camilla Bondareva and Lisa Svensson, then a program officer at the Swedish embassy in Washington, we made our way to Kenth Fjellborg's sled dog kennel. Fjellborg comes from one of Jukkasjarvi's founding families (the fourth one to move to town, once the church was established in the 1600s). Since that tentative start, nine generations of Fjellborgs have eked out a living in the region, through farming, hunting and fishing. "For them, 40 below was a problem. For me, that has been an asset," Fjellborg said. "That has been something people want. If you told my grandfather you're going to take ice from the river and people would come to stay in it, he probably would have thought you should go to the hospital."

Fjellborg grew up playing outdoors, and when he was 12, he became entranced by the dogsled tours that had just started going by his home. After finishing school, Fjellborg moved to raise dogs in Alaska and Minnesota before returning to Jukkasjarvi, where he started his own business in the mid-1990s. Fjellborg provided our transport across the Torne River to the Ice Hotel, in the form of a 15-minute dogsled ride. As the sled skidded to a halt, the hotel's founder, Yngve Bergqvist, came out to meet us, swaddled in many layers, his face encircled with a sort of animal fur that gave him a haloed appearance.

"Welcome to Jukkasjarvi!" he declared, giving us a brief sketch of the town. It took about one minute, which was good, because we were standing outside and freezing after our sled ride. "This is one of the coldest places in Sweden," he said. "It's a way of living."

Bergquist, who had spent years in Jukkasjarvi (pronounced YUK-kas-yair-vey), working as a river-rafting guide and advising a local mining company on environmental practices, started plotting how to lure tourists to his adopted home two decades ago. He called up the tourist chief in Kiruna, a larger town 12 miles away, to see what advice he might have for such a project. "Nothing," he recalls the tourist chief replying. "Give me advice!" Bergqvist pressed him. "Close up," the official retorted. "Everybody knows that place is *koldhala*"—a Swedish word that means, roughly, "a cold spot where nobody wants to go." While another man might have given up at that moment, Bergqvist was un-daunted. He did what any savvy entrepreneur would do: he looked overseas to see how other chilly towns attracted visitors. In 1989, he attended the Hok-kaido winter festival and watched as 35 jumbo jets ferried in tourists from Tokyo to gaze at ice sculptures. The next year, he invited Japanese artists to Jukkasjarvi for a workshop, where they transformed ice taken from the spar-kling Torne River into art. Over time, Bergqvist and his colleagues perfected the art of making an Antonio Gaudi–inspired igloo, cutting more than a thou-sand blocks of crystal-clear ice from the river with industrial saws while spray-ing a mixture of wet snow he has dubbed "snice" onto massive metal forms. By the winter of 1992–93, people started paying to sleep in his well-appointed igloo. Fifteen years later, the Ice Hotel has become a destination of a lifetime.

So much of a destination, in fact, that it comes complete with evening en-tertainment. The modern-day teepee stretched high above my head was glow-ing from the light emanating from the small bonfire roaring in its center. I tried to lean back a bit as Yana Mangi crooned in the language of Lapland's native people, the Sami. She sang of "the little brook between the lakes" and of herd-ing reindeer, a simple life conveyed with the kind of pleasant, ethereal sound I usually associate with the American Southwest. These are towns without cell towers, where people continue to observe rituals that have endured for centu-ries while making few concessions to the modern era. As each song came to an end, the audience of several dozen tourists expressed their appreciation the way one does when the temperature outside is beginning to dip to 35 degrees below zero Fahrenheit: with a muffled clapping, because everyone in the room was wearing mittens.

Mangi's concert—which she has put on three nights a week each season for more than a dozen years—is one of the few warm attractions at the Ice Hotel, the main reason why people across the globe visit Jukkasjarvi, which is 125 miles north of the Arctic Circle. That's because when you build a hotel entirely out of ice and snow, there is no indoor heating. The tepee was packed. After nearly an hour, the show, which included Mangi's husband on keyboards and an audience singalong, was over. I exited with several dozen tourists out into the dark and the snow, to the icy edifice that would be my home for the next two nights. A rush of wind passed over me, and I looked up at the black sky scattered with a few stars. It was only a matter of yards to the white, glowing building that offered some shelter from the Arctic winds, but as I made my way there, I contemplated a simple fact: I wouldn't be that warm again anytime soon.

The Ice Hotel—which gives off an eerie blue glow when spotted from across the frozen Torne River—is a massive, beautiful igloo. Sure, it has cathedral-like ceilings, intricate sculptures and electricity running throughout the building, but make no mistake: it's an igloo. To step inside is to feel as if you have crossed into another civilization that is at once more sophisticated than ours and more severe. Each of the two dozen or so intricately carved suites represents a world of its own. (Sixty other ice rooms without artistic carvings are cheaper to stay in and are reminiscent of actual igloos. Single ice suites range from $400 to $800 per night; simple ice rooms, $325 to $500.) During my stay, one suite, crafted by a Swedish painter, was called Virgin Angel, but the angel in question looked more like a sexy It girl from the 1960s, with pert, snowy breasts and elaborately patterned ice wings. Another, called Projection Room, appeared to have trapped an enormous, twisted tree in ice. (In fact, the two artists who created the latter room, Mark Szulgit and Julia Adzuki, had to methodically chip away at the ice, one after the other, to hollow out spaces to give the impression of a frozen trunk.) A glowing ice chandelier filled with electric lights dipped from the lobby's ceiling, illuminating the room, while a hotel worker quietly cleaned the lobby by sweeping the floor's snow cover.

Everything slows down a bit as you tromp through the Ice Hotel's halls with your boots and swaddled clothing, peering at the designs on the walls and the flower-inspired carvings paying homage to Swedish scientist Carl Linnaeus, who came up with the idea of taxonomic classification of plants and animals (2007 marked the 300th anniversary of his birth).

Part of the hotel's allure stems from its simplicity. Bergqvist and his art director, Arne Bergh, like to talk about the purity of "genuine Torne River ice," and they're not lying. The ice—stacked up in thousands of blocks in a nearby storage facility—is shockingly clear. While occasional cracks make patterns in the blocks, the ice itself is completely transparent—unlike ice made from ordinary tap water—which makes it look otherworldly. So Bergh has a strict rule for the few dozen artists who come each year to create the hotel and craft the suites that amount to individual works of art: they have to work with what nature has supplied, and nothing else. "There are two colors: white and transparent, and then there's the light," he said.

The artists—many of whom have never worked with ice before—take anywhere from a few days to a couple of weeks to complete their given ice suites. The sculpting crew for the 2006–7 season included veterans and novices.

Michael Jermann, a freelance producer and graphic designer from Germany, had never worked with ice or snow before designing the room Flowing Edge, which I stayed in my second night. At first glance, I thought the room was pedestrian because it lacked the intricate carving of other suites. It was only after I had spent some time in it that I realized its simplicity helped put guests in a sort of zone, lulled by the undulating shapes Jermann had sculpted.

In Jukkasjarvi, the Swedes have mastered the art of making do with what nature gives them. "At first, it sounds like an exotic idea—who would come up with something so crazy?" But, Bergh reasoned, it is an obvious response to the Arctic environs. "It's in front of you. What do you have here? It's bloody cold. Darkness. Aurora borealis. The ice and the snow. So those are the ingredients, and you cook them together." The 22 individualized suites were stunning in their originality. One, designed by two graffiti artists from Ireland and England, resembled a traditional English country lord's estate, complete with sitting chairs and a faux fireplace. Another evoked a Turkish bath, complete with pillars. And a third gave guests the sensation of being tucked inside a hot-air balloon, where the bed took on the form of a woven basket and sleepers looked straight into the pillowy, concave form of the balloon's ceiling. The Ice Bar, however, is where visitors actually spend most of their time. Guests chat, dance and drink there until the early hours of the morning, swapping stories and checking one another out. Perhaps this is because they're afraid to go to sleep in their rooms.

I prepared myself as best as I could for my first night, in the Helices suite, shedding my snowsuit but keeping on my thick, high-tech long johns, hat, gloves and wool socks. I laid out the blue thermal sleeping bag the hotel supplies each of its guests, as well as a set of sheets that go inside the bag, and a small pillow. It wasn't as if I were sleeping directly on the ice: on top of the oval ice bed lay a thin foam mattress covered by reindeer skins. I crawled into the sleeping bag, turned out the light with a switch right by the bed. I gazed for a minute at the conical shapes protruding from the ceiling, which made me realize I hadn't seen a patterned ceiling since I tilted my head up in my best friend's freshman-year dorm room and wondered how a single decade such as the '70s could produce so much atrocious architecture. I did a quick check to make sure that only the minimal amount of my body was directly exposed to the frigid air. Just relax, I told myself, you're not going to freeze overnight. Then I promptly fell asleep.

In the morning, a hotel employee came in and delivered my wake-up call with a critical source of sustenance: hot lingonberry juice. Now, you might think that after sleeping in a room that's several degrees below freezing you would prefer a cup of coffee or hot chocolate, but lingonberry proves to be an almost magical aid just after you've awakened, shivering, and need something to propel you out of your bed and a few dozen yards down the hallway to the adjoining, heated building where you've stored your luggage. (That, incidentally, is where the bathrooms are, because the hotel's engineers have yet to master the art of frozen plumbing.) Fortified, I sprinted down the hall to the heated changing room and then ventured up the road to the building that houses both showers and a sauna as well as the main dining room.

Eric had slept in a similar room, and after surviving one evening in the Ice Hotel, he and I felt vindicated. In fact, I've felt colder camping in the Shenandoahs during the fall. We took to tossing our jackets aside as we ran between one of the heated buildings to the Ice Hotel itself. "We're [expletive] reindeers," Eric told me, grinning. Then I opted to sleep in the Ice Hotel for the second night, something that guests rarely do because there are plenty of heated chalets people can rent once they've proved their mettle. I didn't stay the second night to prove a point: I did it because I had come to find the extreme cold relaxing, a way to dial back the stress and hyperactivity that characterize my everyday existence. Some people tout sweaty yoga as a way to center themselves, but that trendy exercise pales in comparison with the soothing balm of a constant—but bearable—freeze.

Each spring the ice hotel disappears. "We take 100 million liters of water from the river a year," Bergqvist says. "That's a loan. We give it back in May, June." Bergh actually likes walking among the ruins of the hotel, when the walls separate and open toward the sky. He is philosophical about the ritual collapse of his work. "You know it's ephemeral. You know it will melt," he says.

At the same time, the warming temperatures globally are a cause of concern for the hotel's operators. Their annual opening on the first weekend in December has not changed, even if it is not getting cold as quickly as it used to in the winter. "We've been more and more hurried opening it, because it always opens at the same time," Bergh says, explaining that they have had to start building it later in recent years. Fjellborg, the sled dog breeder, is more worried about how global warming is jeopardizing the reason people now come to Jukkasjarvi. "Right now, this environment that used to be a problem for my grandfather is the reason we have a good life, because we can make this place interesting for people," he says. "If that goes away, that true winter climate, it's going to affect us all. Not dramatically, but super-dramatically, because we'll be done."

Mitchel Levitas has held numerous senior editing positions at the *New York Times*, including Metropolitan Editor and editor of the Week in Review, the Book Review, and the Op-Ed page. In 1994, he launched a book-development program, with which he remains active as executive associate. This piece appeared in the *New York Times* on November 26, 1995.

The Renaissance of the Marais

Until its reincarnation as perhaps the most fashionable purveyor of tea in Paris—465 kinds—Mariage Frères operated more or less anonymously as a wholesaler. The venerable company, founded in 1854, has been radically transformed in the last decade after its move to the Marais. Now it is crowded with upscale customers in surroundings of acquired antiquarian sophistication— much like the Marais itself. This 310 acres on the Right Bank, where patches of medieval Paris also survive, is rich with 17th- and 18th-century architectural treasures and has become a destination of choice for museumgoers, antique and gallery browsers, and window shoppers of every persuasion. The neighborhood's renaissance—still continuing—has made it a model of urban historic restoration.

These days, behind the counter of Mariage Frères, at 30 rue du Bourg-Tibourg, a half dozen young men in natural linen suits are poised to serve. Along an L-shaped wall, in open compartments from floor to ceiling, black canisters hold exotically scented teas, perfumed, blended teas with mysterious names that hint at some transcendental essence: Vivaldi, Balthazar, Yin Yang, Lover's Leap. Rare teas from the South Seas, Ecuador, Malawi are for sale at heady prices that climb to a peak of more than $100 for 100 grams (about three and a half ounces) of Gyokuro from Japan. After customers have waited in line for the young men to mix and weigh their teas with a silver trowel on a silver scale, they can sample a light lunch in the salon or stroll through the small second-floor museum, with its handcrafted samovars and teapots, picnic boxes of rattan and silver, cups and saucers in every design.

Like the Marais itself, which straddles the boundary between the third and fourth arrondissements, Mariage Frères blurs the line between art and artifice. The new, sophisticated version of the Marais in the fourth arrondissement is now encroaching on the "true," surviving, and slower Marais of the third. Auguste Rodin, who was concerned with the fate of the great Gothic cathedrals of France, warned early in this century: "Don't destroy anymore; don't renovate anymore." The salvagers of the Marais ignored both warnings, with results both wonderful and sad. The struggle is still fierce on the part of preservationists to save what's left of the neighborhood.

Before the Middle Ages, the region was a swamp ("Marais" means "marshy ground"), formed by an alternate bed of the Seine. Henry IV commissioned a residence in 1605 at a grassy square, called it the Place Royale, and gave the rest of the land to 36 noblemen on condition they build nine identical mansions on each side of the 153-yard-long square. Standing above wide arcades at street level, the stone and brick two-story houses, each with a blue slate roof and two high chimneys, frame the oldest and most charming small square, now the Place des Vosges, in Paris. This early example of a planned urban development became a magnet for the entire district, and the Marais boomed for most of the next two centuries. Courtiers, mistresses, ministers and their followers built magnificent homes, or *hôtels particuliers*. Many have been meticulously restored, with great carved doors hiding stone courtyards; to today's visitors, their dimensions are palatial.

After the Revolution of 1789, the neighborhood dropped from favor; as the decline continued into the 19th century, housing became affordable for artisans and the working poor; later waves of immigrant Jews, fleeing persecution in Russia and Central Europe, created a thriving enclave of which scant signs remain. The former ritual bathhouse for women on the rue des Rosiers is now Chevignon, one of several clothing shops in the Marais that sell American-style Western outfits. At 30 rue François Miron, Izrael Skotsky presides over a remarkable international sampling of cereals, spices, sausages, herbs, canned food, dried fruit—you name it, Izrael Epicerie du Monde has it—that crowd the shelves and hang from the ceiling like edible chandeliers. Oddly enough, observed Mr. Skotsky, creating the cosmopolitan cuisine he had always dreamed of had to wait until demographic shifts made the Marais less Jewish.

By the time the Minister of Culture in the de Gaulle government, André Malraux, responded to local initiatives in 1962 with legislation to protect historic neighborhoods, the Marais had lost its grandeur and become a slum. In 1965, the government put the district under its protection as a safeguarded sector, drew up a plan for restoration and banned renovations or new construction that would change its character. By then, said Herbert Lottman, biographer-historian and author of *How Cities Are Saved*, the district "had more substandard housing than any other in Paris; 30 percent of the dwelling units were without running water, 68 percent without private toilets."

Behind the banner of historic preservation, the cadres of revival gathered, stimulated by a housing shortage that real estate speculators were happy to alleviate. The population of the Marais soon shrank from 60,000 to 30,000 as boutiques, art galleries and restaurants replaced low-rent working families. In the loggia of the Place des Vosges, for example, a simple bronze plaque discreetly announces L'Ambroisie, one of five Michelin three-star restaurants in Paris, where the no-frills, three-course dinner is about $130. In a courtyard just off the square is an elegant and expensive 50-room hotel, the Pavillon de la Reine.

Meanwhile, high culture anointed the reborn Marais with five new museums, public and private, whose exhibits have been installed with contemporary French panache behind freshly scoured Renaissance facades. They joined two major museums of long standing, the Carnavalet and the National Archives. The Musée Carnavalet, housed in a magnificent 16th-century residence acquired in 1866, holds the city's historical collections. In 1989, several new exhibits were added in a new wing to mark the bicentennial of the Revolution. They include the one-window (no bars for a King) prison room occupied by Louis XVI before he was guillotined in 1793, and Marcel Proust's cork-walled bedroom-study, where he wrote *Remembrance of Things Past*. Another beautifully preserved palace, the Hôtel de Soubise, houses the National Archives, established by Napoleon in 1808. Its chronological spectrum is wide, from a fifth-century papyrus record left by the tribes who lived on the banks of the Seine to documents and posters of the Liberation in World War II. It also includes four newly restored period rooms whose 18th-century rococo decor is sumptuous. Under construction is the municipal museum of photography; the Paris Museum of Jewish History and Culture will be housed in the large, totally refurbished 17th-century Hôtel de Saint-Aignan.

The huge cultural infusion into the Marais, accompanied by gentrification and hordes of tourists, is not universally admired. Early on, a protest group accurately pointed out that "thanks to the magic wand of the promoters the Marais is becoming the home of millionaires, of landmark zoning, and exposed ceiling beams." Yet as Mr. Lottman observed: "How many cities, regardless of their political system or wealth, had ever managed to salvage a neighborhood for its original inhabitants? One could hope that the vastly improved quality of the surroundings would somehow compensate for the displacements and for the increased incidence of souvenir shops."

Not all is restored elegance. The hectic rue Saint-Antoine, one of the district's main thoroughfares, is lined with specialty food stores, and has a large supermarket where a neighborhood movie house used to be. The Baracane restaurant at 38 rue des Tournelles still serves excellent regional specialties of the Southwest like ox cheeks in red wine and pork with sage; at about $25 for dinner, it's a bargain. The small Place du Marché Sainte-Catherine has two Jewish restaurants, a Korean barbecue and two traditional bistros. The rue des Archives has remained an ordinary shopping street for real inhabitants. And what many consider the best patisserie in the Marais, Pottier, in business since 1974, is still at 4 rue de Rivoli, the busiest street in the quarter. But the Achat des Chevaux, which once sold horse meat, is now a sweater shop. A few doors down, at 37 rue du Roi de Sicile, is the Nantucket Café, where Louis Metz said he's doing a good business in light lunches and sandwiches. Why Nantucket? As a child his parents took him there for vacations.

Few people know the flesh, blood and bones of the Marais better than Alexander Gady, a lanky, exuberant young scholar and author of the district's definitive architectural history. He will point out enthusiastically the battered doorway to the 17th-century house where the philosopher and mathematician Blaise Pascal lived. With the same verve, Mr. Gady denounces a plan to demolish the oldest market in Paris, the 1615 Market of the Red Children (red was the color of charity at the time) on the rue de Bretagne at the corner of the rue Charlot and replace it with underground parking, new shops and a child-care center. "How demagogic!" he exclaims, with the purist's contempt for commercial development.

So authentic is the preservationist's vision that he criticizes the expansion of the International Arts Center, a block from the Seine, which provides modern exhibition space and new ateliers for 100 artists. Another symbol of the new Marais is a small gay population, nonetheless large enough to support a theater and movie house, a café or two and Boy'z Bazaar, a clothing store at 5 rue Sainte-Croix de la Bretonnière that caters to cross dressers.

Mr. Gady is no homophobe but says of the gay presence: "They have no roots here in the Marais. It's just what's happening." On the other hand, he welcomes as "marvelously appropriate" the return of Les Compagnons du Devoir, an international guild of master craftsmen and apprentices that was forced to go underground by a national law banning craft guilds during the Revolution and did not re-emerge until it was deemed acceptable, in World War II. The organization occupies offices in a group of medieval houses near the Seine, close to the Church of Saint-Gervais, which many consider the most beautiful in Paris. A team of 10 Compagnons—ironsmiths and metalworkers—came to New York City a decade ago to help repair and restore the luster of the Statue of Liberty's flame.

As the new Marais of the fourth arrondissement approaches the boundary of the surviving Marais in the third, across the rue des Francs Bourgeois and reaching to the Place de la République, the pace of change slows to normal. Of historic interest are traces of the headquarters of the Knights Templars, the religious order of fighting noblemen founded in the 12th century during the Crusades. Several small textile companies and other kinds of light manufacturing remain, along with ordinary residential buildings; and some antique stores actually leave their wares unpolished and dusty. Mr. Gady concedes that the struggle to hold off the plastic surgeons of progress—gallery and boutique owners, condominium builders—will intensify in the next 5 to 10 years and that finally history will lose.

One of the early outposts of change is the Picasso Museum, a popular destination for visitors to the Marais, which opened in 1985 in the beautifully restored 17th-century mansion of a collector of salt taxes. Actually in the third arrondissement, the museum is around the corner from many buildings with dirty, blemished facades, not yet gutted and rechristened for modern times. Yet compared with the neighborhood that was razed to make way for the Pompidou Center, which has attracted a concentration of undistinguished boutiques and cheap souvenir shops, the salvaging of the Marais is generally conceded to have been a success. Even by Mr. Gady. "Malraux's idea," he says, "was beautiful: to make the Marais a place of intellectual history. But as we have learned, to save a neighborhood, that's a delicate and fragile endeavor."

Christopher S. Wren reported and edited for the *New York Times* for twenty-eight and a half years, including stints as bureau chief in Moscow, Cairo, Beijing, Ottawa, and Johannesburg. These are excerpts from *Walking to Vermont* (Simon and Schuster, 2004).

Walking to Vermont

It was not yet noon and hotter than a July bride in a feather bed when I trudged a half-dozen miles down the wooded northeastern flank of Mount Greylock, which is, at 3,491 feet, about as high as you can go in the state of Massachusetts. The descent, steep and muddy, made my footing precarious under the weight of a pack that felt stuffed with rocks. By the time I emerged from the spruce woods onto Phelps Avenue, a street of tidy wooden houses on the southern fringe of North Adams, I was hurting as hard as I was sweating.

Before I got bitten, I had planned to follow the white blazes marking the Appalachian Trail north across a green footbridge over some railroad tracks and the Hoosic River. Instead, I turned east on Main Street and caught a ride to the regional hospital on the other side of town. Within minutes, I found myself stretched out on a white-sheeted bed in the hospital's emergency ward. It was not where I expected to be.

I had been walking into retirement, from Times Square in the heart of New York City to central Vermont and a house bought eighteen years earlier while I was working in China. My wife and I talked of retiring someday to Vermont, of blending into its crisp mornings and mellow afternoons and worrying no more about fighting Sunday-night traffic back to New York City.

Someday had finally arrived.

Now a few miles short of the Vermont border, I was stopped by a suspected case of Lyme disease. It didn't help that I had passed a restless night on top of Mount Greylock, poring over a worn copy of the *Appalachian Trail Guide,* which, among its earnest descriptions of trailheads, shelters, switchbacks, and sources of drinkable water, found room for dire warnings about snakebites, lightning strikes, and maladies like Lyme disease and a pernicious newcomer called hantavirus ("The virus travels from an infected rodent through its evaporating urine, droppings and saliva into the air.").

Call my walk, interrupted, a rite of passage. After forty years as a working journalist, I had collided with the life change that is the stuff of which dreams and nightmares are fashioned. Once the fizz is gone from the good-bye champagne, how do you enter this next stage of your life with any semblance of style or self-respect? You can press ahead, or you can cling to the past while time keeps stomping on your fingers.

As a scared young paratrooper, I had it screamed over and over at me by foulmouthed instructors that an exit from an aircraft in flight had to be vigorous to clear the propeller blast. Otherwise, the jumper risked being slammed back into the metal fuselage by the screaming wind with such hurricane force as to leave him unconscious—or dead.

My career at the *New York Times* was winding down after nearly three decades as a reporter, foreign correspondent, and editor.

As for exploring retirement at a brisk walk, the notion may have been planted by *The Elements of Style,* the gem of a stylebook compiled by William Strunk Jr. and E. B. White, which serious writers, and even newspaper reporters, rely upon to resolve questions of grammar. I had been sitting at my cluttered desk in the *Times* newsroom a year earlier, consulting the rules about restrictive and nonrestrictive clauses, when Strunk and White caught my eye with an example they cited for enclosing parenthetic expressions between commas: "The best way to see a country, unless you are pressed for time, is to travel on foot." I don't know whether Strunk and White reached their conclusion after setting out on foot themselves, I hope with a picnic lunch, to prove their theorem, which grappled with the eternal problem of when to bracket a phrase between a pair of commas. They did concede that "if the interruption to the flow of the sentence is but slight, the writer may safely omit the commas."

I grew less interested in the commas than in their advice. Were Strunk and White inviting the reader with a wink to interrupt the flow of an uneventful life by taking a hike? Since Strunk and White had brought it up, there was a country that I was curious to see on foot.

After seventeen years abroad as a foreign correspondent, it was time to fill in some blank spaces at home. I must have traveled through more than seventy countries, if you include all fifteen republics of the shattered Soviet Union, but had taken for granted the stretch of New England that separated our Manhattan apartment from the Vermont house where I wanted to retire. We usually drove there at night, more preoccupied with headlights of oncoming traffic than the darkened scenery. What I knew about the countryside amounted to fuel pumps, fast-food restaurants, and takeaway coffee.

The truth was that my walk to Vermont was about more than just walking to Vermont. I had reached the age when regrets set in. My own were blissfully few, involving mostly sins of omission rather than commission. We are likelier to rue what we failed to do than what we did.

If I didn't walk from Times Square to Vermont now, when would I get around to doing it? "Live the life you've imagined," exhorted Henry David Thoreau, the nineteenth-century contrarian whose account of life alone in the woods, *Walden,* I admired, even if I did discard it in his native Massachusetts.

In journeying to Vermont on my terms, I could picture myself, having cooked a simple but satisfying supper, lounging beside a small river, reading *Walden* by the flicker of an evening campfire, falling asleep under a canopy of bright stars. Well, as a Russian proverb reminds us, "If you want to make God laugh, tell him your plans."

Still, I was not to be disappointed by the people I encountered in the five states through which I walked, and sometimes limped. Yes, there were mean-spirited locals who pointed speeding vehicles at me, or balked at letting me use a toilet without buying something, or wished I would go away before they dialed 911. But there were others. A nun at a convent in New York shared old folk songs while she fed me supper. In Connecticut, a shopkeeper had me watch her cash register while she rummaged in the basement for the raisins I wanted. A woman I didn't know in Massachusetts baked me chocolate chip cookies; another stranger let me sleep in his yard and invited me for ice cream on his porch. In Vermont, trail angels left cold drinks and fresh fruit by the wayside. In New Hampshire, a store manager whipped up a frosty milkshake on a hot day and refused to take my money.

I also failed to anticipate the extent to which my experiences as a foreign correspondent would resonate on this journey, evoking memories of memories as I trudged northward at the rate of something over four thousand paces per hour. For better or worse, reminiscences constitute the only acquisitions in this life that remain uniquely our own.

I dithered over what to put in my pack. Should I take a spare can opener or rely on the balky tool on my red Swiss Army knife, which tended to stick from years' accumulation of gunk? Did I need the complete cooking kit, which included a pot, pan, skillet, plate, bowl, cup, and enough utensils to feed an infantry platoon? Every traveler undergoes this exasperating anguish. But what I selected would have to travel on my back for a month or more, not in some overhead luggage compartment.

The most painful decision involved a stack of books I had brought to read in the long summer twilights on the trail. In the end, I limited myself to the copy of *Walden*. Thoreau would hardly have approved of the rest of what I was carrying, which could be generically described as "stuff." "Our life is frittered away by detail," Henry whispered from the pages of my paperback.

Swinging the pack against my thigh and onto my shoulder, I walked as jauntily as I could into a pasture whose white blazes introduced me to the Appalachian Trail. It took me not quite ten minutes to lose my bearings, which was no modest achievement. The Appalachian Trail may well be the most famous footpath in the United States, though not in New York state, where the trail kept petering out until it was indistinguishable from the cowpaths intersecting the mown pastures. I was being passed in both directions by brawny Sunday hikers flexing powerful quadriceps. I forged ahead on the white trail at a retiree's pace, trying not to lose altitude as it led me up and down to the wrought-iron gates of an eerily abandoned graveyard, identified by a metal sign as "Gates of Heaven." The graves, not to mention heaven itself, had vanished under a profusion of weeds.

The trail led to Ten Mile River shelter, a three-sided lean-to built of logs, with a slanted roof jutting out over the fourth side. Inside was a flat platform broad enough to sleep a half dozen hikers. It was typical of shelters on the Appalachian Trail. Some were more elaborate, with open windows and a picnic table or campfire pit outside, but the design had changed little since Abe Lincoln. Except that Abe's lean-to did not have its wooden beams festooned with nylon cords ending in metal cans and jar tops. Their purpose became apparent from the bags of food hanging from the contraptions. They were meant to keep the food supply at a tantalizing distance from mice and insects, leaving these crawlers free to snack on the faces and hands of sleeping guests.

The lean-to was occupied by some young hikers for whom traveling the trail was a way of breaking away from their families and reinventing themselves, with a new identity forged under whatever trail name they chose. A trail name can be whatever you want as long as it isn't your real name, though it should reveal something about you and be catchy. An alias does make sense on the trail, when you are eating and sleeping and excreting and sneezing in intimate proximity to others whom you might not want to appear on your doorstep later. Nor might they relish your looking them up when they are back in their workaday world, clean-shaven with matching socks.

In the course of my journey to Vermont, I acquired and discarded many sobriquets. My trail name ultimately metamorphosed into "Jaywalker," which summed up what I had been doing since I left Times Square.

Only fifty-two miles, hardly 2 percent of the Appalachian Trail, wind through Connecticut, but they seemed to go on forever. It didn't help that I was loaded down like a Himalayan yak. As I walked, mostly up and down, my mind became preoccupied with what I could jettison, or at least mail home from the post office in Kent, the next town upriver.

"Simplicity, simplicity, simplicity!" Thoreau kept reminding me, but I only came up with more reasons for keeping everything I had stuffed in my pack. My *Walden* weighed barely eight ounces, though as I was to learn the hard way, eight ounces here, another eight ounces there add up to a backbreaker.

I was overtaken by an affable youth. He wore his hair in dreadlocks and carried a small knapsack. Lone Wolf said he was from Roanoke, Virginia. He had joined the Appalachian Trail at Harpers Ferry, West Virginia, he said, and kept intending to head for some beach and find a job. He might just hitchhike to the Connecticut coast tomorrow, he told me. Or he might keep walking to New Hampshire or even Maine.

I had covered barely eight miles so far that day, which doesn't sound like much because it was mostly up and down. But I decided to overnight at the next lean-to, tucked into a shady hollow of Mount Algo. I found Lone Wolf reclining on his thin blanket inside the shelter, cupping his hands around a lit candle. He looked longingly at the freeze-dried dinner packet of beef teriyaki and rice that I pulled from my pack.

"Have you eaten?" I asked. He shook his head.

"Do you have anything to eat?" I asked, instinctively knowing what his answer would be. Again he shook his head.

So I fired up my gas stove for the first time, boiled up my beef teriyaki and rice, which the label specified was ample for two hikers, and shared it with Lone Wolf. I don't know which hikers the manufacturers had in mind, because our glop stretched nowhere near as far as the package label promised.

Trail travel gets reduced to the lowest common denominators of survival, meaning nourishment and shelter from the rain and cold. It matters where you choose to camp, how far you travel, how well you're able to feed and shelter yourself. Eating means stoking the human furnace. A thru-hiker, in covering fifteen to twenty miles a day, can burn five thousand calories, or more than twice the daily expenditure of a more sedentary American.

Many people, if pressed, will admit to being afraid in the woods, where dangers are less than on a highway. Statistically, you are more likely to get killed driving home from the supermarket than sleeping on the ground under a bower of hemlocks. Catching a cold, or poison ivy, or the attention of a skunk, is another matter. I feel safer in the woods. I pitched my tent near the rim of a cliff that offered sweeping views to the south. This reduced the odds that some deranged intruder would bludgeon me to a pulp while I slept; he would stumble over the edge first. My concern was irrational, of course, because homicidal stalkers are unlikely to be obsessed with you once you get older, and in any case seldom climb hills in the dark.

The journey of ten thousand miles begins with a single step, says one of those venerable Chinese sages. Two weeks of walking had enlightened me to a painful corollary of this ancient wisdom, which was that a single step should never begin without expensive socks. The socks I wore were cheap cotton. They were chafing fresh hot spots on whatever skin on my heels and toes had not turned raw. A few miles into Massachusetts, I sat down on the roadside grass and peeled off the sweaty socks to inspect the damage. "Tell those who worry about their health that they may be already dead," Henry Thoreau quipped. His feet probably weren't hurting when he wrote it.

Working up a sweat, you need to consume a pint or two of water per hour, so I was low again after walking two hours from a shelter. I knocked on the door of a white clapboard house, but nobody was home. A hand-lettered sign in the window said, "Hikers. Please help yourself to water." It also offered us trail travelers the use of a shower mounted on the other side of the house. This was Vermont, after all.

At last, after five weeks, I trudged up the last winding dirt road toward home. I had indeed walked all the way to my house in Vermont. But the best part was discovering that I had not really finished, because walking to Vermont turned out to be about a state of mind. I felt more tired than triumphant when I dropped my trekking poles and opened the backdoor into what Vermonters call the mudroom. The two cats sniffed at my muddy boots and padded off to the kitchen. First I went into the bathroom, shed my clothes, and stepped on the scale. The needle vacillated back and forth, and concluded that I had lost nineteen pounds during my walk, down to 155 pounds from 174.

I looked at the mirror over the sink. A crusty old guy with tousled gray hair stared back. In walking nearly four hundred miles over the past five weeks, mostly on unpaved roads and trails, I had stumbled upon the secret of how utterly irrelevant chronological age is. Just imagine how old you would feel if your parents never told you how old you ought to be. I donned my shorts, pulled a waiting beer from the refrigerator, and sat, barefoot and shirtless, out on the deck. I had not appreciated until now the delicacy with which the setting sun filters through a curtain of sugar maples and firs on Bragg Hill in the twilight of a summer evening. For not before night approaches can we savor how miraculous the day and the blossoms we gather belatedly have been.

Then I got up and fed the cats.

Martha Mendoza is a national writer for the Associated Press and a winner of the 2000 Pulitzer Prize for Investigative Reporting. This article, published in *Ms. Magazine* in the summer of 2004, was a finalist for a National Magazine Award. She and her husband, Ray, are proud parents of four beautiful and healthy children.

Between a Woman and Her Doctor: A Story about Abortion

I could see my baby's amazing and perfect spine, a precise, pebbled curl of vertebrae. His little round skull. The curve of his nose. I could even see his small leg floating slowly through my uterus. My doctor came in a moment later, slid the ultrasound sensor around my growing, round belly and put her hand on my shoulder. "It's not alive," she said. She turned her back to me and started taking notes. I looked at the wall, breathing deeply, trying not to cry. I can make it through this, I thought. I can handle this.

I didn't know I was about to become a pariah. I was 19 weeks pregnant, strong, fit and happy, imagining our fourth child, the newest member of our family. He would have dark hair and bright eyes. He'd be intelligent and strong— really strong, judging by his early kicks. And now this. Not alive? I didn't realize that pressures well beyond my uterus, beyond the too bright, too loud, too small ultrasound room, extending all the way to boardrooms of hospitals, administrative sessions at medical schools, and committee hearings in Congress, were going to deepen and expand my sorrow and pain.

On November 6, 2003, President Bush signed what he called a "partial birth abortion ban," prohibiting doctors from committing an "overt act" designed to kill a partially delivered fetus. The law, which faces vigorous challenges, is the most significant change to the nation's abortion laws since the U.S. Supreme Court ruled abortion legal in *Roe v. Wade* in 1973. One of the unintended consequences of this new law is that it put people in my position, with a fetus that is already dead, in a technical limbo.

Legally, a doctor can still surgically take a dead body out of a pregnant woman. But in reality, the years of angry debate that led to the law's passage, restrictive state laws, and the violence targeting physicians have reduced the number of hospitals and doctors willing to do dilations and evacuations (D&Es) and dilations and extractions (intact D&Es), which involve removing a larger fetus, sometimes in pieces, from the womb. At the same time, fewer medical schools are training doctors to do these procedures. After all, why spend time training for a surgery that's likely to be made illegal? At this point, 74 percent of obstetrics and gynecology residency programs do not train all residents in abortion procedures, according to reproductive health researchers at the National Abortion Federation. Those that do usually teach only the more routine dilation and curettage—D&C, the 15-minute uterine scraping used for abortions of fetuses under 13 weeks old. Fewer than 7 percent of obstetricians are trained to do D&Es, the procedure used on fetuses from about 13 to 19 weeks. Almost all the doctors doing them are over 50 years old. "Finding a doctor who will do a D&E is getting very tough," says Ron Fitzsimmons, executive director of the National Coalition of Abortion Providers.

My doctor turned around and faced me. She told me that because dilation and evacuation is rarely offered in my community, I could opt instead to chemically induce labor over several days and then deliver the little body at my local maternity ward. "It's up to you," she said. I'd been through labor and delivery three times before, with great joy as well as pain, and the notion of going through that profound experience only to deliver a dead fetus (whose skin was already starting to slough off, whose skull might be collapsing) was horrifying. I also did some research, spoke with friends who were obstetricians and gynecologists, and quickly learned this: study after study shows D&Es are safer than labor and delivery. Women who had D&Es were far less likely to have bleeding requiring transfusion, infection requiring intravenous antibiotics, organ injuries requiring additional surgery or cervical laceration requiring repair and hospital readmission.

A review of 300 second-trimester abortions published in 2002 in the *American Journal of Obstetrics & Gynecology* found that 29 percent of women who went through labor and delivery had complications, compared with just 4 percent of those who had D&Es. The American Medical Association said D&Es, compared to labor and delivery, "may minimize trauma to the woman's uterus, cervix and other vital organs." There was this fact, too: the intact D&E surgery makes less use of "grasping instruments," which could damage the body of the fetus. If the body were intact, doctors might be able to more easily figure out why my baby died in the womb. I'm a healthy person. I run, swim and bike. I'm 37 years old and optimistic. Good things happen to me. I didn't want to rule out having more kids, but I did want to know what went wrong before I tried again.

We told our doctor we had chosen a dilation and evacuation. "I can't do these myself," said my doctor. "I trained at a Catholic hospital." My doctor recommended a specialist in a neighboring county, but when I called for an appointment, they said they couldn't see me for almost a week. I could feel my baby's dead body inside of mine. This baby had thrilled me with kicks and flutters, those first soft tickles of life bringing a smile to my face and my hand to my rounding belly. Now this baby floated, limp and heavy, from one side to the other, as I rolled in my bed.

And within a day, I started to bleed. My body, with or without a doctor's help, was starting to expel the fetus. Technically, I was threatening a spontaneous abortion, the least safe of the available options. I did what any pregnant patient would do. I called my doctor. And she advised me to wait. I lay in my bed, not sleeping day or night, trying not to lose this little baby's body that my own womb was working to expel. Wait, I told myself. Just hold on. Let a doctor take this out. I was scared. Was it going to fall out of my body when I rose, in the middle of the night, to check on my toddler? Would it come apart on its own and double me over, knock me to the floor, as I stood at the stove scrambling eggs for my boys? On my fourth morning, with the bleeding and cramping increasing, I couldn't wait any more. I called my doctor and was told that since I wasn't hemorrhaging, I should not come in. Her partner, on call, pedantically explained that women can safely lose a lot of blood, even during a routine period.

I began calling labor and delivery units at the top five medical centers in my area. I told them I had been 19 weeks along. The baby is dead. I'm bleeding, I said. I'm scheduled for a D&E in a few days. If I come in right now, what could you do for me, I asked. Don't come in, they told me again and again. "Go to your emergency room if you are hemorrhaging to avoid bleeding to death. No one here can do a D&E today, and unless you're really in active labor you're safer to wait."

More than 66,000 women each year in the U.S. undergo an abortion at some point between 13 and 20 weeks, according to the Centers for Disease Control and Prevention. The CDC doesn't specify the physical circumstances of the women or their fetuses. Other CDC data shows that 4,000 women miscarry in their second trimester. Again, the data doesn't clarify whether those 4,000 women have to go through surgery. Here's what is clear: most of those women face increasingly limited access to care. One survey showed that half of the women who got abortions after 15 weeks of gestation said they were delayed because of problems in affording, finding or getting to abortion services. No surprise there; abortion is not readily available in 86 percent of the counties in the United States. Although there are some new, early diagnostic tests available, the most common prenatal screening for neural tube defects or Down syndrome is done around the 16th week of pregnancy. When problems are found—sometimes life-threatening problems—pregnant women face the same limited options that I did.

At last I found one university teaching hospital that, at least over the telephone, was willing to take me. "We do have one doctor who can do a D&E," they said. "Come in to our emergency room if you want." But when I arrived at the university's emergency room, the source of the tension was clear. After examining me and confirming I was bleeding but not hemorrhaging, the attending obstetrician, obviously pregnant herself, defensively explained that only one of their dozens of obstetricians and gynecologists still did D&Es, and he was simply not available. Not today. Not tomorrow. Not the next day. No, I couldn't have his name. She walked away from me and called my doctor. "You can't just dump these patients on us," she shouted into the phone, her high-pitched voice floating through the heavy curtains surrounding my bed. "You should be dealing with this yourself."

Shivering on the narrow, white exam table, I wondered what I had done wrong. Then I pulled back on my loose maternity pants and stumbled into the sunny parking lot, blinking back tears in the dazzling spring day, trying to understand the directions they sent me out with: Find a hotel within a few blocks from a hospital. Rest, monitor the bleeding. Don't go home—the 45-minute drive might be too far. The next few days were a blur of lumpy motel beds, telephone calls to doctors, cramps. The pre-examination for my D&E finally arrived. First, the hospital required me to sign a legal form consenting to terminate the pregnancy. Then they explained I could, at no cost, have the remains incinerated by the hospital pathology department as medical waste, or for a fee have them taken to a funeral home for burial or cremation.

They inserted sticks of seaweed into my cervix and told me to go home for the night. A few hours later—when the contractions were regular, strong and frequent—I knew we needed to get to the hospital. "The patient appeared to be in active labor," say my charts, "and I explained this to the patient and offered her pain medication for vaginal delivery." According to the charts, I was "adamant" in demanding a D&E. I remember that I definitely wanted the surgical procedure that was the safest option. One hour later, just as an anesthesiologist was slipping me into unconsciousness, I had the D&E and a little body, my little boy, slipped out. Around his neck, three times and very tight, was the umbilical cord, source of his life, cause of his death.

This past spring, as the wild flowers started blooming around the simple cross we built for this baby, the Justice Department began trying to enforce the Bush administration's ban, and federal courts in three different cities heard arguments regarding the new law. Doctors explained that D&Es are the safest procedure in many cases, and that the law is particularly cruel to mothers like me whose babies were already dead. In hopes of bolstering their case, prosecutors sent federal subpoenas to various medical centers, asking for records of D&Es. There's an attorney somewhere, someday, who may poke through the files of my loss.

I didn't watch the trial because I had another appointment to keep—another ultrasound. Lying on the crisp white paper, watching the monitor, I saw new life, the incredible spine, tiny fingers waving slowly across my uterus, a perfect thigh. Best of all, there it was, a strong, four-chamber heart, beating steady and solid. A soft quiver, baby rolling, rippled across my belly. "Everything looks wonderful," said my doctor. "This baby is doing great."

James V. Grimaldi, an investigative reporter at the *Washington Post*, won a Pulitzer Prize in 2006 for his coverage of the Jack Abramoff lobbying scandal. This article appeared in the *Washington Post* on March 8, 2005. Hundreds of readers, many of them parents who faced the same issue regarding their infants, contacted Grimaldi after it was published. Later that year, the American Academy of Pediatrics revised its guidance on sleeping infants to include a discussion of strategies for avoiding positional plagiocephaly.

Baby's First Helmet

Like all fathers, I thought we had the perfect baby. So when our son, Xavier, was a couple of months old and my wife asked me, "Does his head look flat in the back?" I rejected the idea. But the question was odd enough that it lingered. Within a week or so, after looking at his head from different angles, I changed my mind: there was a flat surface on his head, on the right-rear part of his skull. His forehead also was protruding and his ears were not symmetrical.

Thus began our odyssey into a little-known but surprisingly common condition in infants: plagiocephaly—literally, an oblique or misshapen head. We were relieved that our son's kind would not require surgery. And there was a remedy. Still, we faced some difficult decisions. The treatment is somewhat controversial, unnecessary in many cases, not always paid for by health insurance, inconvenient for parents and annoying for the infant. A specially fitted helmet—worn 23 and a half hours a day for as long as six months—is used to shape the baby's growing skull. The seemingly extreme remedy posed a dilemma: Do we "fix" our son's head by subjecting him to a helmet for six months? Or do we let him grow up with a flattened head? Because thousands of parents and pediatricians face such questions each year, we decided to share our story.

There are two kinds of plagiocephaly. Luckily, our son did not get the rarer and much more serious form that is caused by craniosynostosis, the premature fusion of the bones in the head. The kind Xavier had—positional, or deformational, plagiocephaly—has skyrocketed to "almost an epidemic" level, as one Harvard medical professor put it. Since 1992, the number of infants with plagiocephaly has increased from one in 400 babies to as many as one in 10, according to numerous medical studies.

What accounts for the spike? The reason is probably the 1992 proclamation by the American Academy of Pediatrics (AAP) that infants be placed on their backs when they sleep in order to prevent sudden infant death syndrome (SIDS). The "Back to Sleep" program is considered a success; SIDS deaths have plummeted 40 percent in the United States. But it's not without consequences.

An infant's brain grows phenomenally in the first six months after birth; the cranium expands to accommodate it. But since babies spend most of this time sleeping, the head of a baby who sleeps mostly on his back can develop a depression. Picture a balloon filled with water sitting on a table: that's how a child's head can look.

Xavier's large size—he was a half ounce short of 12 pounds at birth—placed him at greater risk for certain postpartum problems, including plagiocephaly. He ended up with left torticollis, a shortening of the neck muscle on his left side. A tight neck muscle meant he had trouble turning his head. When he slept, his head naturally rotated to the right, pressing the right side of the back of his head flat. That anomaly would increase proportionally as he grew. Unless we did something about it.

Initially, we didn't know all this, even after the torticollis and deformational plagiocephaly were diagnosed at one of our first well-baby checkups. Our pediatrician, Anne Kuskowski, prescribed physical therapy. The conventional wisdom is that babies can grow out of the asymmetrical-shaped head. Kuskowski also thought that if you eliminate the torticollis, you could minimize the plagiocephaly.

We began a regimen of activities and precautions. We limited the amount of time Xavier spent on his back and added "tummy time," as pediatricians call supervised play on the baby's stomach. While watching him, we would try to place him sleeping on his side, with a blanket propping him up. (The AAP in July 2003 warned that in the "vast majority of cases," parents should not risk placing their sleeping infants on their stomachs unattended. Avoiding the risk of SIDS outweighs the benign risk of an oddly shaped head.)

For nearly six months, Xavier went to a physical therapist, who would stretch his little neck muscles by turning his head to the left and then to the far right until he screeched with pain. My wife, Niki, and I also did exercises with him at home. At night, we tried turning Xavier's head as he slept, but he usually turned it back.

At Xavier's six-month checkup, Kuskowski agreed with us that, despite our efforts, the flattened shape had not improved. She agreed we should explore the helmet option. We were running out of time. Xavier already had passed through some of his first year's largest growth spurts. After a plastic surgeon ruled out a more serious cause for our son's plagiocephaly and a neurologist concurred there was little hope for improvement without the helmet, we knew what we had to do.

The controversy about treatment is related to the fact that medical research offers no clear answers. One study suggests repositioning is just as effective as helmets in mild to moderate cases; another says helmets and such mechanical devices work better. An AAP clinical report in 2003, summarizing the numerous studies on plagiocephaly, concluded that helmets are "beneficial primarily when there has been a lack of response" to repositioning and exercises, but that more studies are needed to determine whether they are worth the significant costs.

We felt reassured that no one could cite any harm to reshaping a baby's head. In fact, we found out, the practice was not new. In some Asian cultures, mothers fashion homemade cushions out of tightly rolled cloth or towels formed into the shape of large doughnuts to prevent flat heads—something we learned from Xavier's physical therapist, who is from India. Several ancient civilizations reshaped the heads of infants to suit cultural mores. The Egyptians, for example, shaped infant heads to elongate them. Picture Queen Nefertiti's head.

The next question for us was what kind of device to use. We found a chain called Cranial Technologies, Inc., which has a clinic in Annandale. In Arlington, we found Eastern Cranial Affiliates, LLC, run by practitioner Joe Terpenning. Another company, makers of a helmet called the STAR Band, did not have a local office. We first visited Cranial Technologies, whose Web site boasts about its Dynamic Orthotic Cranioplasty Band, or DOC Band, treatment. We learned that it was a growing company, sort of the Starbucks of helmets, the largest chain of clinics capitalizing on the plagiocephaly boom. The measurements would be made in Virginia, but the helmet would be made in Phoenix.

Next we visited Eastern Cranial Affiliates. Terpenning is an orthotist, a nonphysician specialist in treating bone deformities, such as clubfoot and scoliosis. Though quite young—he is now 31—Terpenning had designed his own helmet and won approval for the device from the Food and Drug Administration.

We were leaning toward Terpenning, so I called some parents of his patients. One mom, Carolyn Montrose, of Bethesda, said the treatment seemed to work. Montrose said the concept "took me a while to accept. . . . Putting a helmet on your infant is a little hard to swallow." I asked why she finally decided to do it. She said she asked herself how her son would react as a teenager if she told him that she could have remolded his head but didn't. Good point, we thought.

Next we reviewed our insurance policy. We were surprised to find good news on Aetna's Web site: our policy paid for the treatment in moderate to severe cases. Xavier qualified due to the extent of his plagiocephaly. This generally is determined by measuring diagonally from the right base of the skull to the left temple, and then from the left rear to the right front. In a perfectly shaped head, the measurements would be equal. For Xavier, the difference was 13 millimeters. Aetna also requires policyholders to try repositioning and other therapy for at least three months. We'd been trying that for more than six months. Ultimately, we met Aetna's standard. Terpenning's price, a flat rate of $2,200 (since increased to $2,600), included all visits and monthly adjustments. Aetna paid 80 percent of the cost.

To make a helmet for Xavier, Terpenning needed a plaster mold of his head. He put a covering that looked like a ski mask over Xavier's head and applied plaster strips. The process annoyed Xavier, but he was more perturbed at me for holding him down. About a week later I went back to the Eastern Cranial Affiliates office with my older son, Alexander. Terpenning had created a mold of Xavier's head with an addition sculpted onto the back in a "normal" shape.

The idea of the helmet is that it gently contains the areas that are pronounced while leaving room for the head to grow into the areas we wanted to expand.

We went into a back office. It looked more like a carpenter's workshop than a clinic. There were hammers and screwdrivers, welding tools, nuts and bolts. Terpenning told us that for years as a hobby he had fashioned armaments and breastplates, like the kind you see at Renaissance festivals. Terpenning took out a thick sheet of plastic that looked like a cutting board and positioned it over the plaster mold. He put them both in a giant oven. The plastic melted over the mold and took the shape of the clear-plastic helmet in just the shape we desired.

About a week later, we came in for our fitting. Terpenning tried the helmet on Xavier, then went back into his workshop. We heard a noise like a buzz saw. We left with Xavier wearing his new polymer shell, with hinged seams that split the device in half. A long strap fit through a buckle and wrapped around to hold the helmet in place. Xavier tried to take the helmet off, but soon gave up. The first few days, he fussed a little but became distracted or fell asleep. After a while, the helmet began to smell, with the musty odor of a cast when it's removed from a broken arm. We took the device off daily at bath time and washed both it and the baby in mild suds. We also dabbed cotton balls in rubbing alcohol and wiped the helmet down daily.

Seeing Xavier with his headgear strapped on was strange; as much as we'd been reassured we were doing the right thing, the vision of your child topped with a plastic helmet gives you second thoughts. Reactions from others ranged from mean to funny to sweet. While we were out shopping, a boy said, "That baby's head looks funny." A girl with him said, "Shut up. That boy's head is hurt!" At our local bike store, the manager studied the device with interest, thinking it was a new model of bicycle helmet. At a restaurant, an old man walked past our table, thumped the helmet with his finger and said, "Getting ready for takeoff?" The man left the restaurant before I realized what had happened.

Niki coped by developing a familiar routine, going to the same coffee shop, stores and parks on her outings with the baby. Familiar people didn't ask a lot of questions. Wearing the helmet wasn't always a negative. It doubled as a crash helmet, dulling those sharp corners and tabletops that toddlers often bump into. One time, Xavier fell backward off the end of a slide and hit his head; he barely noticed. Another time, his brother's friend Natalie got out her hockey helmet and put it on; he enjoyed bumping his helmet against hers. They giggled hysterically at the inside joke.

At 13 months old, Xavier learned to take the helmet off. It was Mother's Day, and we had driven to the Virginia Arboretum. During the long trip home, Xavier reached up and pulled down on the Velcro strap, winning his freedom. Keeping it on after that required our constant attention. We removed the helmet a couple of times when he had a fever or when the weather was warm. But for the most part, we managed to keep it on constantly (with the daily half-hour breaks). Niki finally gave up as the hottest part of the summer approached. Xavier had worn it for nearly six months.

Terpenning's measurements found that Xavier's "intracranial oblique asymmetry" had been reduced from 13 millimeters to five millimeters. His ears moved about five millimeters back into alignment. Our pediatrician, Kuskowski, declared his plagiocephaly "resolved."

After the helmet came off, it took a while for Xavier to get used to life without it. Bumping into tabletops was now more perilous. One day, we found him gently tapping his head on a wall to feel the vibration.

Last month, I got a call from Craig Cole, a father of twins who was about to go through the same process. (Twins are more likely than singletons to develop deformational plagiocephaly because they are exposed to more risk factors, such as constraint in the uterus and premature birth, and are more likely to have spent time on a respirator.) As he asked questions, I was reminded of all the things we'd thought about: the boy would have a hard time wearing a ball cap or football helmet; his glasses might not sit right; he might have a hard time getting a date. Cole made this analogy to the *Peanuts* comic strip character: "When I boil this down: what was the reason Charlie Brown couldn't get a date? It was his head. Even when your head is considered normal, dating years aren't easy." Life is tough enough without a funny-looking head, Cole said. If you can fix it, why not?

That's pretty much how we feel. We think Xavier, now 22 months old, looks beautiful. More important, he is an adorable, funny, engaging and puckish little toddler who brings us a lot of joy. You'd never know he'd spent six months wearing a helmet. We don't expect our children to be flawless. Life is messy and complicated. We know that. We just want our kids to have a fair shot at success and happiness. Our job as parents is to prepare our children to meet the challenges. We never expected that one of those would be reshaping his head. But we're glad we did it.

Researcher Meg Smith contributed to this article.

Lisa Cohen spent more than two decades in network news, producing newsmagazine reports for, among others, ABC News's *Primetime Live* and CBS News's *60 Minutes*. This text is drawn from *After Etan: The Missing Child Case That Held America Captive*, (Grand Central, 2009).

After Etan: The Missing Child Case That Held America Captive

May 25, 1979

Police hypnotist: About what time is it?
Julie: About 7:00 a.m.
Hypnotist: What do you do?
Julie: Get out of bed.

—*Julie Patz Hypnosis Transcript August 7, 1979*

Nine weeks after Etan Patz disappeared, his mother, Julie, was hypnotized by police to recall the events of Friday, May 25. She was nervous but eager to do anything to add to the nonexistent list of clues. She began to retrace her steps that day, minute by minute. After a stoic first ten minutes, the NYPD hypnotist stopped her, told her she was doing a wonderful job, but that she had to start all over again from the beginning. And this time, he said, she needed to stay completely in the present tense, as if every minute were just happening now. He thought it would help her recall the day more easily. He actually used the word "easily." Julie started again. "The alarm clock is ringing," she said. "Stan is shutting it off."

Her husband, Stan, turns over and goes back to sleep. He had worked late the night before. Julie pulls herself out of bed, unwillingly, but she has a lot to do. Their across-the-street neighbors, Larry and Karen Altman, have invited them to their country place for the weekend. The weather is changeable this time of year—lots to pack. Julie's in-home daycare group will be arriving soon, bringing their daily chaotic mess of arts-and-crafts supplies, spilled Cheerios, and sweet cacophony. The other wild card this morning is Ari, her two-year-old. A playmate of his had slept over the night before, the toddlers snuggled under blankets on the floor in the front room that doubled as the daycare center. This means an extra wiggly body to keep track of. And when Julie peeks in, sure enough they are awake already, "reading" their books amid the bedclothes.

As usual, when Julie wakes Etan, he hops right out of bed. Eight-year-old Shira is a different story. Once awake, Shira might lie in bed imagining ways to get out of having to go to school. Today is really part of the long weekend, she might argue, and then, it's almost the end of the term, and it isn't like anyone's learning anything this late in the year, anyway. Julie has already decided she isn't going to push her daughter that hard.

She goes to her room to throw on a long blue and yellow peasant dress with white flowers and pull her shoulder-length brown hair back in its usual casual ponytail. Then she checks on Etan, who is putting on his blue pants and a T-shirt. While Julie goes to the kitchen, he laces up his racing sneakers, the light blue ones with the fluorescent green lightning stripe on the side. His best friend, Jeff, has just grown out of a blue, wide-wale corduroy jacket, and Etan is now its proud owner, even though the name sewn inside hasn't been changed. He already has on his favorite hat, the Future Flight Captain pilot's cap he bought for a dime at a garage sale and sometimes slept in, as he comes into the kitchen where his mother is making lunches.

Julie watches as, unbidden, he takes the milk out and pours himself a glass. With a naturally contrary older sister, and a typically terrible-two-ish younger brother, Etan is an easy middle child. There are the usual qualifications, of course. He actively tries to please, a refreshing change of pace after Shira, but he knows the secret ways to provoke his sister as only a sibling can. He is fiercely protective of baby brother Ari, but equally jealous. He is sunny and sweet, but has a stubborn, moody streak. He is fanciful and full of stories, planning trips to far-off lands with his imaginary playmate Johnny France-America. For a while, he felt that he could walk on water as Jesus had if only he practiced hard enough, so he spent hours walking flat-footed around the house.

He is on the slight side, but not undersized. His smile reaches up his whole face and through his blue, blue eyes to light up a room. He looks a lot like his mother. She encourages his self-sufficiency, and every morning he fixes his own breakfast of toast and chocolate milk. Now he quickly finishes up both, picks up his cloth lunch bag, the blue one with the white elephants, and heads into the front room to position himself by the door.

Etan has a reason for being one step ahead of his mom. This is a big day. The school-bus stop is two short blocks away, down Prince Street, then a quick right onto West Broadway, in front of the corner bodega. All year he has been begging his mother to let him walk it on his own. A lot of the other kids are allowed, why not me, Etan would say, with classic six-year-old logic. Now first grade is almost over, and he has only a few more weeks to carry out his mission.

Stan and Julie were of mixed minds about this walk-to-the-bus-stop thing, but Etan's pleadings wore them down. It wasn't as if there had been one moment when they decided, yes, this was the day. It just sort of happened. His parents also thought it would be a good confidence builder for him—they were concerned about the tentative streak that coexisted with his thirst for adventure. Etan was particularly fearful of being lost. Once, when he was five, he and his mother rode an elevator, and when the door opened, she made it off but he didn't. She turned as the door closed and would never forget the expression on his face. She could hear him screaming all the way to the top and back down safely to her.

But this morning he is so pleased with himself, acting so grown-up, and just before eight, Julie calculates it's time to go. Etan walks ahead of his mother down the three flights to the front door. He isn't tall enough to reach the lock himself, and has to wait while she opens the door.

Looking up the street, Julie hopes the weather will be better for the next few days, since they plan to spend most of it outdoors on this holiday weekend in the country. She sees the familiar figures of other parents and their children beginning to congregate near the bus stop, which is just barely out of sight around the corner. Mother and son stand in front of their door, heads together, talking briefly about after-school plans. Come home quickly, she tells him, you have to help pack for the trip. She kisses Etan goodbye.

He smiled and waved, turned around and walked away. She watched him, head down, as though he were counting his steps. She waited until he crossed the first of the two streets that stood between their home and the bus stop. If she were wavering at all, well, there were the babies upstairs, unsupervised. She turned and went inside, back upstairs to contain whatever toddler havoc Ari and his friend had wrought in the few minutes she'd been gone.

As Julie relived those few last moments to the hypnotist, she slipped unaware from present tense to past. Living in that exact moment again seemed to be just too hard.

> *Julie*: I'm kissing him and I give him a hug. I say so long, tell him to
>   have a good day. I watched him for a little while and I went in the
>   door and flipped the lock and closed it, I ran upstairs. (Long pause)
> *Hypnotist*: Let me just wipe those away.
> *Julie*: No, that's all right. They feel good. There haven't been enough.
> *Hypnotist*: Well, you can have all you want here.

—Hypnosis Transcript August 7, 1979

The account contradicted one important detail widely reported in the days following May 25. When Julie Patz first told police about her movements that morning, she remembered coming back inside and going out on the balcony fire escape that fronted Prince Street, to watch her son reach West Broadway and turn the corner.

But under hypnosis, she discovered her mind had played a trick on her. Perhaps her unconscious wanted her to have gone out on the balcony so badly, it had given her the false memory. In reality, back upstairs, she eyed the toddlers, then went off to take a quick shower and get ready for work. The rest of "her" kids would be showing up soon, as well as her staff. Julie's in-home daycare made good use of the space. Five days a week, eight kids and two assistants filled the rooms with snack time, rest, and play.

Showered and ready, Julie tidied up, packed Shira off to school after all, and began gathering the weekend belongings before the daycare kids arrived. Karen Altman would be picking up Etan along with her own daughter Chelsea at the bus stop after school, as she often did.

By 3:30 p.m., Etan was still not home, and Julie was a little concerned. She kept sticking her head out the wide expanse of windows in the front, where she was always able to see her children approaching from well up the block. Finally, she phoned Karen Altman, whose own windows looked in on the Patz loft from directly across the street. "Is Etan over there with you?" Julie asked. "No," said Karen. She'd assumed that when Etan hadn't gotten off the bus, he had gone to another friend's, as he often did, for a semiregular playdate. With Julie on the line, she asked her daughter Chelsea whether she knew where Etan had gone after school.

"Etan wasn't in school today," Chelsea said.

Julie tried to contain her panic, but her voice, one of her most revealing features, betrayed her with a tight shake, and she immediately ended the call.

At ten minutes to four on Friday afternoon, at the start of a holiday weekend that would shut the city down for three days, Julie Patz phoned the First Precinct to report her son missing. The officer who answered asked Julie whether she and her husband were having marital troubles—maybe a custody dispute? No, said Julie. Maybe he ran away? No, Julie insisted, her voice rising. The officer promised to send someone over.

Julie hung up and called her husband, Stan, a photographer who was working at a friend's photo studio uptown. By this time she was frantic. Stan, in a moment of pure denial, finished the soggy cheeseburger that was his late lunch, then jumped on the subway downtown.

At the loft, he ignored the elevator, running up the back stairs to the third floor. It was almost 4:30. Stan took one look at Julie and knew nothing good had happened during the time he had been on the subway. She was ashen. Stan's fantasy as he sat on the R train rattling down Broadway, that he would arrive to learn the whole thing was a big misunderstanding, was just that—a fantasy. In between calls to neighbors and friends, his wife had been dialing local emergency rooms and wondering where the hell the cops were.

Time ~ 16:25. No cops yet. Julie was very nervous. She had called everybody for a clue. I called 1st Pct to find out where the cops were. Minutes later two patrolmen were in our place, asked basic questions (marriage, friends, family) and jumped in their car to go down to PS 3 Annex.

—Stan Patz's Account of May 25, 1979
  (written June 1979)

The police told Stan and Julie they needed to confirm that Etan really wasn't in school that day, but on the Friday evening of Memorial Day Weekend, there was no one at the school to call. When one of the officers realized he knew the custodian there, they headed over.

Stan went into his home darkroom. He had no photos of Etan lying around, but remembered that back in March he'd done a lengthy photo shoot of the boy, and there were proof sheets—thirty-six miniature headshots on each page. He grabbed a few of them and ran down the stairs, heading out onto Prince Street to show them to shopkeepers. Stan took his proofsheets to the health food store, the bodega, the M&O Market, and the Eva Deli, then to the Houston Street playground. No, everyone said, shaking their heads as they looked at the tiny pictures, they hadn't seen Etan.

At the P.S. 3 Annex school, a police officer went through the school records to confirm Etan's absence before he finally called back to headquarters to ask for backup. Ten long hours after Etan was last seen, a full-on search for him began.

At 5:15, Detective Bill Butler got the radio call. He and his partner immediately drove to Prince Street, where by 5:30 they were joined by three other detectives from the First Precinct.

Stan showed them pictures of Etan, while Julie repeated the day's events as she knew them. She would recite them again and again, countless times in the days to come.

"He's a very friendly boy," she said. "Very loving, trusting and warm."

By 6 p.m., as if to compensate for the first hour of inactivity, radio patrol cars began to roll up, and through the night some 300 police officers descended on Prince Street. A temporary police headquarters was set up in the Patz loft. Up and down the block, squad cars were left standing in the middle of the street. As the light grew dim, the car doors were propped open and high beams left on to illuminate the evening air. An area diagram was drawn, to divide up and designate the different buildings. Uniformed cops patrolled on foot, moving door-to-door in the streets around Prince, knocking to gain access, to shine their flashlights into dark basements and onto rooftops. Helicopters with floodlights swooped back and forth. Walkie-talkies crackled as false leads and rumors flew.

Peggy Spina, a downstairs neighbor, answered her door to find a policeman politely asking to come in. She examined the card he handed her, ushered him into her home and told him everything she knew, which was almost nothing. She was shocked to find herself following him as he began methodically opening all her closed doors, rummaging behind the clothes in her closets. She wasn't outraged at this invasion, but sickened by the realization that the cops had to think this way in such cases—had to assume a small child might be secreted away in the downstairs neighbors' closet. It must actually happen like that sometimes, she thought, horrified.

Upstairs, Julie Patz sat in the loft surrounded by officers. She felt almost incapable of functioning, although the only outward signs besides the tears were the trembling tic in her jaw and the occasional stumble as she got up to answer phones or to walk across the loft to forage for Etan's toys and other items potentially laden with his fingerprints. His stuffed hippo, Biggie, or his *Star Wars* X-wing fighter. But inside, she quelled the overwhelming urge to vomit and the uncontrollable flood of guilt: why had she let her son walk to the bus stop alone? As night fell, the guilty feelings were supplanted by more damaging fears of the horrors he might be living through, or whether he was even alive.

For Stan Patz, who spent hours conferring with police from the front of his loft turned temporary staging area, the rest of the day and night were as lost to him as his son. It was as if it had all never happened, as if he had never experienced it in the first place. Or maybe, in the way that Julie imagined the balcony scene, remembering was just not permitted.

Karen Altman had already come and gone, taking Shira and little Ari back across the street, where she made everyone soup. There would be no more talk about the trip upstate. Instead, two-year-old Ari Patz watched the goings on from the Altman's front window. This was turning into his second sleepover in a row and his first away from home, but he didn't cry. When Shira and Chelsea stopped playing cards in the other room and drifted off to sleep, Ari stayed at the front window. His face pressed up against the large panes of glass that stretched the length of the Altman loft, he watched his mother and father, moving from the street below to the Patz front room across the way, and back again.

The Patzes' tall windows showcased the blur of activity. From her vantage point over Ari's shoulder, Karen Altman watched Stan too, as his wiry frame paced the length of sidewalk in front of the building, the floodlights illuminating his thin, now pinched face. Karen could see just by the way Stan was holding himself and by the expressions on his face that he was enraged. Not at the cops, not at his wife, but at the gods, she thought. She half expected him to start shaking his fist at the skies.

The gods seemed to be piling on when, shortly before midnight, they began spitting on the searchers in a slow, steady drizzle. By 1:15 a.m., when authorities requested that bloodhounds be brought in from upstate, any traces of Etan—his prints or a scent the dogs could follow—were in the process of being washed away.

"Wouldn't it be awful," whispered Karen's husband, Larry, from behind her and just out of Ari's earshot, "if they never found Etan, and they never found out what happened?"

Juanita Darling of the *Los Angeles Times* left journalism for academia after her semester at Princeton. She is now a member of the International Relations faculty at San Francisco State University and recently published *Latin America, Media, and Revolution: Communication in Modern Mesoamerica* (Palgrave Macmillan, 2008). This article appeared in the *Los Angeles Times* on April 19, 1998. Since then, more than 20,000 people have been kidnapped in Colombia, according to Fundación País Libre. Guatemalan police reported more than 100 abductions in 2008.

A Hostage Crisis Hits Latin America

In life, Beverly Sandoval was the family merrymaker, the oldest daughter who played practical jokes and decorated the Christmas tree. In death, she has become the symbol of a nation's pain and rage. Her burial on a misty day in November resembled a state funeral. Guatemalans filled the long road to a cemetery outside the capital, tossing flowers onto her hearse. Mourners waved banners reading "*Basta ya!*" ("Enough already!"). "What we want is for there to be no more Beverlys," said her stepfather, Gerbert Sole, fighting back tears. The 20-year-old forestry-engineering student died in an epidemic that has stricken thousands of middle-class families like hers throughout Latin America.

She was kidnapped. In Guatemala, kidnapping has spread so rapidly that citizens' groups started keeping statistics on the crime only in 1997. "What I can assure you is that since 1996, [kidnapping] has increased monstrously and become more and more damaging," said Michelle de Leal of Anguished Mothers, one of three antikidnapping organizations here. Colombia has recorded more than 1,000 kidnappings every year since 1993. The number of abductions rose by nearly two-thirds from 1993 to 1997, according to País Libre, an antikidnapping organization.

The toll is also growing in neighboring countries as kidnappers expand operations by exporting their skills. Mexico, Brazil, and Ecuador are suffering rashes of abductions, authorities say. Why the alarming rise? Kidnapping is a simple crime to commit and a difficult one to investigate, making it an easy, quick way to get money. The region's armed conflicts of the 1970s and 1980s left a legacy of former soldiers and guerrillas who know how to use guns and abduct people but have few other skills. Now they are using their wartime training to organize kidnapping rings. Other criminals are learning from their example. Further, critics blame the police and courts for ineptitude and corruption that enable kidnappers to get away with their crimes. The low risk of getting caught makes it worthwhile to abduct for ransoms of $50,000 or less; thus, the pool of potential victims has broadened considerably.

Kidnapping is no longer just a crime against the wealthy. Today's victims are people like Beverly, a leather wholesaler's stepdaughter who was driving through the mountains after a Sunday afternoon in the colonial town of Anti-gua. These victims also include a teenager waiting for a school bus in Guate-mala City; a septuagenarian sleeping in his concrete-block ranch house in northern El Salvador; and a retired teacher bird-watching a few hours' drive from the Colombian capital, Bogotá. "It has gotten to the extreme that all kinds of people are being kidnapped, but the worst of it is that the victims are chil-dren, young people and the elderly," said Juan Jerónimo Castillo, a victims' rights lawyer in San Salvador. "And don't think that these are rich people. These are working people."

Psychiatrists and law enforcement officials warn that so many abductions create societies that are at once fearful and callous. "We are trying to sensitize people with television and publicity campaigns so that we don't just become accustomed to this," said Rubén Darío Ramírez, Colombia's antikidnapping czar. "We have to struggle for freedom and side with those who have lost their freedom." Kidnappings are often brutal, and victims are sometimes killed over ransoms that are less than the winnings from a lucky weekend in Las Vegas. In Pereira, Colombia, kidnappers suffocated 4-year-old Brian Steven Ramírez when his parents failed to come up with a $5,000 ransom in December 1996. Eight-year-old Oscar Suazo was found hanged in rural Honduras in February after his coffee-growing family told abductors that they did not have the $11,000 needed to free him, his father told police.

Because victims are usually killed unless the kidnappers' demands are met, most countries have legalized ransom payments. "Before, the idea was that every family had to offer up its dead, like a sacrifice," said Marta Lucía Aristizabal, a Colombian psychiatrist who has worked with more than 400 kidnapping vic-tims and their families. "But that was cruel." Instead, authorities are trying other strategies. Police departments have set up special antikidnapping units, legis-latures have passed stiffer sentences—including instituting the death penalty for kidnapping in Guatemala—and families have taken precautions, such as sending their children to private school in unmarked buses. Still, the number of abductions remains alarming.

Colombia recorded 92 kidnappings in January, on its way to what appears to be another 1,000-plus year. In Guatemala, the citizens' group Neighborhood Watch recorded 503 abductions from January to mid-March. Guatemalan po-lice officially say those figures are inflated but refuse to provide their own sta-tistics. Privately, officers acknowledge that they receive an average of 10 kid-napping reports a week and believe that fewer than half of all abductions are reported. Law enforcement officials are so concerned that Colombia organized a regional meeting last week to brainstorm and try to find solutions by sharing data and experiences. "This is worrying," said Ramírez, Colombia's antikidnap-ping czar. "It is important enough that there should be an international summit on the problem of kidnappings. This [symposium] is merited to talk about kidnapping, just the way there is a drug summit."

Critics say the problem is that there has been too much talk and not enough action. Guatemala's Neighborhood Watch even advocates a constitutional state of emergency that would temporarily set aside civil rights to permit roundups of suspected murderers, drug dealers and kidnappers. "There may be some abuses," acknowledged Oscar Recinos, the Neighborhood Watch founder. "At first, some of our neighboring countries might be fearful . . . but when they see the results, they will follow our example."

So how did it get this bad? Kidnapping used to be a problem of the very rich. Leftist guerrilla groups throughout the region carefully planned abductions for multimillion-dollar ransoms to finance their causes. Their victims read like a cross between the social register and a sort of Latin American Forbes 400 list. Such abductions became less frequent as the wealthy hired security consultants, installed alarm systems and took other precautions.

Even so, guerrillas still prefer kidnappings that they can justify on ideological grounds. The favorite targets of the National Liberation Army, Colombia's second-largest guerrilla group, are foreign business executives and international oil company employees. The ELN, as the rebel group is known, opposes foreign ownership of Colombian resources. Foreign companies, including Los Angeles–based Occidental Petroleum Corp., still do business in Colombia despite the threat of guerrilla kidnappings. But the increased risks and costs—for security guards, training and ransoms—are reflected in the deals that they make with the government. That ultimately costs the national treasury money. As the civil wars intensified in Central America and Colombia in the late 1970s and the '80s, insurgents, the armed forces and the extreme right all began kidnapping for political reasons: to trade for imprisoned comrades or to "persuade" victims—sometimes by torture—to betray secrets, leave the country or change their behavior.

Colombian drug kingpin Pablo Escobar brought political kidnappings to a new level when he abducted nine prominent journalists and held them for 18 months in 1990 and '91. He used his captives in his successful campaign to force the government to ban extradition of Colombians, a prohibition that was not lifted until last year, four years after his death in a shootout with security forces. Political kidnappings continue. Last year, the Revolutionary Armed Forces of Colombia, or FARC, the nation's largest guerrilla group, enforced its opposition to local elections by kidnapping hundreds of mayors, city council members and candidates for municipal office. On their release, under threat of death, nearly all of the captured candidates withdrew from their races.

Colombian authorities blame the rebels for 60 percent of their nation's abductions. Besides the political abductions, guerrillas also kidnap for ransom. Some victims are targeted, while others just have the bad luck to stumble across the rebels. Central America's experience shows that the end of civil war can be just the beginning for abductions. During the 1980s, when El Salvador was at war, a total of 38 kidnappings was reported to police. Last year alone there were 39. Authorities acknowledge that citizens may be reporting more abductions because of increased confidence in the 6-year-old civilian police force that replaced the military police, but they say they believe that the numbers reflect mainly rising crime.

Throughout the Salvadoran conflict, Luis Navarrete and his family never budged from their ranch near San Jose Cancasque, about 12 miles from the Honduran border—deep in rebel territory. "We did not get involved with either side, and they left us alone," said Luz Navarrete, his wife of 25 years. In February, 10 heavily armed men wearing police uniforms rousted the 70-year-old Navarrete from bed and took him. They left behind his daily heart medication and a note demanding a $500,000 ransom. When family members said they could not pay, the kidnappers cut off communication. "Even if I sold everything, I would not have that much money," said his wife, gesturing toward the laundry sink on the patio, the pig in the paved-over front yard and the concrete-block house. Such modest comforts make the Navarrete family seem prosperous amid the adobe huts of Chalatenango, El Salvador's poorest province. In addition, Navarrete often lent money to other farmers, people in the area say. His wife explained that he could make loans not because he was wealthy but because he harvested sesame seeds at a time when neighbors were planting corn. He would lend them money and, when they repaid him, sow again. "He always tried to help people, and we did not expect that they would do this to us," she said, shaking her auburn braids and dabbing at her eyes with her apron. Now, with planting season approaching, area farmers say they do not know where they will get the money for seeds and fertilizer without Navarrete.

Police say that they are tracking the movements of a gang they suspect in the kidnapping and that they believe the gang members will lead authorities to Navarrete. Then their plan is to rescue him. Their biggest concern, they say, is whether he can have survived this long without his heart medicine. "Criminals know that economically powerful men have bodyguards, and they don't want to take the risk," said Mauricio Rodríguez, chief of the criminal investigations division of the Salvadoran police. Kidnappers instead look for people with less protection, he said.

They choose victims like Paulina, a frail-looking blond who asked that her last name not be published because her kidnappers have not been caught and she is still afraid of them, three years after her abduction. A week before her 18th birthday, Paulina was abducted as she waited for her school bus at a Guatemala City gas station. "Two cars pulled up with eight men with guns," she recalled. "They threw a T-shirt over my face and put a gun to my head." They locked her in a room with a television and VCR, where she lost track of time. They asked her how much her school tuition was and about her family and friends to figure out how much ransom to demand. "They told me my parents didn't care about me," she said. "They said that if I didn't obey them, they would kill me."

Such stories are typical of the early stages of an abduction, said Aristizabal, the Colombian psychiatrist. Captors pump their victims for information, tell them that their families are refusing to pay and constantly threaten them. Victims become afraid to even hope for freedom. "Every day, they said I was leaving," Paulina remembered. "When they finally released me in the street, I thought they were going to kill me."

After her family paid an undisclosed ransom, she was dumped two hours south of the city and walked until a car with teenage girls in it—she was afraid of anyone else—passed her on the highway. She flagged them down, and they took her to a telephone. The effect of kidnapping on victims and their families can be devastating, Aristizabal said. "People are greatly affected, not so much during captivity, because they draw on internal resources to survive," Aristizabal said. "They pull out resources from places they do not have them." The effects show later. Paulina recognizes that the kidnapping changed her. "I don't like superficial things like clothing," she said. "Yesterday, I went to a disco, and I was always looking around to see whether somebody was watching how much I was paying. I was a very secure person, and now I'm not." A few months after she was released, her 3-year-old cousin was kidnapped. "They don't care," she said of the abductors. "For them, it's like work." As Recinos, the Neighborhood Watch founder, said, "Kidnapping has become an industry."

Last year, Colombian police broke up a kidnapping ring that had an office, lawyers and rental cars, Ramírez said. Some gangs are even going international. In January 1997, Daniel Fernando Palacios escaped from the maximum-security prison in Guatemala City. The 30-year-old, who is known as "the Negotiator," had been charged with 20 abductions in Guatemala from 1994 to 1996. Palacios was captured 11 months later—by Salvadoran police rounding up another kidnapping ring in their country. The police believe that Palacios organized the ring that abducted two Salvadorans last year.

Similarly, Guatemalan and Honduran police say an increasing number of the gangs arrested for kidnappings in their countries include people from other Central American nations.

Kidnapping is simply one of the easiest crimes to commit, police officials say. "After drug trafficking, it's the fastest way to make money," Ramírez said. Castillo noted, "Kidnapping is an extremely difficult crime to investigate." To get a conviction, police must nearly always catch the kidnappers in the act, because they disappear afterward and usually leave no trace. But the kidnappers must be caught in a way that minimizes danger to the victim. Now police are trying to make it more difficult to get away with kidnapping. Their main strategy is to try to safely retrieve both victims and ransoms.

"Last year, we had 206 rescues," Ramírez said. Three in five of those kidnapped by criminals—rather than guerrillas—were rescued by police, he said.

But as Beverly Sandoval's family has learned, an arrest does not necessarily lead to a conviction. In recent weeks, Guatemalans have shared the family's outrage as the courts released 14 of the 25 suspects in her kidnap-rape-murder for lack of evidence. At best, critics suspect sloppy detective work; at worst, corruption. "If this can happen in a case this well known, what must happen in other cases?" her stepfather asked. Sandoval's abduction touched Guatemala's heart, providing a focus for the fear and anger against a crime wave that has worsened in the 16 months since a peace agreement ended three and a half decades of civil war. Immediately after Sandoval was kidnapped, abductors demanded a $1 million ransom but eventually agreed to free her for considerably less. Police said the demand for an exorbitant sum is a typical negotiating tactic to panic family members and make them feel relieved about paying a lower amount. In her case, the money was paid, but Sandoval never reappeared.

During the months that followed, Guatemala waited with the family. Somber crowds gathered at the graveside each of the three times that a body thought to be hers was exhumed and examined. After her remains were finally identified, people across Guatemala mourned. They tentatively applauded the arrests early this year of a band accused of kidnapping her and several other people. They have followed the trials, first with interest—and then with bitterness as charges were dismissed. "It has been agonizing to go in and face her killers," said Beverly Richardson, Sandoval's mother. Observers were particularly infuriated at a hearing in February to decide whether two of the suspects would be bound over for trial. With the case file sitting on his desk, the judge told onlookers that he had heard about the existence of a deposition that would give him enough evidence to order a trial. But the deposition was not in the file, he said, and without it he did not have enough evidence to proceed, and was forced to dismiss the charges. Overworked, underpaid Guatemalan prosecutors are routinely bribed to omit evidence, provoking case dismissals. People were shocked, however, at the judge's insinuation that they would do so in such a highly publicized case. "Beverly Sandoval's case has become not only a symbol of public insecurity and the inability of the government to ensure [safety] in compliance with its constitutional mandate but also [of] the impunity that reigns here," said an editorial in the newspaper *La Hora*.

Many potential victims have simply decided that the only way to be safe is to leave their country. Luis Pedro Aguirre, who was kidnapped five years ago, graduated from high school in the United States last year. His parents have been too terrified to bring him back to Guatemala. But many other Guatemalans, Colombians and other middle-class Latin Americans do not have the option of leaving. "Do you know how many hostages there are in Guatemala?" Recinos asked. "Eleven million. All of us. Because none of us knows at what moment he will become a victim."

Kathy Kiely has spent most of her life facing the pressure of daily deadlines. She has covered Congress and national politics for a number of newspapers, including the nation's largest, *USA Today*. Perhaps no story evokes more raw emotion than immigration. She has returned to it again and again in the course of three decades as a reporter. The specifics of the legislation change; sadly, the fundamentals of the problem do not. This story, which appeared in *USA Today* on October 8, 2007, describes how the U.S. failure to come to grips with the problem is affecting young lives.

Children Caught in the Immigration Crossfire

On the phone, Fiorella Maza comes across as a typical American teenager. Her English is unaccented. Her best friend's name is Brittney. Her three most prized possessions are her wallet, her cell phone and, of course, her iPod. Those were the necessities Maza, 19, took when immigration agents arrived at 6 a.m. on March 1 to deport her and her family. The 2006 South Miami Senior High School graduate and her parents now live in her grandmother's house in Lima, Peru—more than 2,600 miles from the place she had called home since she was two. She's searching for language classes "because my Spanish is really bad," and trying to adjust to life in a land where, she says, "I feel like an outcast."

Hundreds of thousands of illegal immigrants' children could suffer the same fate, according to the nonpartisan Migration Policy Institute. They are the lost generation of an underground economy: brought here illegally by parents, they grew up in American neighborhoods, attended American schools and made American friends. As they approach adulthood, most find that their illegal status is a barrier to jobs and education, and their lack of documentation puts them in line for deportation.

Now, Sen. Dick Durbin, D-Ill., is pushing a plan that would give them a way to stay here and become Americans. The measure is triggering another bitter debate over how the nation should deal with its growing shadow population. "The letters and e-mails I get from these young people are just heartbreaking," says Durbin, the number two Democratic leader in the Senate. "They have nowhere to turn. They are without a country." In all but 10 states, students who are not legal residents cannot qualify for in-state college tuition or student loans. They have no right to work. And there's the dread of a knock on the door such as the one that sent Maza's family packing.

It's unclear how many of the 185,431 immigrants removed from the country last year were children who had grown up here. The Department of Homeland Security does not track such statistics, spokeswoman Kelly Nantel says. The Migration Policy Institute, however, estimates that there are 360,000 high school graduates in the United States illegally who would be eligible for conditional legal status under Durbin's bill, the Development, Relief and Education for Alien Minors Act—or DREAM Act, as proponents call it. Another 715,000 younger students could qualify if they graduate high school. "They talk like Americans; they think like Americans," says Bishop Thomas Wenski of Orlando, speaking for the U.S. Conference of Catholic Bishops. "We ought to let them dream like Americans."

Durbin's bill would carve an exemption in the nation's immigration policy for undocumented immigrants who grew up in the United States. It would protect students from deportation and qualify young adults up to age 30 for permanent legal status if they complete high school and at least two years of either postsecondary education or two years of military service. It's one of several pieces of a sweeping proposed overhaul of the nation's immigration laws that proponents are trying to revive following the larger bill's collapse. The other measures, which would allow more foreign workers, have the backing of the agricultural industry and technology companies. The DREAM Act's backers have a different kind of political clout. The Catholic bishops are among several religious groups lobbying for the bill. Democratic leaders in the House and Senate support it. So do senior Republican senators such as Arizona's John McCain and Indiana's Richard Lugar, as well as the nation's largest teachers union.

Even so, the act's passage is far from certain. Many of the groups that torpedoed the immigration bill by arguing it provided amnesty to lawbreakers are targeting the DREAM Act as a backdoor attempt to accomplish the same goal. "It really is an amnesty plan disguised as an education initiative," says Bob Dane of the Federation for American Immigration Reform (FAIR), a group lobbying to reduce legal and illegal immigration. Dane says the bill will "encourage illegal behavior" and force Americans to compete with illegal residents for college slots and scholarships. The bill's opponents aren't out to punish kids, Dane says: "We're merely not rewarding them for the illegal actions of their parents." Such distinctions are lost on many of those caught in the middle of the debate. "I just want to return home where I belong," Maza writes in an e-mail.

"I'm living in limbo," says Marie Gonzalez, 21, a junior at Westminster College in Missouri. Gonzalez, a political science major, has lived in Missouri—"Jeff City," she says, using the nickname for Jefferson City—since she was five. She learned in 2002 she wasn't here legally when an anonymous tipster reported her father. At the time, he was working as a courier in the office of then-Missouri governor Bob Holden, a Democrat. Gonzalez was a sophomore in high school. "I was scared people were going to turn their backs on us," she recalls. "We were the people they talk about on TV." Instead, neighbors in Gonzalez's conservative community rallied around her family. It wasn't enough to save her parents, who were deported to Costa Rica in 2005. Then 19, Gonzalez had to sell the family home and cars. She hasn't seen her parents since, because a visit would mean not being able to return. At Durbin's request, the Department of Homeland Security twice deferred Gonzalez's deportation. However, she says that DHS officials have warned her that if the DREAM Act doesn't pass, she will be deported to Costa Rica in June.

A deportation deadline also looms for Juan Gomez, 18, and brother Alex, 20. Earlier this summer, the two, both students at Miami Dade College in Florida, spent a week wearing orange jumpsuits at the Broward County detention center. Their crime: having arrived here at ages 2 and 4, respectively, with their parents from Colombia. Their parents are to be deported this month. In handcuffs on the ride to the detention center, Juan used his cell phone to send a text message to a friend. The result was the creation of a Facebook group that rallied more than 3,000 supporters to lobby Congress on the boys' behalf. Rep. Lincoln Diaz-Balart, a Republican from Florida, and Sen. Chris Dodd, a Democrat from Connecticut, introduced what is known as a "private bill," used to help individuals with immigration problems. That move gave the brothers two more years in the United States—a courtesy extended by immigration officials to allow Congress time to consider the legislation. "It just shows you what a democratic country we are," says Juan Gomez. "This is the country I've always considered home."

For the Gomez brothers to be able to stay, however, the DREAM Act will have to pass. Diaz-Balart says it's highly unlikely Congress will approve a private bill for the brothers because there are too many similar cases. "We continually run into kids who are in this country because of their parents' choice," he says. Some have younger siblings who are legal. The Constitution says anyone born in the United States is automatically a citizen.

The DREAM Act is one of several pieces of the failed immigration bill now in play in Congress. Other measures that could be part of a year-end immigration deal: one to permit more foreign farmworkers to live in the United States, and another to grant more visas for temporary workers in businesses ranging from high technology to restaurants. By one measure, the DREAM Act would seem the least controversial of the three: When the Senate Judiciary Committee considered it in 2003, the vote in favor was 16–3.

The opposition this year is enough to raise doubts about whether it or any piece of the immigration act can become law in the current Congress. "I just don't think the political wherewithal is there to do it," says Sen. Mel Martinez, R-Fla., the party's national chairman. He supported the immigration overhaul but isn't sure he'll back relief for illegal immigrant children as a separate issue. And though Martinez says it hasn't affected his stance, he says he received "a flood of letters and phone calls" opposing the DREAM Act when Durbin tried to add it to the defense authorization bill. FAIR representatives made 24 appearances on radio talk shows over two weeks to oppose the DREAM Act, Dane says. NumbersUSA, another group that favors clamping down on legal and illegal immigration, urged people on its Web site to call senators thought to be in favor of the bill. Sen. Jeff Sessions, R-Ala., threatened a filibuster. That persuaded Durbin and Senate Majority Leader Harry Reid, D-Nev., to drop their effort temporarily. They say they'll try again to pass the DREAM Act. Responds Dane: "We intend to keep the heat up."

Without the DREAM Act, Tam Tran, 24, is a person without a country. The daughter of Vietnamese boat people, Tran was born in Germany, where her parents ended up after the German navy plucked them out of the sea. The family moved to the United States when Tran was six. When her parents lost their political asylum case, immigration authorities tried to deport the family to Germany, Tran says. However, the Germans refused to take them. For now, Tran is permitted to stay—only because the United States has no repatriation treaty with Vietnam. If the diplomatic situation changes, Tran could be deported to the country of her parents' birth, says Department of Homeland Security spokeswoman Nantel. Tran, who has never been to Vietnam, says that "I consider myself a Southern Californian." She graduated with honors from UCLA in December. Her major: American literature and culture.

For Martine Kalaw, a graduate of Syracuse University's prestigious Maxwell School public affairs program, it took eight years and three lawyers to overturn a judge's order that would have sent her to the Congo, a country she left at age four. Kalaw, 26, is an orphan. Her stepfather died when she was 12. Three years later, she lost her mother. That misfortune may have been her salvation, Kalaw says. Unlike students who fear putting their parents at risk for deportation, she was able to take her case to the public. She first spoke out at an immigration rally where she shared a stage with McCain, and later testified before Congress. "I was scared because I thought there would be a backlash," Kalaw says, who adds that she was treated for clinical depression during her ordeal. "I was extremely ashamed of my situation. Deportation proceedings are the most terrifying, belittling process." On July 4, Kalaw says, her legal odyssey ended. The Board of Immigration Appeals overturned her deportation order and awarded her permanent legal resident status, which will enable her to apply for citizenship in five years. "Now that everything is secure, I'm looking to develop my career," she says. "The sky's the limit."

Geraldine Moriba Meadows is the executive producer of CNN's In America documentary unit. She joined CNN after sixteen years at NBC News, where she served as senior producer for Broadcast Standards, monitoring news reports on all NBC News platforms as an arbiter of NBC news policies, ethics, and style. Moriba Meadows also served as an executive producer on the 2008 election coverage and senior producer on special documentary projects. For the first twelve years at NBC News she was a producer for *Dateline NBC*. She has won numerous awards including five Emmys, a Dupont, and a Peabody.

A Father's Promise

Twelve years ago, NBC News produced an award-winning documentary that began with the delivery of several babies all born the same week at University Hospital in Newark, New Jersey, one of the nation's poorest cities and a place where the rate of absentee fathers was especially high. That week, the fathers of Marquise, Tianna, and Heru all made solemn promises to be there for their children. More than a decade later, MSNBC caught up with the children to find out what happened to them and whether their fathers honored their pledges. What they found is both heartbreaking and revealing. A Father's Promise *premiered on February 8, 2009.*

Today, more American boys and girls than ever are growing up without a father. It is a cultural issue that has emerged at the forefront of American politics. President Obama made it a highly charged national issue in his campaign. Standing before one of Chicago's largest black church congregations, he questioned whether absent fathers bore responsibility for some of the problems afflicting African Americans today. *A Father's Promise* is an attempt to understand this unsettling crisis.

> *Barack Obama*: We know the statistics that children who grow up without a father are five times more likely to live in poverty.
>
> *Heru Kurkland*: Sometime I used to feel like, where did he go? When is he coming back?
>
> *Obama*: They're nine times more likely to drop out of schools, twenty times more likely to end up in prison.
>
> *Marquise Carswell*: He goes in and out of jail, in and out of jail.
>
> *Obama*: They are more likely to become teenage parents because the father wasn't in the home.
>
> *Tianna Thomas*: If I was walking to the store, I would not know who he is if I passed him.
>
> *Obama*: Nowhere is it more true than in the African American community.

Marquise Carswell spends most of his free time thinking about music, making beats for the songs in his head, but he knows he cannot let that get in the way of his long responsibilities at home: "Clean my room, clean the bathroom, take out the trash, wash the dishes, clean the stove, and clean the backyard. Sometimes feed my brother." His mother hopes that engaging her son in chores will keep him from repeating the mistakes his father made.

> *Reporter*: How would you describe your father?
> *Marquise Carswell*: Evil.

It's a decidedly dark remark for a twelve-year-old.

Twelve-year-old Heru Kurkland has a lighter outlook, as evidenced by a camera he turns on himself and his family: "I am Heru Kurkland, and this is my life. That's my mom. My mom's the greatest ever. So this is my family. Indigo, she's my fifteen-year-old sister. She's blind."

A thousand miles from Newark, Tianna Thomas listens to a year-old voice message left by her father. Marquise, Heru, and Tianna are all growing up without their fathers. When Tianna was born, there seemed no happier man on earth than her father, Thomas Lee. He said he and his seventeen-year-old girlfriend, Inesa, had been trying for a long time, and he was afraid they couldn't make a baby: "I've been waiting for this for nine months. I'm going to be there when she take her first steps. I'm going to be there when she have her first day of school. I'm going to be there on her graduation day. I'm just going to be there for her."

At the same time, Keith Kurkland was pledging love to his newborn son, Heru, his second child by his girlfriend, Sonia: "Everything I do now is for them, both of them. It's not for me anymore. Once you commit yourself to being their father, not being there with them, that would be the hardest part."

And so it was for baby Marquise's father. While he wasn't able to be in the delivery room with his fifteen-year-old girlfriend Omega—only her mother was there—nineteen-year-old Rasul Carr professed devotion to the son not yet seen: "I was telling my friends the other night about how I dreamed about him. I mean, that's all I think about is my son. I see myself being reborn into my son. That's me right there. That's my trademark on the world."

As the newborns and their parents began filing out of the hospital on that wintry week twelve years ago, there was no hint of the discord and strife to come. Only jubilation and hope.

A few weeks later, Keith Kurkland, a veteran of the 1991 Gulf War, checked himself into a VA hospital's psychiatric ward for depression: "When I came out of the service, I didn't have a trade that was very much needed. I was a sixteen-inch gunner's mate, and our job, basically, was to blow stuff up! They don't need too many experts in blowing stuff up in the inner city."

We expected Thomas Lee to be alongside his girlfriend, Inesa, to help care for their daughter, but three months later: "No job, no daughter. No job, no daughter. That's basically what it is. That's basically what Inesa's telling me now. If I ain't got no job to take care of my daughter, I can't see her. I'm pissed off about it, man! You just don't know." With few skills, the tenth-grade dropout said he had trouble finding employment: "It could be my handwriting, you know? Or the way I spell or something, you know? Or the way my language is, you know. I really don't know." But he did know his arrest record didn't help. Thomas admitted that he'd sold drugs, like a lot of guys he grew up with; he stopped because he didn't want to risk becoming a father who was behind bars.

> *Thomas Lee*: I ain't asking for a house and two cars. I ain't asking for that! I'm just asking for an opportunity.

Four months after Tianna's birth, Inesa took legal action against Thomas, filing for child support. Soon after, she and Tianna moved on their own to North Carolina.

Marquise and his fifteen-year-old mother Omega would move as well—into a homeless shelter, with Omega's family. Where was Marquise's father? Shortly after he got Omega pregnant, Rasul Carr was arrested on armed-robbery charges, and had been in jail ever since. He heard about his son's birth from a friend: "I just sat in my room and just cried. I was mad. I should have been there. This was my first child, and I was locked up. I wasn't out there to see my son being born."

Rasul was not alone. Back then, according to the Justice Department, there were more than 700,000 African American men who were incarcerated. Today, that number has grown to more than 800,000, and most have children under eighteen, left to grow up without their fathers.

> *Omega Carswell*: All I was thinking about was just having my baby. I didn't think about how I was gonna support him or nothin'.

When Marquise was two months old, Omega agreed to let father and son meet for the very first time. A corrections officer recorded the moment.

> *Rasul Carr*: I never held a kid that was mine. And to just sit there and hold him and look at him and he look at you. It's like he know who you is. He just stared at me the whole time, and I was just staring at him like, this is my son.

When Marquise was six months old, Rasul was released from prison: "This is about it for me. Now it will be the streets or my child, which one means more to me."

By this time, Omega was on public assistance and had moved out of the shelter. Rasul promised to arrive by early afternoon, eager, he said, to meet Marquise for the second time and begin their future together. Omega waited. And waited. But he was back in jail on a new charge: robbery.

Twelve Years Later

> *Omega Carswell*: Twelve years ago, Rasul was incarcerated. Twelve years later, he's still incarcerated.
>
> *Marquise Carswell*: He didn't do nothing for me. That's all I can say about him. He ain't do nothing for me. He should've been in my life, like a father should have. I don't believe in, like, dreams will come true. 'Cause a lot of stuff that you wish for, it never come true. So I just gave up dreaming.
>
> *Rasul Carr*: Dreams aren't really for me.

Rasul says he's remorseful that his absence might have wounded his son. He also says there's a simple reason why many men in the inner city today don't stick around to raise their kids: "People aren't like our parents and grandparents anymore. Relationships might last a year. Two if you're lucky. But they don't really last—there's no substance in relationships anymore. It's 'I like you, you like me. Okay, we're gonna have sex. I don't like you anymore. Let's move on.' But somewhere in there, there was a baby. When I am released, first thing I would say to my son is that I love him and I'm sorry that I've been gone for so long. I will let him know that it was a mistake that I made. Well, it was a choice that I made."

Marquise isn't buying it: "No. He ain't gonna never change. He gonna be always the same, because he gonna keep going in and out of jail, in and out of jail."

Two miles from Marquise, Heru Kurkland reflects on his father's absence. His parents broke up when Heru was still a baby. Keith, diagnosed with posttraumatic stress syndrome, says he periodically disappeared from Heru's life as he shuttled in and out of psychiatric wards. Heru's mother, who is studying to be a nurse, says despite any resentment, she has resisted bad-mouthing her ex: "The kids don't really need that. They have enough pressure of not having their father around."

Heru maintains he has a wonderful relationship with his dad and plainly treasures the good times. Keith told his children he'd stop by on the day we interviewed Heru, but he didn't show.

After moving to North Carolina, Tianna's mother, Inesa, found work as a nursing assistant and bought her first home: "You know Tianna doesn't think that we're poor? I know by standards, maybe we're not poor. We—I mean, we eat regular, where some don't. Tianna hasn't gone without anything. I just try to—I have. I mean, I'll—oh, I hate to say this on camera, but I don't have good underwear. But I'll make sure she has what she needs." Wanting to give Tianna everything she needs, Inesa pushed aside her resentment and encouraged Tianna's father, Thomas, to join them in North Carolina.

This is seventh grader Heru Kurkland's first year of middle school: "My favorite subjects would have to be science and, uh, history." Heru's principal says 80 percent of her students are growing up without their fathers, and that's a worry: boys Heru's age are on the cusp, but what happens when a well-intentioned father is unreliable? Heru's father, who'd failed to keep his promise to see Heru a week earlier, was still out of touch and nowhere to be found.

> *Heru Kurkland*: I don't know if his cell phone has been stolen, so that's why I probably can't reach him.

It's a well-worn pattern. Perhaps one reason Heru is able to cope is that there is someone else in his life who is a steady presence—his mother's husband, Parish, a freelance photographer.

> *Heru Kurkland*: There's not much of a difference between having a dad and a stepdad, cause they're both father figures, no matter what. And they're both fun to have around.

The hurt, anger and disappointment felt by many children of absentee fathers is hard to quantify, but the effects are not. While the large majority of children raised by single parents do fine, fatherless children are at a greater risk than children who grow up in two-parent households to suffer physical and emotional abuse. They're more likely to have emotional and behavioral problems, and are more likely to abuse drugs and alcohol.

Marquise thinks he knows everything he needs to know about his father: "Evil, troublemaker. [*sigh*] That's all I can think." But despite his contempt for his father, Marquise has seen himself starting down the same slippery slope. Often getting into fights. He's now in a special program at school for children with behavior problems.

> *Marquise Carswell*: I need to not get easily mad. And stop fighting because it ain't gonna get me—it ain't gonna get me nowhere except for jail, or dead.

Over the years, Tianna's grades have suffered some, and she's learned to mistrust others. It was particularly hard on her when she was nine and her father stopped showing up altogether: "I remember he said he was gonna come and get me, and he never came. I think the reason he left is because my mom was talking about how she can be both my mama and my father, my grandma, whoever I needed. And I think that's just what made him mad or somethin'. I don't know. Maybe it was me, I don't know."

Now thirty-three, Thomas is on medication for depression, and residing in North Carolina in a maximum-security prison. Why?

> *Thomas Lee*: Let's just say it's a violent crime.

In fact, the crime about which he won't speak is rape and assault by strangulation.

Thomas hasn't talked to Tianna since his incarceration; he tried writing, but the letter just comes back. His only solace is in imagining Tianna is no different today from when he saw her last. While Thomas's ex has told herself that her daughter has no idea where Thomas is, Tianna says she does know—thanks to an awful headline she spotted. Before she could get through the article, she says her mother grabbed the paper away, never to be discussed.

> *Tianna Thomas*: It's—hard to talk about it. Because he's my dad. And I guess it sets a bad example for me or something. I just don't ever talk about it, because it's painful and I don't like it at all.

While she says she hates Thomas, Tianna still keeps a raggedy animal he won for her at a carnival years before: "My momma wants to throw it away, and I told her no. I got mad at her."

> *Thomas Lee*: By the time I get out, my kids'll be kinda old. But if my kids have kids, I look forward to that. Maybe, you know, my kids'll be like, "Okay, well, he wasn't there for me, but he want to be here for my kids, so maybe I'll let him do that."

His projected release date is 2029.

Whatever happens, Heru's mother feels that Heru will be all right—especially since the line of communication is always wide open between her and him.

Marquise would like to be a parent someday. The boy who says he doesn't dream for fear of being disappointed admits there is one dream he does harbor: "I do dream about going to college, but I know I'm gonna go to college. The way I'm heading, the way how smart I am, I know I'm gonna go to college and be successful."

Tianna, who says she got her heart broken by her absent father too many times, seems to want to go in a different direction from Marquise and Heru. She insists she won't ever marry or have children, preferring the company of animals, she says, because they won't lie or hurt her feelings: "I think I just understand animals more than I understand people. Half the time I don't even understand myself."

We started out with three young fathers who are no longer young. Their three children aren't fully counting on anything except their own talents and the love of their mothers, who have always been there and grown up alongside them. In the twelve years we followed these three children's lives, a lot has changed for the better in Newark. Crime and unemployment are down, and while the incidence of absentee fathers has held steady, there are growing numbers of programs that offer education and job training skills, teaching fathers to be more responsible and more involved in their children's lives.

Geraldine Moriba Meadows and Elise Warner were senior producers of *A Father's Promise*; Michael Rubin, vice president and executive producer; Scott Hooker, senior executive producer; John Block and Cameo George, producers.

Athelia Knight was a reporter and manager for the *Washington Post* from 1975 to 2008. This excerpt from a four-part series about an inner-city high school appeared in the *Washington Post* on September 13, 1987, and was a finalist for a Pulitzer Prize in 1988. McKinley closed in 1997 for renovation, reopened in 2004, and graduated its first class of seniors in the restored school in 2008. But McKinley and the District of Columbia school system continue to experience many of the same academic problems described here.

McKinley High School

There was the usual chaos on December 19 when the students of McKinley High School in northeast Washington gathered in the gymnasium for the Christmas assembly. They talked loudly, paying little attention to the McKinley choir's gospel performance. But when Dwayne Hall stood at center court to read the names of the honor-roll students, the crowd quieted enough so that his voice could be heard.

"Please come forward as I call your names," said Hall, who had been invited to the special ceremony as McKinley's top graduate from the previous year. "Valerie Allen. Lisa Anderson. Tracie Andrews. Monica Barnhill. . . . " No one came forward. "Are these people here?" Hall asked. A few students snickered. School principal Bettye W. Topps took the microphone. "I want those people whose names have been called to come forward," she barked. "Front and center, now!" Several students came down from the bleachers. When Hall finished reading the 53 names, about 20 students stood at center court. Topps surveyed the 1,000 students. The crowd grew silent. Topps scolded them for being "the poorest audience I have ever been a part of" and said, "There is something strange . . . when people who have obtained excellence are embarrassed to come forward. I don't understand why you would rather be mediocre than excellent."

What Topps saw that day was an environment that discourages excellence and encourages mediocrity, that inhibits creativity and fosters complacency. To be smart at McKinley is to be different. To be different is to stand out. And standing out, calling attention to oneself, is not cool. "They want to do well," Topps said of her honor-roll students. "But they don't want to be identified as people who do well." "Nobody cares if I'm smart," said 11th grader Irvin Kenny, an honor-roll student whose friends call him "undercover smart." "I hang with people who are not smart. People see me in the hall a lot. I'm loud in class. . . . But I still get my work done."

This is not the McKinley of the 1960s, whose graduates from that period include men and women, nearly all of them black, who went on to distinguish themselves as doctors, lawyers, nurses, research scientists, educators, corporate executives and government officials. That legacy is hardly in evidence now. McKinley's curriculum still includes pre-engineering and science courses that are not available at most D.C. high schools, but the best students go elsewhere. Among the District's 14 high schools, McKinley is neither the best nor the worst; it falls squarely in the middle on test scores and on the percentage of graduates who go on to college. It shares many of the characteristics—and problems—usually found in an urban high school. It is part of a school system in which the majority of students come from poorer families than most of those who attend public school in Washington's more affluent suburbs, the result of several decades of migration from cities to the suburbs.

Although a significant number of black and white families with higher incomes have remained in the District, many have chosen to send their children to private or parochial schools. I spent nearly all of the 1986–87 school year at McKinley, attempting to answer some basic questions about today's urban high school: How do teachers motivate their students? How do the students cope with the pressures they face? Is the school helping the students learn—or standing in their way? The answers came from learning about incidents such as this: One day last fall, teacher Beulah Smith told her first-period senior English class that she was disappointed because more than half of the 30 seniors had done poorly on a writing assignment. She decided to read aloud the best paper, bringing groans from the class. "I know you're going to read Kenny's first," one student said, a reference to Kenneth Jackson. Later, Kenneth stopped by Smith's desk and insisted she not read his papers aloud again. For the remainder of the year, she just tacked his best papers on a bulletin board. Kenneth told me that it wasn't the teasing that bothered him, it was that he saw no reason for the teacher to read his work to his classmates. "It wasn't of interest to them."

On October 10, my second full day at the school, Topps took me on a tour of the 59-year-old building, which was undergoing its first major renovation. She stepped around a hanging plastic sheet and complained: "You won't be seeing a typical school year." As we made our way past several closed-off areas, including some marked "Asbestos Dust Hazard," Topps pointed out some problems: The auditorium, which was supposed to be finished soon after school opened, was nowhere near completion. The public-address system still wasn't working. The main office was closed, and Topps and her four assistant principals were on separate floors. Fifteen classrooms were unavailable, and the heating system wasn't working properly. Topps felt that the school was at a critical stage. The faculty, badly splintered when she took over as principal in 1982, finally had some momentum. They even had a slogan for the year, a theme that seemed to sum up Topps's hopes: "Renewing the Legacy—Listening to the Past, Working for the Future."

The school was designed to fit with the rest of monumental Washington: it has a Greek Revival facade, including six 30-foot columns, and a balcony with a spectacular view of downtown Washington. Inside the main entrance is a marble foyer, which opens onto corridors with terrazzo floors made of polished marble chips set in cement. There is a greenhouse, and a dramatic oval skylight in the library, and most of the classrooms have hardwood floors. But the greenhouse hasn't been used in years and is now filled with debris. The library's skylight is intact, but a 50-year-old mural featuring scenes from American history was removed and replaced with wallpaper. In some classrooms, the windowpanes were so dirty—or had been replaced with plywood or opaque plastic—that teachers showed films without drawing the shades.

Topps ran into music teacher Beatrice Gilkes. In the days when McKinley attracted top-notch music students, Gilkes had more than 40 students; she now has 18. The three pianos—two baby grands and a concert grand that were once used freely by her students—she now keeps locked unless a student asks to use them. Gilkes has seen the school change dramatically since she joined the faculty in 1954, the year that the U.S. Supreme Court issued its *Brown v. Board of Education of Topeka* ruling, ordering an end to the segregated school systems in Washington and throughout the nation. Within a few years, as white families began leaving the neighborhood or sending their children to private school, the all-white school became nearly all black. She saw the introduction of the "track system" in 1956, which grouped students by academic ability, and the demise of that system in 1967 when a federal judge banned such groupings as discriminatory against poor blacks. McKinley's students come from a wide area of northeast Washington that encompasses several poor and middle-class neighborhoods, from public housing on Montana Avenue and Edgewood Terrace, from well-appointed town houses in Fort Lincoln near the Maryland border, from shingled and brick homes in Woodridge and Brookland. After school, many students head off to work; more than half of last year's senior class had half-day schedules so they could work part-time. Topps stopped several times to handle disciplinary problems. She corralled two boys who were in the hall without permission and ordered them to class. She caught two boys who were not McKinley students peeking into a second-floor classroom. She said it was easy to make too much of disciplinary issues. It was more important, she said, to make clear to students that you expect them to behave appropriately. When she first came to the school, she was so disgusted with student behavior at assemblies that she held practice sessions on the proper ways to sit, to applaud, to enter and leave.

The key to a good school, she said, is good teaching. The best teachers are the ones who are knowledgeable, well-prepared and creative. At the same time, a good school could be hurt by a bad image. In the spring of 1986, she said, McKinley was unfairly branded as a drug school after seven McKinley students were charged with selling drugs to a police officer posing as a student. Topps blamed the media for the way the issue was covered. Topps said that if I wanted to write about "bad" teachers and "bad" students, she could give me names and save me time. Was I willing to look at the total picture? I told her that I was, but I particularly wanted to find out what was happening inside the classroom. "Fine," she said. Then she reminded me again: "The whole picture."

The heating system wasn't working again, and Room 107, where Anne Harding's senior English class met, was chilly. Although it was October 14, some students were bundled up in sweaters and coats. Harding, who has taught at McKinley for 20 years, was irritated. The school year was six weeks old and the class hadn't finished a refresher section on grammar. She couldn't seem to get anyone to do the work, even though the class was a requirement for graduation. "It might be elementary and boring," she told them, "but you need to learn it. You should have learned it in the fifth grade." In front of a "Renewing the Legacy" sign, Harding asked for an example of a sentence with a subordinate clause. No one responded. Unable to get anyone to volunteer, Harding had to call on someone. Later she said, "Part of the reason you don't understand is your attention span is too short. You are waiting for the commercial." She hoped that the literature part of the course would stimulate their interest. As a first step, she assigned them to write a brief paper about a "hero"—anyone they admired.

Only 25 of the course's 38 students were there, and only eight said they had written a paper. Harding turned to Katrice Barnes, who usually did her homework. Katrice pulled her paper out of her notebook. "Don't you all laugh," she said, turning to her classmates. "Don't worry about the laughing," Harding said, picking up her pen and indicating that she planned to make a note in her grade book of anyone who teased Katrice. Katrice started to read. Her hero was Sylvester Stallone. A couple of boys put their hands over their mouths to muffle their laughter; Harding looked at them in disgust. No one said anything as Katrice described how she admired Stallone because he played tough characters in his movies. Harding praised Katrice. After four other students read their papers—their heroes were members of their families—Harding addressed the students who had not done the homework. "I can't conduct my class if you don't do what you're supposed to do," she said. "You will need more than a high school education if you're going to succeed in life. You will need more than what I have and what your parents have. . . . I want you to learn something in this class."

On December 18, teacher David M. Messman found only nine of 30 students in his 9 a.m. first-year Spanish class. Attendance had been dropping as the Christmas holiday approached, but this was worse than usual. Messman had a quick explanation. "It's raining," he said. Messman wrote a paragraph in Spanish on the blackboard and led the students through a translation, writing the English version on the board. At 9:15, 15 minutes into the 45-minute class, a boy walked in and strutted to a seat in the back, saying nothing. Two minutes later, another latecomer arrived, without a tardy excuse or books. Messman asked the class to open their books to a Christmas carol. "I don't have my book," one girl called out. A boy who didn't bring his book moved to sit next to a boy who did. Finally, Messman asked how many students had their books. Four of the 11 raised their hands. Messman shook his head, handing out photocopies of the song, which he had handy because he was planning to use it in another class that did not have the same book. It was now 9:20. A few minutes later, a boy and a girl walked in empty-handed. He gave copies to them. At 9:27 a.m., another girl arrived, also without her book, and he gave her a copy. The class was 27 minutes old, nearly two-thirds over, and the students had hardly done any work.

On another day, teacher Liliana G. Chiappinelli stood in front of a student's desk in her 9 a.m. second-year Spanish class, her head bowed as she read from an open book. The lights were off. One girl of the 21 students present seemed to be responding to her questions; the rest were doing something else, including reading a romance novel, drinking soda, chatting, and looking at photo albums. The scene in Chiappinelli's classroom that day was one of the more chaotic I saw during my year at McKinley. It was more typical to see teachers constantly interrupting their classes to deal with students who weren't paying attention.

On the last morning before the winter break, only 50 of the school's estimated 1,200 students were in school. About 500 were at the Cinema Theatre in northwest Washington, watching the Eddie Murphy movie *Golden Child* as part of a school fund-raiser. The whereabouts of the rest was unknown. Movie fund-raisers were popular. The students liked them because they were a break from the classroom and because some teachers gave extra credit to those who went. The teachers liked them because they could usually choose a movie that raised important social issues, which could then be discussed in class. But *Golden Child* was primarily a fund-raiser. Some teachers were bothered by this link between fund-raisers and grades. Still, it seemed harmless enough; during the course of a school year, extra credit for going to a movie wasn't going to change anyone's grade. But then came the incident in which Topps asked students to help the PTA pay off a $500 debt.

It began when the PTA held a Friday-night dance in the gym and fewer than 100 students came. The PTA found itself with a band costing $1,000 and a lot of unsold $8 tickets. At school the following Monday, January 12, Topps told the faculty that "we've got to find a way" to pay off the debt. She held a round of meetings with students. The seniors suggested that students get extra credit— just as some got for going to movies. Topps liked the idea. She came up with the following plan: for a $1 donation, students would receive a "ticket" that could be exchanged for extra credit in a class of the student's choice.

The next day in Anne Harding's senior English class, students seemed even less prepared than usual. Only four of the 21 seniors present handed in a two-page homework assignment. Harding stapled the papers and said: "Nobody can make an A if you don't pass your work in today." At one point, a boy held a ticket aloft and said, "Mrs. Harding, I got a ticket." "That doesn't mean anything to me," she said.

A few days later, an 11th grader came to Topps' office to complain that his algebra teacher wasn't accepting the tickets. "Isn't there another class in which you can use it?" she asked. "I need it in her class," he insisted. Topps said there was nothing she could do. The episode created some bad feeling among faculty members, some of whom confronted Topps and accused her of "selling grades." Others said they saw the plan as a way to promote citizenship and participation. Topps said that some teachers told her that their consciences wouldn't allow them to accept the tickets. Topps said she told them: "That's fine."

In late spring, Topps and the faculty turned their attention to preparing ninth and 11th graders for the national standardized tests. One of Topps's primary goals was to improve test scores; it was also a primary goal of the school system itself. Topps directed teachers to spend part of their class time getting the students ready. On Tuesday, April 14, English teacher Beulah Smith was having trouble with her 11th graders. The students were using copies of old tests to do reading comprehension exercises. Irvin Kenny, the honor-roll student who says he intentionally tries not to act smart, wasn't paying attention. He whispered to a boy who was seated in front of him. He blew big bubbles from his gum. Other students also weren't paying attention. "Instead of paying attention, you are doing other things," Smith said. "This is typical of what happens at McKinley. Some of you are looking around in space. The test is the 5th, 6th and 7th of May. We have not taken this test very seriously."

There was silence. "You hurt my feelings," Irvin said, feigning a sad look. "I'm sorry but that is the way it is," Smith snapped. "You make me feel low," he said, placing his head on his desk.

Smith went on to another exercise. More students were paying attention now. A few minutes later, Irvin lifted his head. He turned to several others and began talking. Smith shot him an angry glance. Irvin went right on talking.

Dan Grech was part of a team that won a Pulitzer Prize in 2001 for its coverage of the INS raid that returned Elian Gonzalez to Cuba. He is the radio director at WLRN–Miami Herald News, and has worked for the *Miami Herald*, the *Washington Post*, the *Boston Globe*, and the public-radio show *Marketplace*. The two pieces below are drawn from longer stories that ran in the *Miami Herald* on February 23 and March 10, 2003.

A Believing Principal Leads a Battle to Save a School

The bass was turned so high the school bleachers vibrated. Cramped students bounced and swayed as one. A disc jockey roamed the gym floor with a microphone. "You ready?" he boomed. "We're ready!" they screamed. Santiago Corrada burst through a door, tore through a banner and hit his trademark split at center court. He was a step slow, the split a touch soft, but still the crowd erupted as Miami Edison Senior High football players strutted in.

Edison—known for having the worst high-school test scores in the state—had not had a winning football team in 11 years. Last fall, the team went 9-1 in the regular season. On this night in November, it was favored in the first round of the state playoffs. You could hear nine wins in the screams. You could feel redemption in the bounce. You could see strength in the strut. This wasn't a pep rally; it was a revival. And the deacon was a diminutive man in a pirate's eye patch and sash.

Santiago Corrada, 38, is Edison Senior High. He hasn't missed a football game in his five years as principal. He swings by senior picnics and Saturday tutoring. He squeezes hands and bumps chests. He knows his kids by name. Last spring, when Edison became one of two high schools in Florida to receive a second failing grade from the state, Corrada took it personally. Corrada, the overachieving son of poor Cuban immigrants, had battled for every perfect report card he brought home from school. He had never gotten an F in his life. Now he had two.

The state doesn't take into account that three out of every four Edison students speak Creole at home, the highest concentration of Haitian students in the nation. It doesn't handicap for each drive-by shooting on Martin Luther King Drive. It doesn't adjust for poverty so severe that students faint from hunger or the burn of a rotten tooth. A single standardized test has branded this school—its teachers, its students, its principal—a failure.

The Florida Comprehensive Assessment Test doesn't count pride or resolve. It doesn't measure the hope in students' eyes as they rock the bleachers of their double-F school. That Friday-night pep rally marked the beginning of the most gut-wrenching 24 hours of Corrada's career. He would lose the big game and bury a beloved student. Heartbreak would test his endurance, his determination, his will.

After he was named Edison's principal in July 1998, Corrada met with community leaders at Grace United Methodist Church in Little Haiti. At the time, Edison was a mess. Its lobby was lit like a closet, stairwells smelled of urine, the halls were infested with fleas. The activists were quietly organizing a boycott of the school. They had gathered the support of 500 families. "There was huge momentum for shutting Edison down," said Jean-René Foureau, director of the Haitian Refugee Center and a social studies teacher at Edison. "The district didn't realize how dangerous and volatile the situation was."

The meeting was held in a stifling back room without air-conditioning. Corrada, who had distinguished himself at Campbell Drive Middle School in Homestead by calming tensions between Mexican migrant children from two feuding labor camps, watched in silence as activists demanded a Haitian principal. With tempers boiling, Corrada was introduced. "Believe me, if I had my way with God," Corrada opened, "I would walk in here as a Haitian speaking Creole." That remark drew a chuckle—and it helped buy Corrada time.

Within a year, he obtained $1.2 million in improvements from the school district: new floors, new lights, new paint, air conditioners, landscaping, 400 computers. He installed 48 security cameras, with monitors in his office. He mended holes cut into the back fence so students couldn't sneak out. "We may not be successful," Corrada told his teachers at their first staff meeting, "but if we keep doing the same old stuff, we're extinct. I'm trying to save us." He revamped the curriculum and started a nursing magnet program. He picked up soda cans and gum wrappers as he walked the halls. He cornered loitering kids and made them go to class. Morale soared. Students started smiling and sticking around after school. "I feel Edison is not a jail no more," one student wrote for class.

By the end of the year, the percentage of students, parents and teachers who rated Corrada effective was well above the district average for principals. FCAT math and reading scores rose as well—just not enough to keep the school from receiving its first F from the state. Corrada was runner-up for Miami-Dade Principal of the Year. Community leaders bestowed on him a title he cherished even more: "Edison's first Haitian principal."

As students filed into the bleachers for the pep rally, Corrada was in his office changing into his pirate uniform. He heard a commotion in the lobby. A mentally disabled girl had pinned her special-education teacher against a wall. Security guards pushed the student into a classroom to cool off until her father arrived. She threw three computer monitors to the floor.

Violence infiltrates Edison. The school, once an all-white football powerhouse and later populated by black children from Liberty City, is now home to poor immigrants fleeing the impoverished island of Haiti. The day before Halloween, a group of young toughs stopped at Edison's front gate to chat with some students. They noticed members of a rival gang driving by and fired four bullets at the car. A few yards away, hundreds of students were eating lunch.

It's a principal's job to get distracted children to sit in class and learn. As Corrada tells it, that takes being a politician, a salesman, a motivator. A magician. "We have 2,300 kids to 150 adults. Those aren't good odds," Corrada says. "If on any given day students refuse to go to class, it's over. But when I tell them they need to go to class, they don't throw rocks or curse. They say, 'Yes, Mr. Corrada,' and they go. A principal chooses his role. I choose to be the person who can communicate with these kids." Corrada does this by touch. He swims through the corridors during class change, poking fun and slapping shoulders. Then he tells students to hurry to class. And they go.

Teachers are Corrada's most guarded resource. He absorbs the fistfights and fallout from the double-F so his teachers can concentrate on class. "Mr. Corrada is our shield," says Mary Beth Thompson, a 16-year chemistry teacher. After the student pinned teacher Jennifer Zirke to the wall, Corrada told Zirke the girl wouldn't be allowed to return. "I need you more than I need her," he said. Corrada later learned the girl had been misdiagnosed. She didn't have a learning disability. She was psychotic.

Corrada's stomach first started hurting at an educators conference in Orlando last year. He was diagnosed with a hiatal hernia and diverticulosis. Corrada lost 60 pounds. The wincing pain sapped his appetite and strength. A once-stocky man who always took for granted an overflow of energy admits that these days it's harder to climb Edison's three flights of stairs.

His mother, Scarlet, looked at her son with sadness during a recent visit to the Kendall Publix where she works as a cashier. "Drink some," Scarlet told him, offering a cafecito. "You look tired." "I am tired," Corrada said, pushing the coffee away.

The pressure of being Edison's principal—a daunting job under normal circumstances—soared when the state gave the school its second F. Corrada flew to Tallahassee to explain to Governor Jeb Bush and his cabinet why Edison was failing and how it would improve. The state checks up on Edison twice a month through conference calls and requires Corrada to file monthly progress reports. "I swallow the stress," Corrada says. "I respond by working harder. I find comfort in doing my very best."

Corrada faces difficult choices. Each year, Edison nominates its best students for the Silver Knights achievement awards. Most Edison nominees have no way to get to the ceremony, so Corrada takes them. One year, his daughter Tiffany's seventh birthday fell on the same day as the award ceremony. His wife, Arlene, had prepared a family celebration. Alvin Smith, Edison's alumni association president since 1986, later asked Corrada why he chose his students over his daughter that night. "He told me he celebrates his daughter's birth every day," Smith marveled.

After the pep rally, Corrada retreated to his office. It was a rare moment away from his Edison family. "Can I keep doing this at this level, with this commitment, with this stamina? Will my body make it? Will my personal relationships make it? It's a sad thing to say, but I am so dedicated to this school I'd come in here on my deathbed and do this job with my last breath. Because I don't like getting licked."

It was the final seconds of the playoff game. Edison was up 10–8. Visiting William T. Dwyer High, a mostly white high school in Palm Beach Gardens, lined up on Edison's two-yard line. The Dwyer quarterback ran for the goal line. He got stuffed for a loss. The home-field crowd bounced and swayed. Dwyer was out of timeouts. The game was over. "Five, four," they joyfully counted down the final seconds. "Three, two." A whistle blows.

The Dwyer quarterback had taken off his helmet in frustration, and the head referee signaled an equipment timeout. Though it's against the rules to make substitutions during an equipment timeout, the all-white referee crew allowed Dwyer's field goal unit to race onto the field.

The referee restarted the clock. The snap, the kick, the ball spinning end over end as a stunned crowd watched in silence. The ball passed through the uprights. The scoreboard clicked three times. Dwyer 11, Edison 10. The crowd let out a roar of protest. Edison players staggered off the field. They threw their helmets, pulled off their jerseys, wept openly. Their jerseys, given shape by the shoulder pads, littered the grass like decapitated bodies.

Some Edison players started toward the cheering Dwyer sideline. Corrada sprinted onto the field to hold them back. Edison fans began throwing souvenir plastic footballs at the Dwyer players. The timekeeper in the press box got on the public-address system and asked for a police escort. The Dwyer players boarded their bus quickly. The Edison players stood cross-armed and watched. As the bus pulled away, someone in the shadows threw a rock that cracked the windshield.

Corrada returned to his office after the game. He leaned his forehead into his palm, just as he had the day he got news of the second F, and read the rule book of the Florida High School Activities Association. It said schools aren't allowed to protest the results of a game or complain publicly about a call. Corrada drafted a letter to the association anyway. He faxed it after midnight. "It's a little bit like the FCAT," Corrada said. "You play by our rules and at the last minute we change them. And if you protest, we fine you. Or give you an F." Corrada sighed deeply. "I get so tired of being beaten up and stomped."

Every principal has bad days. Days when a student is arrested. Days when a gun is fired outside school. Days when the school is given an F. "But the darkest day in the life of a principal," Corrada say, "is to see one of his students pass."

The morning after the football game, Corrada spoke at Poofy's funeral. Poofy was Lucila Simon, class of 2001 and a member of Edison's state-champion girls basketball team. Poofy had been his student at Campbell Drive Middle, and she was the only student Corrada knew when he arrived at Edison. A week earlier,

Poofy stopped by Edison to visit Corrada. That night, she died in her sleep of a heart attack and a brain aneurysm. She was 20.

Inner-city high schools are at the heart of their neighborhoods. They are sanctuaries, symbols, shrines. Above all, they are family. Next to Poofy's casket flew a Red Raiders flag.

"It is the job of a principal to love every student," Corrada told 300 people at Mount Calvary Missionary Baptist Church, six blocks from Edison. "But I especially loved Poofy, a friendly face in a strange school."

Corrada was handed tissues as he returned to his seat. He sat down alone, one of the few white faces in the room. He began to cry. A black man in a mustard-colored pinstripe suit, school custodian Ronald Baker, slid next to Corrada. Baker gripped Corrada's shoulder and took Corrada's hand. For the next hour, he didn't let go.

On dark days, Corrada feels like a failure. He sees no light, no hope. "The principal of a school like this is destined to be squeezed," said English Department head Shawn DeNight, the Florida Teacher of the Year in 1995. "Corrada is forced to spend his precious time doing things that don't matter but are required and not doing things that matter but aren't measured. Corrada's a platoon leader trying to hold down the fort, and he's being attacked on all sides." Corrada fights battles he knows he will lose. He understands the value of small victories in the face of large defeats. And just as his energy is waning, he is revived.

The Florida High School Activities Association refused to consider Corrada's protest over the game. The Edison alumni association took the challenge to circuit court. A week later, a judge denied relief. Corrada returned to Edison from the courthouse and announced that the miracle season was officially over. Then, as is his custom, he went to the lobby to monitor class change. Wide receiver Jackie Chambers, who also plays guard on the basketball team, walked up to his principal. "Don't worry, Mr. C.," he said. "We'll take it out on them in basketball." Corrada's face, a mask of exhaustion and defeat since the game, broke into a wide smile. "Thank God for you, Jackie!"

Edison's Big Loss

With profound relief I learned that Santiago Corrada, the principal of Miami Edison Senior High School and the subject of a *Miami Herald* profile I wrote last month, is leaving the school to become Miami City parks director. Relief because I saw the toll on health and family that being principal of the state's lowest-scoring high school was taking on a man whose greatest sin was to love too much. The same devotion that led Corrada to buy a Mini Cooper in red and black, the school colors, also cornered him, imprisoned him, led a hopeful man to lose hope.

Relief, too, because I feared how this school year would end. Edison students just finished taking the FCAT, and based on past performance, the school is at risk of getting its third failing grade in five years. The first-ever triple-F. The state and district would search for a scapegoat and, inevitably, settle on Corrada, the school's CEO. He does not deserve that indignity.

But beyond the blow to Edison, Corrada's departure is unfortunate because it postpones a showdown between the demands of high-stakes testing and the reality of many inner-city schools. I spent nearly every day for two months at Edison, a school in the heart of Little Haiti. I assure you, this is not a failing school. The school is a safe haven and a source of joy for students living in one of the nation's poorest communities. It does an admirable job of insulating its majority-Haitian student body against street violence and of teaching students English and math and science, not to mention self-respect and dignity and hope.

Edison is a "failure" because of social ills far older than the building. It is a "failure" because students can't score high enough on a standardized test impossibly abstract to the everyday realities of hunger and fear, gangs and drugs, broken families and after-school jobs. It is a "failure" because we have embraced a system that measures Edison against rich suburban schools. Anyone who spends time at Edison or watches Corrada work knows the absurdity of giving Edison Fs. The last thing his students need is another reason to believe that they are destined to fail.

Corrada, in his frustration, has become outspoken about the flaws of the FCAT system. Corrada once called himself a "company man," but he's stopped believing in the company. Why are we allowing this to happen? Why have we adopted a system that exchanges life lessons for test prep? Why are we defeating our bravest educators? Can't we find a way to instill high standards without demoralizing schools? Corrada offers a solution: measure the progress of low-scoring schools against their own past performance, not on an absolute scale. We shouldn't demand that perennially underachieving schools suddenly catch up; we should expect them to get better.

My mother taught art in inner-city Philadelphia for 35 years, so I understand why some people are drawn to hard-luck schools. As one Edison teacher told me, "Some of these kids need hugs and kisses more than chemistry." The opportunity to reach students, improve their lives and lead them down a better path is so much greater in the ghetto than in a gated community. We should all mourn the loss of Santiago Corrada and hundreds of others like him, of the big hearts and the giving souls, of the educators for whom teaching our state's neediest children has started to hurt too much.

T. R. Reid has worked around the world in almost every form of journalism: print, radio, television, documentary films, and the Internet. In his book *Confucius Lives Next Door* (Random House, 1999), he argues that the admirable social statistics in East Asian countries—low crime rates, low divorce rates, excellent education—result from the region's continuing allegiance to ancient Confucian values. Those values came home when the Reid family lived in Tokyo and sent two of their children to a Japanese public school. This text is excerpted from the book.

Yodobashi No. 6

I can still remember the look on our daughters' faces, and the you're-just-kidding-aren't-you-Daddy tone in their voices, when we told the girls they'd be going to a Japanese elementary school. The kids raised all the standard objections. But we had done our homework, so we had the answers.

But we'll have to go to school all through summer vacation!

Not exactly true. All Asian countries, true to that Confucian tradition, consider schooling a full-time occupation for younger members of the society. Thus the schools are in session pretty much year-round. In Japan, China, and most other East Asian nations, there are about 240 school days per year. That makes the school year one-third longer than in Western countries like the United States, where the average is 180 days per year, with a long break in the summer. (And thus it's not quite so surprising that Asian students score so much higher on standardized tests than their peers in other countries.) Japanese kids go to school all of June and July. But in August, when the weather is hot and muggy over most of the archipelago, there's no school. The break lasts about four weeks, and comes complete with daily homework assignments. Still, it is a summer vacation.

But we'll have to wear a uniform!

Not exactly true. Japanese school students—like Japanese adults in many lines of work—are generally required to wear a uniform. This enhances the group feeling and gives each student the security of knowing that she'll never be in the uncomfortable position of sticking out from the crowd. In public schools, the uniform is usually a dark blue Prussian army outfit for boys, complete with a blue chauffeur's cap, and a blue sailor suit for girls. Private schools, in contrast, have dumped these military-style outfits and hired world-class designers to create new uniforms for the new millennium. The trendy new look in school uniforms is junior executive: blue blazer, blue tie, and gray slacks for the boys; blue blazer, blue bow tie, and pleated tartan skirt for the girls. But uniforms are generally required only for junior high and high school students; most elementary schools don't have uniforms. At least, not in the classroom. On the way to and from school, though, the kids in the primary grades are all required to have the same leather backpack (a handsome, sturdy piece of gear available in any Japanese department store for a mere $160) and a colorful bonnet—sky blue, red, or bright yellow. But that's not exactly wearing a uniform.

Even if we hadn't had such ready answers, though, we probably would have made the girls go to the school anyway. After all, I had made a promise to Abe-sensei. Abe Masako, a square-faced, intense, no-nonsense woman of about fifty, was the principal at a public school near our house called Yodobashi Dai-Roku Shogakko, or Yodobashi No. 6 Elementary School (now called Nishi-Shinjuku Shogakko).

She was not a person who suffered fools gladly. When I first met her and told her that we lived in Subsection 3 of the Hiro-o neighborhood, she mentioned that we were pretty near Yodobashi No. 6. In any case, Abe-sensei had the idea that it would be a good experience for her students to have some *gaijin*—foreigners—in the classes to help them adapt to an international age. So she suggested that our girls join the third and fifth grades, respectively, at Yodobashi No. 6. My wife and I were intrigued by the idea. With some misgivings, we decided to give it a try. It would be an interesting cultural experience for the girls, we thought. The school would certainly sharpen their Japanese-language skills, we figured, not to mention that famous Japanese educational rigor in math, science, and geography. And so we trundled the girls off to Yodobashi No. 6 when their international school was on summer vacation. In the process, we got both more and less than we had bargained for.

To some extent, Yodobashi No. 6 did provide substantive learning for our daughters; even today, back in an American Catholic school, they draw on concepts from the math or science classes at Yodobashi. But the strongest lesson our kids took away from that Japanese school was something we hadn't counted on. They were taught to be little Confucians. That public school, like all Asian public schools, devoted endless time, energy, and ingenuity to the teaching of moral lessons: community virtues, proper social conduct, appropriate behavior as a member of a group. Confucius and his followers, after all, had insisted that virtue can be taught—indeed, must be taught if the society as a whole is to be a virtuous and civil community. Moral education was much too important to be left to parents, or churches, or Boy Scout troops. It was a job for the whole society to engage in. And this is what the schools do, to this day, in East Asian societies. They teach reading, writing, arithmetic, science, and so forth, but at the same time they are busily turning out Confucian citizens.

Of course, for all the emphasis on citizenship, on civility, on proper group-membership skills, the Japanese schools have a dark side. Two of them, in fact. And both probably stem from that inordinate focus on the group.

One of these problems is called *taibatsu*. My pocket Japanese-English dictionary provides the formal translation "corporal punishment" for this term. To me, *taibatsu* has a more painful connotation than that, perhaps because the word is formed from two characters that mean "beating up the body." In Japanese schools, teachers or principals are known for beating their students—spanking, striking, or slugging children who act up or refuse to fit in with the others. Kids who cause problems, after all, are violating the school's collective *wa*, and that deserves punishment. Corporal punishment has become highly controversial in Japan in modern times, and today the school system prohibits *taibatsu*. Officially, that is.

A far greater concern for anybody thinking about sending children to a school in Japan is the notorious *ijime* (rhymes with "Fiji May"). For this word, that same rather understated dictionary of mine offers the translation "teasing"—you know, boys will be boys, and all that. But *ijime* frequently takes on a more malignant flavor; in many cases, the better translation would involve words like "bullying," "harassment," "persecution," or, occasionally, "murder." *Ijime is* what happens when a Japanese group—it's usually, but not always, a group of children—decides that one member doesn't fit in. The outsider becomes an object of torment, emotional or physical. In the schools, *ijime* can go on for months. It doesn't end until the wretched victim finds a way to fit in with the group or a way to get out—switching to a new school, running away, or, sometimes, committing suicide.

The fact that *ijime* happens to a relatively small number of students in Japan is totally irrelevant if one of the victims is your own child. And of course, the risk of being tormented as an outsider is greater if you really are an outsider. In a sea of black-eyed, black-haired kids named Hanako and Hiroshi, my two blond, blue-eyed girls named Kate and Erin would be outsiders with a vengeance. We were worried.

And so I told Abe-sensei we would be happy to have our girls attend Yodobashi No. 6, on two firm conditions: (1) no *taibatsu;* (2) no *ijime*. I had expected a polite but unsatisfactory answer, with the principal promising evasively to do her best. But the stern Abe-sensei was not the evasive type. She gave me that all-business look of hers and said, "No *taibatsu*. No *ijime*. None at all. I won't allow it."

And so it was that we set out one morning, taking a bus, a train, and finally one more bus that dropped us at the stop called "In Front of Yodobashi No. 6." And there was the school building, a three-story concrete structure of a nondescript architectural style that seemed to blend elements of aging prison and aging factory. The building was gray, of course.

The school's immediate neighborhood—now known as Nishi-Shinjuku, or the area west of Shinjuku station—is Tokyo's equivalent of Madison Avenue. The little concrete schoolhouse is shadowed today not by lush green trees but by the world's most expensive real estate—soaring towers of glass and steel that house great corporations, banks richer than most countries, and five-star, $500-per-night hotels. The school's dominant vista today is not a distant mountain but rather a next-door neighbor that has become a famous symbol of

Japan's leap to global financial power: Tokyo's New City Hall. This stupendous structure, reaching toward the heavens directly in front of Yodobashi's front door, is the magnum opus of Kenzo Tange, the patriarch of postwar Japanese architecture. It was specifically designed, at the height of the so-called bubble economy of the late 1980s, to show the world that Japan no longer took a back seat to the United States or Europe in architecture or anything else. Tange conceived his mission to be the creation of a great urban cathedral. So he built a twenty-first-century copy of the West's most famous cathedral, Notre Dame, complete with twin bell towers 797 feet tall and modern-day flying buttresses connecting the mayor's office to the city council chamber. It is all done in a blue-and-gray grid pattern that suggests the surface of a microchip, and it is one of the most beautiful city halls on earth—to me, at least. Unfortunately for Tange, however, and for the politicians who hired him, the huge new monument has sparked huge controversy among the citizens of Tokyo, who had to pay for the thing. When the New City Hall opened in 1991, it was quickly dubbed "Takusu Towah"—that is, Tax Tower—because the construction bill came in higher than a billion dollars. That billion-dollar city hall became a symbol of bubble-era excess.

It wasn't just urban cathedrals that were built with tax money during Japan's rich bubble era, however. True to the Confucian dictate that education is one of the prime duties of the state, Tokyo took advantage of a big increase in tax revenues to pour massive investment into schools. The result was that Yodobashi No. 6, like countless other aging, gray, concrete schools all over the city, became a gleaming, state-of-the-art educational facility—once you stepped in the door. By the time our kids got to No. 6, the school had hallways of polished white pine, a gleaming new outdoor swimming pool, a bright, comfortable library, and computers all over the place. In a corner of the play hub, the school had its own zoo, with rabbits and roosters; each classroom was required to feed and care for one of these. The school had a fleet of 150 unicycles for gym class. In the music room, every square inch of free space was stacked with shiny new instruments—drum sets and tubas and racks full of recorders, one assigned to each student in the school. One item that confounded me at first was the student desks in the music room. They were bigger than any other desks in the school—bigger than the desktops in the classrooms, bigger even than the desks in the art room. Why such big desks in music? I figured it out when I lifted a desktop and found that inside every student desk there was an 88-key Yamaha keyboard.

A piano for every student! At first, this struck me as another example of the bubble era's wretched excess—until I came to realize that those keyboards were installed out of necessity. They were necessary because of the basic philosophical belief underlying elementary education in Japan, to wit: every student can master every subject. If the year-end exams at Yodobashi No. 6 ever showed that, say, 298 out of the school's 300 students were reading at grade level, this would be a failure; it would prompt a furious round of meetings and special sessions and worried investigations of the cause.

The secret to success is considered to be hard work. Why does one student get straight As in math, science, geometry, and language, while her best friend gets all Cs? In the United States, almost everybody answers that question by saying that the all-A student is smarter. In Japan, almost nobody would answer that way. The reason some kids do well in school and others don't is almost universally considered to be effort. If you work hard, you'll get As; if you didn't get As, you didn't work hard enough. I've visited hundreds of Japanese class-rooms over the years, and virtually every one has the word *doryoku* framed on the wall. The word means "effort."

And that's why the school needed a piano for every student and its own fleet of unicycles. Every kid at Yodobashi learned to read music and play the piano. Every kid was expected to balance on a unicycle. The school would provide the equipment, the teachers would provide the training, and the students were required to provide the effort.

But little things like balancing on one wheel or playing a Chopin étude are simple compared with the enormous amount of effort required for the major academic challenge of Japanese elementary school: learning to read and write. Japanese schools are famous around the world for their achievements in math, science, and geography. As a group, Japanese students regularly rank in the top two or three worldwide on standardized tests at every grade level in these sub-jects. For my money, though, the greatest achievement of Japan's school system is teaching people to read and write Japanese.

Through a series of historical accidents, Japan has been stuck with an ab-surdly complicated written language. Take a look at a single page of any Japa-nese newspaper, and you'll see not just one alphabet in use, not just two, not just three, but four different alphabets (actually five, if you count the Arabic numerals as another alphabet.) It is "possibly the world's most difficult writing system," the Harvard scholar Edwin O. Reischauer noted.

And yet Japan has a literacy rate higher than 99 percent.

That's a government statistic, but I'd guess it's pretty accurate. I've never met a Japanese adult who couldn't read and write. When I used to have trouble making sense out of the orthographic jungle that is a Japanese newspaper, I would occasionally ask some nearby Japanese person for assistance. I was usu-ally too hung up to ask a serious business type, so I directed my queries to less-imposing people: janitors, cleaning ladies, subway ticket punchers. I al-ways found that they could read any word, in any of the four alphabets, with-out a moment's hesitation.

How can one language have four different alphabets? Here's how it works:

- The Japanese have an indigenous alphabet with 47 characters—that is, one character for each of the 47 distinct sounds used in the Japanese language. Since each of the characters represents a whole syllable (*ka, sa, ta, na,* etc.), this collection is sometimes called a syllabary. But it works the same as any other phonetic alphabet.

- In addition to that one 47-letter alphabet, there's a second, completely different Japanese alphabet; this one uses 47 different letters to represent those same 47 sounds. It, too, is used regularly in books, magazines, and so forth. The main purpose of this second syllabary is to write words that come from foreign languages—such as "ham-ba-gah" or "hotto doggu"—but it is also widely used to write plain old Japanese words as well.
- The Japanese also use Roman letters for many purposes, so students have to learn our alphabet as well. You can write any Japanese word or name in Roman letters. That means there are at least three different ways—the first Japanese phonetic alphabet, the second Japanese phonetic alphabet, and the Roman alphabet—to write a Japanese word. But it gets more complicated than that.
- The primary Japanese "alphabet," imported by Buddhist priests from China in the sixth century A.D., is composed of Chinese characters. These constitute an alphabet that contains not 26, not 260, but well over 2,600 different letters. (Chinese characters are often known in the West as *kanji*; that's a Japanese word meaning "Chinese character.") Unlike our Roman letters, and unlike the letters of the two Japanese syllabaries, the *kanji* have no phonetic value. That is, you can't just look at a character and know how to pronounce it. There's no way to sound them out. You have to memorize the pronunciation of every one of them—thousands of them.

It is sometimes possible to discern the meaning of a character you've never seen before. All the Chinese characters started out about three thousand years ago as pictures. Some of these pictographs are straightforward, some complex. The character meaning "tree," for example, is a simple picture of a tree, with a trunk and four branches. That's an easy one to learn. And if you subsequently come upon a *kanji* that combines three of these "trees," that's the character for "forest." Most people have to put in year after year of hard work to learn all the characters, but some lucky ones—both Occidental and Oriental—seem to have an innate ability to break the code of the ancient Chinese wordsmiths, to know what characters mean with no study. The American poet Ezra Pound was a master of this art form. The day Pound first came upon this *kanji*, 馬, he knew immediately what it meant. "Any fool can see," he said, "that it's a horse." He was right, of course, because he was able see the ancient picture embedded in this *kanji*. The elements of the character, reading from top to bottom, show the horse's mane flying in the wind, the four flying hooves at the bottom, and a long tail hooking around behind the hooves. Any fool can see that it's a horse.

Filip Bondy is a sports columnist for the *New York Daily News* and the author of *Chasing the Game; America and the Quest for the World Cup* (DaCapo, 2010). He has authored or coauthored books about baseball, figure skating, and basketball. This article appeared in the *New York Daily News* on August 24, 2008.

Sports: The Glue for Lost Kids

Beijing. A dozen yellow softballs are behaving very badly inside Sunshine Hall at Sun Village, where children of Chinese prisoners come to reclaim the playtime that is their birthright. One boy smashes a window with a batted ball, and recoils in Norman Rockwellian horror. Another boy throws one of the official-sized softballs right across an upright piano, where a girl is too engrossed in her classical piece to notice. Large mitts are flying everywhere. Helmets are bouncing off the floor. Bats are being swung at odd angles atop a makeshift stage. And then there is this one girl wearing purple sandals and a toothy grin, who knows exactly how to bring it.

Li Yu Feng is 8 years old from Hubei Province, and just a few minutes earlier she did not look very happy while the adults in the room discussed her family history. Her father is in jail, for reasons that nobody wants to detail. Her mother has disappeared. Li simply says through a translator, "She's working all over the place." But then a softball materializes in her hand, and the Olympics come to Sun Village, the way they have come to all of China—even here in rural Beijing north of the city. Li winds up, whips the ball like a New Jersey travel-team pitcher. She hurls strikes to an American visitor, again and again. She is beaming now, a long way from that conversation about her mom and dad.

Li is so good at this that she was invited by the International Softball Federation to throw out the first pitch at the U.S.-Canada match two weeks earlier. ISF officials spotted her form while delivering all this equipment to the village, and then suddenly she was making her Olympic debut at Fengtai Softball Field in front of thousands. "When I first came on the field, I was nervous and I tried not to see anything," Li says. "I couldn't tell east from west. I was looking for my friends, but I couldn't see them." Now she is back in Sun Village among friends who are using this odd sports equipment the best they can. A potted plant becomes just another victim of a wild pitch. Ah Duzhang, 8, throws a pitch overhand past a batter and tells the boy, "I'm bigger than you. I'm better than you."

There is one instructor at the place, Yin Er Chin, who knows a little bit about the game, but not all the rules. Everybody is doing the best he can, which really cuts to the core value of this community. The village is the brainchild of Zhang Shuqin, who worked for 10 years as a deputy editor in chief of a newspaper published by the Shaanxi Province Prison Administration. She has since founded and organized four Sun Villages across the country. The idea is simple and humane: to restore dignity and security to children whose parents are imprisoned for 10 years or more, and to provide jailed parents motivation for reform.

ISF president Don Porter says these are the children of political prisoners, but the parents have been arrested for a wide range of crimes—some gruesome, others perhaps nonexistent. According to official state literature, there are about 400,000 criminal cases in China each year, and 70 percent of those convicted are married with children. "Theft, drug trafficking, violent crimes, some minor crimes," Zhang says, without offering specifics. "It is important for the inmates, particularly the women. It gives them hope." Zhang doesn't discriminate or determine eligibility by arrest record or political bent. All around the village, there are stories of survival and accomplishments posted on the wall.

Jin Na from Changping has been here since 2001. She is the daughter of a woman whose death sentence was stayed, and now Jin attends a local high school outside the community. Zhang Lu's mother killed her father, and now Zhang is a graduate of Xi'an Fanyi University. There are small babies in the village, as young as four months old, born to parents arrested in the Beijing area.

The 130 children at this center are here from 10 provinces, many of them rural and impoverished. Some arrived in ill health, with respiratory, digestive and skin diseases. For that reason alone, sports have become central to the daily regimen. The kids play basketball, badminton, table tennis. They practice the high jump and martial arts.

And now they play softball. A little bit, anyway. "We have intramurals between houses," says Wang Qian, who is in charge of activities in the village. "There are 16 or 17 kids in each house, and they compete together against other houses for a sense of solidarity. They have no parents, so it is important to feel solidarity within the unit." The houses are metal barracks, painted colorfully, with neat piles of children's shoes resting outside in cubbies. A playful cat stops to be petted by three kids along a winding pathway. Many of the kids drop the softball bats and move on to badminton rackets. They are running around like crazy, oblivious of the midday heat. Li is playing with a much older child, Ma Yiang Hua, 16, from Hebei, who has been at Sun Village for four years. Ma loves to watch the Olympic divers on television and wants to be an actress. She is practiced and polished already with her lines. "Exercise trains my body, enriches my life," she says.

It is a slogan, like "One dream, one world," the Olympic motto that is painted on the side of the main building. But it is also the truth for a nation of 1.3 billion enthralled by the Summer Games. Sport is the glue at Sun Village, even if it means a broken window or two. "It's normal," Zhang says, of the spiderweb crack on the pane of glass. "If it were an adult who did it, that would not be okay. Something like this already happened last week, when an Olympic official visited and a child hit the car with a tricycle." Zhang laughs. She has seen a lot of pain in her life, and hopes to make things a bit better for a few lost children and for some desperate, imprisoned parents. The corporate sponsors have helped, and so have some private donors. These softballs and bats are gravy, some capricious fun.

Li is enthralled with the stuff. She still wants to pitch, and is looking for someone to play ball. Li has been in Sun Village only since last summer. She remembers that when officials dropped her off, she was wearing a sundress. She is a wiry, resilient kid. And Li has now thrown out the first pitch at an Olympics, after "O Canada" and "The Star-Spangled Banner." They picked me because they liked my pose," Li says proudly. The Summer Games don't end on Sunday night, after all. They keep right on going, until Li Yu Feng stops playing catch.

Ken Armstrong is an investigative reporter at the *Seattle Times*. He previously worked at the *Chicago Tribune*, where he cowrote a series on the death penalty that helped prompt the governor to declare a moratorium on executions and to empty death row. This story appeared in the *Seattle Times* on January 29, 2008, in a four-part series, written with Nick Perry, that reexamined a celebrated football team and explored the consequences of our sports-crazed culture.

Curtis Williams — Victory and Ruins

When Curtis Williams took the field for the Huskies' 2000 season opener, the University of Washington's media guide described him like this: "Senior, strong safety, 5-foot-10, 200 pounds. Named, in 1999, the team's best hitter. Led team in solo tackles. Went to high school in Fresno, Calif., where he was a top recruit. The seventh of eight kids. Pursuing a degree in American ethnic studies."

Here's what the media guide didn't say: When Williams played against Idaho, he had a warrant out for his arrest. He'd been arrested every year he was here: 1996, 1997, 1998, 1999, 2000. He was a convicted felon who'd served time for choking his wife. Two other assault charges were pending against him. He was accused of cutting his wife's face, breaking her arm, breaking her nose. Ordered to pay $283 a month in child support, Williams had paid nothing. Earlier in the year, he'd flunked two classes. If not for Swahili, a notoriously easy class at the UW and a favorite of football players, he would have been ineligible to play.

In the season's first game, played at Husky Stadium in front of 70,000 fans, Williams recorded eight tackles and forced a fumble on a kickoff return. The UW beat Idaho, 44–20. Williams could certainly play. The question was why was the UW allowing him to?

When Curtis Williams arrived at the UW in the summer of 1996, he was a father, husband, student and football player, all at the age of 18. Michelle, his 20-year-old wife, was with him. So was their daughter, one and a half years old. They'd met in California. Michelle was a swimmer and cheerleader at her high school, Curtis a football star at his. Once, he bought new speakers for her car and picked her up, with her favorite song playing. A few weeks before arriving on campus, they got married in Alaska, Michelle's home state. They saw a flier for a minister who married couples for $50, provided they came to his house. So that's what they did. Afterward, they ate at Denny's.

In Seattle, Michelle planned to work while Curtis played football and studied. Later, she'd pursue her dream of becoming a physical therapist. In August 1996, the *Seattle Times* ran a profile of Curtis that mentioned his marriage to Michelle: "In the storybooks, they might live happily ever after; in reality, Williams's story is just beginning." Two weeks after that story ran, a UW graduate student called 911. He'd heard a woman in a neighboring housing unit say, "No! No!" followed by a scream. Another neighbor heard the woman say, "I can't take it anymore!" followed by, "That hurts." Police, from the outside, heard a woman crying upstairs. They knocked. The crying stopped and the light, upstairs, went off. For 25 minutes the knocking continued. Finally, police threatened to force the door. Only then did Curtis Williams and his wife answer. Nothing's going on here, the couple told police. Police documented the call and left. In the next three months, police were summoned to Williams's home three more times. One of those times, Williams was charged with misdemeanor assault. Jan Zientek, the grad student who'd called 911, said Michelle sometimes "looked like a punching bag," with bruises, a black eye, and marks on her arm. He says he was so disturbed he called Jim Lambright, the UW's head coach. "He thanked me for being concerned," Zientek says.

Then, in December 1996, a fifth call came in. A neighbor heard shouting, thumps against a wall and a woman crying. The fourth time that police knocked, Curtis answered, wearing only sweat pants. Officers saw specks of blood on his stomach and arms. Upstairs, blood puddled on and around the bed, and droplets ran to the bathroom. When Michelle came out of the bathroom, her nose appeared broken. An officer asked whether police had ever been called out to the couple's home before. Curtis lied, saying no. When police questioned the couple separately, their accounts made little sense and failed to match.

Police arrested Williams and took him to jail. He was charged, for a second time, with misdemeanor assault.

A victim advocate in the prosecutor's office met with Michelle. Curtis did not break her nose, Michelle insisted. She said she didn't want charges filed, because it would ruin his reputation as a football player and he would lose his scholarship. The victim advocate learned that Michelle had previously broken her arm while pregnant. Although Michelle denied it, her family suspected Curtis was responsible. The advocate wrote a report, saying: "I feel victim in serious danger."

In May 1997, Williams appeared in King County district court and cut a deal. If he completed batterers' counseling and stayed out of trouble, prosecutors would drop the two assault charges. The hearing lasted only minutes. Judge Douglas J. Smith accepted the deal and lifted a no-contact order that had kept Williams away from Michelle. Then the judge and Williams talked football. The two chatted about spring ball, weightlifting, the advantages of redshirting and the previous year's game against Notre Dame. "OK. As long as you don't play [against] the Irish anymore, we can root for you," Smith told Williams. "Except against the Cal Bears, too, I have a problem with that."

Four days after this hearing, Michelle Williams called 911. When police arrived, she was crying. Her face was red, her hair disheveled. An officer saw marks on her throat and the side of her neck. She and Curtis had argued, Michelle told police. He wanted to go out with teammates. She wanted him to stay home. She worked two jobs, 75 hours a week, supporting the family. She'd typically start at 7 a.m., working day care. Then she'd put in a full shift at the mall, at either Footlocker or Gymboree. This was her one day off. Curtis demanded the family car, but Michelle had hidden the alarm deactivator. He grabbed her by the throat and choked her until she passed out, Michelle told police. She awoke, coughing and vomiting. He choked her again and drove away, the alarm sounding. Michelle said Curtis had choked her before and cut her face with a key. She also confirmed her family's suspicions, saying he'd broken her arm, too. "He has told me not to tell anyone what happens," Michelle said, "but I cannot take it anymore."

Police took Williams to the King County Jail. Unable to make bail, he stayed there for the next 74 days. Williams had to withdraw from all his classes, making him ineligible to play in the upcoming season.

In September 1997, Williams pleaded guilty to third-degree assault, a felony. A probation officer who prepared the sentencing report interviewed Lambright, the head coach. The coaching staff seemed oblivious of how many times Williams had attacked Michelle and how dangerous he could be, the officer noted. Williams was sentenced to 90 days in jail, a sentence he'd already served, with credit for good behavior. The judge placed Williams on probation and ordered him to stay away from his wife and daughter.

The felony conviction negated Williams's deal in the two other assault cases. One week later, Judge Smith convicted Williams of those charges and moved straight to sentencing. Williams told the judge: "Well, I feel bad because I do, on the felony, you know, I hurt Michelle and I'm real sorry about that. I know that I need to get into counseling and I need to get my life back together because I lost it." Smith sentenced Williams to an additional six months in jail. But Williams appealed the misdemeanor assault convictions and remained free in the meantime.

In December 1997, authorities learned that Williams was living with Michelle and their daughter, Kymberly, despite the no-contact order. Michelle's mother told a probation officer that Curtis had threatened to kill his wife and daughter if Michelle left him. Prosecutors filed two more charges against Williams, pushing the total to five since he had arrived at the UW. He was arrested and stayed in jail for 15 days. Williams was let out after two assistant UW coaches went before a judge and vouched for him, urging his release.

In the summer of 1998, Lambright, the Huskies' head coach, decided he'd had enough. Williams had yet to play a down for the team. He'd sat out his first year, to preserve all four years of his eligibility. He'd been off the team his second, the year he spent two and a half months in jail. He was a felon and a lousy student. And now his estranged wife and her mother were contacting coaches, asking why they'd kept Curtis on the team. Michelle wanted Curtis to get a job, to help pay for their daughter's support. Lambright wanted Williams's scholarship taken away so that he could give it to someone else. He provided the university with a report that cited Williams's problems "socially, academically and athletically." Though light on details, Lambright's report noted Williams's felony conviction, saying he'd had "an altercation" with his wife. Lambright said the team had ordered Williams to attend counseling, only to discover he'd blown off most of his appointments.

At the UW, the Athletic Financial Aid Committee decides whether a student-athlete's scholarship can be revoked. The committee was headed by Eric Godfrey, then an assistant vice president, now vice provost for student life. In September 1998, Godfrey wrote Williams, telling him the committee had ruled in his favor: his scholarship would not be lifted. Williams had recently completed a summer course that had pulled up his grades, Godfrey wrote. Plus, the coaches had sent Williams mixed messages, first getting him out of jail, then saying he was unfit for the team. Godfrey's letter referred to Williams's marriage as the principal source of his troubles. But now his wife was gone. "Your personal difficulties appear to have been eliminated, largely because your wife has relocated to Alaska," Godfrey wrote.

Curtis and Michelle separated in 1998 but never got divorced. At this point, Williams had three assault convictions, two on appeal. Two other charges were pending against him. For Williams and his wife, there was no "happily ever after." But what story there was, a top recruit convicted of assaulting his wife, didn't make the newspapers. In 1997, when Williams served time on the felony, the *Seattle Post-Intelligencer* ran a brief note, saying Williams "is off the team with what Lambright called 'personal problems.'" For the next three years, other newspapers, including the *Seattle Times* and the *News Tribune* of Tacoma, attributed Williams's missed season to "academic and unspecified off-field problems," or "family and academic problems," or "academic and personal problems."

When Williams returned to the team in 1998, after the team failed to get his scholarship lifted, Lambright went on his weekly radio show and said, "He's actually gotten all his academic credentials, and he seems to have his social life under control." Williams's "off-field problems" were spelled out in court records. But reporters didn't read the files or, if they did, they didn't write about them.

To remain eligible to play, UW football players are supposed to maintain a 2.0 grade point average, the equivalent of a C. In 1997 and 1998, Williams finished four straight quarters with a GPA below that line, placing his scholarship in jeopardy.

But then came Swahili. At the UW, athletes get to sign up for classes before regular students. Athletes flock to Swahili in such numbers that other students can wait three or four years to get into the class. The course is easy, football players say. When Robert Aronson, a law professor, served as faculty representative to the Athletic Department, he noticed that Swahili seemed to appeal to those football players who struggled academically. "It was awfully suspicious to me," he says.

Seyed Maulana, the UW's sole Swahili teacher since 1985, says athletes have typically accounted for about half his students. During away games, he faxes the exams to coaches, and they fax the answers back. After a year's study, most students can speak some Swahili, Maulana says. "They are able to do greetings. I tend to focus more on the structure of the language." In the summer of 1998, Williams took Intensive Swahili, a class worth 15 credits. He earned a B, pushing his GPA to 2.06, just enough to let him keep his scholarship. Afterward, Williams continued to take Swahili, earning a C, an A minus and a B plus. He earned 30 Swahili credits in all, nearly a fifth of his UW total. With those Swahili grades, Williams managed a final GPA of 2.05, just high enough to keep him playing.

After being convicted in 1997 of choking his wife, Williams was placed on probation for two years. In June 1999, a probation officer wrote that Williams still did not accept responsibility for his violence: "He is as narcissistic as ever, does not feel the rules apply to him and decides which rules he will follow." When Williams was sentenced in 1997, a judge ordered him to complete two kinds of treatment: batterers' counseling, to protect the community, and victim-awareness counseling, because he lacked compassion for the suffering he'd caused.

Time and again, Williams failed to enter the two programs, or missed individual sessions, or showed up late. Plus, he repeatedly missed appointments with probation officers. He usually blamed these lapses on the demands of football practices, games and school. Probation officers reached out to the courts for help. One officer, who wrote that Williams showed an "absolute blatant disregard" for his court-ordered obligations, asked that Williams be jailed 240 days for violating his probation. But a superior court judge instead gave Williams 15 days, time he had already served. Williams never completed victim-awareness counseling. Twice, he entered the program. Twice, he dropped out. But he was released from probation anyway.

In 1999, after two years of off-and-on counseling, Williams finished batterers' treatment. On a scale of 0 to 9, with 0 the most dangerous, 9 the least, Williams scored a 2: "able to recognize his controlling behavior." This same year, Williams received an extraordinary break in two other cases. In the summer of 1999, a judge reversed Williams's two misdemeanor assault convictions, based upon a screwup in the clerk's office. Police records crucial to the case were supposed to be in the court file. But they "were inexplicably removed or lost or destroyed," the judge wrote, throwing out the convictions and ordering a new trial. Prosecutors now had to start over with those two charges. The missing records allowed Williams to avoid six months in jail and to keep playing football.

Williams first played for the UW in 1998, starring on special teams. When Rick Neuheisel replaced Lambright as coach in 1999, Williams was named a starting safety on defense. Teammates loved Williams's ready smile, the way he joked around in the locker room. Neuheisel's staff loved how he never shied from contact.

Williams preferred playing without a mouth guard, standard gear that protects teeth and jaws. He wanted to intimidate, teammates say. Protective gear whispered fear. A mouth guard also garbled his words, and when Williams taunted an opposing player, he wanted to be understood. He would go for the ballcarrier's mouth, hitting him, face mask to face mask, and then get into his ear. "Curtis would run up, hit you in your mouth, take your lunch money and tell you you ain't nothing," says Hakim Akbar, a fellow safety. Hitting another player helmet to helmet comes with risk. Football has worked since the 1970s to reduce such blows, after they led to scores of deaths from brain or spinal-cord injuries. Tackle with your shoulder, coaches typically tell players. A hit becomes particularly dangerous if a player leads with his helmet and dips his head.

In the 2000 season, the Huskies' fifth game was at home, on October 7. The game program included a profile of Williams, titled "Designated Hitter." The story started: "On the football field, Curtis Williams just likes to hit. There is not much about which you can ask Williams that will get him to open up. That is, until you mention laying a hit on an opposing player from the safety position. Then his eyes light up. 'It's just a good feeling,' the 5-foot-10, 200-pound senior says. 'You can get all your frustrations out on that guy. Hitting a guy real hard like that, that's what the game is all about.'" Williams now appeared to have a legitimate shot at the NFL.

Off the field, Williams's struggles continued. He flunked biology in the winter quarter of 2000 and astronomy in the spring. In October, Williams hired Mike Hunsinger, a Seattle lawyer who'd represented lots of other Huskies. The state was coming after Williams for unpaid child support. Two years before, Michelle had obtained a court judgment requiring Curtis to pay $283 a month. Hunsinger maintained that Williams hadn't been notified of his obligation. But the state said that wasn't true. Williams had written in court documents that he couldn't afford to pay anything, being in school: "When I was living with Michelle she supported all three of us. So why does she need money from me for just her and Kym at this point?"

Williams also had an outstanding warrant for his arrest. He'd kept missing court hearings to review his probation in one case or to prepare for his new trial on the two reinstated assault charges. Each time, the judge would issue an arrest warrant. In mid-October, Hunsinger helped Williams get an appearance bond so that the latest warrant would be dropped. Then the two went to lunch. Hunsinger found he liked Williams. He seemed like a guy who was 22 going on 30. "He'd been a terrible father," Hunsinger says. But Williams knew it and was looking forward to turning that around. Williams had tattooed "Kymberly," his daughter's name, in cursive across his heart. He'd picked his number 25 to match the day of her birth. He hadn't seen Kymberly for a year but talked to her on the telephone twice a week.

Curtis Williams mouthed the words: I can't breathe. That's what teammate Anthony Kelley remembers, Williams lying there, looking up at him, trying to talk, while another player ran up and told Williams, "Shake it off, shake it off, hop up." The UW was playing at Stanford on October 28. Kerry Carter, Stanford's 235-pound running back, had cut into the line. Williams came flying in, beating Kelley to the tackle. Williams's head dipped, just a little, before the hit, which was helmet to helmet. Kelley knew it was a bad hit—he knew it right away. Williams bounced off, but his body was already rigid, as though it was frozen in air. After Williams fell, he just lay there. Then his body started to shake, his eyes started to roll: I can't breathe.

Kelley remembers telling Williams: "Relax, relax." A photographer remembers Kelley screaming: "Curtis! Don't you stop. Curtis! Don't give up. Curtis! Keep fighting."

For about 15 minutes, a medical team attended to Williams on the field. He responded only with his eyes. Awareness and panic, that's what one doctor saw. A driving rain soaked the field. The official attendance said 31,300, but all those empty seats said the number was smaller. The afternoon was gray, but Husky fans cut through it, making a wedge of purple in one end zone. The Huskies gathered on the sideline, and Kelley led a prayer: "I just lifted him up to God, telling Him to heal him, take care of him, look over him, and to bring him back to his family." Medics put Williams on a stretcher and into an ambulance. When play resumed, Kelley struggled to keep it together. Crying, he almost jumped offside, he was so desperate to hit someone.

With the game almost over, the UW trailed Stanford, 28–24. The Huskies had 80 yards to go and 47 seconds to get there. "We could have curled up," says Matt Fraize, an offensive lineman. "But we did what we thought Curtis wanted us to do, to keep fighting, to finish what we started." In three plays, in 30 seconds, the Huskies scored, keeping their Rose Bowl hopes alive.

The day after the game, Neuheisel and another coach visited Williams in the hospital. Williams, with a ventilator in his mouth, could respond only with his eyes. He was paralyzed from the neck down. "We told him we were going to play our tails off for him. When I said that, he blinked his eyes several times," Neuheisel said afterward.

The next week, 70,000 fans chanted "C-Dub," Williams's nickname, across Husky Stadium while the marching band formed the letters below. A few days later, the UW created a fund that raised more than $300,000 for Williams's medical care. At season's end, the team named Williams its most inspirational player and carved his initials into every Rose Bowl ring.

Williams became the focal point of the Rose Bowl season, with dozens of stories written about him. The *Seattle Post-Intelligencer* never reported his criminal history, while the *Seattle Times* mentioned it twice in passing. Without saying that Curtis had served time for assaulting Michelle, a *Times* sports columnist wrote: "Friends of Curtis said Michelle was more abusive than he.

It was a bad marriage." When Michelle read that column, she couldn't believe it. "A lot was written about what a great football player he was. With the other issues it was like, 'Don't ask, don't tell. Don't look, don't see.'"

After getting injured, Curtis moved in with his brother David in California.

"He got to sit back and reflect on his life a bit," David says. "Some days he would be laughing, other days he'd be crying." On May 6, 2002, his body shut down. Two days after his 24th birthday, and 18 months after he crumpled on the field, Williams died in the quiet of the night, sometime between midnight and dawn.

The UW painted his number on the sidelines of Husky Stadium and awarded him a posthumous degree. At Williams's funeral, some 600 people filed into a Fresno church. The mourners included more than 30 current or former UW football players—Marques Tuiasosopo, Anthony Kelley, Jerramy Stevens—and a half-dozen coaches. A Husky helmet and pictures of Williams, in uniform, flanked the altar. Purple and gold flowers covered the casket. A video showed football highlights. At a graveside service afterward, Neuheisel took Williams's number 25 jersey from atop the casket and presented it to Williams's parents. Michelle also attended the funeral, along with Kymberly. To this day, Michelle wishes Curtis were alive and part of his daughter's life to teach her how to drive, to be there when she graduates.

Emilie Lounsberry is a faculty member at The College of New Jersey following many years as a staff writer at the *Philadelphia Inquirer*. This article appeared in the *Philadelphia Inquirer* on January 14, 2007.

Arson Science — To Their Rescue?

The fire swept quickly through the redbrick rowhouse. It consumed the sofa and love seat and caught the curtains, burning so brightly that an orange glow filled narrow Carver Street in northeast Philadelphia's Summerdale section. Daniel Dougherty, a 26-year-old mechanic with a drinking problem, ran out of the fiery home, cried for help, and grabbed a garden hose to try to douse the flames. But it was no use. The fire was relentless, and its choking smoke soon reached his two sons, Danny Jr., 4, and John, 3, upstairs in their beds. Nearly 22 years later, from a cell on Pennsylvania's death row, Dougherty is fighting to prove he did not set the blaze that took the boys' lives—and is counting on an evolving science to save his own. New methods of analysis and computer simulation are transforming arson investigators' understanding of how fires start and spread. Some of the old axioms have been debunked; others have been shown to be true much of the time, but not always. On the morning of August 24, 1985, an assistant Philadelphia fire marshal examined burn patterns and concluded that the Carver Street inferno had three points of origin, a classic indication of arson. Today, though, burn patterns are known to be potentially deceiving.

In a petition filed in November in the Philadelphia Court of Common Pleas, Dougherty's lawyers cite such advances in the hope of discrediting at least some of the evidence that convinced a jury he was guilty of first-degree murder. Recalling the impact of DNA on criminal justice, legal experts expect the case to be part of the leading edge in a surge of appeals by convicted arsonists, some behind bars since the 1970s. The new fire science is not as definitive as DNA testing, by any means, but it can raise significant doubts about past investigations. One nationally known fire scientist, John J. Lentini, estimates that between 100 and 200 people may be "doing hard time" for arsons that weren't.

In 2005, according to the National Fire Protection Association, 31,500 structure fires were deemed intentional; they caused 315 deaths and $664 million in property damage. Even with so many advances in fire investigation, worries persist that the new science is not practiced widely enough. "There's still a lot of old wisdom that turns out not to be so wise being employed," said David L. Faigman, a professor at the University of California's Hastings College of the Law in San Francisco, who has written extensively on the role of scientific research in legal decisions.

The Philadelphia assistant district attorney who prosecuted Dougherty expressed confidence last week that there had been no mistake about what happened on Carver Street, and that the death-row inmate was where he belonged. "There's no question," John Doyle said, "and the jury so found." However, three arson experts who reviewed the case for the defense, including a former New York City fire marshal, found the original investigation to be so flawed that it was impossible to tell whether the fire was arson. "There's no credible evidence that it was a set fire," said Lentini, one of the analysts and the president of a Florida company that conducts fire studies.

In Pennsylvania alone, at least a half-dozen other cases have been called into question, either in court filings or experts' studies. Among the accused are a 71-year-old Korean immigrant serving a life sentence for the 1988 fire that killed his daughter during a Poconos vacation, and a former Dickinson College student in prison for life for a 1972 fire that led to the death of a woman involved with her boyfriend. In New Jersey, Centurion Ministries—a Princeton group that works to free the unjustly imprisoned—has gotten inquiries from about 50 convicted arsonists whose cases could be affected by a scientific reexamination of the evidence, said Kate Germond, the assistant director.

Yet while new looks at old fires are generating legal challenges across the country, courts generally have been slow to overturn convictions, even when science undermines investigators' initial findings. Although the rethinking of conventional arson wisdom began more than two decades ago, many judges and lawyers are only beginning to grasp its import. "Courts are understandably cautious" about opening the floodgates to appeals, Faigman said. "But I do think they have to act for the greater needs of justice. I think it's going to take some time." Still, there have been reversals.

In 2004, for instance, an inmate who spent 17 years on Texas's death row was released after prosecutors acknowledged that his conviction had been based on unreliable arson indicators, including burn marks. Ernest Willis collected nearly $430,000 for his time behind bars. That same year in the same state, Cameron T. Willingham was executed for the 1991 fire that killed his three children. Afterward, a panel of experts commissioned by the Innocence Project—another group dedicated to exonerating the wrongly convicted—concluded that the fire was mislabeled as arson, again based on outmoded beliefs about burn patterns. The people most at risk for being wrongly accused of arson are survivors of fires that kill close relatives, said John D. DeHaan, a California forensic scientist who was among the first to urge a more scientific approach. "When there's a death involved, there's a lot of pressure on investigators to solve it," DeHaan said.

Consider what happened to Paul Camiolo. He called 911 and yelled for his parents to get out when fire erupted in their home in Upper Moreland Township, Montgomery County, in September 1996. He tried to fight the flames, he said, but while he managed to rescue his sickly 57-year-old mother, his 81-year-old father perished inside. His mother died two months later of injuries suffered that morning. For more than two years, investigators and fire officials debated whether the fire had been set, since traces of gasoline had been found in the hardwood flooring but not in the carpet. They opted for arson and murder, and in January 1999, Camiolo was charged. He spent 10 months in the county jail before prosecutors dropped the charges. Camiolo's lawyers had shown that the gasoline was leaded, which meant it hadn't been commonly available for 15 years, and said it had been added to the hardwood floor's finish in the 1970s. "Where do you go to get your name back?" asked Camiolo, now 41 and a computer software specialist living in Bucks County. "The mere accusation is so disgusting." Steven Avato, a supervisory agent with the U.S. Bureau of Alcohol, Tobacco, Firearms and Explosives, investigated the Camiolo fire and contended from the start that it had been accidental—possibly ignited by a cigarette or a dropped match. Camiolo's mother was a smoker. Others are probably in prison because of faulty arson findings, but "my gut tells me it would be a small number," Avato said in a recent interview. "The question is, is even a small number acceptable?"

Letters from inmates come in at a fairly steady pace to the office of Philadelphia's fire marshal, Robert J. Ruff. He feels sympathy for those trying to get arson convictions overturned, he said, and sends them what information he can. "You never want to see an innocent person in prison, let alone on death row," said Ruff, who has been in the post six years. As in any other type of criminal investigation, he said, science is having an undeniable impact on fire investigation. But he isn't ready to close the book on the practical knowledge that generations of fire marshals have gleaned from the ashes. "I think the scientific method has been around—it just wasn't called the scientific method," Ruff said. "It was just years of experience."

The first shadows of doubt were cast on that anecdotal wisdom in the 1980s, when maverick investigators such as DeHaan began setting test fires and watching what happened, often in amazement. Early on, he and some colleagues tested the long-accepted notion that a smoldering cigarette took two hours to ignite a sofa. They dropped a cigarette into a couch and went to lunch, figuring they had plenty of time. Instead, it took mere minutes—and they had to race back to douse the blaze.

This is how fire science slowly changed, one test at a time. For example: fires were always thought to burn upward. Now it is known that they can burn down from a ceiling as well. Fires ignited by flammable liquids were believed to reach very high temperatures. Research has shown, though, that temperature is affected mostly by the ventilation. Finely crackled glass was viewed as a sign of rapid heating caused by an accelerant. But scientists have found that the "crazed" surface results from the rapid cooling when water hits hot glass. Burn patterns on a floor also were considered a reliable indicator of an accelerant.

Today, investigators are careful not to read too much into those marks because they are common when a room is engulfed, even in an accidental blaze.

Fire science took a quantum leap into the 21st century when researchers began understanding a naturally occurring phenomenon known as "flashover." As an interior fire burns, it spews heat and gases to the ceiling until the temperature there reaches about 1,100 degrees. At that critical moment, everything in the room suddenly ignites. The effects of flashover can look like evidence of arson. It can produce multiple burn patterns, much like those found on Carver Street.

Dan Dougherty was supposed to go to an Alcoholics Anonymous meeting on the night of August 23, 1985. Instead, he went to a neighborhood bar, where his girlfriend tracked him down. Furious, she told him that they were through and that she wouldn't return to the two-story rowhouse they shared, even though her family owned it. After their argument at the bar, Dougherty told police, he went home and heated up a roast beef sandwich on the range. He then got into another quarrel, this time with his ex-wife. Only then, he said, did he fall asleep on the sofa. When he awoke, he said, he saw the curtains on fire. Dougherty ran outside to get a neighbor's hose to drench himself and then raced to the backyard. He tried twice to climb a ladder but couldn't get inside. Judy Sorling, a neighbor, heard Dougherty cry for help and watched as he turned on the hose. Only a trickle came out. He looked drunk, "staggering and slurring," she recalled in a recent interview. Flames, meanwhile, engulfed the house. "It was horrifying, something that stuck in my head for all this time," said Sorling, who described Dougherty as "distraught and heartbroken" as the fire was being extinguished. A police officer at the scene reported that Dougherty stated, "My name's mud. I have to die for what I did."

From the start, Philadelphia assistant fire marshal John J. Quinn suspected arson. Now retired and living in Carbon County, Quinn declined to comment on the case last week. But in his 1985 report, he concluded that three fires had been set: in an overstuffed sofa, in a love seat, and under the dining-room table. He wrote that his investigation had "disclosed a fast fire, indicative of direct application of an open flame." Quinn's ruling was arson.

Nonetheless, 14 years passed before Dougherty was arrested. He had remarried, had another child, gotten divorced, and, by 1999, was involved in a custody dispute. His second ex-wife told police that he had confessed to her that he set the fire. At Dougherty's trial in October 2000, the prosecution contended that he had set the fire in an enraged act of vengeance against his girlfriend and his first ex-wife. Two inmates testified that Dougherty had confessed to them. Yet the most pointed evidence was the expert testimony of John Quinn. The jury took three hours to find him guilty and three and a half hours to send him to death row. In 2004, the Pennsylvania Supreme Court upheld the conviction and death sentence.

Now a new group of lawyers from the Center City firm Ballard Spahr Andrews & Ingersoll is representing Dougherty at the next level of his court fight. It will put him back before Judge Renee Cardwell Hughes, who presided over his trial. In the November filing, the legal team, led by David S. Fryman, contends that Dougherty's original defense lawyer was ineffective for failing to call fire experts to challenge Quinn. Dougherty's conviction rested on "nothing more than fire marshal folklore propped up by lying snitches," the petition asserts, and Quinn's conclusions were based "upon pure speculation amounting to old wives' tales passed down from fire marshal to fire marshal."

Arson scientists who reviewed the case said they could find no credible evidence that the fire had started in three places. Each raised the possibility that what had looked to Quinn like arson had merely been the result of flashover. "Because the three alleged points of origin were all connected by contiguous areas of burning," Lentini reported, "it is impossible to state . . . to a reasonable degree of scientific certainty that there were three separate ignitions." The district attorney's office is expected to file a response to the petition in March.

As the court battle proceeds, Dougherty, a hulking 6-foot-4, is well into his seventh year on death row. When the *Inquirer* requested an interview with him at the State Correctional Institution in Greene County, south of Pittsburgh, his attorneys declined. Dougherty, they say, is a mix of emotions—anger, sadness, impatience. "It has taken its toll," said Shannon D. Farmer, one of those representing him. "There's a growing sense of injustice and having been wronged by the system." Dougherty has reestablished contact with a son by his second wife, who died last year. Fifteen-year-old Stephen Dougherty lives with a relative in California. He talks by phone often with his father, he said last week, adding that he hoped to visit his father in the summer. Stephen said his father spent his time in his cell listening to radio music from the '60s and '70s—the Eagles' *Hotel California* is a favorite—and watching old westerns on TV. "I'm hoping that he gets out," he said. "He's a good guy."

Elisabeth Rosenthal, MD, is a journalist for the *New York Times* and the *International Herald Tribune*. This story, which she covered from Barcelona, appeared in the *New York Times* on August 3, 2008.

Stinging Tentacles Offer Hint of Oceans' Decline

Blue patrol boats crisscross the swimming areas of beaches here with their huge nets skimming the water's surface. The yellow flags that urge caution and the red flags that prohibit swimming because of risky currents are sometimes topped now with blue ones warning of a new danger: swarms of jellyfish. In a period of hours, 300 people on Barcelona's bustling beaches were treated for stings, and 11 were taken to hospitals.

From Spain to New York, to Australia, Japan and Hawaii, jellyfish are becoming more numerous and more widespread, and they are showing up in places where they have rarely been seen before, scientists say. The faceless marauders are stinging children blithely bathing on summer vacations, forcing beaches to close and clogging fishing nets.

But while jellyfish invasions are a nuisance to tourists and a hardship to fishermen, for scientists they are a source of more profound alarm, a signal of the declining health of the world's oceans.

"These jellyfish near shore are a message the sea is sending us saying, 'Look how badly you are treating me,'" said Dr. Josep-María Gili, a leading jellyfish expert, who has studied them at the Institute of Marine Sciences of the Spanish National Research Council in Barcelona for more than 20 years. The explosion of jellyfish populations, scientists say, reflects a combination of severe overfishing of natural predators, like tuna, sharks and swordfish; rising sea temperatures caused in part by global warming; and pollution that has depleted oxygen levels in coastal shallows.

These problems are pronounced in the Mediterranean, a sea bounded by more than a dozen countries, which rely on it for business and pleasure. Left unchecked in the Mediterranean and elsewhere, these problems could make the swarms of jellyfish menacing coastlines a grim vision of seas to come. "The problem on the beach is a social problem," said Dr. Gili, who talks with admiration of the beauty of the globular jellyfish. "We need to take care of it for our tourism industry. But the big problem is not on the beach. It's what's happening in the seas."

Jellyfish, relatives of the sea anemone and coral that for the most part are relatively harmless, in fact are the cockroaches of the open waters, ultimate maritime survivors who thrive in damaged environments, and that is what they are doing. Within the past year, there have been beach closings because of jellyfish swarms on the Côte d'Azur in France, the Great Barrier Reef of Australia, and at Waikiki in the United States.

In Australia, more than 30,000 people were treated for stings last year, double the number in 2005. The rare but deadly Irukandji jellyfish is expanding its range in Australia's warming waters, marine scientists say.

While no good global database exists on jellyfish populations, the increasing reports from around the world have convinced scientists that the trend is real, serious and climate related, although they caution that jellyfish populations in any one place undergo year-to-year variation. "Human-caused stresses, including global warming and overfishing, are encouraging jellyfish surpluses in many tourist destinations and productive fisheries," according to the National Science Foundation, which is issuing a report on the phenomenon this fall and lists as problem areas Australia, the Gulf of Mexico, Hawaii, the Black Sea, Namibia, Britain, the Mediterranean, the Sea of Japan and the Yangtze estuary.

In Barcelona, one of Spain's most vibrant tourist destinations, city officials and the Catalan Water Agency have started fighting back, trying desperately to ensure that it is safe for swimmers to go back in the water. Each morning, with the help of Dr. Gili's team, boats monitor offshore jellyfish swarms, winds and currents to see whether beaches are threatened and closings are needed. They also check whether jellyfish collection in the waters near the beaches is needed. Nearly 100 boats stand ready to help in an emergency, said Xavier Duran of the water agency. The constant squeal of Dr. Gili's cell phone reflected his de facto role as Spain's jellyfish control-and-command center. Calls came from all over.

Officials in Santander and the Basque country, on the Atlantic coast, were concerned about frequent sightings of the Portuguese man-of-war, a sometimes-lethal warm-water species not previously seen regularly in those regions. Farther south, a fishing boat from the Murcia region called to report an offshore swarm of *Pelagia noctiluca*—an iridescent purplish jellyfish that issues a nasty sting—more than a mile long. A chef, presumably trying to find some advantage in the declining oceans, wanted to know whether the local species were safe to eat if cooked. Much is unknown about the jellyfish, and Dr. Gili was unsure. In previous decades there were jellyfish problems for only a couple of days every few years; now the threat of jellyfish is a daily headache for local officials, and is featured on the evening news. "In the past few years, the dynamic has changed completely—the temperature is a little warmer," Dr. Gili said.

Though the stuff of horror B movies, jellyfish are hardly aggressors. They float passively with the currents. When they bump into something warm—a human body, for example—they discharge their venom automatically from poison-containing stingers on mantles, arms, or long, threadlike tendrils, which can grow to be yards long. Some, like the Portuguese man-of-war or the giant box jellyfish, can be deadly on contact. *Pelagia noctiluca*, common in the Mediterranean, delivers a painful sting, producing a wound that lasts weeks, months or years, depending on the person and the amount of contact.

In the Mediterranean, overfishing of both large and small fish has left jellyfish with little competition for plankton, their food, and fewer predators. In contrast to Asia, where some jellyfish are eaten by people, here they have no economic or epicurean value. The warmer seas and drier climate caused by global warming work to the jellyfish's advantage, since nearly all jellyfish breed better and faster in warmer waters, according to Dr. Jennifer Purcell, a jellyfish expert at the Shannon Point Marine Center of Western Washington University. Global warming has also reduced rainfall in temperate zones, researchers say, allowing the jellyfish to better approach the beaches. Rain runoff from land would normally slightly decrease the salinity of coastal waters, "creating a natural barrier that keeps the jellies from the coast," Dr. Gili said. Then there is pollution, which reduces oxygen levels and visibility in coastal waters. While other fish die in or avoid waters with low oxygen levels, many jellyfish can thrive in them. And while most fish have to see to catch their food, jellyfish, which filter food passively from the water, can dine in total darkness, according to Dr. Purcell's research.

Residents in Barcelona have forged a prickly coexistence with their new neighbors. Last month, Mirela Gómez, 8, ran out of the water crying with her first jellyfish sting, clutching a leg that had suddenly become painful and itchy. Her grandparents rushed her to a nearby Red Cross stand. "I'm a little afraid to go back in the water," she said, displaying a row of angry red welts on her shin. Francisco Antonio Padrós, a 77-year-old fisherman, swore mightily as he unloaded his catch one morning last weekend, pulling off dozens of jellyfish clinging to his nets and tossing them onto a dock. Removing a few shrimp, he said his nets were often "filled with more jellyfish than fish." By the end of the exercise, his calloused hands were bright red and swollen to twice their normal size. "Right now I can't tell if I have hands or not—they hurt, they're numb, they itch," he said.

Dr. Santiago Nogué, head of the toxicology unit at the largest hospital here, said that although 90 percent of stings healed in a week or two, many people's still hurt and itched for months. He said he was now seeing 20 patients a year whose symptoms did not respond to any treatment at all, sometimes requiring surgery to remove the affected area.

The sea, however, has long been central to life in Barcelona, and that is unlikely to change. Recently, when the beaches were closed, children on a breakwater collected jellyfish in a bucket. The next day, Antonio López, a diver, emerged from the water. "There are more every year—we saw hundreds offshore today," he said. "You just have to learn how to handle the stings."

Felicity Barringer has been reporting for the *Washington Post* and the *New York Times* on domestic and foreign issues for three decades. In February 1991, two years after her overseas tour in Moscow, she returned to see what the Soviet government had actually done to help the victims of the Chernobyl nuclear-power disaster. The Soviet empire was already crumbling; eight months after this reporting, it was no more. The pieces from which the following account is drawn appeared in the *New York Times* in April 1991.

Chernobyl: The Danger Persists

Eight-year old Sasha Danilkin left the hospital late last summer and came home to the wooden cottages and muddy roads of Tarasovka, a farming village in southeastern Byelorussia. Since then, the scar left after doctors in Minsk removed his cancerous thyroid gland has faded. His energy has returned. In the light snow of a February afternoon, Sasha chases his sisters around a decrepit green cart.

Watching him, his mother, Nadezhda, says over and over, "See how healthy he is." Although Sasha's thyroid received a large dose of radioactive iodine in the days after the explosion at the Chernobyl nuclear-power plant in April 1986, his mother claims the accident has not affected her life. In a high-volume, peremptory tone that turns a sentence into a declaration, she repeats: "We knew everything. We were protected. Our officials took care of us."

Then, for a brief moment, Nadezhda Danilkina's strident optimism subsides. "Why could they not do more for the children?" she asks. "Why could they not at least protect the children?" The moment passes as abruptly as it came. She repeats her earlier words like a mantra. "We were told everything. All of our needs have been secured. Look how healthy he is."

Five years after the Chernobyl disaster spewed at least 50 tons of volatile radioactive particles—10 times the fallout at Hiroshima—across Byelorussia, western Russia and the Ukraine, Nadezhda Danilkina clings furiously to the remnants of the old illusion: that the consequences could be controlled, that the harvest could be made safe, the food clean and the future secure.

She craves such assurance, but she knows her son's future is uncertain. In the days after the accident, his thyroid gland received a dose of 200 rads from radioactive iodine—in terms of cancer risk, the equivalent of thousands of chest X-rays. Four years later, a malignant tumor developed. The cancer has metastasized to his lymph nodes.

While the worst of the radiation danger passed within weeks of the accident, while the iodine-131 and other short-lived particles died out, there is still significant residual gamma radiation from cesium particles. In many villages like Tarasovka, which is about 95 miles northeast of the reactor, the radioactivity will linger for a generation.

In Tarasovka, there is only one way to reduce the risk: pack up and leave. But the Danilkin family has nowhere to go.

In 1986, when the Chernobyl myths were being made, I was a correspondent for the *New York Times* in Moscow. Those were days of martial metaphors, harking back to the suffering and triumphs of World War II. Radiation was the enemy: insidious, invisible, stubborn, powerful. But the firemen who extinguished the blaze, the helicopter pilots who dropped sand, lead and boron to smother the smoldering remnants of the reactor and the soldiers who cleaned up the territory were a powerful army. People had to be moved—about 135,000 from an area within an 18-mile radius of the reactor. But their health would be monitored. They would be safe.

I returned in February, nearly five years after the accident, to find the region littered with the remnants of those illusions and with anger, cynicism, doubt and fear. Far more land was poisoned than can ever be cleaned—or evacuated. Far more illness is evident than Soviet officials ever predicted. Far more clean food, far more medical care, far more money is needed than the country can give.

The numbers of those at risk of radiation-related illness are numbing: 600,000 workers were involved in the cleanup, and many were exposed to high doses of radiation. Some 200,000 people have been evacuated from contaminated areas, many after receiving between 20 and 100 rads (units of measurement of absorbed radiation), a nonlethal dose that nonetheless increases the risk of developing cancer. An additional 2,000 still occupy areas where the contamination measures, on average, 40 curies per square kilometer—up to 300 times the background levels in Byelorussia. Perhaps 75,000 more, like Nadezhda Danilkina, occupy regions where the levels are several times that of normal background radiation.

It was mid-1989 when Byelorussian and Ukrainian leaders revealed how much was left undone. The nation was then transfixed by its experiment in quasi-democratic elections. Ethnic violence was flaring in the Caucasus and Central Asia. There was little energy left to help the new Chernobyl victims; there were few resources. Reckoning with these truths and uncertainties has left the region crippled, environmentally, economically and psychologically. Many of those with the most marketable skills, like teachers and doctors, have moved away from cities where radiation lingers. Those who can't, or won't, flee the contaminated areas live in places they are told people should not live, and eat food they are told they should not eat. With a thousand different versions of the truth available, people believe whatever story best fits their fears.

"Back at the time of the accident, all I remember is that they told me there was radiation," recalled 9-year-old Tamara Klatsman, a patient at the Radiation Medicine Clinic in a Minsk suburb. "Radiation. Radiation. Simply that. An invisible thing." Doctors have found abnormalities in her thyroid; her dose of radioactive iodine was in excess of 200 rads. Tamara, from the town of Svetlogorsk,

75 miles north of Chernobyl, was 5 when the reactor exploded. "We first didn't know there was an accident," she said. "Then we thought some kind of machine had exploded. Or just everything had exploded. We didn't know."

The children of Svetlogorsk were not alone. The nuclear experts who were running a low-power experiment at the plant that night in 1986 also knew less than they thought. The wishful thinking that has characterized the history of Chernobyl began within minutes of the series of blasts in the hall of reactor No. 4 at 1:24 a.m. on Saturday, April 26. From the first, senior engineers in the control room refused to believe what had happened. Grigory Medvedev, one of the nuclear-power engineers sent from Moscow to investigate the accident, described the scene in his book *The Truth about Chernobyl*. According to his account, a few seconds before the explosions, a panicked engineer watched "in amazement" as the dials on his control panel began to glow, "as if they were red hot." Moments later, he sent two other young engineers to the reactor hall to lower by hand the control rods that had jammed before the blast.

When they got there, there were no control rods left to lower. The reactor lid, weighing tons, was canted crookedly above absurdly twisted girders and a mass of searing, intensely radioactive fuel burning blue and red. The reactor was gone. They surveyed the scene for a minute or two—long enough to have their skin turn brown from lethal doses of radiation—and returned to report that the reactor had been destroyed. Their superiors in the control room refused to believe them. The two young men, like 29 others, would perish of radiation sickness within 10 weeks. Two plant workers died in the fire and explosion.

Medvedev reports that the plant's director, Viktor Bryukhanov, and chief engineer Nikolai Fomin were called at their homes, where they were asleep, and told there had been an accident but that the reactor was intact. They passed the lie on to Moscow. These refusals to accept the truth had two results: a delay of days in finding a workable way to quench the radioactive volcano and in evacuating the small high-rise city of Pripyat, two and a half miles away. As they had refused to believe the reactor was destroyed, Bryukhanov and Fomin also refused to believe the plant's radiation monitors were registering radioactivity off the scale.

The following Saturday, there were soccer games in Pripyat. Women gardened. Children played in the sand. Weddings were held. Finally, late Saturday night, Moscow officials agreed to an evacuation. On Sunday afternoon, the city's population of nearly 50,000 boarded 1,100 buses and left.

Militiamen and soldiers, like Yevgeny Zhuk, whom I met on the streets of the small town of Khoiniki, were called in to keep order. But the radiation didn't dissuade thieves. As fast as cleanup workers could bury radioactive cars and ambulances, Zhuk added, they were dug up and stripped, the parts taken away for resale. Zhuk shook his head as he spoke, leaning on a cane and smiling sadly. Zhuk, now 24, was one of the soldiers put to work controlling access to the zone. His comrades buried chunks of radioactive graphite blown out of the reactor, plowed under radioactive topsoil, chopped down contaminated trees and built a "permanent" sarcophagus that is already obsolete. The 600,000 workers, many of them conscripts like Zhuk, were shuttled in and out of fields pulsating with the radioactive elements strontium, cesium, and plutonium. They came to be called *likvidatory*, a name drawn from words spoken by Mikhail S. Gorbachev: "Work to liquidate the consequences of the accident now remains the immediate task." Like the village children, more and more likvidatory are falling sick. But according to Zhuk, whose legs are stiff and whose knees give him constant pain, "the local doctors, they send us away. They want nothing to do with us. I have become a person of no use to anyone."

In the Supreme Soviet, there is a thirst for accountability. Aleksei Yablokov, a scientist who is now vice chairman of the Supreme Soviet's committee on the environment, is leading a parliamentary investigation. It seeks to determine whether the lies of the early years resulted from arrogant ignorance or a policy of deceit.

Where are the victims? One must start looking in the fields and woodlands of western Russia, Byelorussia and the Ukraine, where villages rise up like tiny islands in a vast and empty plain. Along their muddy streets, people wait with angry stoicism as the men with the clicking Geiger counters come and go.

Soviet and American maps trace the current levels of contamination, the active remnants of the short-lived radioactive particles that rained down on millions of people immediately following the accident. The largest area of persistent contamination was made by cesium-137, one of the longest-lived radioactive elements emitted in the Chernobyl explosion. It was carried on the wind and fell where the rain did. Across the southwestern edge of the Soviet Union, more than four million Soviet citizens live on ground that, while generally clean, has scattered pockets where the radiation is 5 to 20 times the normal background radiation for this area.

Thyroid cancer is extremely rare among children. In the United States, according to the Centers for Disease Control, it is almost unknown in people under the age of 25. Yet health officials in Byelorussia reported 19 cases of malignant thyroid cancers in children, including Sasha Danilkin, in 1990. In the Ukraine, there were 21 cases.

The woodlands region of southern Byelorussia and the northern Ukraine have long been known as a "goiter belt," notorious for a lack of iodine in the environment, and for the resulting thyroid abnormalities. Health officials say childhood thyroid cancer had never been seen here. But when the accident happened, they say, the children's thyroids, thirsty for any sort of iodine, greedily absorbed the damaging radioactive iodine. While no individual case of cancer can be linked to radiation exposure with certainty, most Western experts believe that the children here struggling with thyroid cancer owe their disease to Chernobyl.

Doctors today, five years later, are more concerned about the internal doses in people who consume tainted milk, grain and meat. Both the Ukraine and Byelorussia have established supply lines to get clean produce to the people living in areas where contamination exceeds 15 curies per square kilometer. In theory, good food goes in and no bad food comes out. In practice it doesn't work that way. Refrigerated train cars filled with radioactive meat have turned up in Georgia in the south and Karelia in the north. In Leningrad, city officials found they had bought tons of mushrooms that they had to discard as radioactive waste.

Quarrels among experts who speak only to one another leave the village people feeling like guinea pigs. "We were given dosimeters at work. We wore them for a month. Then they took them away from us and no one told us what dose we received," said Vera Zborovskaya, a 30-year-old combine operator in a Byelorussian village about 35 miles north of the reactor. "All these counters, they lie, they lie," cried a querulous group of portly grandmothers, crowding around her in the local bread store, kerchiefed heads wagging and metal teeth flashing. "I have two children," Zborovskaya said. "I can't get them checked." Her 10-year-old daughter, Oksana, has developed abnormalities in her thyroid gland. Every six months or so, Oksana, like other children in "periodic control zones" is taken away for a month, to the "clean" regions in the north, east or west. "When they come back, I am told they are sick. But here, no one checks their health. In Bragin, they put a stamp on a piece of paper and said the kids were examined. They didn't examine them."

Indifference from medical personnel is nothing new. In a country that has few material comforts and public amenities to offer its citizens at the best of times, these areas have the bare minimum. Roads are narrow and pocked with potholes. Telephones and indoor toilets are rare. Interiors are warmed by whitewashed peasant ovens that double as hearths; their broad shelves serve as sleeping nooks. Even bare-bones Soviet-made cars are a luxury; in some villages, horse-drawn carts with rubber car or tractor tires make their way past women drawing water from wells.

"Our children go to schools here, but there's no heat," said Zborovskaya. "Then they come home and play in the streets. Clearly it's dangerous, since they want us to move out of here." "I worked as a combine operator this past summer," she said. "We were sent to work in the places left empty when people were resettled. If I refused to go there, I would be punished. There are no people there, but I am forced to go to work. I cannot check my dose. To what end do I harvest contaminated wheat? We feed the cattle with it."

In the crowded halls of the Diagnostic Center for Radiation Medicine in Minsk, mothers, their hair covered by scarves, hold the hands of children wearing dark, knitted tights. Young men sit on benches, elbows on knees. Their complaints are the same as those found in any other clinic: listlessness, stomach pains, heart troubles, sore joints. It would be an unremarkable assembly of aches were the patients not likvidatory and residents of contaminated regions.

There is sharp divergence among Western experts about the eventual Chernobyl toll. Dr. Marvin Goldman, a radiation biologist, says the Soviet Union will see between 1,000 and 7,500 new cancers in the next 50 years, a rate he says will be undetectable against a backdrop of hundreds of thousands of cancers that will have occurred anyway. But John Gofman, professor emeritus of biophysics at the University of California at Berkeley, estimates the toll in Soviet Union will be between 50,000 and 250,000 deaths.

The effort to get reliable health data is a source of continuing frustration to Westerners working with the Soviets. And the exodus of doctors from the contaminated regions has left those remaining carrying a heavy workload. "In the woodland regions, we used to have 60 or 70 percent of the doctors we needed. Now we have 30 percent," said Yuri Spizhenko, the deputy Minister of Health in the Ukraine. "This kind of medicine needs to be very sophisticated," Spizhenko added. "But our doctors are diagnosing things by eye, by ear, by touch, the way they did 100 years ago. We need ultrasound equipment. We have almost no blood analyzers."

While the government struggles to define what is "safe" and how to make people safe, some pay no heed. "I was born here," said Tatyana Leonenka, who came back to her home in the evacuated village of Krasnaya Gora two years ago. "I lived here during the war. I lived here till they resettled me. I was not happy there." "I've been back two years," said her neighbor, 74-year-old Vasily Osipenko. "I'm healthier here than I was where they evacuated us. There's no danger here. I drink, I eat my bread, I keep a cow, I drink her milk."

Between the extremes—those who fear everything and those who fear nothing—people wait. The 5,000 people of Narodichi, 50 miles west of the reactor, are slowly being moved out. The village of Nozdrishche is already empty. On the outskirts, authorities have built a barbed-wire fence. It curves between an apple orchard and a hayfield. A sign at the gate warns "Danger—Radioactive Zone." The fence offers a pretense of demarcation. The apples on one side are bad, the hay on the other is good. But the fence is rusted, the lock broken. The gate hangs open. Through it, headed toward the distant reactor, a stream of footprints is etched in wet and muddy snow.

Now, in the confusion of a decentralized Soviet Union, the old illusions spawned by the government are disappearing, but homemade myths arise in their stead. In a country of storytellers, Chernobyl has become everyone's story.

Jeffrey Bartholet is the Washington bureau chief for *Newsweek*. He previously served as the magazine's foreign editor and as a correspondent based in Tokyo, Jerusalem, Nairobi, and Cairo. This article was published in *Newsweek* on August 13, 2001.

Alaska: Oil's Ground Zero

A trip to the Arctic National Wildlife Refuge is a confrontation with choices: to drill or to preserve one of the last wild places.

If you want somebody to fly you over the towering peaks of the Brooks Range and drop you onto the spongy tundra of the Arctic National Wildlife Refuge (ANWR), Dirk Nickisch is your man. Dirk is a former rodeo rider and crop duster, a wiry fellow with sharp eyes and prickly whiskers, whom some in his home state of North Dakota have likened to a coyote. He meets clients at a gravel airstrip in a Gwichin Indian village just south of the range. Dressed in oily pants and a baseball cap, he kicks the tires on his 1952 single-prop de Havilland Beaver, shoulders the rear rudder back and forth to be sure it's still in working order and tells you, if you ask him, that he reckons his Pratt & Whitney engine has been overhauled "a few times." He doesn't have much time for people who stand around asking questions without making themselves useful, however. So he rolls four plastic barrels of fuel under the plane and puts you to work with a hose and a squeaky hand pump.

Nobody would mistake Dirk Nickisch for a tree hugger. But as he takes off and flies over the northern mountains of Alaska—into one of the last unspoiled wilderness areas of America—he explains (if you ask him) why he doesn't want multinational oil companies to explore and drill for oil in any part of the refuge. "I moved up here because it's the last place like this," he says, looking out the windscreen over the southern reaches of the 19 million-acre refuge. Then he nods toward the peeling plastic of the dashboard, where a black-and-white photo of his two kids is stuck among pinwheel gauges measuring altitude and direction. "My little boy was 3 months old when he first saw the caribou come through the coastal plain," he says. "I don't want to leave him and his kids a bunch of old oil wells and some empty promises."

Minutes later, with snow-streaked peaks a few hundred feet below us, the vintage engine starts to cough and sputter. Dirk turns a worn red handle to switch gas tanks, and adjusts the throttle. The engine finds its voice again, and from here on in, the ride is smooth. We cross the range and glide between the Sadlerochit Mountains to our left and the white sluice of a small glacier to our right, cushioning down toward a 1.5 million-acre plain that has, from above, the tawny, matted appearance of buffalo hide. "This is the wildest place left in Alaska," Dirk says after landing on a strip of knee-high willow shrubs near the

Jago River, "the wildest place left in the United States." Then he climbs back in his Beaver and flies off, leaving me and three companions (two photographers and environmentalist Dan Ritzman) in a seemingly lonesome land, silent but for the wind and the rushing river—the sort of quintessentially Alaskan place that touristy T-shirts in Anchorage refer to as "the last frontier."

America's founding myths are largely about taming wild places. The frontier shaped the American character even as we shaped it, moving from the Allegheny Mountains to the Mississippi and onward to the Missouri, the Rocky Mountains and the Pacific. But the frontier is all but gone now, and what remains occupies a unique place in the American psyche. Alaska has the largest area of wilderness lands in the country by far—an area roughly the size of Maine, New Hampshire, Vermont, Massachusetts, Rhode Island, Connecticut, New Jersey, Delaware and Maryland combined. Yet it also has the nation's two largest oil-fields, and is second only to Texas in proven reserves of crude. Alaskans use more energy per capita than any other people in the country, and scientists who study global warming say that no state is more affected by climatic change. As it is, average temperatures in Alaska have spiked close to 5 degrees since the 1960s, and the polar sea ice has thinned by 40 percent over the same period.

A trip to Alaska's Arctic refuge is a confrontation with choices: should we drill or protect wilderness? Which do we value more: greater American oil production or a landscape largely untouched by the hand of man? In this debate, Alaska itself has taken on a symbolic heft beyond its value as a wilderness preserve or as a source of oil. Once again, the way Americans engage their frontier will reflect, in no small measure, the national character. Are we energy gluttons, or hopeless romantics wedded to a utopian vision of the natural world? Are we conservationists or materialists? In a country where most people support government conservation efforts, yet sales of gas-guzzling SUVs are soaring, some might argue that we're simply a people who hope and believe that we can have it all.

Most Americans who want to protect the Arctic refuge will never see it, and there's good reason for that. In February, when the sun hardly comes up, temperatures drop to an average of about 4 degrees below zero. And in the endless days of July, visitors can hardly breathe without sucking mosquitoes down their throats. Some Alaskans familiar with the refuge, like oil consultant Ken Boyd, don't understand the attraction of the place. "You can't see the end of the world from there, but you're pretty darn close," says Boyd, a geophysicist who once directed Alaska's Division of Oil and Gas.

Nobody really knows how much petroleum there is under the ANWR coastal plain. Although oil seeps out of the tundra in some places—staining bogs with a bluish-black sheen—some scientists believe the seeps are evidence that a potential reservoir underneath has been crushed and ruined over geologic time. The most recent study by the U.S. Geological Survey, published in 1998, concluded that several oil deposits—what some geologists call a "string of pearls"—are located mainly in the west of the ANWR coastal zone. The survey gave a wide range of estimates for how plump those pearls might be. Environmentalists often cite the USGS study to argue that the refuge will likely produce 3.2 billion barrels of oil—less than half of what the United States burns in a single year. That assessment is based on a future oil price of about $20 per barrel. At about $15, it could become uneconomical to produce any oil at all. Then again, the USGS estimates for oil that is "technically recoverable"— if oil prices and cost weren't a factor—range from 5.7 billion to 16 billion barrels. "It's got billions of barrels of potential and a lot of unknowns," says Boyd.

Keeping ANWR off limits has undoubtedly increased America's reliance on oil imports, even if only marginally. Slightly more than half the oil Americans consumed last year was imported, compared with 37 percent in 1980. And the Energy Information Administration projects that dependence on foreign oil will surge further in the decades ahead.

So if we don't drill in ANWR, where will we drill?

Environmentalists have their own win-win argument: Americans could save far more oil by increasing energy efficiency, they say, than could ever be drilled in places like ANWR. And those savings would reduce U.S. dependence on foreign oil, limit U.S. production of greenhouse gases and husband America's resources for another day. As it is, although Americans account for just 4.5 percent of the world's population, they consume nearly a quarter of the world's energy. Europeans pay roughly twice as much at the pump for premium gasoline, and American cars use one-third more energy than European cars. The Natural Resources Defense Council, an environmental organization, estimates that increasing fuel-efficiency standards for new cars to 39 miles per gallon over the next decade would save 51 billion barrels of oil over the next 50 years, many times more than even the most optimistic predictions for the Arctic refuge. But the House of Representatives last week, at the same time it approved ANWR drilling, rejected a proposal to substantially boost fuel-efficiency standards for SUVs.

Defenders of the refuge as a wilderness area believe, in any case, that the ecosystem has an intrinsic value beyond oil. They point out that it is one of the last places in the United States where a visitor can still witness a great migration of animals—in this case, caribou. The 130,000-strong Porcupine Herd, named so because it winters near the Porcupine River in Canada, moves every summer into the coastal plain, where the cows usually give birth. The caribou favor the ANWR coast as a natural maternity ward because predators are more scarce here than in the foothills and mountains. Nutritious grasses also are plentiful, and offshore breezes help fend off summer mosquitoes. (Alaskan officials maintain that drilling would have no significant effect on the caribou; conservationists disagree.)

In three days and nights camping on the plain in June, we saw about 20 caribou—the full herd didn't make it to its traditional calving ground at the usual time this year because of unusual weather conditions. We also spotted an arctic peregrine falcon, plovers and several other species of birds, arctic ground squirrels and, during our flight out, a herd of shaggy musk oxen. Despite plentiful scat around our campsite, we encountered no grizzlies. But we did find the elusive arctic woolly bear caterpillar, which can live for up to 14 very frigid years before blossoming into a moth.

Geologists argue that with new technologies, including 3-D seismic mapping and horizontal drilling over long distances, they can exploit ecologically sensitive areas with minimal disruption. Conservationists dispute that, but many also argue that the petroleum geologists miss a larger point: that global warming from the burning of fossil fuels presents an even greater potential danger to arctic ecosystems. Polar bears may or may not be affected by seismic thumping, but they surely will suffer from the rapid melting of their habitat. As it is, several animal species are mysteriously declining in Alaska—including a species of sea lion and harbor seals in the Gulf of Alaska—and some scientists attribute that to warming trends.

Arctic drilling will also directly impact local peoples, for good and bad. The 260 Eskimos who live in the village of Kaktovik support onshore oil drilling. And it's not hard to see why. "We don't have any other economy up here," says Kaktovik mayor Lon Sonsalla, who hails from Wisconsin and married into the local community after coming to the village during a military stint in 1977. "If you take away the oil money, you've got a subsistence way of life. All of a sudden you'd be trying to find food, stay warm, keep out of the wind. That would be your main occupation: staying alive."

Yet opponents of oil exploitation in ANWR include a separate group of native Alaskans who live to the south of the refuge. The Gwichin Indians of Arctic Village worry that oil development will harm the Porcupine caribou herd, which they have hunted for generations. That doesn't mean they aren't open to outside influence: the Gwichin live in electrified homes, watch satellite TV and drive all-terrain vehicles they call "four wheelers." Yet they equate the potential loss of the caribou with the destruction of buffalo herds for the Sioux, a prelude to cultural catastrophe. "If there were no caribou, we wouldn't have lived here for thousands of years," says Trimble Gilbert, 66. "That's who we are and where we came from."

It's clear that a nonnative like Dirk Nickisch, who flies for a living, needs oil as much as the next guy. But he's also made a conscious choice to lead an austere life. "I have a lot of time up here to think about things," he says. "A lot of people want their high ideals as long as it doesn't cost them anything. They want to save the environment, but they also want to drive their SUVs." Last winter Dirk and his wife, Danielle, sold their three-bedroom, one-and-three-quarter-bath ranch-style house in Fairbanks in favor of a 16-by-24-foot cabin with a loft and a wood stove. "We have a simpler life and have come to enjoy the simpler things."

Many Americans appreciate that sentiment, but would not want to live that life. They may be willing to accept modest changes in their lifestyles, but for how long and to what extent? For an environmentalist out on the coastal plain of the Arctic refuge, in that brief but beautiful season between the harsh winter and the full onslaught of the mosquitoes, the choices seem simple enough. "In 50 or 100 years, would you stand out here and look back and think to yourself, 'Thank God we opened this area for oil'?" says Dan Ritzman. "No, you wouldn't. You'd say, 'Thank God we had the foresight to recognize that there are some places with more value than that.'" Three thousand miles and a world away, in the air-conditioned corridors of Washington, the battle is still on.

With Adam Rogers in Washington and Michael Hsu in New York.

Craig Duff is a videojournalist and director of multimedia at Time, Inc. In 2005, he visited five countries with territory above the Arctic Circle to report on the future of the Arctic Ocean. His reporting, along with that of *New York Times* correspondents Andrew Revkin, Clifford Krauss, Steven Lee Myers, and Simon Romero, was included in a four-part newspaper series called "The Big Melt." To accompany the series, Duff wrote and produced a television documentary called *Arctic Rush*. It aired on the Discovery Times Channel and CBC Canada, and won the 2006 National Association of Science Writers' Science in Society Award. What follows is based on that documentary.

Arctic Rush

Narrator: Alaska is special among American states. Its spectacular landscapes lure tourists to mingle with the wildlife and to marvel at the ice. At Kenai Fjords National Park, daily boat tours take tourists to the glaciers, pausing to watch masses of ice break off into the fjord.

Tim Fleming (captain, Kenai Fjords Tour): It is hard not to get excited when there is such a wide variety and people are so excited. [*announcing to tourists*] More pieces coming down. Keep watching that area. A big crack has developed across the face.

Narrator: Huge pieces of ice fall naturally from a glacier as it moves downhill, but at other glaciers at Kenai Fjords, global warming is taking its toll. Park ranger Mike Tetreau has been monitoring the glaciers at Kenai Fjords since the 1980s.

Mike Tetreau (ranger and resource manager, Kenai Fjords National Park): Glaciers can actually be a very good indicator of changing climate, especially lower-elevation, lower-latitude glaciers, which respond pretty dramatically to changes in climate.

Narrator: The so-called Exit Glacier is the star attraction at Kenai Fjords because it is the only glacier reachable by car. Although the glacier has been retreating since the 19th century, Tetreau worries about how thin it is getting and how fast it is retreating.

Tetreau: Within our time frame, even within the last decade, you can see dramatic changes. They are right in front of our faces. This is not a geologic time scale; it's now.

Narrator: What is happening in southern Alaska is magnified as you travel north. People who live and hunt on the ice in the Arctic region, the Saami people of northern Europe and the Inuit of Alaska, Russia, Greenland and Canada, all have tales to tell. Pitseolak Alainga

has been hunting since he was a youngster on the ice outside of Iqa-
luit, the capital of Canada's semiautonomous Inuit territory of
Nunavut.

Pitseolak Alainga (hunter): I learned how to hunt from my father. From
years back to today I have noticed how the ice formation and the
strength of the ice have changed.

Narrator: The Inuit know their ice. The indigenous peoples of North
America—originally called Eskimos by Arctic explorers—have long
adapted to the harsh Arctic climate. Inuit leader Sheila Watt-Cloutier
says that the people of the high north are among the first to feel the
effects of global warming, but she warns that as the Arctic warms up,
the rest of us will eventually feel it, too.

Sheila Watt-Cloutier (chair, Inuit Circumpolar Conference): Even
though we've come to become wage earners, working nine to five
during the week, we are still avid hunters and fishermen. Our environment is our supermarket. We are witnessing the melting of the
planet faster than anyone else because we are on that ice and snow
every day.

David Barber (chair, Arctic System Science, University of Manitoba):
You know it is a remarkable time when a society like the Inuit in
northern Canada develop a word for sunburn. They never had a
word for that before.

Narrator: There may not be adequate words in any language to describe what may ultimately happen in the Arctic. Scientific predictions are forcing people to imagine a North Pole without ice. Leading polar scientists say that the next hundred years will see an
unprecedented melt.

Andrew C. Revkin (science reporter, *New York Times*): You would have to
go back 15 million years to find the last time the Arctic Ocean was
routinely free of sea ice.

Robert Corell (chair, Arctic Climate Impact Assessment): It is really happening now and has been happening seriously for the last 30 years.
We have places in the Arctic that are warming five to ten times faster
than rest of the planet, and that will continue.

Narrator: In the Arctic Climate Impact Assessment, some 300 of the
world's top Arctic scientists from eight countries analyzed computer
models of climate and Arctic sea ice. Their forecast shows that the
polar ice cap will melt away during the summers as the planet
warms.

Corell: Our models project that a complete emptying of ice that could
take place as early as midcentury or by the end of the century, depending on the model. That is a gigantic change from anything we
have ever anticipated.

Narrator: The predicted melt means a new ocean will emerge. While some warn of environmental catastrophe, others are calculating the benefits of open Arctic waters.

Watt-Cloutier: As long as there is ice, nobody cares except us, because we hunt and fish and travel on that ice. It is our homeland. But the minute the ice starts to thaw and become water, then the whole world is interested. They see it as a potential benefit, while we see it as one of the biggest intrusions into our homeland.

Narrator: In the push to the north, there will be winners and losers. The resources in the region might be worth trillions of dollars, and with more open waters, shipping routes will blossom. The long-held and mythic wish for a shortcut across the top of the globe will come true.

Sen. John McCain: If there is any good news, it is that the long-sought Northwest Passage will finally become a reality. Those of us who studied history remember that maritime nations long dreamed of a trade route to China.

Narrator: The pursuit of the Northwest Passage is part of the fabled lore of the north. Spellbound explorers became icebound as they tried to conquer the frozen channels. Many met icy deaths, but tales of the treacherous passage could eventually be relegated to history books.

Revkin: I looked in all the old books about what Arctic exploration used to be like; it was horrible. People froze to death, or they got stuck in the ice for one or two winters before they could even think about getting through the Northwest Passage. The idea of its being open water has been a dream of civilizations for a long time.

Barber: The idea of opening up the ocean is complicated. It has many different facets, pros and cons. If you are a shipping company and you want to take products from Europe to Asia, you would really like to see the Northwest Passage navigable, even for a few months a year, because the top and bottom of the planet are the skinny parts, while the middle is the fat part. You can get over the Northern Hemisphere much more quickly, which means at much less cost. Today ships travel from Asia to Europe through the Panama Canal. Sailing the Northwest Passage through the Canadian archipelagoes would trim thousands of miles off the trip.

Michael Byers (Liu Global Institute, University of British Columbia): Companies are looking at the north and saying okay, when can we go? When is the risk sufficiently low of going through the north?

Barber: On the problem side, you cannot predict what kind of disasters will be caused by shipping accidents or natural hazards. There is increased storminess. All these factors complicate the issue. There is no straightforward answer.

Narrator: To look for answers, one of Canada's top polar scientists, David Barber, is leading a team of researchers in Churchill, Manitoba. As the spring begins to thaw the ice near Churchill, the team drills into the sea ice of Hudson Bay to monitor temperature changes.

Since the 1920s, there have been dreams for Churchill to be a viable port, but it remains icebound for eight months a year with its tugboats and silos dormant. A railroad company called OmniTRAX has plans that could turn Churchill into a boomtown. The company has made a $50 million investment in order to be first out of the gate in the race for Arctic shipping routes. They are calling it an Arctic bridge: a route from Churchill to Murmansk, Russia.

Barber: This has been a dream in Manitoba for a century. The initial ideas for the port began around the turn of the century. We are now into the next century, and it is just starting to look like a realistic proposition. Hudson Bay is opening up very rapidly. We can already see this from satellite images.

Here in Churchill, we work very closely with the OmniTRAX people, who own the port of Churchill. They are very interested in what is going on with Hudson Bay sea ice. But what is good for shipping isn't necessarily good for the environment. The sea-ice season is getting shorter each year. Because it's shorter, the oceans absorb more solar radiation. After the sun warms the surface of the ocean, it takes longer to freeze the next fall. Climate change is happening very rapidly, but we have not really prepared for it. We do not know the answers, and we are not even sure what some of the questions are.

Narrator: As the sea ice season shortens here, some believe the so-called Arctic bridge could be viable in less than a generation.

Corell: I think some of that is going to open up on time scales over the next decade or a few decades. From what we can see, it is not a century sort of issue.

Narrator: Churchill mayor Mike Spence worries that even though more ice-free months may bring more ships to town, it can also hurt the town's biggest moneymaker: tourism. Churchill is best known for its polar bears, which come through town each year as they migrate to their northern hunting grounds on the Hudson Bay ice. It has been called the polar bear capital of the world, but polar bears need ice to survive.

Byers: If you extend the period where Hudson Bay is ice free, you put increased stress on the polar bears, and at a certain point, they starve and Hudson Bay no longer has bears.

Narrator: Can the bears adapt to it? It would be hard for Churchill to adapt without them. At the other end of the proposed Arctic bridge, 3,700 miles from Churchill, the port city of Murmansk tells another

side of the tale. As countries sharpen their elbows to stake out domi-
nance in the Arctic, Russia's long shipping history puts it in a strong
position. Russia also has its own Arctic shipping lane, a rival to the
Northwest Passage, called the Northern Sea Route. In the Soviet era,
the country built nuclear-powered icebreakers to open up the passage for shipping. That route connects Asia to Europe across the
north of Siberia.

Artur Chilingarov (arctic explorer and vice chair, Russian parliament): In
the Soviet era, there was a system. There were special aircraft that
flew twenty-four hours a day and recommended routes for the icebreakers, which in turn were followed by other transport boats. That
all collapsed with the end of the Soviet Union.

Narrator: The Murmansk shipping company still operates the nuclear
icebreakers. They plow through the Northern Sea Route during the
four months when ice is thinnest. Researchers predict the route will
open up to more shipping sooner and faster than the Northwest Passage over North America. This will give Russia a head start over
Canada.

Corell: The place where the ice is receding most rapidly is along the
coastal margins of Russia, what we call the Northern Sea Route.
There is now only one little choke point left. That pathway used to
be open two or three weeks a year; soon it will be open for two or
three months and finally as many as six months a year.

Chilingarov: It will be wonderful, like the Suez Canal.

Byers: We are not quite there yet, but as the ice melts, we are going to
be there in the next five or ten years. Some companies are already
building ice-strengthened freighters and tankers, supertankers, to
make that passage.

Narrator: Look at the top of the globe, and you see how many of the
world's most powerful countries are remarkably close to one another.
Arctic nations are girding themselves for a fight over every inch of
ocean territory. Turf battles over the Arctic will be handled through a
treaty called the United Nations Convention on the Law of the Sea.
Under the treaty, nations can claim the ocean bottom beyond their
200-mile exclusive economic zones.

James Watkins (chair, U.S. Commission on Ocean Policy): The Convention on the Law of the Sea was established to pull nations together
and see if we could set up a system, a structure, that would make
some sense, so we could govern the oceans of the world as the
human resource we all desperately need.

Larry Mayer (marine geologist, University of New Hampshire): The
Arctic is potentially very, very resource rich. There has been a tremendous amount of interest in countries' mapping the Arctic in

order to claim an extended continental shelf, as it's called in the treaty.

Narrator: Here is where Arctic countries currently stand. Canada has potential claims on a huge area to its north. The United States can petition for a swath of ocean as large as the state of California. Denmark, which oversees Greenland, could claim the North Pole because its shelf connects to an undersea mountain range. And Russia has submitted a claim covering half of the Arctic Ocean. It is not very different from the arbitrary lines Joseph Stalin drew.

Chilingarov: Stalin drew a line from Murmansk to the North Pole and then to Churchill and proclaimed it USSR polar region. At the time, nobody worried about it, but today, with gas and oil fields in the shelf, it has become a very important issue. Russia will, of course, follow all the conventions and the laws of the sea.

Revkin: Russia was first to stake a claim, making its case for virtually half of the Arctic Ocean right up to the North Pole. The commission basically said, "We don't think you have enough data to support your claim," and sent the Russians back to redo their homework.

Narrator: The clock is ticking. Countries have only ten years after ratifying the treaty to map the sea floor and stake their claims. But critics say the world's only superpower could be left out of the discussion as nations divvy up the ocean floor. That is because the United States Senate has yet to ratify the treaty. At stake for the United States: $1.5 trillion in resources, according to one estimate. The rush for territory is being driven in great part by a thirst for oil and gas.

Watkins: We need to be at the table, talking about fisheries management, mineral extraction, freedom of navigation. That's why it is essential for the United States to have membership in the bodies that are set up within the Law of the Sea Convention.

Byers: There is an incredible irony in all of this. The melting of the ice facilitates the rush to extract petroleum. At the same time, the ice is melting, at least in part, because of the consumption of fossil fuels.

Narrator: Scientists warn that not all of the anticipated impacts of Arctic warming will be local. The Arctic Ocean plays a crucial role in climate systems that ultimately affect the entire globe.

Watkins: The Arctic is the engine that drives the conveyor belt of ocean waters. It drives world climate. Let us come together on this and understand the Arctic, because if we do not, we will never understand world climate.

Corell: During this century, the sea level will rise almost a meter. That doesn't sound like a lot, but if you live in Bangladesh, that is 60 percent of the country. If you live in southern Florida, it's gone; the Keys are underwater.

Barber: Global warming is all about people; the planet itself will continue, but we are the ones affected, both economically and politically.

McCain: What is the cost of climate change? It is the destruction of the ecosystem in the Arctic. It is the melting of the ice caps, which will have profound effects around the globe. We do not know all the effects on the earth's ecosystem.

Watt-Cloutier: The Arctic is the early warning for the world. What we are trying to say is that what is happening now in the Arctic will, in time, affect the rest of the world.

Narrator: Whatever the final costs, one thing is clear. Because of changes we have set in motion, the Arctic of our lore and imagination—that place of frozen vistas where few humans tread—is already history.

Thomas E. Weber is a veteran business and technology journalist. He is a former *Wall Street Journal* columnist and bureau chief; more recently, he was editor of SmartMoney.com, a personal-finance Web site. At Princeton, he was chairman of the *Daily Princetonian*. In 1997, Internet pornography was mostly causing giggles, but writing for the *Wall Street Journal* allowed him to give the topic serious treatment and stumble upon lessons that still apply today. This piece, which appeared in the *Wall Street Journal* on May 20, 1997, is a reminder of how business journalism relentlessly cuts through to the bottom line.

The X Files

When rapper Ice-T auditioned firms to design his new site on the World Wide Web, everyone wanted to charge $10,000 or more for the project. Everyone except Babenet Ltd.

Babenet, of Chatsworth, California, promised a site so compelling that Internet users would pay to see it, and it even offered to do the job free of charge if Ice-T would agree to split the earnings. The secret ingredient: X-rated pictures online. And so Ice-T's Forbidden Zone recently opened its virtual doors, zapping images of bare, undulating bodies onto the computer screen of anyone with a credit card. "This site could make $4,000 to $6,000 a day," says Ice-T's manager, Jorge Hinojosa. "The whole adult thing," he adds, "is pretty cool."

Pretty profitable, too. Cyberporn is fast becoming the envy of the Internet. While many other Web outposts are flailing, adult sites are taking in millions of dollars a month. Find a Web site that is in the black and, chances are, its business and content are distinctly blue.

That has legions of entrepreneurs rushing to cash in, from former phone-sex marketers gone digital to new-media mavens to a onetime stripper whose thriving Web site brings in so much revenue that she has given up the stage and nude photo shoots. "I'm out of the modeling business for good," says the former exotic dancer, Danni Ashe, creator of Danni's Hard Drive. "The site is all I do now."

How can X-rated fare rack up profits online when so many mainstream Web sites continue to struggle? The obvious reason: sex sells. And on the Internet, customers can view racy fare without having to slink into a sleazy bookstore or even visit the back room of the neighborhood video shop. Customers can peruse raunchy fare in the privacy of the home—or office.

But beyond sex, Internet pornographers deploy savvy tactics that mainstream sites would do well to imitate. Adult sites sharply target their marketing, placing notices in electronic discussion groups devoted to sexual topics and tastes, and running ads that pop up on the Yahoo! Internet directory whenever a user types in a search that includes the word "sex."

They also are masters of "upselling," charging for admission when most Web sites are free, then racking up extra revenue by selling accessory services. And the X-rated sites eagerly take up innovative technology that others are too timid to embrace, zapping encrypted credit-card numbers despite widespread fears of hackers and swiftly turning live video transmissions into digital peep shows.

The Internet has always trafficked in dirty pictures, but in the past year, amateur swapping has given way to commercial ventures. Nearly 900 adult-related pay and free sites on the Web are indexed at Persian Kitty, an online guide to cyberporn. The commercial sites vary in size from small outposts with just a few hundred paying members to major networks with thousands of subscribers.

One site, Amateur Hardcore, produced by WebPower Inc., of Lake Worth, Florida, ranked 16th among the Web's most frequently visited sites in a recent survey by PC Meter, a Port Washington, N.Y., company that tracks Web usage. Amateur Hardcore's ranking puts it well ahead of Web offerings from big mainstream brands like Disney and CNN. Industry revenue, pegged conservatively at $50 million last year by Forrester Research Inc., of Cambridge, Massachusetts, could grow fivefold by 2000, and even those numbers may understate the market.

All of this commerce comes despite some technological drawbacks. Internet pictures don't yet approach the clarity of magazines, film or television. Photos take awhile to appear on-screen, and video images, confined to the size of a baseball card, can be blurry. Yet customers don't seem to mind.

Any government crackdown may be unlikely, given recent federal-court rulings granting the Internet the broadest possible First Amendment protection. And for now, this market is being shaped by newcomers. Some of the biggest names in traditional pornography have only a limited presence in cyberspace.

"There are a lot of computer nerds emerging as porno kings," says Bob Guccione, publisher of *Penthouse* magazine.

When Mr. Guccione's General Media, Inc. established the premium Penthouse Live service online, it turned to a more seasoned Web publisher—23-year-old Seth Warshavsky. His company, Internet Entertainment Group, which he formed two years ago on the bankroll he earned from running a phone-sex business, is the real operator of the Penthouse page.

Mr. Warshavsky claims IEG will hit the $20 million mark in revenue this year from about 200,000 customer accounts splayed across nearly two dozen Web sites; of that amount, about 20 percent goes to partners like *Penthouse*. Short, scrubbed and apple-cheeked, Mr. Warshavsky looks hardly old enough to shave, let alone direct a sprawling adult-entertainment operation.

A Queens, New York native whose family moved to the Seattle area when he was six years old, he jumped into the phone-sex business after graduating from Bellevue High School in Bellevue, Washington, Class of '91. Soon he was processing hundreds of calls each day. In 1995, he started cruising the Internet, spotted one of the early adult sites and figured he could do better.

"People on the Internet didn't have the aggressive posture you need to market," he says.

IEG employs a staff of two dozen and leases offices in a tony downtown Seattle tower. But Mr. Warshavsky's biggest single revenue generator—an offering that has the entire adult-Web industry abuzz—springs from an operation several minutes away. There, behind a locked door at a converted warehouse a few blocks from the Kingdome, women hired by IEG cavort nude before video cameras beaming their images out onto the Web.

"This is it. This is huge," Mr. Warshavsky says. "This combines the interactivity of phone sex with the visuals of television." Known simply as "live video," it features exotic dancers in full color on the computer screens of users, who can even call on the telephone to chat with the performers in mid-gyration. Customers of IEG's live service can click their way to different "rooms." In the "health club," the performer works out on a step exerciser, sans workout togs. The images may be grainy and a little jerky, but the experience is completely private.

On a recent afternoon at IEG's studio, a performer wearing only her underwear waits to begin her shift and watches a wall of video monitors as another woman, the camera operator, works a joystick on a control panel, zooming and panning cameras on the various sets. Nearby, doorways lead to two of the rooms: the health club and the "bedroom," where another dancer, tall, thin and naked, rolls around energetically on an expansive mattress.

For Mr. Warshavsky, the best part of the show plays in glowing text on a lone computer monitor: a list of the nine customers currently paying $49.95 to watch the 30-minute show. That translates into almost $450 in revenue. The dancer's pay for the segment: $10, or $160 for an eight-hour shift. For an entire day's worth of live-video programming, IEG usually sells to about 500 customers—nearly $25,000 in daily revenue.

The live-video feature is available at all the sites IEG runs. Club Love is Mr. Warshavsky's flagship site, and E-Zine mimics the format of print magazines like _Penthouse_ or _Hustler_. AlleyKatz emphasizes hard-core sex images, while another site features gay porn. Coming soon: Mistress X, with a domination theme.

Despite their different names, nearly all IEG sites follow a common formula. First-time visitors see a splashy front page beckoning them to click their way into the site (but only if they are 18 or older, the pitch warns). Visitors who wander into a free "guests" area see a few freebie photos and a description of the offerings.

Then comes a pitch to sign up for a membership. Monthly dues for Club Love are $9.95. "Hardcore photo archives . . . the world's most extensive photo search engine . . . exotic shows," the site promises. Joining takes a minute.

Would-be members simply type in their name, address, telephone number, electronic-mail address and birth date, then punch in a credit-card number. IEG receives the credit-card information in a scrambled format, then instantly verifies it. Once signed up, users are automatically billed each month unless they cancel their membership.

What the new member has really purchased is the opportunity to spend more money. This is the art of the upsell. A Club Love customer quickly encounters pitches for merchandise (massage lotion, $6.95); taped "bedtime stories" played back through computer speakers (99 cents a minute); pay-per-view movies (now showing for $4.95: *The Cable Girl*); personal ads ($4.95 for each day of access); and online games (Strip Blackjack for $7.95 a day—win a hand and an article of clothing disappears from the photo of your "opponent").

The typical member spends nearly double the minimum $9.95-a-month fee. These extras generate about 30 percent of IEG's revenue, and live video provides another 40 percent; membership fees account for the remainder.

To build all of IEG's Web offerings, Mr. Warshavsky and a partner have invested a small fortune: $3 million for computers, phone equipment, software, the video studios and hundreds of X-rated photos for use and reuse at the various sites. (Though big players like IEG commission their own photo shoots, some smaller sites flagrantly violate copyright laws, ripping off content from printed porno magazines and scanning the pictures into their Web pages.)

But Mr. Warshavsky and other operators say the budding entrepreneur can get started for as little as $20 a month. Put up a simple Web page through a consumer online account and create an electronic "link" to an existing IEG site. When a customer visits via that personal page, its owner will get a third of the revenue.

"Virtually anyone can put up a Web page, and virtually anyone can promote one," says Steve Becker, a consultant to phone-sex firms and other 900-number ventures.

At Albamar, Inc., in New York, partners Madeleine Altmann and Steffani Martin launched their live-video site, Babes4U.com, for $200,000, double what they had initially hoped to spend. Yet after eight months, Albamar already is showing a profit, the two owners say. Break-even "is about a hundred guys a night. And that ain't much," says Ms. Martin, a former adult-film distributor.

Yet as compelling as the live video seems, most mainstream Web sites haven't yet chosen to offer it, in part because the moving images remain fuzzy and choppy. Adult sites are almost the only ones jumping on the new technology. So while IEG and Albamar lure Web surfers with the promise of full-color moving pictures, America Online, Inc. and other big mainstream nonporn services continue to offer live celebrity appearances that confine stars to tediously typing out messages that appear as text on users' screens. No pictures, no sound, no video.

"The adult firms are simply more willing to try new technologies," says Marc H. Bell of Bell Technology Group Ltd., a New York firm that provides Internet services to businesses. His mainstream clients include MSNBC, the Web site jointly run by Microsoft Corp. and General Electric Co.'s NBC network, but when he wants to recommend something new, "we go to the 'adult' people first." His latest project: a Web video site for *Penthouse* that will mimic cable television, piping different channels of adult and mainstream video over the Internet.

Without live video and other bells and whistles, the fledgling pornographer can launch a basic membership site for less than $10,000, including computers, software, phone gear and photos.

Danni Ashe, the former stripper and soft-core video actress, started Danni's Hard Drive with a do-it-yourself approach. She spent $8,000 for two computers, a scanner and some networking equipment, plus $1,400 for freelance programmers. But before long, Ms. Ashe scrapped the programmers, bought a few books on Hypertext Markup Language, the computer language used to build Web pages, and started doing the work herself.

Ms. Ashe, 27, originally perceived Danni's Hard Drive as an extension of her fan club, the marketing apparatus by which many prominent dancers promote their videos, autographed photos and other merchandise. She didn't charge for access, instead posting messages to various discussion groups and waiting for users to click in and buy something. It worked.

"For years I just ran my fan club part time out of the house, and I made $1,500 a month," Ms. Ashe says. "I went on the Web, and it went immediately to $10,000 to $15,000." That prompted her to add Danni's HotBox, a premium membership service giving users access to a library of nude photos and interviews with nude models for $9.95 a month.

Now the pay site boasts 17,000 members, putting Ms. Ashe on pace for more than $2 million in revenue this year, she says. Of that, 30 percent comes from outside the United States. Ms. Ashe says the site is profitable but won't reveal specifics. Judging from the customer e-mail she receives, she believes she is tapping a new market. "I think a lot of these guys," she says, "have never even bought an adult magazine."

Gilbert M. Gaul was a reporter for thirty-five years, including at the *Washington Post* and *Philadelphia Inquirer*. He won Pulitzer Prizes in 1979 and 1990 and has been a Pulitzer finalist on four other occasions. He is currently writing books and is a senior contributor to *Kaiser Health News*. A longer version of this story, the first of a two-part series, appeared in the *Washington Post* on November 30, 2009.

Internet Gambling

Whenever Todd Witteles signed on to an Internet poker site, the first thing he did was look around for inexperienced players. One day in August 2007, the Las Vegas poker pro thought he had found an easy mark on AbsolutePoker .com. A newcomer using the name "Greycat" was making unusually big bets off weak hands. "He seemed like a bad player who had just been getting incredibly lucky," Witteles recalled. "When you see someone like Greycat, you stop everything you're doing to play." But in a series of one-on-one games, Witteles quickly found himself down $15,000. Worse, Greycat began taunting him. Soon, some of Witteles's online poker friends began wondering publicly whether Greycat was cheating. It was almost as though he could see Witteles's hole cards. It turned out that was exactly what Greycat was doing. After months of pressure from a small group of players who took it upon themselves to investigate the claims, AbsolutePoker was forced to admit that a cheater had cracked its software, and it refunded $1.6 million to Witteles and dozens of other players.

It appeared to be a huge victory for the players and the self-policing nature of the Internet. Yet just weeks later, rumors of a new scandal rocked the world of online poker, this time at AbsolutePoker's sister site, UltimateBet.com. The stakes were dramatically higher: more than $20 million cheated from players over four years. The alleged culprits included a former world poker champion and UltimateBet employees who had hacked into the site.

Even as Internet gambling grows in popularity and profits, with millions of players and billions of bets, the two biggest cheating scandals in online gambling are raising fresh questions about the honesty and security of a freewheeling industry that operates outside of U.S. law. Unlike brick-and-mortar casinos, which undergo rigorous security checks, many Internet gambling sites operate in a shadowy world of little regulation and even less enforcement, a joint investigation by the *Washington Post* and CBS's *60 Minutes* has found. Dozens of these sites are located in countries with no reporting requirements. The licensing agencies there essentially operate as pay-as-you-go boutiques, generating millions of dollars in fees while showing little interest in policing rogue sites. As it has given birth to Amazon.com, eBay and scores of other 21st-century businesses, the Internet has also spawned its own gambling boom, with estimated revenue more than tripling over five years, to $18 billion annually, including about $4 billion from virtual poker.

Millions of the bets originate in the United States, where online poker and gambling sites are banned, forcing players to reach out across the Internet like modern-day bootleggers. Yet players have little way of knowing who is watching their bets or where their money is going. Often, owners hide behind multiple layers of limited partnerships, making it difficult to determine who controls the sites or to lodge complaints about cheating. In the AbsolutePoker and UltimateBet cheating scandals, players decided to investigate the matter themselves after managers and regulators did not respond to their complaints. "No one would listen to us," said Serge Ravitch, a 28-year-old lawyer turned poker pro who played a key detective role.

AbsolutePoker and UltimateBet operate out of a shopping mall in Costa Rica, run their games on computer servers housed on an Indian reservation near Montreal, and are licensed by a Mohawk tribe that has no background in casino gambling and does not answer to federal or provincial regulators. Joseph Tokwiro Norton, who owns both Web sites, is the former grand chief of the Mohawk tribe of Kahnawake, which collects millions in fees each year by licensing Internet gambling companies and hosting the Web sites on servers inside a high-tech building converted from a mattress factory.

AbsolutePoker's origins are sketchy. Records and interviews point to a poker aficionado named Scott Tom, who attended the University of Montana in the late 1990s. After graduating, Tom and several partners headed to Costa Rica and started the business.

A number of online gambling sites already existed. But it was not until a few years later that Internet poker exploded. The impetus was a former Tennessee accountant and aptly named player, Chris Moneymaker. In 2003, Moneymaker came from nowhere to win the main event at the World Series of Poker in Las Vegas. His $2.5 million victory was televised on ESPN and is widely credited with igniting a worldwide surge. "When I am being glib, I refer to it as the Moneymaker effect," said David G. Schwartz, director of the Center for Gaming Research at the University of Nevada at Las Vegas.

Soon, scores of sites began popping up in Antigua, Costa Rica, Malta, the Isle of Man and other exotic locations. The Kahnawake alone license 450 sites run by 60 permit holders. By 2007, Internet gambling sites had revenues of $18.4 billion, up from $5.9 billion in 2003, according to Christiansen Capital Advisors, a New York firm that tracks online gambling. Thousands of those players found their way to AbsolutePoker, which boasts on its Web site that it has handled more than 300 million hands since it started accepting bets and that, at its peak, accounted for as much as 5 percent of the multibillion-dollar online-poker market. "It was probably pulling in between $150,000 and $250,000 a day," estimated Bobby Mamudi of the Gaming Intelligence Group, which tracks worldwide gambling issues from England. Hundreds of customer-service employees worked at its office in a mall in San Jose, Costa Rica, and at a smaller office in Panama.

Generally, Internet poker is divided into two types of games: cash games, in which winners collect the money on the table, just as in a live casino game, and tournaments, in which players put up an entry fee and the winning pots are divided based on play. A key difference is that games are played on computers, not face to face. Players cannot see one another to gauge expressions or tics. The online style of play is also faster and more aggressive than that of live games. Some players may have four or five games going at once. Poker sites use a variety of payment methods, including prepaid debit cards, electronic transfers and bank wires. In addition to tournament fees, Internet poker sites make money from advertising and by taking a small percentage of the pot, called a rake. The rake can be as little as pennies but adds up over millions of pots, industry analysts say.

One of the regulars at AbsolutePoker was Witteles, a former computer scientist whose screen name is "Dan Druff." At 36, he jokes that he is often the oldest player in Internet games. "It's a very young crowd," he said. "Most of them are in their early 20s."

Witteles said he plays almost exclusively in cash games. When he squared off against Greycat in 2007, it was to play Texas hold 'em, currently the most popular poker game, in which bluffing is critical. "So if the other guy can see your cards," Witteles said, "it's a real disaster. I quickly got slammed for $6,000."

Witteles waited for Greycat's luck to run out. But he continued to make one unlikely winning bet after another. Witteles's losses mounted to $15,000. Although frustrated, he didn't yet suspect cheating. And had Greycat not taunted him—ridiculing his skills in the game's instant-message box—Witteles said he might have gone undetected. "There was a real arrogance and vindictiveness to the thing," he said.

It is not uncommon in Internet poker for other players to follow the games. Some started to post comments on a popular poker forum about Greycat's improbable winning streak and several other suspicious accounts on Absolute-Poker. Witteles wondered whether Greycat somehow had access to a "super-user" account, which would allow him to use the site's software to spy on his cards. But when he complained to AbsolutePoker, Witteles said, "I got a different story every time."

A few weeks later, in September 2007, a 21-year-old player named Marco Johnson paid $1,000 to enter a tournament sponsored by AbsolutePoker. Johnson, who uses the screen name "Crazy Marco," reached the final against a player called "Potripper." They played 20 hands, and Potripper won them all, collecting $10,000. At first, Johnson shrugged off the loss. But others watching the final games online insisted that he, too, had been cheated. Johnson requested his hand histories for the games. Poker sites generally promise to keep players' archives for as many as five years. A few days later, Johnson received a confusing Microsoft Excel spreadsheet containing 65,000 lines. At first, he set it aside.

While players heatedly debated Potripper's play in poker forums, the management at AbsolutePoker released the first of several statements denying the cheating allegations. "While we are continuing with our investigation, we have yet to find any evidence of wrong doing," the first statement said. "A super-user account does not exist in our software," stated the second. "Absolute Poker remains a 100% secure place to play."

Players continued to attack AbsolutePoker in online forums, complaining that they could not get answers to their questions or tell who owned the site. A few frustrated players decided it was time to start their own investigation.

Although players can be fiercely competitive during a match, it is not unusual for them to share information afterward. "Most of the top players know one another," said Ravitch, who plays on his laptop from his home in Queens. "If I don't know someone in the seat next to me, chances are I know his friends." Ravitch is a graduate of the University of Michigan Law School who realized he enjoyed playing poker more than filing legal briefs. "Sunday is my work day," he said. "That's when all the big tournaments are." Each week, Ravitch said, he averages about 20 hours of play while spending an additional 10 hours studying a large database of hand histories he has compiled, searching for competitors' tendencies. "Poker has become mathematically much more sophisticated," he said. Among the successful participants, he added, "there are no dumb players."

Ravitch offered to help analyze the suspect hand histories. He was joined by Nat Arem, a former auditor in the Philadelphia office of the consulting firm Deloitte & Touche. Like Ravitch, the 26-year-old Arem is good at math and with computers. In 2006, he attended Emory Law School in Atlanta for a semester but dropped out after selling a software program that players use to track the results of poker tournaments. He now lives in Costa Rica, where he develops poker-related businesses.

In the fall of 2007, Arem and Ravitch obtained copies of Marco Johnson's spreadsheet file and started analyzing the data. Arem wrote a software program to decode the information. Joined by a handful of other poker detectives, they quickly identified improbable betting patterns for Potripper and several other suspect accounts. The patterns suggested that the players with improbable win rates could somehow see their opponents' facedown, or hole, cards. "Obviously, if you can see your opponents' hole cards, you have a huge advantage," Ravitch said. "That helped to explain how the suspect accounts never seemed to lose."

One of the first things the poker detectives noticed was that Potripper was playing exclusively in "nosebleed stakes," games with the biggest pots. "He got caught because it was easy to catch," Ravitch said. "There are only a handful of other players playing those stakes, and everyone knows one another." Instead of losing a few hands to deflect attention, Potripper continued to win every time. "It would have been so easy if he had just lost a few hands. No one would have ever suspected a thing," Ravitch said.

Who was the cheater? By mid-October 2007, the poker detectives were fo-
cusing on an employee at AbsolutePoker's Costa Rica office. They posted their
findings online, setting off a new wave of charges and increasing pressure on
AbsolutePoker's management and the Kahnawake Gaming Commission to address the cheating. Shortly thereafter, the commission announced that it had
hired Gaming Associates, a small Australian computer-security firm, to audit
the poker site's software. Two days later, AbsolutePoker released an e-mail acknowledging that it had identified "an internal security breach that compro-
mised our systems for a limited period of time." It added: "The cause of the
breach has been determined and completely resolved."

The company's statement did not detail how the breach occurred, how many
players were cheated or how the cheater was able to spy on cards without being
noticed.

Unbeknown to the players, AbsolutePoker had already cut a secret deal
with the cheater, whom it characterized as a "consultant with managerial responsibilities." The company agreed not to release his name in return for a "full
and detailed explanation" of how he cheated, according to company officials
and other interviews. AbsolutePoker also agreed not to sue the cheater or turn
him over to Costa Rican authorities, company officials told the *Post*.

"Of course we considered going to the police, but we decided that it was in
the best interest of our cheated players and of AP to get the perpetrator to tell
us how the cheating was done," company officials wrote in response to questions from the *Post*. "We also recognized that prosecutions for white collar
crimes in Costa Rica can be time-consuming and sometimes unsuccessful."
(The name of the alleged cheater has circulated widely among poker players on
the Internet. The *Post* is not publishing his name because even though he purportedly confessed to AbsolutePoker, the company did not release its records
and would not discuss the matter. The alleged cheater declined requests to be
interviewed.)

Witteles and other players said they were appalled by AbsolutePoker's decision not to seek prosecution of the cheater. "Yeah, we were paid back," he said.
"But they made absolutely no attempt to bring any of the people to justice. If
someone stole that amount of money from a casino, they would be thrown in
jail." AbsolutePoker said it fired the cheater on October 20, 2007, the day before it started sending $1.6 million in refunds to the cheated players.

In January 2008, the Kahnawake Gaming Commission released a four-page
report on the AbsolutePoker scandal. It said a single cheater using several
screen names had taken advantage of a flaw in the software to spy on players'
cards during a six-week period starting in August 2007. It fined Norton's firm
$500,000. But it also declined to name the cheater, contending that there
"would be no material benefit to the affected players." "I don't know about
that," said Frank Catania, the former New Jersey gambling official who helped
the Kahnawake write their Internet gambling regulations, and who was hired

by the commission last summer to investigate Norton and his poker sites. "Maybe what they should have done is named the person."

A day after the Kahnawake commission released its report about Absolute-Poker, managers at UltimateBet were alerted to new allegations of cheating involving a player using the screen name "NioNio." One of those who had played against NioNio was David Paredes, 29, a Harvard graduate and lawyer turned hedge-fund employee. As a childhood math whiz, Paredes had been good enough at chess to travel to national tournaments. In high school, he and his friends played poker for as much as $100 a game. During breaks from law school at New York University, he played at the Foxwoods Resort Casino in Connecticut and in the city's network of underground clubs.

Paredes started playing online around 2005. "I made money almost from the start," he said. Over time, he said, he used his winnings to pay off his law school bill, rent a Manhattan apartment and pay private tuition for a high school student he mentors. In July 2007, Paredes lost $70,000 to NioNio in a series of games. NioNio had played recklessly, Paredes recalled, making one improbable bet after another, yet winning most hands. Paredes said he did not suspect cheating until he discussed his hands with another player who also had lost to NioNio. They did a statistical analysis of hand histories, and what they found shocked them: during one brief stretch, NioNio had managed to win $300,000 while rarely losing. Another poker detective calculated that his win rate was about equal to winning the Powerball jackpot three days in a row. Moreover, it appeared that NioNio was not the only unusually lucky player. Their investigation turned up seven other suspicious accounts that had won a total of $1.5 million on UltimateBet. Later, UltimateBet officials determined that the cheaters had used as many as 88 screen names to avoid detection. It was as though the cheaters were playing against a "bunch of blind men," Catania recalled. "I mean . . . you're the only one that can see. Everyone else is blind." In news releases, UltimateBet said that former employees had secretly installed a back door in the software, allowing them to spy on players' cards.

To date, UltimateBet has issued $6.1 million in refunds and has promised to reimburse players an additional $15 million, at which point it is likely to lose its license or be sold. The gaming commission fined UltimateBet $1.5 million "for its failure to implement and enforce measures to prohibit and detect fraudulent activities."

The Kahnawake now say they operate one of the most secure Internet gambling operations in the world, with "cutting-edge security systems that make us the safest site in the industry." But Frank Catania does not expect cheating to stop: "I'm sure there are people out there right now figuring out, let's say, 'Here's a way we can do it again.'"

Steve Kroft, Ira Rosen, and Sumi Aggarwal of *60 Minutes*, along with special correspondent Gary Wise, contributed to this report.

Charles Lewis founded and for fifteen years directed the Center for Public Integrity, where he coauthored five books. A former producer at *60 Minutes*, he is now a professor at American University and founding executive editor of the Investigative Reporting Workshop in Washington, D.C. This article appeared in the Spring 2008 issue of the *Nieman Reports*.

Seeking New Ways to Nurture the Capacity to Report

> [You journalists live] in what we call the reality-based community. [But] that's not the way the world really works anymore. . . . When we act, we create our own reality. . . . We're history's actors . . . and you, all of you, will be left to just study what we do.
>
> —Unidentified senior advisor to President George W. Bush, as quoted by Ron Suskind in the *New York Times Magazine*, October 17, 2004.

Controlling information and public perceptions is hardly a new phenomenon; a powerful few have been doing this literally for centuries. But the global reverberations and almost immediate human impact of decisions made by those now in power are new. And when the truth is deliberately, effectively obscured by secrecy, lies and public posturing, it distorts the government decision-making process, mutes popular dissent and sometimes fatally delays the inevitable, cold dawn of logic, reason and reckoning so fundamental to an open democracy. In an open, pluralistic society, in a democracy, we expect that journalists will safeguard the broad public interest and ultimately provide truth and accountability to citizens. But unfortunately, in this 24/7 "warp speed" information age, the myriad and imaginative ways in which to propagate a palatable but false reality have substantially increased in recent decades, far outpacing the ability of reporters and other independent truth-tellers to hold up those lies to the harsh light of day.

Each successive White House occupant has been more adept at controlling the message of his administration, technologically but also in terms of additional public relations money, personnel and "outreach." And the intricacies of the Bush White House communications efforts, specifically the extent, substance and sophistication of its "on message" coordination and internal discipline, remain substantially murky, thanks in no small part to the apparent and possibly illegal destruction of millions of White House e-mails. We do know that, as *Newsday* reported, the Bush administration in its first term hired an additional 376 public affairs officials to package information, at an annual cost of $50 million. And, separately, $254 million was spent on "faux news" contracts, nearly double what the Clinton administration had spent during the preceding four years. Positive video news releases were sent out to hundreds of commercial TV stations and viewed by millions of Americans, often with no on-air identification or disclosure. Government Accountability Office comptroller general David Walker criticized the practice as "illegal propaganda," and the Federal Communications Commission has recently begun issuing fines to broadcasters who have aired such messages without disclosure.

Unfortunately, the problem of finding verities instead of verisimilitudes beneath the varnish has been exacerbated in recent years throughout America because there are, quite simply, fewer varnish removers—investigative reporters—actually devoted daily to monitoring those in power. Of course we all know too well that the meticulous information gathering and editorial quality control essential for serious, high-quality news require time and money—finite resources that many news organizations are increasingly unable or unwilling to expend.

Indeed, in recent years nearly all of our media corporations have been reducing their commitment to journalism, reducing their editorial budgets, early "retiring" thousands of reporters and editors from their newsrooms in order to keep their annual profit margins high and their investors happy, harvesting their investments from a "mature" industry. The net result of this hollowing-out process: there are fewer people today to report, write and edit original news stories about our infinitely more complex, dynamic world. While more and more newspapers transform themselves into "print-Web hybrids," as columnist Robert Kuttner and others have written, online advertising revenue must increase considerably if newsrooms are going to be able to remain near their current editorial payroll levels. That prospect is uncertain at best, and layoffs in the immediate years ahead seem likely. International reporting and investigative reporting, always time-consuming and expensive, increasingly have come to be regarded by management as high-risk, high-maintenance, high-priced impracticalities.

The global reach of the new technologies; the versatility, range and depth of what is possible journalistically because of multimedia convergences, computer-assisted reporting and other technical advances; the ease and relative affordability of high-speed communications in this information age, are all terrifically exciting and historically unprecedented. And the quality of some of the best reporting and writing breaks new ground with each passing year. What gnaws is the realization that there ought to be more, much more, of this unprecedented quality of journalism. Thus far, however, most of the emerging online commercial media ventures are noticeably light when it comes to their commitment or their capacity to publish original reporting. The highly successful Web search engines, such as Google or Yahoo! merely aggregate, automate and repackage other people's work. While the world's blogs continue to proliferate and will develop further as a content form before our eyes, hardly any of them at present are solely devoted to responsible reporting and fact-based journalism. Perhaps new, stand-alone, advertising-supported, profitable, original news-gathering and storytelling venues—beyond password-protected, subscription-based, specialized niche publishing—will robustly evolve in the digital age, but that hasn't really happened yet.

If, like an endangered species, serious, independent, high-impact, "truth to power" national reporting will be seen only rarely, will this kind of vital, no-holds-barred truth telling become a thing of the past, like the dodo bird? No, but what is needed are new, sustainable economic models for in-depth news and a new, much greater ownership and management commitment to publishing it "without fear or favor."

In State of the News Media 2004, a survey (by the Project for Excellence in Journalism) of 547 journalists and news-media executives, 66 percent felt that profit pressures were hurting national coverage—up 25 percent since the question was first asked, in 1995. As the world is becoming infinitely more complex, 86 percent of national journalists whose newsrooms have undergone staff reductions believe the news media is "paying too little attention to complex stories." It is deeper than just numbers, though.

My particular interest has been very simple since 1977, when I began working as an off-air investigative reporter, hired by ABC News in Washington in the wake of the Watergate scandal, later as a producer at 60 Minutes, and for 15 years as the founder and executive director of the Center for Public Integrity. All I have wanted to do is to find an unfettered place to investigate and expose abuses of power. I became frustrated in the 1980s and quit commercial journalism to start a nonprofit investigative reporting organization. Too often, investigative reporting did not seem to be particularly valued at the national level, regardless of media form. Occasionally, I had seen investigative-reporter friends' and colleagues' stories unjustifiably resisted, reduced or rebuffed by their respective news organizations. National news organizations often seemed to report only reactively the various systemic abuses of power, trust and the law in Washington—from the Iran-Contra scandal to the Housing and Urban Development scandal to the Defense Department's procurement prosecutions, from the savings-and-loan disaster to the "Keating Five" influence scandal to the first resignation of a House Speaker since 1800.

In Washington, there was very little aggressive investigative journalism about these or other subjects and, equally galling to me, smug denial by the incurious national press corps despite its underwhelming, lackluster pursuit of these major instances of political influence and corruption. Regarding the decision by George W. Bush and his administration to initiate a preventive war in Iraq in March 2003, it was unfortunately not particularly surprising that most national reporters and their news organizations were figuratively embedded in official propaganda and misleading statements. There were a few notable exceptions in Washington to this pattern, certainly, such as the fine independent reporting by the Knight Ridder bureau. Some major news organizations have publicly eaten crow, acknowledging without necessarily apologizing that their coverage was perhaps not sufficiently critical of government pronouncements and information.

Such uncharacteristic humility does not ameliorate the tragic consequences of an unnecessary war and the tens of thousands of slain or wounded soldiers and innocent civilians, including women and children. Could such a controversial war of choice have been prevented if the public had been better informed about the specious official statements, faulty logic and breathtaking manipulations of public opinion and governmental decision-making processes? On the five-year anniversary of the invasion of Iraq, that might be too searing a question to ask, but it nonetheless will likely haunt our profession for years to come.

All of this underscores the fundamental necessity of serious journalism to any functioning democracy predicated upon self-government of, by and for the people; without an independent news media, there is no credibly informed citizenry. But what does it say about the current state of the commercial news media that it took a nonprofit investigative-reporting organization to research and post online all of the Iraq and Afghanistan contracts and the windfalls of war to the penny, company by company, first revealing Halliburton's bonanza? Why did it take that same nonprofit organization to analyze all of the 935 false statements made by the president and seven of his top officials over two years about the supposedly imminent threat posed by Saddam Hussein's Iraq, in a 380,000-word, searchable, online public and private Iraq War chronology? It was the Center for Public Integrity that posted those massive reports in 2003 and 2008.

Why in the Philippines was the corruption of the president, spending tens of millions of dollars to build lavish mansions for his mistresses, uncovered and documented by a nonprofit investigative reporting organization, the Philippine Center for Investigative Journalism, resulting in his removal from office? There are many nonprofit organizations committed to investigative reporting in the United States and in the world, none older than the Center for Investigative Reporting, begun in California in 1977, and none newer than ProPublica, which just emerged in January 2008, with former *Wall Street Journal* managing editor Paul Steiger as its president and editor in chief. All are limited in various ways, from the caliber or number of experienced personnel to the quality and frequency of their publications or documentaries, to their ability to fully utilize the exciting new technologies and means of distribution.

The net result is that important subjects desperately requiring responsible investigation and public education simply go unaddressed. When that happens, the public is not as well informed as it could be; important truths do not emerge in a timely, relevant fashion or at all; and accountability of those in power, essential to any democracy, does not occur. These trends are universal, irrespective of geography, climate or the country's economic or democratic condition.

Yet amidst the current, deteriorating state of original, investigative and otherwise independent journalism in America, new, very energizing forces are at play. There are talented and highly motivated journalists, mindful of the stakes involved; entrepreneurial nonprofit and for-profit leaders with vision, a commitment to community and financial wherewithal; new media platforms and technologies revolutionizing the means and cost of production; and, every day, more and more signs of what is possible journalistically, particularly with the new social-networking connectivity of the Web and related, constantly improving technologies.

All of this has set the stage for the recent emergence of some new hybrid entities to emerge, such as the cluster relationships between university-based centers and major commercial news organizations committed to high-quality journalism that have occurred at the University of California (Berkeley), at Brandeis University and at Columbia University. The possibilities represented by these new approaches explain why—working closely with veteran reporter, editor and American University journalism division director Wendell Cochran and the dean of the School of Communication, Larry Kirkman—I have decided to start and lead, as executive editor, an exciting new enterprise, the Investigative Reporting Workshop at American University in Washington, D.C. In addition to doing significant, original, national and international investigative reporting for multimedia publication or broadcast, the workshop will also serve as a laboratory incubator to develop new models for conducting and delivering investigative journalism. We will also partner with other nonprofit institutions or with investigative journalists.

What both journalism and democracy need right now are new economic models—fit to meet the full range of our contemporary challenge—to support the work associated with in-depth multimedia news. These models will succeed if they can nurture a more hospitable milieu for investigation and exposure of abuses of power and provide real-time truth and accountability to citizens. Because those in power should never be able to create their own false reality, or to even think it is possible.

Roberta Oster Sachs, an Emmy Award–winning network news and documentary producer, worked for two decades at ABC, CBS, and NBC News. She reported on the impact of the Taliban on Afghan women, the September 11 terrorist attacks, famine in Ethiopia, public education, poverty, racism, and gender inequality. She was awarded a John S. Knight Fellowship for Professional Journalists at Stanford University. Oster Sachs also taught journalism at Tufts University, where she directed the Media and Public Service Program, and at the Columbia University Graduate School of Journalism. She is now associate dean for external relations at the University of Richmond School of Law. Her profile of Sarah McClendon appeared in the *Columbia Journalism Review* (May–June 2003). Her tribute to Ed Bradley was published in the *Richmond Times-Dispatch* on November 11, 2006.

Role Model: Sarah McClendon

Her booming voice—shouting "Mr. President! Mr. President!"—is a sound White House reporters who worked with Sarah McClendon over the fifty-seven years she was there are unlikely to forget. What will also be remembered is how, with every question, she embodied the very idea of a free press in a democracy. When a Texas battle-ax in comfortable shoes, armed only with her personality and a press pass, can shout down presidents on behalf of her readers, something is right. McClendon never forgot whom she was working for.

Nor did many of the young women she trained as interns. I was one of them. I remember her shaking her finger in my face, and barking in her East Texas drawl, "Don't be afraid to ask the president a question. It's his job to answer your questions, and your responsibility to ask them." The citizens, she would say, including veterans, minorities, welfare mothers, and children, have a right to know what their government is doing.

Back in 1981, I was a Georgetown University senior struggling to keep up with a seventy-one-year-old McClendon, who raced around town in a broken-down Toyota and never missed a news event or a cocktail party where she could work her sources. She was the only full-time employee in her one-person news bureau, the McClendon News Service. Sarah often worked past midnight, pounding out stories that were syndicated to newspapers across the country. She wrote stories about real people struggling with real issues and problems, from veterans' and women's rights to racism and unemployment. She often got results.

For me, this was a kind of journalistic boot camp. A typical day began with a phone call from the boss at 6:30 a.m. with marching orders. Basically, I was to cover nearly every news event in town, from a briefing in an obscure office of the Agriculture Department to a presidential press conference. Long before mentors were in fashion, McClendon fashioned herself as mine. "Women can make a difference, and you must use your education to be a voice for the little people," she used to say. "The men don't want us in here, so we're just going to have to push our way in.".

When she was five, Sarah's mother would take her to women's suffrage rallies; she taught her daughter, the youngest of nine children, to stand up on the kitchen table and belt out suffragette speeches. The family was poor, but one of Sarah's sisters scraped together the tuition for Sarah to attend Tyler Junior College. She went on to get a journalism degree from the University of Missouri. Sarah married and joined the Women's Army Corps, serving as a public-relations lieutenant during World War II. Her husband abandoned his pregnant wife, and she was honorably discharged when her daughter, Sally, was born. McClendon then headed to Washington as a single mother, and in 1946, she started the McClendon News Service. She often took her daughter to work—at the White House, at the Capitol, even to political conventions.

I recall Sarah saying she was shy when she covered her first president, Franklin Delano Roosevelt, but soon she realized she had to shout questions to be heard. The press corps was nearly all male, and some colleagues didn't take her seriously. But that didn't stop her. McClendon broke new ground at many press conferences; in 1974, she asked President Nixon a question the mainstream press was ignoring about delays in processing tuition checks for Vietnam veterans. The president fixed the problem immediately and publicly thanked Sarah.

I am a student again now, but when I was teaching journalism at Columbia, I honored Sarah by starting every class I taught with a few McClendon principles in hopes that my students would come to believe that they wouldn't have to be part of the pack, that they could ask questions that might be unpopular, or unsexy, or, good heavens, embarrassing to the administration. I recall one student who said she couldn't get her idea across in an all-male editorial board meeting. It was Sarah's voice I heard inside of me telling this frightened young woman to fight for her story.

At ninety-two, McClendon was still working on her weekly column in a nursing home just weeks before she died, in January. Her tenacity, commitment to her readers, and fearlessness inspired me to become a journalist and, I expect, other women as well. Women journalists know they can make a difference, and we're a chorus now. When I read Jill Abramson or watch Andrea Mitchell or Christiane Amanpour, or take in the solid journalism of any number of less famous but equally dedicated women, I think of Sarah McClendon shouting to be heard.

Remembering a Friend: Ed Bradley Was a Gift to Journalism

This week we lost one of the great journalists of our time. A brilliant man with a velvet voice and a kind heart, Ed Bradley was one of my mentors when I was a young producer at CBS News. Bradley was a voice for human rights, for ethics in journalism, and for using media for positive social change.

In his full but too-short life, Bradley was a schoolteacher, radio DJ, war correspondent wounded in Cambodia, CBS's first African American White House correspondent, and a gourmet chef who loved music, skiing, and life. Most of all, he loved a good story.

I recall when Bradley and I went on the road with B. B. King in Florida, and one of the concert stops was a prison where King's daughter Patty was incarcerated for drug trafficking. King told Bradley, "I have 15 children . . . This is the first time I ever did a concert with a family member in trouble." In front of Patty, Bradley asked, "What kind of father do you think you were?" King shook his head and answered, "Not the best. Not the best. I love my family. I love my children. I wish I could have been a better father." Bradley stroked his close-cropped beard and listened intently for more.

King later told me that he could not have shared that story with any other reporter, but he trusted Bradley and knew he understood the pain of the blues. "King of the Road" aired in 1993 on CBS's *Street Stories*, a newsmagazine that Bradley helped create. *Street Stories* was pure Bradley. Ahead of its time, the program was hip, raw, and real—an edgier alternative to the staid *60 Minutes*, where Bradley continued to be a reporter. B. B. King's story won one of the 19 Emmy Awards that sit on a cluttered bookshelf in Bradley's office at CBS in New York.

Traveling with Bradley was the hard-news equivalent of traveling with a rock star. I remember one time I went to meet him at an airport gate. He was swamped by a group of women ranging in age from 18 to 80—Bradley groupies desperate for a chat, a snapshot, or just a handshake. Flashing his signature grin, eyes twinkling, Bradley said he wished he had more time but he was there on business, and made a quick but courteous exit. As we headed to the car, he leaned over to whisper, "What they don't know is, I'm really very shy."

Perhaps it was that singular blend of shyness and showmanship that made Bradley one of the best in the business, a man of extraordinary compassion, depth, and dignity. Bradley skillfully wielded a tool most reporters rarely employ—silence. He would ask a question and then sit and wait for an answer, and after the answer, he continued to wait, compelling people to dig deeper, to reach, and to be honest.

Bradley inspired me to teach young people to use media for positive social change. When I taught a documentary course at Tufts University, I showed clips of Bradley's work to teach aspiring journalists how to ask probing questions and to listen carefully. We analyzed Bradley's stories on the effects of nuclear testing, Chinese forced-labor camps, and the controversy between the parents of a deaf child and a deaf association.

Viewers know Bradley's hard-hitting journalism. I saw his softer side. When the editor of the B. B. King story, my friend Lisa Orlando, was battling cancer,

Bradley raced out of a busy newsroom to come to a birthday party in her honor. He sat in the middle of a group of 12 women who were in tears, and cried along with us. When Lisa saw Bradley recently, he remarked, "We are both survivors." That was optimistic Ed. Even then leukemia was consuming him.

Ed Bradley was a gift to the profession of journalism, to my young students, to my dear friend Lisa, and to me. I hope that the next generation of reporters will learn to listen as he did.

Ralph J. Begleiter teaches journalism and political science at the University of Delaware after working more than thirty years as a broadcast journalist. From 1981 to 1999, he was CNN's world affairs correspondent, a job that took him to ninety-five countries. During that time, the news media became a transnational force in politics and public opinion. In this text, he reflects upon the changing role of reporters in an arena of technology and globalization. It is an excerpt from a longer article that appeared in the *Brown University Journal of World Affairs* (Winter 2002), more than a year before the start of the war in Iraq in March 2003.

Whose Media Are We?

You are the ranking naval officer aboard the U.S.S. *Enterprise*. Your sailors and aviators are actively engaged in the undeclared "war on terrorism." Bombing runs and surveillance flights are taking off hourly from the decks. At the request of the Pentagon, you already have on board a media "pool" of journalists and photographers representing ABC, NBC, CBS, CNN, the *New York Times*, the *Washington Post*, the Associated Press and *People* magazine. Also aboard are journalists from Reuters and the BBC, two of Britain's most reputable news organizations. You have been told these are "responsible" journalists, carefully selected by their organizations and vetted by the Pentagon for this extraordinary duty during military action.

The media pool is one of many scattered around the Afghanistan theater, dispatched pursuant to an agreement reached between the news organizations and the Pentagon after the 1991 Gulf War. These journalists have agreed to guidelines governing their safety and the flow of information to and from the *Enterprise*.

A senior officer approaches you with a fresh message from Washington. It is a request that you accept another group of journalists in your media pool. The message says it's up to you; the Pentagon will support your decision. The applicant reporter and crew are from al-Jazeera, the Arabic-language all-news network operating out of Qatar. It is the same network that, on the first day of U.S. bombing of Afghanistan, received and aired a lengthy videotape from Osama bin Laden, Washington's primary target since the attacks on the World Trade Center and the Pentagon.

Do you welcome the al-Jazeera team on board the *Enterprise*, along with the other media in the pool? You know that since the fighting began, al-Jazeera has broadcast several statements by bin Laden and his associates. You can see the network in your cabin, because its signal is distributed by satellite throughout the Middle East. It looks like a CNN pretender. Your public-affairs officer says al-Jazeera has been generally sympathetic to the Arab cause and frequently criticizes U.S. policy in the region.

Your first responsibility is to the American people and, among them, your own service personnel. You are as outraged as anyone by the World Trade Center and Pentagon carnage of September 11. Bin Laden's venomous video-taped messages were pure propaganda, serving no purpose but to inflame en-emies of the United States. It is hard even to give the media-pool request seri-ous thought.

You remember, though, that CNN, Fox, and other news networks also aired the bin Laden tapes. You also recall the public statements made by your com-mander in chief. The president said the United States is at war with terrorists and those who harbor them, not with the Afghan people, or with Islam. You know Secretary of Defense Donald Rumsfeld has been making the rounds of key friends in the region, including Egypt, Saudi Arabia, and Pakistan—all countries with predominantly Muslim or Arab populations. He has been trying to shore up support for the war on terrorism, and he has been telling leaders that they and their people have nothing to fear from the U.S. military deploy-ment. If the White House wants to get messages to the Muslim and Arab worlds, you think, they'll get more from al-Jazeera than from an item in *People* maga-zine or the *New York Times*.

You decide to take on the al-Jazeera team, issuing instructions that they are to be subject to the same restrictions imposed on the rest of the media pool. You privately decide to agree to an interview if they ever ask for one. You have a few choice words you'd like bin Laden—and the rest of the Muslim and Arab world—to hear. You send a cable to Washington, explaining your rationale for accepting the Arabic-network crew on board. The message Washington wants to get across includes the following elements:

- The United States will retaliate for the barbaric attacks on the World Trade Center and the Pentagon.
- The United States will use its considerable military and political might to fight the war on terrorism.
- The United States is not engaging in a war against Islam, against Arabs, or against the people of Afghanistan or Pakistan.
- The United States will use its most sophisticated and careful military techniques to wage this war, designed to avoid civilian casualties.
- The United States will behave in a compassionate and humanitarian way toward those not responsible for the terror attacks but will be ruthless in its assault on those who are responsible and on those who assist them.

You suspect the people who should hear this message are not regular read-ers of the *New York Times* or viewers of ABC News. They are more likely to be viewers of al-Jazeera, whose broadcasts are in Arabic and whose programs are often picked up by other media in the Muslim and Arabic world.

You know that even the American news organizations aboard your ship are denied access to the most sensitive information about your operations, and you know that even if al-Jazeera were not aboard, some of the material filed by American journalists would end up being seen on the Arabic network anyway.

Finally, you suspect that information delivered over al-Jazeera will be considered more credible in the Arab and Muslim world than material from Western media. So you decide that if you can tell the U.S. story directly to an al-Jazeera crew, at least some of it will reach its most important audience without being considered tainted by Western news organizations.

Global Media/National Media

The globalization of the news media has added new twists to old assumptions about media issues in times of war, not only for the U.S. government, but also for journalists themselves. These new twists prompt anxious debates within and about the media. Simple answers fail under scrutiny.

It seemed natural when, on September 11, U.S. news organizations instantly adopted patriotic red, white, and blue symbols for their print and broadcast products about the terror attacks. American networks unfurled graphic flags on their screens, and newspapers flew banners such as "America under Attack." Patriotism soared, encouraged and assumed by the news media. Television stations across the country devised patriotic on-screen logos and musical themes; some news anchors suddenly sported flag pins and other symbols of national unity. The all-news cable TV channels were no exception.

As events unfolded for the first couple of days, CNN's live, continuous coverage from New York, Washington, and abroad was simulcast over the network's domestic and international signals. But as the red, white, and blue motif became increasingly prevalent, managers of CNN's international network balked. Viewers in Pakistan, the Middle East, and elsewhere (including the Muslim world from Manila to Casablanca) would not relate well to news programs being draped in the American flag. They had become accustomed to the global network as an independent news service, albeit one tied intimately to American journalistic and social values and economic principles.

CNN International broke away from CNN USA's programming. It adopted a neutral color and logo scheme and reverted to its normal programming production environment, based on internationally oriented producers, writers, and anchors. Gone were the "we" and "our" being used by domestic network anchors to refer to the American people and government. In its place, the extent of reporting from abroad increased.

The challenges quickly became more sophisticated and more difficult. On Sunday, October 7, when bin Laden's first videotape coincided with the start of American bombing of Afghanistan, U.S. networks and newspapers treated the tapes as news. Most either played the tape in its entirety or published extensive excerpts. After all, it was the first time since the World Trade Center and

Pentagon attacks that the world was hearing from the man accused by the United States of orchestrating the worst terrorism in history.

In the almost frenzied atmosphere of patriotism that had developed by then, however, some Americans considered the playing of bin Laden's recordings a near treasonous act. A caller to a National Public Radio talk show in which I was a participant on October 8 declared that because most Americans were unaware of the profound hatred felt by bin Laden and his supporters toward the United States, they should not be subjected to his videotaped bile spewing out over American TV news channels. I agreed 100 percent that most Americans were unaware of the depth of bin Laden's hatred; that is precisely why they should hear every word he uttered on the tape.

Within days, the White House was pressuring the networks to refrain from publishing bin Laden's tapes, and government officials were darkly suggesting the messages might contain secret instructions to his loose al-Qaeda network. By the time bin Laden's third recording was released a month later, the Fox News Channel was puffing that it would not dream of airing the "propaganda" of a terrorist. Even CNN had been cowed by public and governmental pressure into reducing the tape to a fifteen-second excerpt. A top ABC News executive issued a public apology for suggesting he was unsure whether the Pentagon could be considered a legitimate military target of terrorists.

American news organizations had not balked at playing up the Pentagon's own carefully government-edited night-vision videotape of U.S. troops rummaging through Mullah Omar's sock drawers at Taliban headquarters in Kandahar. The extent to which the U.S. government intended to manipulate the American news media became apparent two months later when, in early December 2001, yet another bin Laden videotape surfaced. The Pentagon edited it and distributed the tape to U.S media outlets. The tape, said to have been discovered in Afghanistan by U.S. troops, showed bin Laden chuckling and gloating about the World Trade Center attack, which killed thousands. The U.S. government had it translated and, superimposed English subtitles on the tape before feeding it to broadcast and print media. In this reversal of policy, the U.S. government was openly encouraging the broadcast of bin Laden's rhetoric. Despite the U.S. government's goal of influencing Arab publics, the Pentagon did not distribute an unedited Arabic-language version to Middle Eastern media.

Information Challenges within the Military

The military itself confronts challenging new questions of information management only partly related to the news media. Consider this scenario: new technology allows tiny video cameras on helmets and on guided missiles to relay almost instantaneous field information about the Afghanistan campaign. Who gets to see those pictures? Some of the answers are obvious, but others really are not. Field commanders, for sure, must see what those "electronic eyes" can show them, and so should theater commanders. Should the Pentagon see them? Some military leaders would prefer not to have the Joint Chiefs of Staff electronically peering over their shoulders at all times. Does the White House get to see real-time images from the battlefield? After all, the President is the commander in chief. If civilian leaders see them, what about Congress, which has the constitutional power to declare war? Would you want 535 elected representatives constantly second-guessing military operations? How about the CIA? Do intelligence analysts see live pictures from the field?

If live pictures from the war front are being transmitted back to Washington, when (if ever) do the American people or the news media get to see them? When the Pentagon says it's OK? (Would that have been a satisfying rule during the Vietnam War, in instances such as the U.S. storming of My Lai?) If the media get to see the pictures, even occasionally, what happens if a 14-year-old computer hacker in Canada figures out how to tap into the military's video stream from the battlefield? Are the images posted on the Internet? Do they become available to al-Jazeera?

These examples only hint at some of the information tests facing news organizations and governmental and military leaders in an age of global media. Consider satellite photography, for example, which is directly related to the media. Americans cheered when CNN managed to broadcast live from Hainan Island, China, earlier in 2001 after a U.S. military-intelligence aircraft was forced to land there. Chinese authorities had held the American crew for days by the time CNN's ground staff succeeded in showing pictures, and a correspondent near the secret Chinese base also made available (via Space Imaging, Inc.) a crystal-clear photograph of the American plane sitting on the runway, guarded by Chinese military vehicles. Print journalists and broadcasters alike used both kinds of images. China objected not only to the espionage effort by the U.S. government, but also to the intrusive journalism of American news organizations, which had neither sought nor obtained China's permission to show scenes from the top-security military base.

A year earlier, the *New York Times* had spectacularly used satellite imagery to disprove the Russian government's claims that it was acting with restraint against the rebel stronghold of Grozny, in Chechnya. Unable to get reporters on the ground into Chechnya, the *Times* bought two images of downtown Grozny, taken by a private firm two months apart. The images powerfully exposed Moscow's lies about that war. Grozny had been literally pulverized in a withering air campaign between December 1999 and February 2000.

Space Imaging also captured clear satellite photos of the southwest Asian region where the war on terrorism is being fought. The Pentagon, however, outfoxed the news media by buying exclusive rights to all such satellite imagery, effectively censoring the media's ability to report on the war from the sky (denying the media the ability to use such photos to verify U.S. and Taliban claims about the military campaign and to determine the extent of refugee streams resulting from the war).

Presumably, Americans would not have cheered if newspapers and broadcasters had shown independently acquired aerial images of the war on terrorism, as they had of the Chinese air base or of the Chechen capital.[1] Imagine the outcry if nongovernmental satellite images had been used by the news media to report on the Gulf War in 1991.

The media widely published the limited overhead pictures of U.S. bombing raids issued by the Pentagon, showing the success of those raids at destroying Taliban air bases and alleged terrorist training camps. The Pentagon did not reveal the casualties suffered during some of its operations in Afghanistan until weeks after they occurred.

Global Audiences

The question of a global audience is among the most difficult for today's news organizations. Should a news product designed for consumption in the United States be the same as one intended for global consumption? That does not matter very much to the most popular American television networks (ABC, NBC, and CBS), whose programs are not widely seen abroad. Nor does it matter to local newspapers or television stations, whose product is tailored purely for domestic consumers. But it is of crucial importance to organizations such as CNN, whose exposure to 160 million households in more than 200 countries and territories vastly outnumbers even its potential audience within the United States. That is why flying the American flag on an anchor's lapels or over news video is unacceptable to CNN International, even though it might seem natural to a network with a U.S. audience.

The notion of a global audience has other important implications; it raises questions about national security and national loyalty.

National Security and National Interest

Today's global media managers often find themselves negotiating with foreign leaders about the content of news broadcasts and publications. For years, China's government sent its ambassador to Atlanta to demand that CNN stop repeating video of the Tiananmen Square massacre. This was important to China outside of the United States as well. China's worldwide image was shaped in part by CNN's visual reminders of the bloody events of 1989.

Today, in a phenomenon nonexistent as recently as five years ago, major news organizations also publish their product on the Internet, in a form viewable by people far from the political epicenter of the newsroom's headquarters country. The *New York Times*, the *Washington Post*, and CNN are just a few of the Web-based media outlets whose Internet audiences now form a significant portion of news consumers. Whose national interest should these Internet media consider in the content of their product? U.S. allies? Enemies? Economic friends?

When news organizations were more clearly identified with and tied to their countries, when audiences more consistently were of a single nationality, and when the media were confined by technology and politics to the security of their own country, many of these difficult notions of mixed media loyalty did not exist. But as the technology and economy of globalization pervade the news media, and as people around the world come to depend on the same media for news and information, these questions of national interest will become increasingly troublesome for media managers and governmental leaders alike. Patriotic citizens everywhere will have to come to new, perhaps more sophisticated understandings of how the news media work, especially in times of political, economic, and military conflict.

Note

1. Private American companies that acquire and sell satellite photographs are licensed by the U.S. government, which retains the right to exercise "shutter control" in national-security instances. Another unique licensing rule limits the photographs that may be taken of Israel. To date, the Pentagon has not exercised its right to control the shutter. Foreign companies (and other governments) acquiring and selling satellite images are not subject to such U.S. national-security limitations.

Daoud Kuttab, a Palestinian journalist and an activist for freedom of the press, is the founder and director of Community Media Network, a not-for-profit media organization that includes Radio Al Balad in Amman, AmmanNet, and PEN Media, a television NGO that produces *Shara's Simsim*, the Palestinian version of *Sesame Street*. In this article, published in *Al-Hayat* on November 21, 2004, he confronts the way Western media affect society in the Arab world and provides a glimpse of the development of new media in the Arab world.

The West and the Arab World: The Case of Media

This is the BBC from London, Voice of America from Washington, Deutsche Welle from Germany, Monte Carlo Radio from France. According to Reuters, AP wire service, UPI news . . . This is CNN. You are watching the Disney Channel, Hollywood Channel, History Channel. Tonight's feature is *The Terminator*. Follow the latest episodes of *The Bold and the Beautiful*, *Dallas*, *Friends*, *The Practice*, *NYPD Blue*, *Law and Order*.

The above is a small sample of the barrage of media outlets and programs that fill every moment of every day for Arabs and Muslims. The powerful media outlets provide us with the news, chosen, directed, and spun by Western media practitioners in New York, Washington, Atlanta, London, and Paris. Open any newspaper in cities like Cairo, Casablanca, or Islamabad, and you will read more news and see more photos coming from Western wire services than from any other.

We are also drenched with entertainment written and produced by creative talents from places like Hollywood and Orlando. These shows receive awards with names like Oscars and Emmys from cities like Los Angles, California, and Cannes, France. View a television station in Riyadh, Algiers, or Manila, and you will no doubt see programs originally written in American English, about people living in American cities, dealing with issues of interest to Americans. Attend any cinema hall in Amman, Beirut, or Jakarta, and you will see a flick starring blue-eyed, blond white men or women crushing bad guys who have black hair and brown eyes.

Western media in all its forms is a major import item in the Arab and Muslim worlds. This is not restricted to powerful media carriers (CNN, BBC, and Monte Carlo). Western media is also a major producer of fiction, as well as nonfiction, content.

In a region that is very young (the majority of the population in the Arab and Islamic world is under 25), this modern cultural colonialism has created a huge desire to emulate the West. News and analysis from the Western world is taken at face value, film stars are bigger than life, and fashion trends seen in movies and television quickly become adopted by a young, hero-less Arab and Muslim population.

What has happened to us? How did we find ourselves on this slippery slope? Where are the alternative media outlets, films, and heroes that reflect this region's rich culture and traditions?

To answer these questions, we have to recognize that we are not in this problem alone. Western media hegemony is not restricted to the Arab and Muslim worlds, but is global. But where other regions, nations, and communities have realized this problem and have attempted to remedy it, our region continues to consume Western culture without any reservations, hesitations, or efforts to look for other sources of strength within our own societies.

Part of the problem comes from political and military defeat. Many defeated nations are fascinated with their victors and often study them ad nauseam. Blacks in South Africa knew their oppressive white-minority government much better than the whites understood the black-majority population. Palestinians know more about Israel and Israelis than the other way around. A look at how many people around the world speak English and how many English speakers speak another language supports this assumption.

To change this imbalance, an extraordinary effort must be exerted to change the flow of information from the present flood of West to East, to a more equitable, two-way relationship. There is no doubt that both East and West have a lot to offer each other. Lessening this asymmetry requires a multilayered approach. The present Western hegemony must be balanced by a serious attempt to get the peoples of the East to better represent themselves in the eyes of the West.

The twentieth century's colonial policy of divide and rule has left its effect on media consumption. With the Arab and Muslim region divided and weak, the West has ruled it not only politically, but also in the media field. The media industry (and we should never forget that it is an industry) is expensive. Erecting powerful transmitters, creating quality programs, and supplying firsthand news is an expensive operation. Small countries are unable to compete with these multinational conglomerates, thus leaving powerful media carriers with a virtual monopoly on both media transmission and media content.

Not only have Arab and Muslim peoples been divided and splintered, but they have also been cursed with undemocratic political regimes that have confiscated the popular will of their own people. These autocratic regimes have hijacked media and media content, forging it to fit their own political desires and ambitions of staying in power. Media ownership in the Arab world has been almost totally in the hands of the ruling powers. Cultural production and other creative endeavors have also been hijacked to the degree that artists have become mere cheerleaders to kings, emirs, presidents, and prime ministers.

The hegemony of Western media has reached dangerous proportions, and counteracting it requires a strong, unified, and serious strategy. This strategy needs to work on two tracks. It must provide the peoples of the region with credible and independent media outlets, and at the same time, a unified effort must be exerted to begin the hard process of creating alternative media content that can be taken seriously by an ever-skeptical public. Arabs have a major advantage over many other peoples. All Arab nations speak, read, and understand the same language. For an independent media to develop, attention to professionalism is paramount. The success of the Arab network al-Jazeera has as much to do with the professionalism of its staff members and their ability to work independently as to any other factor.

The success of networks such as al-Jazeera, MBC, LBC, and al-Arabiya is also the result of smart Arab media entrepreneurs using modern technology and proven international media standards to produce quality television. In our search for a unique media, independent from that of the West, we need not reject the latest internationally available techniques and technologies developed in the West. We are not obliged to reinvent the wheel in order to produce genuine Arabic media.

A strong Arab media also needs to pay attention to everything that is local and indigenous. When Arabs start looking inwardly in a critical way, the rest of the world will take both the Arab media and Arabs much more seriously. We cannot expect to participate in a serious dialogue with the West unless we first develop a genuinely independent media that pays attention to our own issues. Only when we have the courage and willingness to dialogue with each other can we succeed in organizing a dialogue with the rest of the world.

Joel Stein is a columnist and a regular contributor to *Time*. The following pieces appeared in the *Los Angeles Times* on January 2, 2007, and in *Time* on August 6, 2001, and July 10, 2000

Don't E-mail Me

That address on the bottom of this column? That is the pathetic, confused death knell of the once-proud newspaper industry, and I want nothing to do with it. Sending an e-mail to that address is about as useful as sending your study-group report about Iraq to the president.

Here's what my Internet-fearing editors have failed to understand: I don't want to talk to you; I want to talk at you. A column is not my attempt to engage in a conversation with you. I have more than enough people to converse with. And I don't listen to them either. That sound on the phone, Mom, is me typing.

Some newspapers even list the phone numbers of their reporters at the end of their articles. That's a smart use of their employees' time. Why not just save a step and have them set up a folding table at a senior citizen center with a sign asking for complaints?

Where does this end? Does Philip Roth have to put his e-mail at the end of his book? Does Tom Hanks have to hold up a sign with his e-mail at the end of his movie? Should your hotel housekeeper leave her e-mail on your sheets? Are you starting to see how creepy this is?

Not everything should be interactive. A piece of work that stands on its own, without explanation or defense, takes on its own power. If Martin Luther put his 95 Theses on the wall and then all the townsfolk sent him their comments, and he had to write back to all of them and clarify what he meant, some of the theses would have gotten all watered down and there never would have been a Diet of Worms. And then, for the rest of history, elementary school students learning about the Reformation would have nothing to make fun of. You can see how dangerous this all is.

I get that you have opinions you want to share. That's great. You're the Person of the Year. I just don't have any interest in them. First of all, I did a tiny bit of research for my column, so I'm already familiar with your brilliant argument. Second, I've already written my column, so I can't even steal your ideas and get paid for them.

There is no practical reason to send your rants to me. If you want to counter my opinion publicly, write a letter to the editor. If you want me fired, write a letter to the publisher. If you want a note back, write a letter in lipstick on the bathroom mirror. Or you could just write mean things about my column on some blog. Don't worry, I'll see them. I have a "Joel Stein" RSS feed that goes straight into my arteries. But don't make me feel like you expect a return e-mail. Because this takes my assistant four to five hours every week. I know this because my assistant is me.

Huge portions of my e-mails come from people who haven't even read my article. They're just assuming, based on a headline or an excerpt on a blog, that I'm unpatriotic or irreligious or lecherous. Sure, they happen to be right, but it would have been nice if they had clicked on my column and moved me up on that "most-read articles" list.

A lot of e-mail screeds argue that, in return for the privilege of broadcasting my opinion, I have the responsibility to listen to you. I don't. No more than you have a responsibility to read me. I'm not an elected servant. I'm an arrogant, solipsistic, attention-needy freak who pretends to have an opinion about everything. I don't have time to listen to you. I barely have time to listen to me.

Part of the problem is that no etiquette has yet been established for the hyperinteractive world. And I, born before MySpace and e-mail, don't feel comfortable getting a letter and not answering it. And then, if I do, suddenly we're pen pals, with all those pen pal responsibilities.

And I don't want a pen pal who already has strong opinions about me. What fun is that? I want a pen pal named Simone who lives in Grenoble and is trying to learn English while I learn French, and teases me with vague promises to come visit over summer break even though she never does.

So I'm going to establish a new etiquette. I'm asking my editors to build a page on opinion.latimes.com where, instead of e-mailing me, you can write about how arrogant I am. And maybe on this site, one brave person will write about how I'm right to stand up against this world of false, easy community where columnists pretend they think their essays are no more valuable than yours, and friendship is a stranger who thanks you for the MySpace add.

And I hope that this brave someone else is smart enough to think of a username and IP address that doesn't reveal that it's obviously me.

Millions of Women Weep

I had two major reasons for never wanting to get married. The first was that you can't have sex with other people. The second was that marriage is really just a legal method for the patriarchy to possess and subjugate women. You would not believe how long it took me to come up with the second reason.

I didn't want to get married because, basically, I don't like thinking any further into the future than what I'm going to eat and how I'm going to get sex. Anything else is a hassle. Also, as an optimist, I like the thought of not knowing how the future will work out, the future of course consisting of what I'll eat and whom I'll have sex with. Once you know those things, all that's left is when you're going to die. And there's a Web site that calculates that.

Still, because I've been living with my girlfriend, Cassandra, for some time, everyone was on my case about getting married. When I was interviewing the

Wu-Tang Clan, even Inspectah Deck and Cappadonna, who were emptying out a Dutch Masters cigar and refilling it with marijuana, starting laying into me. "You got to marry her," Cappadonna told me. "You got to step up and be a man. Take some responsibility." Deck nodded in agreement. I never needed a puff of a Dutch Master quite so much.

But after three and a half years of explaining to Cassandra that I was too young to get married and getting almost enough mileage out of my damaged understanding of commitment to make my parents' divorce worth it, I started to feel that being married would be nice, a relief from contemplating what to do, a comfort in being able to plan the future. Plus, I realized the odds were slim of finding someone else who would let me write about her.

Now, I've never proposed before, but I had some theories. Women, it seemed to me, like to be proposed to. It puts them in a good mood. It's a can't-miss. So, the way I saw it, you should use it as an opportunity to go somewhere she wouldn't normally enjoy. Not only will you both have a good time, but she'll also have positive associations with that place. That's why so many guys do it at baseball games. I had my eye on Scores, the premier strip club in Manhattan.

But then I thought that I'd rather not do it somewhere that's all glitzy and forced romantic, like Tahiti or Scores, places that don't represent our real life together, which is actually full of tedium and drudgery, though a really pleasant tedium and drudgery. So I made her a big tofu dinner in our studio apartment. Then I woke her up at 1:30 a.m. and told her that over the past six months, I've been tearing up over *Friends* episodes about marriage and the ending of *What Women Want*. I told her that my life was perfect and that I wanted to freeze it. She seemed to want me to get to the point so she could go back to sleep.

I gave her the ring, and she cried, and we consummated our engagement in a way that, because of the late hour and general excitement, didn't last all that long. Afterward she said, "If this is what it's going to be like, I'm not sure I want to marry you." That's when I knew I had made the right decision.

People keep asking if I'm excited, and I feel bad that I'm not. But I am happy. And calm. And relieved. And so much more sure than I thought a person could be. And I finally realized that I'd happily trade the excitement of the unknown for all that.

The Lessons of Cain

Angola, Louisiana

Howard has just served us four plates of the best chocolate-chip cookies I've ever eaten when Warden Burl Cain tells us that Howard killed a man and is going to die an old man in prison for it. It's flat as that, but it exposes the most intimate, relevant detail of Howard's life. I don't want to look at him, but I do, and Howard doesn't flinch. Howard's sad eyes don't change, don't feign remorse or regret, just stay sad, and his gold-plated teeth are the only thing that hints he was once a man who wouldn't let himself be stared at. "I don't know how Howard killed somebody, and I don't care," says Cain about his favorite prisoner. "I care about how he is now." Even though Louisiana offers no hope for parole, Cain says he believes Howard is rehabilitated and should be freed if he can meet the family of the man he killed and receive its forgiveness. Howard nods in agreement, because justice is as simple and brutal as that, even if he is going to die here in Angola prison.

Heaven and hell and sin and redemption are just philosophy to me, a system to make sense out of life. But here in Angola, heaven and hell and sin and redemption aren't philosophy. They are the answers to why you're here and who you are and where you are going to end up.

There are 88 men on death row, and Burl Cain has killed more people than most of them. He has set five down by lethal injection, and he has held each of their hands as they died. One man had track marks so bad they had to shoot the poison into his neck, and he kept bolting upright, so Cain had to push his shoulder down with his right hand while letting the man hold Cain's left for comfort. The table has five straps on the gurney—two leg manacles, two wristbands and one chest belt—making a horizontal cross, the only thing in Angola that isn't pointing toward either heaven or hell. Cain says he stayed quiet when he killed his first man and didn't give him a chance to confess and get right with God, and Cain felt him go to hell, felt it in his hand surer than anything he'd ever known, and it made him commit his life to Christ. "My wife, she doesn't like that she's married a killer," he says. "This is probably going to end my marriage."

One of Cain's predecessors, Warden C. Murray Henderson, was recently convicted of shooting his wife five times, and he's most likely going to wind up in Angola for it. At 18,000 acres, it's the largest prison in the United States, with the lowest-paid guards, few of whom have graduated from high school. It's a place that *Collier's* magazine once called "the worst prison in America," where, in 1951, in an effort to protest the brutal conditions, 31 prisoners sliced their Achilles tendons so they couldn't be sent to work.

At the prison museum Cain has built, where all the T-shirts, coffee mugs and videos have the name ANGOLA printed in big letters, Cain points his thick fingers at pictures of the men he has executed. "They're special people to me," he says.

There are 88 more men waiting to be made special. They've got their own building with their own lawyers meeting room, which has a mural of an eagle and another of Scooby-Doo. Everyone spends all day on his bed, silent, reading the Bible or playing chess against a neighbor he can't see except for the hand that reaches through the bars into the hall to move pieces. Jenny Jones is on the TV, and she is looking good, but no one looks. Instead the inmates study the Bible, which they know better than some preachers.

These men, like most prisoners, don't get many visitors. "The first people to stop visiting are your buddies who you committed the crime with," explains Cain. "The next is your wife. Your father dies. Your mom and your sister are the only ones who keep coming. Your momma is the only one who loves you." So Cain says his main job is to give the 5,108 hopeless men on this former slave-breeding farm hope, even though 86 percent of them will stay here for "life and one dark day." The dark day is the one after they die, when their body gets embalmed and waits to go home and get buried, although the truth is that when they die, no one comes, and they get buried right here on the Farm. Cain thinks he can summon hope through a four-year Bible college, or the amateur rodeo the prisoners put on every year, or having them pick cotton by hand in the fields that were once a real plantation, and still really are, for 4 cents an hour.

A few months ago, though, some prisoners lost it, lost the hope, and one of them took a guard hostage. Burl Cain couldn't talk the hope back into him, and they had a shootout. "He got one of ours, and we got one of theirs," he says. "It all worked out in the end." And wrong as that sounds, in Angola that's how it is, and there's no hiding from it, and I feel so lucky to go back to a place where heaven and hell and sin and redemption are just philosophy to me.

Charles Lane, an editorial writer at the *Washington Post* and a former editor of the *New Republic*, was a Japan Society Media Fellow in 2003–4. This piece appeared in *Foreign Policy* (May–June 2005).

A View to a Kill

Tamaki Mitsui was a bit surprised one Friday when his boss gave him his instructions for the following Monday: to serve as a witness at two hangings. Mitsui, an official of the Nagoya High Court Prosecutor's Office, which handles criminal appeals, had argued for the death penalty in three cases himself. He knew that Japanese law requires representatives of the prosecutor's office to witness executions. But he had thought this duty would be assigned by lottery. Still, he accepted it. Part of the job, he thought.

When Monday came, Mitsui took a subordinate with him to the Nagoya Detention Center. It is one of seven Japanese jails where capital offenders await execution—and then go to the gallows. Shortly after 9 a.m., Mitsui, his deputy, the director of the detention center, and another prison official sat in a row behind a floor-to-ceiling glass barrier. On the other side of the glass was the death chamber: an empty room, about 18 feet square, with bare white walls and a polished floor of light brown Japanese cypress wood. Dangling from the ceiling, illuminated by floodlights, was a noose. The only sound was the pre-recorded chanting of a Buddhist sutra. Mitsui found the setting oddly serene. "It's bizarre to say this, but it was a beautiful place," he recalls, "like a Noh theater."

Then, a set of double doors on the far side of the execution chamber swung open. The prisoner, escorted by a pair of guards, walked in. It was November 19, 1998, and Tamaki Mitsui was about to see something very few people in the world ever have. In Japan, a high wall of secrecy surrounds the gallows. Perhaps only the Imperial Palace is more insulated from public view. No member of the press is allowed to witness hangings. Nor are the families of either the condemned prisoner or his victims. No official descriptions or accounts are published. Executions are not announced until after the fact, and even then official spokespeople say only that they have occurred. (The names of the people hanged leak out from lawyers and family members.) Civil servants ordered to witness executions are required by law to keep silent. Even members of the Diet, Japan's parliament, get no access. When a nine-person delegation from the Diet visited Tokyo's gallows in 2003, it was the first such tour in 30 years. The lawmakers were forbidden to see a hanging or to take photographs.

I spent two months reporting on the death penalty in Japan during the summer of 2004, and Mitsui's was the only eyewitness account of a relatively recent execution I could find. Mitsui, 60, is a trim, slightly nervous man with an officious air and, it must be acknowledged, a controversial figure in Japan. He was arrested in 2002 on charges of accepting expensive entertainment from gang-sters and falsifying a residency certificate in order to obtain an illegal tax break. But the arrest came on the very day he was about to tell a Japanese television program about rampant slush-fund abuses in the prosecutor's office. He pleaded not guilty, accusing his former colleagues of a politically motivated prosecu-tion. In February 2005, the Osaka District Court acknowledged that his claims of selective prosecution should be investigated, but nonetheless convicted him on five of six bribery counts. He is free on bail pending his appeal.

Clearly, Mitsui has an ax to grind. And our meeting was arranged by Forum 90, Japan's leading anti-death-penalty organization. But his conflict with the Ministry of Justice is unrelated to capital punishment. Although he evinced some ambivalence about what he saw in the gallows, he indicated that he is not an active opponent of the death penalty. His account squared with the few de-tails about the Japanese gallows that have trickled out through other sources. Nobotu Hosaka, a former opposition member of the Diet who joined the delega-tion that toured the Tokyo gallows in 2003, says the place he and his colleagues visited matches Mitsui's description of the Nagoya death chamber, except that in Tokyo the floor was covered by a carpet. Government officials confirmed certain aspects of Mitsui's description. "On the death penalty, he would seem to have no reason to lie or puff," says David T. Johnson, a professor of sociology at the Uni-versity of Hawaii, who interviewed Mitsui as part of a long-term study of Japan's criminal justice system.

Mitsui's story has special relevance now. Not only is Japan the only member of the Group of Seven industrialized countries other than the United States to retain capital punishment, but it is also increasing its use of the death penalty. Thanks to declining murder rates and concern over recent death-row exonera-tions, death sentences are on the wane in the United States, reaching 130 in 2004, the lowest number in any year since the United States Supreme Court reinstituted capital punishment in 1976. But in Japan, the authorities have re-sponded to a recent surge in street crime, and to such events as the 1995 sarin poison-gas attack on the Tokyo subway, by seeking more death sentences. The 18 death sentences issued by Japanese trial courts in 2002 were the most in a single year since 1961, when 29 people were sentenced to die. Brushing off criti-cism from the United Nations Human Rights Commission, the Council of Eu-rope, and Amnesty International, Japanese trial courts sentenced 55 people to death between 2000 and 2003, as many as in the previous 11 years combined. Two men were executed in Japan in 2004, a typical rate for recent years, though two or three times that number is not unusual. This figure is far below the rate in the United States, where 59 people were executed in 2004. But it appears that in the coming years, more and more people will be led to Japan's gallows.

Although the conflict between the United States and Europe over capital punishment is well known, Japan's determined retention of the death penalty shows that the global death-penalty debate is not strictly transatlantic. There is also a wide gap between Europe and the democracies, established and emerging, of Asia. Of the Asian countries with freely elected governments, India, Indonesia, the Philippines, South Korea, Sri Lanka, Taiwan, and Thailand all have capital punishment. This list, to be sure, encompasses a range of death-penalty policies. Taiwan is in the process of phasing out capital punishment, while in Thailand, a nation of 65 million people, there are almost 1,000 men and women currently under sentence of death, many for drug offenses.

The man stepping through the double doors on that November morning six years ago was 61-year-old Tatsuaki Nishio. In his younger days, he had been a gang leader. Between 1976 and 1977, he committed three crimes in the Nagoya area: he directed a subordinate to strangle a 48-year-old employee of a Nagoya construction company, and attempted two other murders. The Supreme Court of Japan denied his last appeal in 1989. On the day of his execution, prison guards awakened him and informed him it was his time to die. In Japan, death-row prisoners are not told in advance of their execution dates, a practice international human rights organizations condemn as a form of psychological torment.

But the government argues that the process is compassionate and prudent, insisting that advance notice would create unnecessary anxiety when prisoners should be adjusting to the inevitable. "A death row inmate is every day waiting for death, so it is easily understood that he may easily be emotionally destabilized," says Satoru Ohashi, an assistant director of the Ministry of Justice's Correction Bureau. "And if he becomes emotionally destabilized, he may commit suicide, escape, or harm the prison staff." Additionally, it is said, publicity about individuals on death row would invade the privacy of their families, who feel shamed or ostracized because of their criminal kin.

Death-penalty opponents say the Ministry of Justice's real purpose is to break the inmates' will, to discourage extended appeals. "If you have no one to help you and you have access to clergy who say, 'You committed a crime, so accept death,' and you live every day staring at a wall, who wouldn't begin to want to die?" says Yuichi Kaido, a prominent defense lawyer who represents capital defendants. "This kind of treatment induces them to give up retrial petitions." Japanese opponents of the death penalty note that at least some death-row inmates, or their families, were given notice of their pending executions until about 30 years ago. According to a 2001 article by Kaido, condemned inmate and murderer Kiyohachi Horikoshi was actually permitted to meet his mother the day before his execution in December 1975. But a month later, Kiyoshi Okubo, another convicted murderer, was executed without warning, and no one else has been given advance notice since then. The timing of the change, opponents argue, shows that it was meant to counteract a 1975 decision by the Supreme Court of Japan that loosened the requirements that death-row inmates must meet to win a new trial. The court decision encouraged many new retrial petitions, which were previously rare.

If that was the government's true intent, it did not entirely succeed. The eventual result of the 1975 ruling was the exoneration and release of four men who had been on death row since being convicted of murder and sentenced to death in the decade after World War II, but who had always insisted on their innocence. In each case, there were serious questions about the handling of evidence and the methods authorities used to extract confessions. Perhaps the most notorious such miscarriage of justice involved Sakae Menda, who in 1948, at the age of 23, was convicted of a double ax murder. The conviction was based on the contradiction-riddled testimony of a prostitute and Menda's own confession, extracted after spending 80 hours in a police station without sleep.

The Ministry of Justice tightened its procedures after those cases, which were part of the reason Japan suspended executions for 40 months between November 1989 and March 1993. Yet some problematic aspects of Japan's death-penalty system remain essentially unchanged. Perhaps the most basic— the authorities' reliance on confessions—is not unique to capital cases.

Traditionally, Japanese courts have treated a defendant's own admissions as more persuasive than other evidence, including circumstantial evidence or even forensics. Although suspects have a theoretical right to remain silent, they may also be held and questioned without access to a lawyer for up to 23 days. Even after they have contacted an attorney, they are not entitled to have counsel present during questioning. As a result, the Japanese criminal justice system has been plagued by allegations of physical and psychological abuse during interrogation. From an American perspective, it seems incredible that confessions are not given to the court as either tapes or verbatim transcripts. Rather, they are rewritten and summarized by the authorities themselves.

As it happens, there was no serious question of Tatsuaki Nishio's guilt, though the government waited to execute him until he exhausted his legal claims. That is standard Ministry of Justice policy; however, the authorities reserve the right to proceed with an execution if they feel an inmate is simply filing repetitive or baseless appeals. By the time Nishio appeared before Mitsui, he would also have been offered a final meal or some sweets, a cigarette, and a meeting with the clergy of his choice. The government says the condemned may draft a last-minute will, but anti-death-penalty campaigners say this is sometimes nothing more than a few words hastily murmured to a guard.

When he stepped through the double doors, Nishio was blindfolded and dressed in a white cotton robe, Mitsui says. His hands were bound behind him. His feet were bare. The guards led him to a square marked in the middle of the floor, directly beneath the noose. One guard placed the noose around his neck. Nishio stood there for a moment, silent, seemingly calm, bathed in lamplight.

Then, without warning, the square beneath Nishio's feet, a trap door, swung open. He dropped straight down. The noose tightened. Nishio's neck snapped, and he stopped moving. His body now hung in a separate room downstairs.

As Nishio dangled there and the minutes dragged by in silence, Mitsui began to grow uneasy. What were they waiting for? Eventually, he turned to the director of the detention center and asked, "Why so long?" Japan's prison law refers to a minimum hanging period of five minutes. But the director replied simply that this was the way things are done. The witnesses returned to their silent vigil.

Finally, after 30 long minutes, the director ordered Mitsui and a prison doctor to go downstairs and examine Nishio. On the lower level, Mitsui noticed that there was no theater-style floor, just bare concrete. With the guards' help, Mitsui and the doctor laid Nishio down and stripped off his robe and blindfold, in accordance with the prison law, which provides that "the countenance of the dead shall be inspected after hanging." They rolled the body back and forth, noting that it was unscathed except for a bruise on Nishio's neck. There was no question: the sentence had been carried out.

As I listened to Mitsui, it was clear that he had been made extremely anxious and uncomfortable by that 30-minute wait, for reasons that he could not quite articulate. His disquiet made me wonder what the Japanese public would think if they knew, in detail, what he knows. Toyoko Ogino, an interpreter I worked with in the coal-mining town of Omuta, was surprised when I told her that prisoners were hanged. "I thought that was just an expression," she said. Perhaps greater information would make no difference: polls indicate that public support for capital punishment is even stronger in Japan than in United States—more than 81 percent in a February 2005 survey.

Nor is the use of hanging as a method of execution controversial in Japan. It has been all but abandoned in the United States, in part because of fears it might subject prisoners to unnecessary suffering, especially if the noose fails to work as designed. But, apart from a 1961 decision by the Supreme Court of Japan, which found that hanging does not violate the postwar Japanese Constitution's ban on "cruel" punishment, Japan has not reconsidered a form of execution first adopted by the Meiji-era Grand Council of State in 1873. Mitsui said he was untroubled. "They die instantly," he assured me. "There is no agony."

Indeed, Japan adopted hanging during the Meiji Restoration as a reformist alternative to decapitation. A new debate over hanging does not seem to be in the interest of either the Japanese government or the country's small anti-death-penalty movement. The former does not wish to hash out any aspect of the death penalty in public; the latter does not want to appear to accept the death penalty's legitimacy by arguing over how it is carried out.

As Mitsui describes it, the hanging of Nishio seemed to happen all by itself. The man stood on the trap door; the trap door opened; he went down. This was by design. Ordinary prison guards operate the gallows. They may not refuse the job, even if they have a conscientious objection. Officials understand this system can create stress. "As you can imagine, it's a very emotionally demanding task," says Satoru Ohashi of the Correction Bureau. So, Ohashi said, a solution has been found. Five guards press separate buttons simultaneously. Only one of these is the button that actually opens the trap door. And all of this takes place outside the witnesses' field of vision—offstage, as it were. There is a hanging, but no identifiable hangman.

For Mitsui, it was a long day at the gallows. After Nishio had been hanged, guards brought in Masamichi Ida, 56. Ida used to work for a car repair shop in Aichi Prefecture, near Nagoya. He took out a life insurance policy on a 20-year-old customer and then, in November 1979, went sailing with the young man and pushed him overboard. He was also convicted of two other murders near Kyoto in 1983. Ida was executed in exactly the same manner as Nishio, Mitsui says, including that excruciating 30-minute wait.

In the early afternoon, Mitsui returned to his office and wrote up a report to the Ministry of Justice in Tokyo, confirming that the prisoners had been duly executed. His officemates had thoughtfully spread salt on the floor before his return; in Shinto tradition, death is impure, and salt is thought to purify those who have had contact with the dead. But he and his coworkers did not actually discuss what he had seen. His boss gave him the rest of the day off. Returning home, he did not tell his wife about his day either.

Even now, though, Mitsui muses about the strange beauty of the death chamber, that secret theater of polished floors and tasteful lighting. The condemned man enters blindfolded. "Why do they prepare such a beautiful place, but the prisoner is not able to see?" he wondered in our interview, then answered his own question: "Maybe it is for the benefit of the witnesses, to make them feel calmer."

Roger Cohen, a columnist for the *International Herald Tribune* and the *New York Times*, is the author of *Hearts Grown Brutal: Sagas of Sarajevo* (Random House, 1998). These excerpts are drawn from a longer piece, written on the occasion of the fiftieth anniversary of the Cuban revolution and published in the *New York Times Magazine* on December 7, 2008.

Cuba: The End of the End of the Revolution

On my first day in Havana, I wandered down to the Malecón, the world's most haunting urban seafront promenade. A *norte* was blustering, sending breakers crashing over the stone dike built in 1901 under short-lived American rule. Bright explosions of spray unfurled onto the sidewalk. I was almost alone on a Sunday morning in Cuba's capital city of 2.2 million people. A couple of cars a minute passed, often finned '50s beauties, Studebakers and Chevrolets, extravagant and battered. Here and there, a stray mutt scrounged. Washing flapped on the ornate ironwork balconies of crumbling mansions. Looking out on the ocean, I searched in vain for a single boat.

It was not always so, 90 miles off the coast of Florida. In 1859, Richard Henry Dana Jr., an American lawyer whose *To Cuba and Back* became a classic, sailed into Havana. He later wrote: "What a world of shipping! The masts make a belt of dense forest along the edge of the city, all the ships lying head into the street, like horses at their mangers." Over the ensuing century, Cuba became the winter playground of Americans, a place to gamble, rumba, smoke *puros* and sip *mojitos*, the land of every vice and any trade. Havana bars advertised "Hangover Breakfasts." They were much in demand. The Mafia loved the island, the largest in the Caribbean; so did the American businessmen who controlled swathes of the sugar industry and much else. Then, a half century ago, on January 1, 1959, Fidel Castro brought down the curtain on Fulgencio Batista's dictatorship. America's cavorting-cum-commerce ceased. Miami became Cuba's second city as, over the years, hundreds of thousands fled communist rule.

I noticed over subsequent days that Cubans perched on the seafront wall rarely looked outward. When I asked Yoani Sánchez, a dissident blogger (www.desdecuba.com/generaciony), about this, she told me: "We live turned away from the sea because it does not connect us, it encloses us. There is no movement on it. People are not allowed to buy boats, because if they had boats, they would go to Florida. We are left, as one of our poets put it, with the unhappy circumstance of water at every turn."

It is unnatural to perceive the sea and a distant horizon as limiting. But in Cuba, a lot of things are inverted, or not as they first appear. A repressive society long under a single ruler develops a secret lexicon of survival. Through a labyrinth of rations, regulations, two currencies and four markets (peso, hard currency, agro and black), people make their way. Stress is rare but depression rampant in an inertia-stricken economy. Truth is layered. Look up, and you see the Habana Libre, which began life as the Hilton. The seafront Riviera hotel, now so communist-drab it seems to reek of cabbage, once housed a rakish casino.

Diplomatic relations between the United States and Cuba have been severed since 1961; a U.S. trade embargo has been in place almost as long; the Cold War has been over for almost two decades. To say the U.S.-Cuban relationship is anachronistic would be an understatement. But changing it won't be easy. There is something about this proximate island, so beautiful yet so remote, so failed yet so stubborn, that militates against the exercise of U.S. reason.

Lealtad (Loyalty) Street runs from the Malecón down through the densely populated district called Centro Habana. I first went there at night. The city is dimly lighted, but one of Fidel's achievements, along with an impressive education system and universal health care, is security. It might be said that's because there is very little to steal, but that would be uncharitable. The revolution, anything but puritanical, has nonetheless instilled a certain ethical rigor.

A residential street, Lealtad beckoned me with its silhouettes lurking in doorways, its clatter of dominoes being banged on tables, its glimpses through grated windows of lush interior courtyards, its old men playing cards in high-ceilinged living rooms of brocaded furniture and sagging upholstery, its melancholy.

The next day, I came back and, dodging boys playing baseball with a ball made from tightly rolled paper, stopped at a chicken-egg-fish store with nothing in it. Antonio Rodriguez, 50, the affable, bald Afro-Cuban running it, explained to me the mechanics of rationing, in which he is an often-immobile cog. Every month, each Cuban is allocated 10 eggs; a pound of chicken; a pound of fish; and half a pound of an ersatz mince, the whole lot for no more than 25 cents. That may sound like a steal, but there are catches. Rodriguez, after 17 years at the store, where the broken cash register is of prerevolutionary vintage and the antique refrigerator of Soviet provenance, earns $15.40 a month. The average monthly salary is about $20. I asked him when some chicken or eggs might arrive. Beats me, he said. As many as 15 days a month, he's idle, waiting for something to be delivered so he can announce it on the blackboard behind him and get to work crossing off "sales" in his clients' frayed ration books. Rodriguez pointed to a man outside. "That guy standing on the corner, and me working, there's no real difference," he said. "We get paid almost nothing to spend the day talking."

Luiz Jorrin, the man in question, approached. "This is all due to the U.S. blockade," he said, pointing a finger at me and using the exaggerated term that Cubans favor for the embargo. This was too much for Javier Aguirre, a slim fellow who helps Rodriguez. "We're wrecked, and after three hurricanes, we're even more wrecked," he said. "I just don't believe in the system. Give me

Switzerland! Of all the Cubans who have gone to the United States, how many want to come back?" The question prompted a silence. Aguirre, it transpired, tried twice to escape, only to be caught, once by the Cubans and once by the U.S. Coast Guard. Under the current "wet foot, dry foot" policy, most Cubans who reach U.S. soil are allowed to stay, while most intercepted at sea are repatriated. Go figure.

Now 29, Aguirre, an aspiring artist, is waiting. Cubans are used to waiting. Along with baseball and quiet desperation, it's the national sport. They talk; they joke at the Beckett play that is their lives; they tap their fingers to the beat of drums and maracas; and they try to make sense of the senseless. "This is not communism or capitalism," said Aguirre, "it's a Cuban mess."

The more I learned of the centralized Cuban economy, the more that seemed a fair summary. Cuba has two currencies, one for communism and one for a limited, state-dominated capitalism. The pesos that people get their salaries in are essentially good for nothing but rationed or undesirable items. By contrast, the convertible dollar-pegged pesos known as CUCs (pronounced "kooks") are good for international products. Pass a dimly lighted peso store, and you might see a bicycle tire, a yellowing brassiere and a set of plastic spoons. Pass a convertible-peso store, and you will see cell phones, Jameson whiskey and Heineken in a bright, air-conditioned environment. As a result, many Cubans spend their lives scrambling to get in on the convertible-peso economy, which largely depends on getting access to foreign visitors. Cubans see access to the CUC universe of tourists as salvation.

A kind of economic apartheid exists. People are stuck in a regulation-ridden halfway house. They want to escape the socialist world of Rodriguez's store for the capitalist world of the mini Cancún east of Havana, a hotel-littered ghetto of white sand and whiter Scandinavians snapping up Che Guevara T-shirts without worrying too much about what Che wrought on Lealtad Street.

The Cuban government gave me a courteous welcome. I was escorted to a few official meetings, but otherwise left without a minder (as far as I could see) to do what I wished. One official stop was with Elena Alvarez, who was 15 when Fidel's revolution came and now, at 65, works as a top official at the Ministry of Economics. She tried to make sense for me of the voodoo economics I'd seen. Here's what she wanted me to grasp. Cuba, at the time of the revolution, was "one of the most unjust, unequal and exploited societies on earth." Illiteracy was running up to 40 percent, a quarter of the best land was in U.S. hands, a corrupt bourgeoisie lorded it over everyone else. Fidel's initial objective was a more-just society, but U.S. pressure radicalized his revolution and pushed it toward all-out socialism within the Soviet camp.

Alvarez reeled off some numbers, among them these: there were 6,000 doctors in Cuba at the time of the revolution; there are now close to 80,000 for a population of 11.3 million, one of the highest per capita rates in the world.

Despite scarcities, attributable in large part to the embargo, it's a society that wants to protect everyone. The rationing system guarantees that all citizens have a minimum. Everyone gets low-cost food at work. Free health care and education mean a $20 monthly salary is the wrong way to view the quality of Cuban life. Life expectancy for men and women in Cuba is 76 and 80 years, respectively, on par with the U.S. figures. The probability of dying before the age of five is 7 per 1,000 live births in Cuba—nearly as good as in the U.S. Illiteracy has been eliminated; 93.7 percent of Cuban children complete high school, far more than in the United States or elsewhere in the Caribbean. That raises the question: Why educate people so well and then deny them access to the Internet, travel and the opportunity to apply their skills? Why give them a great education and no life? The bottom line, of course, is that the authorities are scared: opening the door to capitalism on an island 90 miles from Florida is very different from doing that in Asia.

"The revolution has been a success," Alvarez said. "It overthrew a tyrannical regime. We got our national sovereignty. We got our pride. We survived aggression by the most powerful country in the world for 50 years. We preserved the essence of what Fidel fought for." But did he really wage guerrilla war in the Sierra Maestra so that countless talented Cubans might sit idle, plotting means to get out? The challenges were great, Alvarez said, but Cuba would again prove Miami wrong. "We are an example to others," she said, "an example to all those looking for an alternative to capitalism."

I did sense something hard to quantify, a kind of socialist conscience, particularly among doctors. When I met Dr. Verena Muzio, the head of the vaccine division at the Center for Genetic Engineering and Biotechnology—another official stop—she said her commitment to the revolution's achievements outweighed the knowledge "that I could go to Chicago and earn $300,000 a year." Her salary is $40 a month.

Tour buses are a frequent sight, ferrying groups that take in Hemingway's Havana bars (La Floridita and La Bodeguita del Medio) and the Che memorial in Santa Clara before heading back to the beach. Although this invasion has brought Cubans more contact with foreigners, its impact has been limited by the fact that the Cuban government does rigorous background checks on any job seekers in the international sector. Over all, most tourists seem happy with sun, sand, rum and cigars—and to heck with totalitarian politics. Meanwhile, Cuba's dissidents are marginalized. The press is muzzled. State television is a turgid propaganda machine. But of course Cuba is not totalitarian East Germany. "There's a very intelligent repression here, a scientific repression," Yoani Sánchez, the dissident whose blog is now translated into 12 languages, told me. "They have killed us as citizens, so they do not have to kill us physically. Our own police is in our brains, censoring us before we utter a critical idea."

At 33, Sánchez represents something new: digital dissent. The authorities seem unsure how to deal with it. A slight and vivacious woman, she started her blog in 2006. It was, she told me, "an exorcism, a virtual catharsis." Now her biting dissections of the woes of Cuban life have a wide international following—to the point that "the intelligence services know if they touch me there will be an explosion online." Still, they harass her. When she won Spain's prestigious Ortega y Gasset prize for digital journalism in April, she was prevented from going to collect the award. She would like to take up an invitation from New York University, but permission has been denied without explanation.

When I returned to Lealtad Street, I found a flurry of activity: the chicken had arrived! Rodriguez, in his green overalls, had the news up on his blackboard. He was unpacking frozen chicken legs and thighs. Chicken breast is available only on the convertible-peso market. He held up the box with a big smile. It said "Made in U.S.A." Since 2000, when Congress bowed to the farm lobby, it has been legal to sell food and agricultural products to Cuba. That means everything from chicken legs to telephone poles. In fact, the United States is now the largest exporter of food to Cuba, earning upward of $600 million this year. It's among Cuba's five biggest trading partners. So much for the embargo; it's as arbitrary as the wet-foot, dry-foot policy toward Cubans trying to escape. While America took in hundreds of millions of dollars from Cuba, it sent back 2,086 seaborne refugees in fiscal 2008. Principle has nothing to do with current Cuban policy. It's just an incoherent mess.

A gentleness inhabits Cuba, the island that Columbus, landing in 1492, called "the most beautiful land that human eyes have ever seen." It is the gentleness of time passing very slowly. The absence of visual clutter—no ads, no brands, no neon signs—leaves the mind at peace. Fidel's colossal stubbornness has delivered a singular aesthetic, striking in the age of globalized malls. I found myself thinking of a phrase of Pico Iyer's in the excellent *Reader's Companion to Cuba*, edited by Alan Ryan: "Cuba catches my heart and then makes me count the cost of that enchantment."

History may be gentler on Fidel than the ruinous state of Cuba would suggest. Fidel is a brilliant, romantic and towering figure; as such, like his country, he tends to enchant even as the cost of that enchantment mounts. Framing his revolution as being about independence—*patria* more than *socialismo*—and casting that independence as being above all from the United States, has been one of Fidel's most ingenious ideas.

And how will history judge U.S. policy toward Fidel's Cuba? Badly, I think, especially since the end of the Cold War. If the embargo had come down then, back in 1989, I doubt the regime would have survived. But the grudges were too deep, and a mistake was made. Today the policy makes little sense.

I drove out to the town of Guantánamo. There were no road signs and no road markings. Cubans say they are waiting for Obama to send paint. I passed tractor-trailers crammed with people; Chinese buses imported by Raul Castro have not yet met needs. At Guantánamo, slogans abounded: "Our duty is to be victorious" and "This is the first trench in the anti-imperialist war." From a hill,

I could see the control tower of the U.S. naval base glimmering in the distance. The land before me, and this further stretch of empty sea, had been carved from Cuba at its independence. And now Guantánamo had become synonymous with some of the most egregious acts of Bush's war on terror, acts that have tarnished America's name. Yes, Fidel's communist revolution has carried a terrible price for his people, dividing the Cuban nation, imprisoning part of it and bringing economic catastrophe. But as I gazed from Cuban hills at Guantánamo, and considered the promise of Obama's administration, I thought the wages of guilt in the Americas might just have found a fine enough balance for good sense at last to prevail.

Jane Mayer is a staff writer for the *New Yorker*, specializing in political and investigative writing. She is coauthor of *Landslide: The Unmaking of the President, 1984–1988* (Houghton Mifflin, 1988) and, with Jill Abramson, who is also represented in this anthology, of *Strange Justice: The Selling of Clarence Thomas* (Houghton Mifflin, 1994). This text is excerpted from *The Dark Side: The Inside Story of How the War on Terror Turned into a War on American Ideals* (Doubleday, 2008).

Guantánamo

As the first anniversary of September 11 approached and the White House braced for what was considered to be the very real threat of a second major attack on America, frustration practically radiated from the military's prison camp in Guantánamo Bay, Cuba. It had been three-quarters of a year since the first orange-jumpsuit-clad detainees had been unloaded from the war zone in Afghanistan, and the U.S. government had learned almost nothing of importance. In some cases, the government had learned literally nothing at all. When White House staff members had asked to see the prisoners' files, they had been astounded to discover that for some detainees, there were no details of any sort. Not even a name. There was just an assigned prisoner number and a silently uncooperative detainee.

The detainees had been described by Secretary of Defense Rumsfeld as "among the most dangerous, best-trained, and vicious killers on the face of the earth." They would "gnaw through hydraulic lines in the back" of a military plane "to bring it down," in the memorable phrase of General Richard Myers, the chairman of the Joint Chiefs of Staff. They were all "unlawful combatants," Rumsfeld had declared as they arrived on the island on January 11, 2002, with "no rights under the Geneva Convention." But the decision to sweep away the Geneva Conventions, and with them the Article 5 status hearings formerly required for each prisoner of war, had left the government with an ominous blank slate. In Afghanistan, the military had tried to sort the prisoners, but Michael Gelles, a Navy psychologist, described the process as "pure chaos."

The CIA, concerned by the paucity of valuable information emanating from the island, in the late summer of 2002 dispatched a senior intelligence analyst, who was fluent in Arabic and expert on Islamic extremism, to find out what the problem was. After spending several hours with each of about two dozen Arabic-speaking detainees, chosen in a random sampling, he concluded that an estimated one-third of the prison camp's population of more than 600 captives at the time, meaning more than 200 individuals, had no connection to terrorism whatsoever. If the intelligence haul was meager, his findings suggested, one reason was that many of the detainees knew little or nothing.

One man was a rich Kuwaiti businessman who took a trip to a different part of the world every year to do charity work. In 2001, the country he chose was Afghanistan. "He wasn't a jihadi, but I told him he should have been arrested for stupidity," the CIA officer recalled. The man was furious with the United States for rounding him up. He mentioned that every year up until then, he had bought himself a new Cadillac, but when he was released, he said, he would never buy another American car. He was switching to Mercedeses.

There was also the pitiful tale of an Iraqi Shiite who had fled from Saddam Hussein. He had escaped to Iran, where he worked in a shoe factory. He was working there alongside many Afghan immigrants when the Iranians expelled them all to Afghanistan. The Taliban then jailed him as an American "spy" for having supported the U.S.-backed opposition to Saddam Hussein. After September 11, when the United States defeated his Taliban jailers, he fled to Pakistan. But, for a $5,000 bounty, the Pakistanis arrested him as a foreign terror suspect and turned him over to U.S. officials, who in turn shipped him to Guantánamo. There, in Guantánamo along with him, was the Taliban member who had accused him of being a U.S. sympathizer. "I could barely keep a straight face, listening to him," the CIA officer recalled.

Beneath the dark tales of human folly and bad luck was a potentially toxic political problem. "I was very concerned about the system," he said. By imprisoning innocent Muslims indefinitely, outside the reach of any legal review, "I thought we were going to lose a whole damn generation" in the Arab world. Instead of helping the war on terror, Guantánamo was making the world more dangerous.

Rather than heeding the cautionary warnings about detaining the wrong suspects, the Department of Defense pushed for greater "flexibility" in Guantánamo to interrogate the detainees more forcefully. It was understandable that in the midst of the confusion and upset surrounding September 11, large and damaging mistakes would be made. But what is less comprehensible is the intransigence, and even belligerence, with which unbiased evidence of error was met months and even years later. Those who shared the goal of defeating terrorism, but saw the administration's extreme response as shortsighted and self-defeating, were shunned and excluded. Meanwhile, the sense of peril inside the top rungs of the administration fed on itself. Controversial techniques such as hooding, twenty-hour interrogation sessions, the use of military dogs to increase fear, the removal of clothing, and stress positions became familiar features of military interrogations in Guantánamo, Afghanistan, and Iraq.

The immediate cause for ratcheting up the military's techniques was a twenty-six-year-old Saudi detainee who, by late spring of 2002, had been identified as one of the few held in Guantánamo who were of genuine interest. His name was Mohammed Mani' Ahmad Sha'Lan al-Qahtani, but American officials merely referred to him as "detainee number 063." He had been captured near Tora Bora in Afghanistan in December 2001, which was a suspicious time and place for any Saudi national to be.

He claimed he'd been in Afghanistan to pursue an interest in falconry. But in July 2002, visiting FBI agents ran a routine fingerprint analysis on 063 and discovered that the pattern of whorls on his thumb matched the print of a long-sought Saudi suspect who had made an unsuccessful attempt to get through U.S. customs a month before September 11. The wanted Saudi man had a surly manner, a one-way ticket, and $2,800 in cash—barely enough to pay for a return ticket. When pressed, he had refused to identify where he was staying or who was picking him up at the airport. On August 3, 2001, an astute customs agent in Orlando, Florida, said the man gave him an unsettling feeling. On the grounds that the Saudi might be an illegal immigrant, he refused him entry into America. Through an interpreter, the Saudi vowed menacingly, "I'll be back."

As soon as the identification was made, FBI counterterrorism experts flew to Guantánamo to find out more. They knew already that on the same day that 063 was refused entry, a phone call had been placed from the Orlando Airport to one of the central Al Qaeda telephone numbers they were monitoring, in the United Arab Emirates. The FBI agents then obtained surveillance camera footage for that day of all the airport parking lots and, with meticulous detective work, identified the rental car driven by September 11 ringleader Mohammed Atta, who had apparently come to pick up Qahtani.

It seemed likely that he was the fabled twentieth hijacker, suspected of having been meant to round out the team of four on United Airlines Flight 93. It was the flight on which the passengers had valiantly overpowered the hijackers, crashing in Pennsylvania and thereby sparing its alleged intended destination, the U.S. Capitol. The three other hijacking teams each consisted of five men, fueling theories that one "muscle" man was missing.

Now that the case looked serious, the FBI sent in Lebanese-born Ali Soufan, one of only eight FBI agents who spoke Arabic fluently in 2001. He was also a Muslim who had steeped himself in the details of Islamic extremism, rocketing to the top of the bureau's terrorism investigations before reaching the age of thirty. An admirer of Khalil Gibran, he was of a philosophic bent and loved to argue religion and politics with terror suspects, drawing them out in the process. He would sit on the floor and drink tea with them, and learn about their families and their concerns. "Ali was phenomenal, and he was making lots of progress on Qahtani," recalled Gelles. "But he wasn't moving fast enough for the intelligence community."

By September, the FBI had reportedly ascertained that Qahtani had in fact intended to join the other hijackers. Qahtani had also reportedly disclosed that he had attended the key Malaysia planning meeting in 2000, along with the two future hijackers who had afterward slipped into America, unknown to the FBI. He also mentioned a relative living near Chicago whom U.S. officials were subsequently able to identify as Ali Saleh Kahlah al-Marri, an alleged "sleeper cell" agent who was already in U.S. custody as a material witness. Al-Marri was subsequently declared an "enemy combatant" and imprisoned without access to a lawyer in the U.S. naval brig in Charleston, South Carolina.

Top Pentagon officials were increasingly desperate for actionable intelligence on pending Al Qaeda attacks. They worried that Qahtani's relative in Chicago may have been part of a planned "second wave." Al Qaeda appeared more threatening than ever. U.S. officials believed the suspect was hiding more, and that tougher measures were called for to make him talk.

Documents and interviews suggest that Rumsfeld and others at the highest levels of the Pentagon were closely involved in Qahtani's case from late 2002 on. In addition, the highest-ranking civilian leaders of the Pentagon, including Rumsfeld's top lawyer, William Haynes, received a stream of information—some of it quite disconcerting—as early as the summer of 2002 about abuse of detainees in Guantánamo. Colonel Brittain Mallow argued to no avail that coercion was counterproductive and produced unreliable intelligence: "It's immoral, unethical, and it won't get good results."

By September, military officials held a series of brainstorming meetings in Guantánamo about how to crack through the resistance of detainees such as Qahtani. One source of ideas was the popular television show 24. The fictional drama was written by a Hollywood conservative who had no military or intelligence expertise whatsoever. But on Guantánamo, as everywhere else in America, its macho hero, Jack Bauer, who tortured his enemies until they talked, was followed with admiration. On 24, torture always worked. It saved America on a weekly basis. Lieutenant Colonel Diane Beaver, the top military lawyer in Guantánamo, said quite earnestly that Jack Bauer "gave people lots of ideas" as they sought for interrogation models that fall. Beaver explained that even in Guantánamo, "We saw it on cable . . . It was hugely popular."

A team of interrogators in Guantánamo went to work on Qahtani while several FBI and Criminal Task Force members warned strongly that the cruel and degrading interrogation approaches under contemplation for Qahtani were "potentially illegal." The tactics in fact touched off wrenching debates within the FBI in which one agent, who cannot be named, accused the military of criminal behavior. "When I became an agent, I swore to uphold the Constitution against all enemies, both foreign and domestic." The military officer argued that he was defending the country and the Constitution. "Not the same Constitution that I read," said the agent.

The Pentagon argued that Qahtani's interrogation was always "humane." An internal investigation strained not to disagree, proclaiming his treatment "degrading" and "abusive" but, ostensibly, not inhumane. Yet the psychological manipulations, packaged under names such as "You're a Failure Approach," read like the hazing rites of a sadistic fraternity. He was moved in shackles to a room with red lights, where he was required to stand as the national anthem was played. His head and beard were shaved, and he was also given "a birthday party" in which a party hat was placed on his head while the guards sang "God Bless America." The log notes, "Detainee became very angry." He was also shown a "puppet show" that the logs said satirized his involvement with Al Qaeda. He was subjected to loud music and told that his family was in danger. He was also told that his mother and sister were whores and that he was a homosexual. He was forced to observe foraging banana rats outside his cell, whose status was likened to his. He was made to stand so much that his feet and hands swelled and had to be wrapped in bandages and elevated. He was forced repeatedly to view film footage of the September 11 attacks, as well as photos of the victims, some of which were taped to his pants.

By the end of Qahtani's interrogation, the Pentagon proclaimed that it was all worthwhile. A Defense Department spokesman told *Time* magazine that he had become "a valuable source of information." The *New York Times*, too, quoted an unnamed "senior Bush administration official" saying that the harsher techniques used on Qahtani had produced important information about an unspecified "planned attack" and "financial networks used by terrorists."

But Cal Temple, chief of intelligence operations for the CIA, which supervised and manned much of Qahtani's interrogation, later conceded that all they really got from him was a bit of interesting information that was "contextual in nature, confirming in nature. Did it help catch Osama Bin Laden? No."

The final verdict, ironically, may have been rendered by Qahtani's former Al Qaeda commander. A year and a half after Qahtani's interrogation, when the CIA captured Khalid Sheikh Mohammed, they asked him about the twentieth hijacker. Mohammed, who had organized the September 11 attacks, had no means of checking his testimony with that of Qahtani. Mohammed was snidely condescending about Qahtani, describing him as "too much of an unsophisticated Bedouin," an "extremely simple man" who had no understanding of the Western world. He had not known what a visa was and had trouble with codes. After Qahtani failed to talk his way past U.S. customs, Mohammed said, he had "no further use or patience for him." Qahtani knew he was bound for a suicide operation in the United States, but beyond that "did not know the specifics of the operation." He had been a last-minute addition who joined the plot "very late." He was brought in near the end as muscle, to round out the numbers on the hijack teams. Mohammed said Qahtani flew to Florida unaccompanied and was given "very limited information about his points of contact" in the United States. He had not been told who was going to meet him at the airport. In other words, the gap-ridden story Qahtani had told his interrogators, which caused them to disbelieve him and push him to the point of medical emergency and, in the view of some colleagues, criminal excess, had been true from the start.

In May 2008, the Pentagon announced that it was dismissing charges against Mohammed al-Qahtani, apparently because the inhumane treatment to which he had been subjected during his long interrogation in Guantánamo, all of which had been authorized by Rumsfeld, had destroyed the credibility of his confession, hopelessly tainting the case.

The CIA, meanwhile, quietly investigated seven or more allegedly mistaken renditions of innocent victims and sent several homicide cases resulting from prisoner abuse to the Justice Department for possible criminal prosecution, but not a single officer was charged. Instead, President Bush gave George Tenet, who presided over the creation of the CIA's interrogation and detention program, the Medal of Freedom. By the last year of the Bush presidency, growing numbers of former administration insiders had abandoned the government with the conviction that in waging the war against terrorism, America had lost its way. Many had fought valiantly to right what they saw as a dangerously wrong turn. Bush, Cheney and David Addington, the chief architect of Bush's idiosyncratic interpretation of American law, were still in power, but change was in the air.

From Charlottesville, Virginia, Phillip Zelikow, who had served as executive director of the 9/11 Commission and later as an aide to Secretary of State Condoleeza Rice, took stock after returning to teaching history at the University of Virginia. In time, he predicted, the Bush Administration's descent into torture would be seen as akin to Roosevelt's internment of Japanese Americans during World War II. It happened, he believed, in much the same way, for many of the same reasons. As he put it, "Fear and anxiety were exploited by zealots and fools."

Ethan Bronner is Jerusalem bureau chief of the *New York Times*. These articles appeared in the *Times* on November 5, 2008, and January 25, 2009.

The Promise

Gaza

From far away, this is how it looks: there is a country out there where tens of millions of white Christians, voting freely, select as their leader a black man of modest origin, the son of a Muslim. There is a place on Earth—call it America—where such a thing happens. Even where the United States is held in special contempt, like here in this benighted Palestinian coastal strip, the "glorious epic of Barack Obama," as the leftist French editor Jean Daniel calls it, makes America—the idea as much as the actual place—stand again, perhaps only fleetingly, for limitless possibility.

"It allows us all to dream a little," said Oswaldo Calvo, 58, a Venezuelan political activist in Caracas, in a comment echoed to correspondents of the *New York Times* on four continents in the days leading up to the election. Tristram Hunt, a British historian, put it this way: Mr. Obama "brings the narrative that everyone wants to return to—that America is the land of extraordinary opportunity and possibility, where miracles happen."

But wonder is almost overwhelmed by relief. Mr. Obama's election offers most non-Americans a sense that the imperial power capable of doing such good and such harm—a country that, they complain, preached justice but tortured its captives, launched a disastrous war in Iraq, turned its back on the environment and greedily dragged the world into economic chaos—saw the errors of its ways over the past eight years and shifted course. They say the country that weakened democratic forces abroad through a tireless but often ineffective campaign for democracy—dismissing results it found unsavory, cutting deals with dictators it needed as allies in its other battles—was now shining a transformative beacon with its own democratic exercise.

It would be hard to overstate how fervently vast stretches of the globe wanted the election to turn out as it did in order to repudiate the Bush administration and its policies. Poll after poll in country after country showed only a few—Israel, Georgia, the Philippines—favoring a victory for Senator John McCain. "Since Bush came to power it's all bam, bam, bam on the Arabs," asserted Fathi Abdel Hamid, 40, as he sat in a Cairo coffeehouse.

The world's view of an Obama presidency presents a paradox. His election embodies what many consider unique about the United States, yet America's sense of its own specialness, of its destiny and mission, has driven it astray, they say. They want Mr. Obama, the beneficiary and exemplar of American exceptionalism, to act like everyone else, only better, to shift American policy and somehow to project both humility and leadership.

And there are others who fear that Mr. Obama will be soft in a hard-edged world where what is required is a clear line in the sand to fanatics, aggressors and bullies. Israelis worry that he will talk to Iran rather than stop it from developing nuclear weapons; Georgians worry that he will not grasp how to handle Russia. An Obama presidency, they say, risks appeasement. It will "reassure Europeans of their defects," lamented Giuliano Ferrara, editor of the Italian right-wing daily *Il Foglio*.

Such contradictory demands and expectations may reflect, in part, the unusual makeup of a man of mixed race and origin whose life and upbringing have touched several continents. "People feel he is a part of them because he has this multiracial, multiethnic and multinational dimension," said Philippe Sands, a British international lawyer and author who travels frequently, adding that people find some thread of their own hopes and ideals in Mr. Obama. "He represents, for people in so many different communities and cultures, a personal connection. There is an immigrant component and a minority component."

Francis Nyamnjoh, a Cameroonian novelist and social scientist, said he saw Mr. Obama less as a black man than "as a successful negotiator of identity margins." His ability to inhabit so many categories mirrors the African experience. Mr. Nyamnjoh said that for America to choose as its citizen in chief such a skillful straddler of global identities could not help but transform the nation's image, making it once again the screen upon which the hopes and ambitions of the world are projected.

Shi Yinhong, a professor of international relations at the People's University of China, said Mr. Obama's background, particularly his upbringing in Indonesia, made him suited to understanding the problems facing the world's poorer nations. He and others say they hope the next American president will see their place more firmly within the community of nations, engaging in what Jairam Ramesh, junior commerce minister in the Indian government, called "genuine multilateralism and not muscular unilateralism."

Assuming Mr. Obama does play by international rules more fully, as he has promised, can his government live up to all the expectations? "We have so many hopes and wishes that he will never be able to fulfill them," said Susanne Grieshaber, 40, an art adviser in Berlin who was one of 200,000 Germans to attend a speech by Mr. Obama there in July. She cited action to protect the environment, reducing the use of force and helping the less fortunate. In essence, she wants Mr. Obama to make his country more like hers. But she is sober. "I'm preparing myself for the fact that peace and happiness are not going to suddenly break out," she said.

Many in less developed countries—especially in the Arab world—agree that Mr. Obama will not carry out their wishes regarding American policy toward Israel and much else, and so they shrug off the results as ultimately making little difference. "We will be optimistic for two months but that's it," predicted Huda Naim, 38, a member of the Hamas parliament here who said her 15-year-old son had watched Mr. Obama's rise with rapt attention.

But some remain darkly suspicious of the election itself. They doubted that Mr. Obama could be nominated or elected. Now they doubt that he will govern. The skeptics say they believe that American policy is deeply institutionalized and that if Mr. Obama tries to shift it, "they"—the media, the corporate robber barons, the hidden powers—will box him in or even kill him. "I am afraid for him," said Alberto Müller Rojas, a retired Venezuelan Army general and the vice president of President Hugo Chávez's Unified Socialist Party. "The pressures he will face from certain sectors of society, especially from white Anglo-Saxon Protestants, will be enormous."

Part of that fear stems from genuine if distant affection. "He has charisma, he's good-looking, he's very smart, he's young and he knows how to make people like him, to the point that when he went to bow down to the Israelis, people here still made excuses for him," said Nawara Negm, an Egyptian writer and blogger. There is another paradox about the world's view of the election of Mr. Obama: many who are quick to condemn the United States for its racist past and now congratulate it for a milestone fail to acknowledge the same problem in their own societies, and so do not see how this election could offer them any lessons about themselves.

In Russia, for example, where Soviet leaders used to respond to any American criticism of human rights violation with "But you hang Negroes," analysts note that the election of Mr. Obama removes a stain. But they speak of it without reference to their own treatment of ethnic minorities. "Definitely, this will improve America's image in Russia," said Sergey M. Rogov, director of the Institute for U.S.A. and Canada Studies in Moscow. "There was this perception before of widespread racism in America, deeply rooted racism."

In Nigeria, a vast, populous and diverse collection of states, Reuben Abati, an influential columnist, has written, "Nigerians love good things in other lands, even if they are not making any effort to reproduce the same at home," adding, "If Obama had been a Nigerian, his race, color and age would have been an intractable problem."

So foreigners are watching closely, hoping that despite what they consider the hypocrisies and inconsistencies, the nation they once imagined would stand as a model for the future will, with greater sensitivity and less force, help solve the world's problems. There is a risk, however, to all the extraordinary international attention paid to this most international of American politicians: Mr. Obama's focus will almost certainly be on the reeling domestic economy, housing and health care. Will he be able even to lift his head and gaze abroad to all those with such high expectations?

Reporting was contributed by Rachel Donadio from Rome; Steven Erlanger from Paris; Nazila Fathi from Tehran; Isabel Kershner from Jerusalem;

Nicholas Kulish from Berlin; Clifford J. Levy from Moscow; Sarah Lyall from Reykjavik, Iceland; Lydia Polgreen from Dakar, Senegal; Simon Romero from Caracas, Venezuela; Somini Sengupta from New Delhi; Michael Slackman from Cairo; Sabrina Tavernise from Istanbul and Kiev, Ukraine; Edward Wong from Beijing; and Robert F. Worth from Sana, Yemen.

Gaza Notebook: The Bullets in My In-Box

Gaza

Faisal Husseini, a Palestinian leader who died at the start of this decade, used to tell a story about his first visit to Israel. The 1967 war had just ended, borders were suddenly opened and he took a drive to Tel Aviv, where at some point he found himself detained by an Israeli policeman. Questions and answers ensued. At one point the policeman said to him, "As a proud Zionist, I must tell you . . ." At which Mr. Husseini burst out laughing. What's so funny? the policeman asked. "I have never in my life," Mr. Husseini replied, "heard anyone refer to Zionism with anything but contempt. I had no idea you could be a proud Zionist."

I have written about the Arab-Israeli conflict on and off for more than a quarter century and have spent the past four weeks covering Israel's war in Gaza. For me, Mr. Husseini's story sums up how the two sides speak in two distinct tongues, how the very words they use mean opposite things to each other and how the war of language can confound a reporter's attempts to narrate—or a new president's attempts to mediate—this conflict in a way both sides can accept as fair.

Among Israel's Jews, there is almost no higher value than Zionism. The word is bathed in a celestial glow, suggesting selflessness and nobility. But go anywhere else in the Middle East, and Zionism stands for theft, oppression, racist exclusionism. No place, date or event in this conflicted land is spoken of in a common language. The barrier snaking across and inside the West Bank is a wall to Palestinians, a fence to Israelis. The holiest site in Jerusalem is the Temple Mount to Jews, the Noble Sanctuary to Muslims. The 1948 conflict that created Israel is one side's War of Independence, the Catastrophe for the other.

After Israel's three-week air, sea and land assault in Gaza, aimed at halting Hamas rocket fire, it is worth pausing to note how difficult it has been to narrate this war in a fashion others view as neutral, and to contemplate what that means for any attempt by the new Obama administration to try to end it.

It turns out that both narration and mediation require common ground. But trying to tell the story so that both sides can hear it in the same way feels more and more to me like a Greek tragedy in which I play the despised chorus. It feels like I am only fanning the flames, adding to the misunderstandings and mutual antagonism with every word I write because the fervent inner voice of each side is so loud that it drowns everything else out.

George Mitchell, the former Senate majority leader who is Mr. Obama's new special envoy to the Israeli-Palestinian dispute, could find something similar when he arrives here. Even though an understanding crystallized a decade ago over the outline of an eventual solution here—Israel returning essentially to its 1967 borders and a Palestinian state forming in the West Bank and Gaza—the two sides' narratives have actually hardened since attempts to reach a peace foundered. So Mr. Mitchell, who once led a commission tasked with finding a solution to the conflict, will begin this latest effort grappling with two separate wars fought here, based on two very different sets of assumptions.

Opponents of Israel feel the Gaza fighting has demonstrated (again) everything they have always believed—that Israel is a kind of Sparta that dehumanizes the Palestinians and will do anything to prevent their dignified self-determination. The ways in which Israel attacked—the overwhelming force, the racist graffiti left on walls—are what one has come to expect of that state, they say; those Hamas rockets were no challenge to the Israeli military behemoth, and, after all, who could blame the resistance fighters for launching them to protest the blockade and everything else about Israel's longstanding occupation? Those for whom Israel is the victim and never the aggressor likewise saw in this war a reaffirmation of their beliefs—that Hamas, an Islamist terror group, hides its fighters behind women and children; that Israel's army was an exemplar of restraint and respect, holding its fire when civilians were in sight, allowing tons of humanitarian aid in even while at war (what other army would be so decent?).

Abroad, people care deeply about this conflict. That should make it easier for a reporter to cover, because the actors and place names and history are familiar. But it turns out that, like the actors themselves, the audiences have utterly distinct and contrasting sets of assumptions. Every time I fail to tell the story each side tells itself, I have failed in its eyes to do my job. That adds up to a lot of failure.

What's more, the competing war narratives are part of a larger narrative disconnect. One side says that after thousands of years of oppression, the Jewish nation has returned to its rightful home. It came in peace and offered its hand to its neighbors numerous times only to be met with a sword. Opposition to Israel, this side argues, stems from Muslim intolerance, nationalist fervor and rank anti-Semitism, all fed by envy at the young state's success. Every time I write an article about the conflict that does not mirror this story line—if, for example, I focus on Palestinian suffering or alleged Israeli misdeeds or quote a human rights group like Amnesty International—I have proved myself to be a secret sharer with the views of the enemy. As one recent complainer wrote, "To read your paper, all the questions and criticism are directed at Israel, and it is all based on a collection of anti-Semitic organizations masquerading as humanitarians."

The other side tells a different story: there is no Jewish nation, only followers of a religion. A group of European colonialists came here, stole and pillaged, throwing hundreds of thousands off their land and destroying their villages and homes. A country born in sin, Israel has built up an aggressive military with help from Washington in the grips of a powerful Jewish lobby. Every time I fail to allude to that story—when, for example, I examine Israel's goals in its Gaza war without implicitly condemning it as a massacre, or write about Israel in ways that do not call into question its legitimacy—I have revealed my affiliation and can no longer be trusted as a reporter.

Since the war started, on December 27, I have received hundreds of messages about my coverage. They are generally not offering congratulations on a job well done. "Thanks to you and other scum like yourself," said one, "Israel can now kill hundreds and you can report the whole thing like it was some random train wreck." "Bronner," said another, "you're back to your usual drivel about only the poor filthy Arabs—who voted for the Hamas people who got them into this predicament—with incessant indiscriminate rocket fire on innocent Israelis." There are also blogs and chat sites on both sides that spend time accusing all the journalists here of having agendas because our articles mention facts or trends that they consider a diversion from the real story.

Because Israel barred foreign journalists from entering Gaza until the war ended, the *New York Times* relied on my Palestinian colleague here, Taghreed el-Khodary, for on-the-ground coverage of the fighting. We would speak several times a day as she cautiously went out. Her first stop was usually Shifa Hospital, to get a sense of civilian casualties. Early in the war, at the hospital, she witnessed the murder of an alleged Israeli collaborator by Hamas gunmen. They shot him in the skull more or less in front of her. One of the gunmen told Taghreed that she should never mention what she saw to anyone. She told him there was not a chance she would stay silent, then made some calls to find out about other such events and sent me the information, which we published the next day. A couple of Arab bloggers went after Taghreed with the worst insult they could come up with—Zionist. She was a Palestinian Uncle Tom doing the bidding of her white-man bosses at a newspaper that, as one reader said in an e-mail message, "is fully complicit in the atrocities that Israel commits against Palestinians in Gaza and the West Bank. You make it sound guiltless and reasonable. That's your assignment."

At the same time, Israeli officials and their backers declared that keeping reporters out of Gaza was the right move because no independent journalism could possibly occur in an area run by Hamas, which controls every utterance here. Have any of these people ever read Taghreed's work? Or any of our work out of here? Many have, but it doesn't matter, because their belief in their own view is so overpowering that anything that contradicts it becomes a minor detail. As another reader put it, "Basically, you are aiding terrorists and causing the increase in bloodshed while telling one-sided stories, totally ignoring the whole picture." He did say one thing I agree with: "You should not be a reporter if you are not telling the whole story, not just the parts that sell." I would offer a mediator the same advice.

Chris Hedges spent two decades as a foreign correspondent for the *Dallas Morning News* and the *New York Times,* covering conflicts around the globe, including seven years in the Middle East, where he was the *Times'* bureau chief. These are excerpts from "A Gaza Diary," published in the October 2001 issue of *Harper's* magazine.

A Gaza Diary

Thursday morning, June 14, Jerusalem

The artist Joe Sacco and I are driving up through the Jerusalem Hills to Beit Agron, the government-run press building. Beit Agron was the first place I visited in 1988, when I moved to Jerusalem as the Middle East bureau chief for the *Dallas Morning News.* I had no office, no staff, and no experience in the Middle East. I had arrived from Lausanne, where for four months I had studied Arabic. My teacher, an Egyptian, used to write on the board phrases such as "The Arabs are good. The Jews are bad." I later took the Hebrew University conversational Arabic course, taught by a kind and gentle Palestinian professor, Omar, who became a close friend.

Arabic is a delicate and beautiful construct. The language is poetic, magical, with calls and responses, ornate greetings and salutations, for everything from eating to entering a house. When someone brings you food you say, "May God bless your hands." If offered a coffee you say, "Coffee always," meaning may we always drink coffee during moments like this. Seven years later, now the Middle East bureau chief for the *New York Times,* I had spent 600 hours of study and reached the conclusion that mastery of Arabic was a lifelong pursuit. A little of it, though, goes a long way. After being captured by the Iraqi Republican Guard in Basra in 1991 during the Shiite uprising following the Gulf War, I was able to recite strings of bad Arabic jokes and talk about my family. I wrote Omar a thank-you note when I was released.

Joe and I pass the rusting hulks of crude Israeli armored vehicles, left as a monument to the 1948 war that made possible a Jewish state. We skirt the old walled city, its quadrilateral shape and network of streets laid out by the Roman emperor Hadrian. In the distance stands the Jaffa Gate, where, in 1538, in ornate and cursive Arabic, an inscription was placed by Suleiman, the second Ottoman ruler of Jerusalem: "In the name of Allah the Merciful, the Great Sultan, King of the Turks, Arabs, and Persians, Suleiman son of Selim Khan—may Allah make His Kingdom eternal—gave the order to build this blessed Wall."

In Beit Agron, I run into familiar Israeli press officials. They are efficient: our press cards are ready in minutes. They welcome me back. They ask about New York. They hand out cell-phone numbers and tell us to call if we need assistance.

Thursday afternoon, June 14, en route to Gaza City

We come to the Erez checkpoint, in the north of the strip that separates Gaza from Israel. Israeli soldiers hunker down in concrete bunkers, the black nozzles of their machine guns poking out between the sandbags. Gun battles between Palestinians and Israelis are frequent here, especially after dark. I hoist on my body armor, which has the word PRESS emblazoned across its front. The twenty-six pounds of Kevlar plating make me feel as if I were wearing a body cast.

At the last Israeli guard post, the blue-and-white flag with the Star of David on a pole overhead, the young soldiers peer out and tell us jokingly to have a nice trip.

I point to the word PRESS on my chest.

"Shoot me here," I say, laughing.

And then I point to my head.

"Not here."

Friday morning, June 15, Gaza City

In the morning, we are joined by my friend Azmi Kashawi. Azmi—who with his girth could easily play Falstaff, were he not a devout Muslim who does not drink—is a fellow reporter. We have been through a lot together. Without Azmi many doors remain shut. I am grateful that he has agreed to accompany us to Khan Younis.

Friday afternoon, June 15, Abu Holi

Joe and I lift our body armor into the small trunk of Azmi's car, where Azmi keeps his own vest and a television camera, and head down the coast road for Khan Younis. Azmi beats the wheel with his fingers and hums along to a tape of the Egyptian singer Abdel Halim Hafez. He keeps urging us to look at the coast; he himself drives with his head turned to the side, watching the rolling white surf, praising the sea. We weave around trucks and buses. One must trust Allah and Azmi's horn—used in lieu of brakes—when one climbs into Azmi's small, yellow car.

The gaiety of our drive is cut short when we reach the Israeli-controlled junction at Abu Holi, about fifteen miles outside of Gaza City. The landscape here is lunar. For acres around, fields have been bulldozed, houses demolished, and olive trees felled and hauled away. In the distance sits a conical cement tower manned by Israeli soldiers. On either side of the checkpoint, long lines of cars wait to cross. The coast road is the only way to get to southern Gaza and Khan Younis, and at this point it crosses a highway used by Jewish settlers and the Israeli army. When the settlers speed by in their white armored cars, all Palestinian traffic is stopped. Weeks can pass with the intersection closed or the soldiers letting through only a thin trickle of traffic. One of Azmi's friends, who lived in Khan Younis and worked in Gaza City, gave up trying to make the commute and moved in with friends in Gaza.

Azmi shuts off his tape player. He insists that everyone open a window. We do not speak. We unbuckle our seatbelts. In all war zones, everyone needs a door and a swift way to roll out onto the ground if shooting breaks out. We creep forward in the stop-and-go traffic until we face the tower. Azmi leans forward over the wheel. He narrows his eyes and concentrates on a disembodied hand poking out of a slit in the bulletproof glass. The flat palm means stop. A bad read, a lurch past the tower when the Israelis do not want you to move, could see your vehicle raked by gunfire. Suicide bombers, who conceal explosives in donkey carts, view spots like these as prime targets. We do not move. We wait. Finally the hand behind the thick Plexiglas flutters, motioning us through.

Azmi, sweating now in the heat, begins to drive cautiously over the speed bumps. Joe sketches the scene in his notepad. We cross the settlers' road—Palestinians are not allowed to use it—and pass the long line of cars waiting on the other side. It is several minutes before Azmi agrees to roll the windows up and restore the air-conditioning. None of us feels like talking.

Friday afternoon, June 15, Khan Younis

Khan Younis is a dense, gray, concrete shantytown, the black waters from sewers running in thin rivulets down the middle of alleys. There are no gardens or trees. There is no place for children to play, other than the dunes in front of the neighboring Israeli settlements. Vendors in small, dingy stalls sell roasted corn on the cob or falafel. Hunks of meat hang on giant hooks, alongside wooden tables piled with tomatoes, potatoes, green peppers, and green beans. During the rains, the camp floods with wastewater. Only the lonely minarets, poking up out of the clutter, lend a bit of dignity to the slum.

Khan Younis is one of eight refugee camps in Gaza. It is surrounded on three sides, like a horseshoe, by Israeli military positions. The soldiers there fire down on the roofs of the concrete shacks—asbestos mostly, held down by piles of rocks, cement blocks, and old tires. Bands of Palestinian gunmen, who often initiate the shooting, fire back.

We turn down a crowded alley and come upon a group of older men seated on chairs in a patch of sand, playing backgammon. A black plastic water tank and a TV antenna loom over them. A radio, perched on a window ledge behind metal bars, plays Arabic music. At dusk these men, and the families that live along the perimeter, will move deeper into the camp to seek safety with relatives and friends. Bands of Palestinian gunmen will creep up to shoot at the Israeli positions, and the crackle of automatic fire will punctuate the night air.

Saturday, June 16, Khan Younis

The Israeli positions on the dunes virtually surround the Jewish settlements, whose whitewashed villas and manicured lawns and gardens look as if they have been lifted out of a southern California suburb. Inside the fence are warehouses where cheap Palestinian labor once stitched together clothes for export or tended rows of vegetables in huge greenhouses.

We set off to find Fuad Faqawi, who runs the United Nations Relief and Works Agency (UNRWA) for Palestinian Refugees office in Khan Younis. The Palestinians in Gaza, 1.1 million of them, most of whom lack the means to leave, live in a 147-square-mile area. Twenty percent of that territory belongs to the sixteen Jewish settlements, home to about 6,000 Jewish settlers. In other words, one-fifth of Gaza is in the hands of 0.5 percent of the people who live there.

Faqawi brings out a worn pouch and tenderly unfolds sepia documents. The papers, from the government of Palestine, then a British mandate, permitted Faqawi's father to sell tobacco and food in his grocery in Jaffa. He holds out the Register of Lands document, issued under the land-settlement ordinance of 1928, that proves title to his father's house. "Our house in Jaffa exists," he says, offering me the paper. "I have all the documents. Two Iraqi Jewish families live there. I visited them in 1975. We had coffee. They told me they knew it was my house. They said they had left four houses in Iraq. They told me to go to Iraq and take one."

As a boy growing up in the camp, Faqawi lived with his eight brothers in a tiny concrete shack. His family built a new structure on the foundations of the old one about fifteen years ago. The boys shared one bedroom. He had no shoes, no schoolbooks, and was plagued by disease and insects.

"U.N. officials would come to my elementary school and tell us to open up our shirts," he says. "They would douse us with DDT. . . . When I saw pictures in magazines of the way other people lived I was jealous. I was especially jealous of children who could have long hair. We could not let our hair grow because of the lice."

As we speak, a homemade mortar, launched a few blocks away, rips through the air. It, or one fired later, is sure to bring an Israeli response. Groups of Palestinian men and boys are already at the dunes, throwing rocks at the Israeli jeeps patrolling the Gani Tal Jewish settlement. The soldiers will open fire and wound eight Palestinians, five under the age of eighteen. At about the same time in Halhoul, a town north of Hebron in the West Bank, Israeli soldiers will wound seven Palestinians, including two medics. The shooting will take place as Palestinians try to dismantle a barricade, built by Israeli soldiers, across the main road leading into the town.

Faqawi goes into his house again, a cigarette dangling from his mouth, and returns with twisted scraps of Israeli munitions, including black, dartlike needles known as fléchettes. The fin-tailed fléchettes are packed inside shells and spray out in a deadly mass when the shells detonate. Three women in Gaza were killed by fléchettes a few days ago.

Faqawi sighs. "We are seeing a lot of divorce, a lot of fighting in the homes, and a lot of shouting in the street," he says. "But I still believe in negotiations." He looks at his two sons, who grimace when he speaks of compromise. As we leave the house, Faqawi leans toward me and says quietly, "I can never say that the way to fight the Israelis is to blow ourselves up. I can't allow my children to think like this. I will always disagree with them." He stops, his eyes weary. "If I did agree," he says, "I could never tell them."

Sunday afternoon, June 17, the dunes

I sit in the shade of a palm-roofed hut on the edge of the dunes, momentarily defeated by the heat, the grit, the jostling crowds, the stench of the open sewers and rotting garbage. A friend of Azmi's brings me, on a tray, a cold glass of tart, red *carcade* juice.

Barefoot boys, clutching kites made out of scraps of paper and ragged soccer balls, squat a few feet away under scrub trees. Out of the dry furnace air, a disembodied voice crackles over a loudspeaker. "Come on, dogs," the voice booms in Arabic. "Where are all the dogs of Khan Younis? Come! Come!" The invective continues to spew: "Son of a bitch!" "Son of a whore!" "Your mother's cunt!"

The boys dart in small packs up the sloping dunes to the electric fence that separates the camp from the Jewish settlement. They lob rocks toward two armored jeeps parked on top of the dune and mounted with loudspeakers. Three ambulances line the road below the dunes in anticipation of what is to come.

A percussion grenade explodes. The boys, most no more than ten or eleven years old, scatter, running clumsily across the heavy sand. They descend out of sight behind a sandbank in front of me. There are no sounds of gunfire. The soldiers shoot with silencers. The bullets from the M-16 rifles tumble end over end through the children's slight bodies. They kill an eleven-year-old boy, Ali Murad, and seriously wound four more, three of whom are under eighteen. Children have been shot in other conflicts I have covered—death squads gunned them down in El Salvador and Guatemala, mothers with infants were lined up and massacred in Algeria, and Serb snipers put children in their sights and watched them crumple onto the pavement in Sarajevo—but I have never before watched soldiers entice children like mice into a trap and murder them for sport.

Monday morning, June 18, Khan Younis

In the morning, we attend the boy's funeral. It is easy to find. Trucks with mounted loudspeakers tour the camp, urging residents to attend and giving the street address. The boy's father, Murad Abdel Rahman, stares vacantly as he stands up from one in a long line of purple plastic chairs placed in the street and shakes the hands of mourners. "This is what I worked so hard to prevent," he says, his voice hoarse and low. "I took Ali with me every day to my restaurant at 6:00 in the morning on al-Bahar Street. I made him promise he would not go to the dunes to throw rocks. Yesterday he asked to go home at 3:00. He said he had to study for the makeup sessions they are holding because of all the school closings this year."

"We all threw rocks," says Ahmed Moharb, ten. "Over the loudspeaker the soldier told us to come to the fence to get chocolate and money. Then they cursed us. Then they fired a grenade. We started to run. They shot Ali in the back. I won't go again. I am afraid."

Every new death pushes the voices of moderation deeper into the background. Azmi, who has Israeli friends, says he no longer speaks of them for fear of being branded a collaborator. Those moderates who keep open the channels of communication are often the first to be silenced by their own side. As in most conflicts, all dialogue has been reduced to a scream.

Thursday afternoon, June 21, Jerusalem

Joe and I cross back over Erez, our heavy body armor slung over our shoulders. We climb into an old taxi, which we have arranged to meet us, and start for Jerusalem. The wide expanse of highway, the gleaming gas stations, the roadside restaurants, the stucco homes, the lush valleys filled with vineyards and crops, seem shockingly unfamiliar now.

The afternoon light casts a soft golden glow over Jerusalem, on the crest of the hill before us. It is hard not to be moved by the city, by all it has endured and will endure. It has seen its share of zealots, those who killed in the name of causes now forgotten. They, too, believed they were faced with an insoluble human dilemma.

I have been invited to dinner with a friend, a surgeon, and his family in their affluent home in West Jerusalem. His father fled Vienna for Palestine shortly after the Nazis took over Austria. They are liberal Israelis, no friends of Sharon and no friends of the growing religious right. They support the creation of a Palestinian state. I worry about them every time a suicide bomb explodes in the city.

At the table, I try to make them grasp, just for a moment, what I felt watching the children on the dunes in Khan Younis. I tell the story. They admit that it is wrong, and then add, "But you have to understand, the Palestinians are brainwashed." I concede the point, hoping only to impart the raw cruelty of what I saw. I try again. I fail. I fall silent.

War has an alluring simplicity. It reduces the ambiguities of life to blacks and whites. It fills our mundane days with passion. It promises to rid us of our problems. When it is over, many miss it. I have sat in Sarajevo cafés and heard that although no one wished back the suffering, they all yearned for the lost spirit of self-sacrifice and collective struggle.

War's cost is exacting. It destroys families. It leaves behind a wasteland, irreconcilable grief. It is a disease, and in the night air I smell its contagion. Justice is not at issue here: war consumes the good along with the wicked. There will be no stopping it. Pity will be banished. Fear will rule. It is the old lie again, told to children desperate for glory: *Dulce et decorum est pro patria mori.*

Paul Salopek is a journalist based mostly in Johannesburg, South Africa. As a foreign correspondent with the *Chicago Tribune*, he won two Pulitzer Prizes and a George Polk Award. The dispatches below are typical of dozens written over a decade of war reporting across the globe. Dashed out in an hour or two after filing the day's main news story, they often captured the textures of life in a war zone better than what appeared on the front page.

In Horses, a Personal Refuge

Pec, Kosovo, June 25, 1999

They are fine-looking animals, the horses of Kosovo. This is an inexpert opinion. I grew up around horses in Mexico and the Southwest and know them as partners in work, nothing else. I've always liked the way they smell. I like the way they warm your palm when you stroke their backs. I like their honest bigness. But I'm no authority. Mostly, I just like their associations in memory with mountains and open country.

So I say again, with these caveats, there are good-looking horses in Kosovo. I was driving the other day on the newly opened road between Pec and Kosovska Mitrovica, running over the rubble to avoid the mines planted alongside the asphalt, feeling tense. The landscape was beautiful, a lot like the San Juan country of southern Colorado, but completely devoid of people.

In a place like Kosovo this is cause for alarm. Here, people—even armed ones—offer at least the illusion of safety. You can argue or plead with a man with a gun, but with silence, with the tracking barrel of a sniper, there's no argument at all. For almost 13 miles, past scorched farms and villages, not a soul stirred. This was disagreeable.

But there were horses. Strong, big-haunched cart horses wandered in loose herds along the blacktop. They had the road to themselves, and they shined in the sun the way horses do. I looked at the size of their hooves (big as saucers; flatland animals), and I admired the healthy polish of their summer coats. I immediately and irrationally felt better.

Later, after covering another bad stretch of road to a remote Kosovo Liberation Army base (the guerrillas in the back seat insisted the road had been demined; by instinct, I uncurled my thumbs from the steering wheel—my own private terror is having my thumbs ripped off while being blown out of a car), horses again came to the rescue. Waiting to interview the rebel chief, I saw a guerrilla walking a draft horse down a village road. He cut a very romantic figure: sunburned fighter, chest draped with ammo bandoleers, leading a stout white mare harnessed for work. She was to pull a truck out of a pothole.

I tried talking with the man. This was difficult, because the translator was a city girl who didn't know the words for fetlocks, frogs and withers, but we managed. I showed him how people shoe an ornery animal in the Sierra Madre, using a length of rawhide rope. He proudly displayed the ornate leather harness. His blunt farmer's fingers roamed over the animal with skillful familiarity. In the few minutes we chatted, I learned more about the nature of this peasant army than a half-dozen interviews with military eggheads in Western capitals.

Horses are pretty much everywhere in Kosovo these days. This was farm country, and people here owned tractors, but many kept horses too—for tradition's sake. Today, the animals roam the ruined streets of cities, poking their heads into the gaping windows of empty houses or bolting out of the path of NATO tanks. Some have stepped on land mines. Others have been shot by Yugoslav troops or eaten by feral dogs. The ones that survived—those are my personal refuge.

There is this one horse. It was here in Djakovica. A large family—a mom and dad, a big family of uncles, aunts and cousins—was showing me where its favorite boy had been shot down by the Yugoslavs. This was supposed to be an interview. But first one and then another began to cry, and soon the whole crowd was weeping. About 20 people stood on a dirt street, completely undone, just wailing. I closed my notebook. But the father insisted. Even though he couldn't get a coherent word out between his ragged sobs, he wanted his son's story told.

Finally, I had to look away. There was a horse. It was white, chewing on grass in an empty lot. An unexceptional animal. I will never forget it.

Hints of Lives Are All That Remains

Shomali Plain, Afghanistan, December 4, 2004

What happened to you, people of Rabat? You who baked wheaty nan in kitchens where iron stoves rust, punctured by shrapnel? You who dug fine irrigation canals, mending leaks with fistfuls of mud and carefully placed stones? American B-52s have turned the canals into graves for the Taliban. On the morning of the final attack, the harsh ordinariness of your lives lay exposed to the sun: old buckets, a woman's white-heeled shoe, a rotting sweater, a turban unraveled like a fleeing snake. In one mud-walled alley, a plastic whistle lay—once blown by a favorite daughter or son?

The advancing Northern Alliance rebels ignored your ghosts. Tough Solangis, they slogged under the weight of their ammunition past your ruined homes, joking and singing on the footpaths your men had trod to barley fields: just another day's work to be done. One platoon of rebels took cover in the court-yard of a rich man's house, shitting in full view of one another beneath dead plum trees. Like the rag ends of village life scattered in the dust, there were no secrets left to hide.

These hard men cared nothing for you, people of Rabat. The sunny yards where your sticky harvests of raisins dried, or the flat mud roofs where you kept noisy pigeons in cages of wire, these were just more places to die on the road to Kabul. But I remember. I know which block on your main street dips across a broad, sandy gulch that floods during the rains, but is good for a soccer match after school. I know where your oldest vineyard grows, behind a wall with a blue door that now hangs crazily on its hinges.

Who lived in the mud fortress where commander Bashir directed machine-gun fire at the Taliban front line? He must have been a tall man. The steps up to his shattered watchtower are steep.

And your poorest must have huddled in the maze of small, unkempt houses across the field from the mosque—where a Solangi's feet were blown off by a booby trap that exploded with a dirty brown pop. The Solangis walked out of your village in the tracks left by their tank, headed south. That was November 12, the day before Kabul fell. Advancing on the Taliban trenches, some held hands firmly, as people falling from buildings do.

Where are you, people of Rabat? Wheezing in some camp in Pakistan? Sell-ing sweets on a Tehran street corner? Or are you dead beneath your fields? Leaving Afghanistan the other day, I pressed my face against the window of a United Nations mercy flight, searching for your emptied homes. I distinguished nothing. The dusty Shomali Plain stretched below like the page of a crumbling manuscript that has been written on and erased, too many times.

Now They Execute Polite Shuffles: There's a Strange Sameness in the Stories of Baath Party Members in Iraq

Mosul, Iraq, April 15, 2003

They show up singly or in pairs, quiet men in cheap, shiny suits, most of them scared, a few robotic and in shock, virtually all of them excessively polite in the fussy way of palace courtiers. This is how Saddam Hussein's men come to surrender.

"He is a good guy," Farhan Sharafani, the negotiator, will say in the parlor of his family's modest home, which is crawling with former Baath Party members. "This one has an interesting story." And they do. Up to a point. Because no matter who they are—generals who have just walked away from a Baghdad army division (as one is) or the secret policeman who taps local phones (as one is)—there is a strange sameness to all their stories. I did this. I did that. No violence. No repression. Nothing to really feel contrite about: it was just a job, shuffling troops or papers.

All this may be true. We have heard it all before: the banality of evil. Just taking orders. "To be frank, we expected a popular uprising," says the mild-mannered chief of the local Muhkabarat, Hussein's fearsome security police. "Some segments of society were discriminated against." Maybe he means the minority Kurds. At least 100,000 of them were discriminated against with extreme prejudice. As in butchered. Or perhaps the majority Shiites, who were bombed out of their southern swamps with napalm. Raising these issues seems a bit rude over sweet tea and cigarettes. They always gaze back steadily. As if their honor had been questioned.

The most honorable man in Sharafani's way station for police-state castoffs is, without question, Sharafani himself. A Kurdish tribal leader with impeccable clothes and connections, he says he will help none of the 55 U.S.-named war criminals in Hussein's regime. Most here are small fish, like the wiretapper who calls himself "only an electrical engineer." The army general was the biggest catch so far. He walked and hitchhiked two days from Baghdad. Sharafani called the Americans on his cell phone, as if he were delivering a pizza. More come every day. Everyone trusts Sharafani. "I serve my people," he says modestly. Then he orders more tea. Imagine a dashing young Omar Sharif in Kurdish pantaloons and cummerbund. Sharafani is cooler.

This is how the war ends in Mosul. Not with a bang but a whimper. Hussein's secret policemen sit on a tattered couch in a dim parlor, awaiting their fate. They watch Egyptian soap operas in complete silence. The broken clock on the wall doesn't tick. It always shows a few minutes before midnight.

In Land of Ruin, a House of Stone Shelters Delight

Luanda, Angola, March 26, 2004

We are living in the house of a 100-year-old woman. True, she is actually 97. But she carries herself like 100—someone who walks the planet regally, in weary triumph, with a sense of ownership, a queen who knows the world's secrets and finds them dull. She sips her guava juice alone, at her own table. Once, she was young and rich and beautiful. She employed a Portuguese driver—a white. This is still commented on. Dona Maria Eulalia Augusta Leal: Even her burnished name makes her the matriarch of Casa Soleme.

The house is made of stone. Six middle-age daughters—the five Marias and Margarida—rent out its clean and simple rooms. A hive of granddaughters mop, cook, tap at the computer, book your appointments, translate, drive your car, buy your plane ticket, shame the police officer who extorts the bribe, repair your faith and your shoes. A house of women. Efficient. Protective. Savvy. Always talking. Laughing. Singing. The lilt of Cape Verde bouncing in their veins. Only the parrot in the cage is quiet. He is overwhelmed.

So are we. The Portuguese engineer, the American Bible thumper, the Polish journalist traveling the globe to write about waterfalls—the guests. Even before we meet, we are not cold strangers. "Hello, I am calling from South Africa to reserve a room." "So sorry, sir, but we are full," granddaughter Rita's wiry voice says from 1,000 miles away. "But if you like, you can stay at my Auntie Mila's house." After one hour we are friends—dandling slobbery babies whose names we mispronounce, sharing YES cigarettes, helping cut fruit. After three days, if we have not yet married one of the granddaughters, we are family anyway. "You skipped your dinner!" huffs Maria Eugenia, a former language professor and baker of custard tarts. "I will send pasta to your room!" "Why look so worried?" asks Maria Eulalia, the accountant who years ago fell in love with Angola's most famous reporter—a near disaster, but let's not talk about that. "You work too hard!" she says. "Slow down!"

Every day we stumble in, dazed. We are beaten down by the glassy heat of Angola. By the ruinscape of the capital, with its endless slums and cheap new oil-boom office buildings. By the arrogant politicians. By the haunted countryside, ticking with 10 million mines. By injustice. By the absence of so many war dead—they have hardened Angola's heart.

But not at Casa Soleme. Soleme—"Solo Leal y Monteiros." Only Leal and Monteiros. The family names of the six sisters in charge. "No, we will never expand," says Maria Antonia, the jolly social worker who studied in France. "Life is beautiful. This is as good as it gets." And it is true: inside the stone house, we breathe easy. We feel human. We begin to smile again.

Remember the way. Turn right off the Atlantic waterfront where the captured pirate boats rot at anchor. Go up the hill past the parliament, with its honor guards in their toy-soldier uniforms, and then left. There it is. A patio teeming with children in every hue of brown. A silent parrot in its cage. Music. Inside, a century-old woman will be sitting stiffly in a parlor stuffed with sepia photographs and dark Portuguese furniture; a dim, cool place closed to the outside world, like those old-fashioned lockets women used to wear on their breasts.

Thanassis Cambanis covered Middle Eastern turmoil for five years, first for the *Boston Globe* and later for the *New York Times*. He followed the invasion and occupation of Iraq from 2003 to 2006, and then shifted his focus to Lebanon during the 2006 war with Israel. His book *A Privilege to Die: Inside Hezbollah's Legions and Their Endless War against Israel* was published in 2010. In 2005, a sectarian civil war and several uprisings against the American occupation tore apart Iraq. Yet most Iraqis lived, as ever, on the fringes of history, playing bit parts but usually paying the heaviest personal price. The first piece is the story of one Iraqi clan on the timeless periphery; the second provides a penetrating account of the psychology of a Hezbollah fighter. They appeared in the *Boston Globe* on March 21, 2005, and December 30, 2006.

Iraq: Transformation Bypasses the Heartland

Buaraif, Iraq

Regimes come and go, but decades of political revolutions in Iraq have hardly changed a thing for the destitute tribesmen who cultivate wheat and dates here on the east bank of the Euphrates. This is the fiefdom of Sheik Humaid Sagban, 77: a patch of chicken-scratched farmland that's only a half hour by car from Najaf but feels like an Iraqi village from a century ago.

For almost half a century, Sagban has presided over a clan of 1,500 whose way of life has barely changed since the reign of King Faisal II ended in 1958. The sons of Buaraif village die in Iraq's armed forces—once as Saddam Hussein's conscripts forced to fight in Iran and Kuwait, now as volunteer soldiers slain by insurgents who revile them as traitors. Buaraif's women are kept out of sight in back rooms when men visit. And Buaraif's farmers cannot remember a time that they could afford enough water to fill their irrigation canals and eke out more than a subsistence crop from their fields.

This forgotten place clings to the margins of Iraq's history. About a third of the country's population lives in rural areas, according to United Nations statistics, and as many as 5 million Shiites live scattered in backwaters like Buaraif. It's the other Iraq, the one that rarely gets the attention of politicians in Baghdad.

American officials point to rural areas such as this one when they argue that Iraq's heartland is not in turmoil. While it is true that most cataclysmic violence of the current war has bypassed Buaraif, so too have most of the positive developments of the past five decades, including the fruits of Iraq's most recent transformation.

"Life always has been hard, and we always have been poor," Sagban said as he received visitors in his dirt-floored living room, which doubles as a tribal headquarters. Government power has shifted hands countless times since

Sagban was born, in 1927, when British colonialists still held sway. Each new regime brought its own flavor, he said, some more tyrannical, some more prosperous, but all equally unpleasant for the denizens of Buaraif. Iraq's historic elections probably will not change much for his rural tribesman either, said Sagban, whose grip on politics is so hazy that he is not even sure for whom he voted January 30, when he cast his ballot at a school across the river. What he does know is the seemingly inescapable fate dealt the villagers of Buaraif—a dual dose of bad luck that seems to strike the village's sons and its fields, whatever the era and whatever the government in Baghdad.

Late last year, 12 young men from the village were massacred on a road north of here, on their way home after signing up to join the Iraqi National Guard. Their killers apparently targeted them because they were Shiite Muslims. A pair of bereaved fathers paid Sagban a visit on a recent morning, in part to bemoan the killing of their sons, in part to discuss a proposed marriage of another child, and in part because there is not that much to do in Buaraif. "Today is better than Saddam's time. We just need security," said Dawood Salman Shiah, 55, the older of the two visitors. One son was killed in the roadside massacre; his other son still fights in the Iraqi Army. "We come to the sheik for advice when we have business, and when we need his advice," Shiah explained. "They come to me for everything," the sheik said, laughing. "He comes to me to ask what color dishdasha he should choose before he goes to the tailor."

It is easy to see why the men visit Sagban every day. His eyes brim with tears of sympathy while he tells stories to his visitors. Usually, the tales end with an impromptu stream of rhyming verse and a bellow of laughter from Sagban, even if he doesn't mean the story to be funny. "There was a lady from Amarra Province who had lost four sons in the army," Sagban began, in a tone suggesting he was telling a joke. One day she found herself standing before Saddam, he said, and as the dictator watched, she began a mourning ritual. Sagban in pantomime started pounding his chest rhythmically with a closed fist. The woman listed the fates of her sons: one had died in the battle of Shib, another in the battle of Tib—both during the Iran-Iraq war—a third was tortured to death, and the last disappeared after deserting from the army. Sagban told the story in metered rhyme, then broke out into roaring laughter that he seems to deploy like defensive gunfire to keep defeatist grief at bay. Still wheezing, he added: "It's a true story. She was my cousin. Saddam had her executed."

The time of Iraq's kings, from 1921 to 1958, was the best, the three men agreed, because the royal military would draft only one son from every family. Wars, uprisings, and revolutions have swept through their rural Shiite region every five or 10 years for as long as Sagban can remember. "There have been so many times when you couldn't stick your hand out the window without being shot," he said. Without self-pity, Sagban looks back on a tenure as tribal chief that began when his father died in 1960 and has been marked throughout by unrelenting poverty and spikes of bloody chaos.

His mud-brick house on the riverbank gets two hours of electricity a day. The latrine drains into an open pit, 20 feet from his front door. The back of the house overlooks the river; a small flock of geese and chickens forage beside a pile of sheep manure.

He wears a dirty navy blue raincoat, and when he is cold, wraps a brown wool blanket over his shoulders. He wears a checkered head scarf held in place with a leather band. If he looks like a poor cousin to the other clan heads of the mammoth Bani Hassan tribe, which claims 800,000 members from Basra to Jordan and whose shawls are often embroidered with gold thread, that's because he is. Some of his 32 children still live in his compound. Two sons, Abbas and Hussein, serve tea and biscuits to the visitors. Sagban has four wives, the maximum allowed under Islam.

Somehow, modernity seems to have passed by the 500-odd people living in this cluster of homes, although in view just across the river, the county seat of Abbasiyat district boasts the trappings of a developed town: new schools, a police station, and a shopping strip. Here in Buaraif, unchanging tribal mores control life. Sagban's main job as clan head is to resolve disputes through the timeworn tribal right of 'fassil, retribution payments that eliminate the need for vengeance. "For a murder, you must pay 2 million Iraqi dinar," Sagban said, an amount equal to $1,400. "A kidnapping costs the same as a murder. If you shoot someone in the leg, you pay 1 million dinar. If you beat someone and draw blood, you must pay 150,000 dinar." Tribal law is rigid and not always fair. "If you shoot a man and his hospital bill is 10 million dinar, you still only have to pay him 1 million," Sagban said.

Beyond life-and-death matters, the village's main problem is water. No water pipes run to people's homes, and health officials have warned that the Euphrates water is too polluted to drink. But because there are no alternatives, the locals dig wells in their front yards or draw silty brown water directly from the river. There also is not enough water for the fields. With only two hours a day of electricity to power the pump, irrigation ditches that should be knee-deep with water are dry. Mohsen Toman Shiah, 51, the sheik's next-door neighbor, has a half-acre plot across the street. Small clumps of wheat grow in the field, but he says he loses 40 percent of his crop every year for lack of water. Fertilizer prices are up, price controls are gone, subsidies fading. It costs more to plant wheat than the crop will fetch at market, Mohsen said. "It's always been a struggle for a farmer to make a good living," he said.

For all the deference shown by his kinsmen, the sheik has little power other than his ability to keep them laughing sometimes, despite their lot in life. So Sagban stays focused on the problems he can solve—marriages, quarrels, property disputes. The greater and more painful issues that have persisted throughout his lifetime, he leaves to God. "Most of us are poor," he said. "Suppose we are not happy. What can we do?"

Hezbollah Fighter Strove to be a Martyr

Thanassis Cambanis met Rani Bazzi on a battlefield during a brief truce in the war between Israel and Lebanon. Perhaps motivated by the specter of death, Bazzi talked at length about his family life and his devotion to Hezbollah. His unexpected confidence offered an unvarnished glimpse of Hezbollah's usually impenetrable community.

Bint Jbail, Lebanon

In unguarded moments, Rani Ahmed Bazzi expressed his fear that he would not achieve martyrdom. On a battlefield in southern Lebanon, in the middle of last summer's month-long war between Hezbollah and Israel, he broke down weeping as he spoke with a pair of reporters: "I'm afraid I won't die," he sobbed. Bazzi was a resolute Islamist, a charismatic pillar of Hezbollah's militia, the kind of trainer, recruiter, and fighter that the Shiite movement depends on to maintain its popularity in southern Lebanon and southern Beirut. And when he died on the last weekend of the war—apparently rushing an Israeli position in a suicidal charge, fighters with him later told his family—he achieved the immortality of "martyrdom," the most vaunted status for an Islamist fighter.

A rare, personal glimpse of Bazzi's public and private faces tells the story of Hezbollah's battlefield strength, its fanaticism, its religious potency, and its deep cultural hold over Lebanon's Shiites. In death, Bazzi is a political instrument—Hezbollah airs video clips of his "martyr's will" on its television station and plasters posters of Bazzi and other martyrs all over the country. In this way, the Islamist movement seeks to build on its perceived success against the Israelis to strengthen its political hand in Lebanon's power struggle. But in life, Bazzi also had a personal story, one colored by warmth and a compulsion to befriend strangers and win their confidence, and proselytize for Hezbollah's cause.

During the war that began July 12, Bazzi fought as a Hezbollah field commander with a specialty in antitank mines. He fought first in his hometown of Bint Jbail, a heavily contested border town, and in the last weeks of the war in Ghandouriyah, where he was killed. On July 31, during a two-day suspension of Israeli bombing in the middle of a punishing war, Bazzi called out to passing reporters from a half-destroyed mosque in downtown Bint Jbail. He wanted to talk, which he did for more than two hours, in perfect English he learned in Kuwait, where he grew up. He gave a fake name, "Hussein," and said he was three years older than his age, 39. He led reporters to a destroyed building, where Hezbollah fighters had clashed with Israeli soldiers, and he fished out Israeli night-vision goggles from the wreckage. By turns delirious, hectoring, and affectionate, Bazzi talked of dead comrades with glee in his eyes—"They've gone to paradise!"—and wept about the destruction of his hometown under Israeli shelling.

He toed Hezbollah's political line when he talked of the war, but he also displayed humanity. After excoriating Israel and America as countries "where people treat animals better than they would treat a Muslim," he cried and described sharing one of his last cans of tuna with a starving stray dog during one battle. He said he fought not only because he opposed Israel, but also because as a devout Muslim he was obliged to resist any force that opposed Islam. He said he made all his decisions based on his faith and the Koran.

After the war, a reporter visiting Bint Jbail needed only a few minutes to learn the real identity of "Hussein the fighter": the well-known engineer Rani Ahmed Bazzi, 39, who left a wife and two sons. "I always had fights with him about religion. I am open-minded, and he was very strict," said Ali Bazzi, a cousin and dentist who immigrated to Sydney more than two decades ago and was home for his annual visit during the month of Ramadan. Rani Bazzi was part of a well-off family that gave him a good engineering education and encouraged him to stay in Kuwait. But he turned down high-paying engineering job offers in the early 1990s to move back to his family's ancestral village of Bint Jbail, which at the time was still under Israeli occupation. Family members assumed Rani Bazzi had joined the Islamic resistance, or was collaborating with the Israelis, Ali Bazzi said.

Rani Bazzi never talked about his work for Hezbollah, his relatives said. But his ties to the resistance were no secret. In 1996, his wife and other relatives recalled, the Israeli occupation forces arrested Rani Bazzi and destroyed his house, accusing him of storing weapons there. He was released after less than a year from the notorious Khiam Prison in southern Lebanon, run by Israel's proxy the South Lebanon Army. He and Farah were married that year.

Farah had known Rani Bazzi from Kuwait, where their families prospered. Farah Bazzi was studying art and teaching in Beirut, and said she fell in love with her husband for his warmth and for the patriotism that had brought him back to Bint Jbail from Kuwait. Within a year, they had their first son, Amir, which means "prince"—as in prince of the martyrs. Farah Bazzi was pregnant with a second child when her husband was arrested again, in 1999. This time he stayed in Khiam prison for more than a year, until the Israeli withdrawal from south Lebanon in May 2000. "They practiced so many ways of torturing us," Farah Bazzi said. For example, she said, his captors told him that his second son was stillborn, and he believed the child had survived only when his wife brought him photographs in prison. He told her then to change the boy's name from Mohammed to "Shaheed," Arabic for "martyr." The second term in prison hardened Rani Bazzi, his wife recalled. After his release, he would regularly spend time away, supposedly teaching engineering in other cities, but in fact doing military training for Hezbollah. From then on, she and other relatives said, he became increasingly religious. He taught his children to eat the healthy diet of the "digestive jihad," and he regularly talked with his wife and others about the afterlife.

When Hezbollah kidnapped a pair of Israeli soldiers on July 12, it took less than a day for all-out war to engulf Lebanon's south. Israeli bombs and shells turned Hezbollah strongholds like Bint Jbail into hellholes. Farah Bazzi and her children stayed in the village for six days before fleeing to Beirut. Her husband telephoned regularly. "He would cry, he would say the angels were helping them fight," his cousin Mariam Bazzi recalled. In the last week of the war, Rani Bazzi was seen in Ghandouriyah, on the eastern side of the front, delivering a truckload of mines. According to his wife and cousins, some fighters who were with him visited her later and told of his final day.

Israel and Lebanon had agreed on a cease-fire, the fighters told Farah Bazzi. Her husband shaved his head and asked his companions if any were ready to join him in paradise. One said yes, and together they rushed an Israeli commando position. They were shot dead just a few yards from the Hezbollah position.

Rani Bazzi is buried in a single row of 16 graves in the Bint Jbail cemetery, reserved for fighters who fell during Operation Truthful Promise, Hezbollah's name for the war of the summer of 2006. "The Martyrs with God have the honor and the light," his tombstone says. The Martyr's Association has publicized the images and tales of dead fighters like Bazzi, and it will also fund a private education for his sons Amir and Shaheed. The boys are shy and tearful, although with prompting from their mother, they also parrot Hezbollah slogans about glory and death.

Farah Bazzi said her husband was terrified of growing old. She teeters between certainty about his cause and sadness over his death. "I am proud of what he did, but I miss him," she says, crying quietly in her living room, decorated with pictures of Iranian leader Ayatollah Khomeini, Hezbollah leader Sayyed Hassan Nasrallah, and her husband.

She has moved to Beirut and resumed working as a high school painting teacher, and her kids have enrolled in school there. In addition to a written will for his wife, Rani Bazzi left behind a videotape, just under 8 minutes long. In it, he faces the camera and speaks of heaven and hell, Hezbollah's cause, and the "joy of martyrdom." Then, eyes downcast, he addresses his family members, consulting a piece of paper in his hands. "This life is not for rest. It is for patience and endurance," he tells his wife. His sons, he says, must follow the path of Hezbollah and never forget the significance of their names.

Peter Maass is a contributing writer at the *New York Times Magazine* and the author of *Love Thy Neighbor* (Knopf, 1996), and *Crude World* (Knopf, 2009). In the summer of 1992, as the war in Bosnia got underway, Serbian forces established a network of prison camps. This excerpt from *Love Thy Neighbor* chronicles the author's visit to several of those camps.

Love Thy Neighbor: A Story of War

I never thought that one day I would talk to a skeleton. That's what I did at Trnopolje. I walked through the gates and couldn't quite believe what I saw. There, right in front of me, were men who looked like survivors of Auschwitz. I remember thinking that they walked surprisingly well for people without muscle or flesh. I was surprised at the mere fact that they could still talk. Imagine, talking skeletons! As I spoke to one of them, I looked at his arm and realized that I could grab hold of it and snap it into two pieces like a brittle twig. I could do the same with his legs. I saw dozens of other walking skeletons of that sort. I could break all of their arms, all of their legs. Snap. Snap. Snap.

We were given 15 minutes to wander around, and technically speaking, we were free to talk with whomever we wished. But guards with Kalashnikov assault rifles and Ray-Ban sunglasses sauntered through the grounds, and I could talk for no more than a minute or so before one of them would creep up behind me and start listening to the conversation. A few guards had slung their rifles across their backs and started snapping pictures of us as we talked with prisoners. They were not subtle; they were in charge, and they wanted us to know it. If there's one thing that all bullies have in common, it's the fact that they want you to know they are bullies. One skeletal prisoner had just enough time to unbutton his shirt, showing off a mutilated chest with a few dozen fresh scars from God-knows-what torture, before a look of horror came over his face. He was staring, like a deer caught in a car's headlights, at a spot just above the top of my head. I looked around. A guard stood behind me.

I walked on. A prisoner tugged at my sleeve. Follow me. I followed, trying to pretend as though I wasn't following. He led me to the side of the school building and, after glancing around, darted through a door. I followed. Where was he taking me? Why? I feared not only the trouble that I might be getting into, but also the trouble that he might be getting into. The door closed behind me. The room was small, dark. My eyes took a moment to adjust. People were whispering beside me. I looked at the floor. Two bodies on the ground. Corpses? Not yet. I was in the infirmary, the sorriest infirmary you could imagine. No medicine, no beds. I was not supposed to be there.

The doctor, also a prisoner, motioned for me to crouch down so that guards could not see me through the window. He began peeling off a filthy bandage from the leg of one of the two men. Puss oozed out. The man had an infected hole the size of a baseball just under his knee. A bone-crushing blow from a rifle butt. In a few days, the leg would turn gangrenous, and the man would die. The doctor whispered his explanations to Vlatka, my interpreter, who whispered them to me. I handed my notebook and pen to her. Ask the questions, write down the answers, I told her, we don't have time for translation. Vlatka had worked for me and other journalists long enough to know the right questions. She was the best.

I looked at the other body, barely alive. The man seemed to be in his late thirties or early forties. It was hard to tell. His face was cut and bruised, colored black and red, and swollen, as though I was looking at the kind of grossly expanded reflection you get from a trick mirror at a circus. I looked at his naked torso—more bruises, more swelling, more open wounds. He didn't move, and I doubted that he was still alive. I didn't need to ask questions about what had happened to this poor man, or what was going to happen to him. His agony would be over soon, for if his wounds didn't finish him off in the next twenty-four hours, then the guards would. As I learned later, guards routinely killed prisoners who could not recover quickly from the beatings. Prisoners who could neither talk nor walk were of no use.

We slipped out after a few minutes, Vlatka first, me a few seconds later. An eighteen-year-old youth came up to us. He had just arrived at Trnopolje after two months at Omarska, the worst camp of all. His skin was stretched like a transparent scarf over his ribs and shoulder bones. "It was horrible," he whispered. "Just look at me. For beatings, the guards used hands, bars, whips, belts, chains, anything. A normal person cannot imagine the methods they used. I am sorry to say that it was good when new prisoners came. The guards beat them instead of us."

I slipped into his hand a sandwich from my shoulder bag. It was a ham sandwich. "I'm sorry, it's all I have," I said. "Will you eat it?" He stared at me, as though I were a naked fool. Of course he would eat it. It was food. Allah would look the other way as he devoured the forbidden pork. I approached another skeleton, this one too afraid to talk, turning away after whispering a single word, "Dachau."

It was time to go. The guards started rounding up the journalists. I forget my parting words as I broke off my conversation with the last prisoner. What do you say in a situation like that? See you later? Good luck? You are leaving the condemned, the half dead, and the fact that you spoke to them probably puts them in greater peril than they already were. You had a good breakfast that morning, a couple of eggs, some toast, lots of jam. He had half a slice of stale bread, if he was lucky. Your money belt contains five thousand dollars, and there is always more where it came from. He has nothing. You have an American passport that allows you to walk into the camp and walk out unmolested. He has no passport, only two eyes that watch you perform this miracle of getting out alive. You have a home somewhere that has not been dynamited.

You have a girlfriend who has not been raped. You have a father who has not been killed in front of your eyes.

Whenever I returned to a normal place after an assignment in Bosnia, friends would ask me what it was like to suddenly leave a war zone and then be in a place where bombs are not falling. I would say that it was no big deal, which was the truth. Going from Sarajevo to London in a day is a piece of cake in psychological terms. I would feel relief, splendid relief. It didn't compare to the experience of mixing with death-camp inmates and then walking away, a free man with a future. The misery of Bosnia is not half a world away at places like a prison camp; it is staring right at you, less than a foot away, watching you as you get into a van and drive away, and it notices that you don't look back.

The next stop was Omarska. I was to have the privilege, if you can call it that, of meeting some of the worst torturers of the twentieth century. During its heyday, Omarska was ground zero for atrocities. The existence of the camp and of the horrors there had become known a few days before we arrived. As a result, the Serbs had begun playing a shell game: most prisoners were shipped off to other locations or executed, the camp was cleaned up, food rations were improved for those left behind, and then foreign journalists were ushered in.

When we pulled up to the camp gates, no more than 250 prisoners remained of the thousands who had been there, and those on display were recent arrivals, not yet emaciated or bloodied. They were kept there for the benefit of journalists like myself, so that we would report to the outside world that the camp was small and conditions were tolerable. Omarska was a changed place, and it was going out of business, but one thing was unaltered, the terror in the prisoners' eyes. They had plenty of reason to be afraid.

Every imaginable degradation had been played out at Omarska during the previous months. It was not a death camp on the order of Auschwitz. There was no gas chamber to which the prisoners were marched off every day. What happened at Omarska was dirtier, messier. The death toll never approached Nazi levels, but the brutality was comparable or, in some cases, superior, if that word can be used. The Nazis were interested in killing as many Jews as possible, and doing it as quickly as possible. The Serbs, however, wanted to interrogate their Bosnian prisoners, have sadistic fun by torturing them in the cruelest of ways, and then kill them with whatever implement was most convenient, perhaps a gun, perhaps a knife or scissors, perhaps a pair of strong hands wrapped around an emaciated neck. If the Germans had used the same approach, they would have needed decades to kill 6 million Jews.

About fifty prisoners were washing themselves at an open spigot at a side of the building. They were surrounded by guards with submachine guns. It is a neutral term, "guards," and it implies a certain amount of discipline, a sense that the camp had rules, and that these men whom we call "guards" enforced the rules. Nothing could be further from the truth. There were no rules at Omarska except for one: the guards were omnipotent. It might be accurate therefore to refer to them as gods rather than guards. They could kill as they please, pardon as they please, rape as they please. Their subjects, the prisoners, prayed to them for forgiveness, for a favor, for life.

We were marched into the building and up a dark stairwell to the second floor. Into that room, we were told by Simo Drljača, the local police chief, who motioned us toward a door at the end of the hallway. We went. It was a stuffy office, with stacks of papers in the corners, a few books on a shelf, a table, chairs, a desk. A calendar hung behind the desk. It showed a half-nude woman who had a pair of huge breasts. The camp's "chief investigator" was sitting behind the desk.

The session was forgettable, and so I have forgotten much of it, even the face of the chief investigator. This man, like dozens of other war criminals whom I interviewed during my time in Bosnia, was not going to pour his heart out to us. He said the prisoners were interrogated to learn what role they had played in the "Islamic insurrection," and that they were released if the investigators decided they had played no role. The ones who were involved in the fabled insurrection were transferred to "other facilities" for trial. Torture? He laughed. Of course not.

"Interrogation is being done in the same way as it is done in America and England," he said.

What I find most remarkable about the session is that I cannot recall the chief investigator's face. It is a total blank, gone from my memory, or sealed in a corner I cannot reach, no matter how long and hard I think about Omarska, no matter how firmly I close my eyes and try to recall. It is as though my subconscious is playing a trick on me, perhaps trying to send me a message, that the man's identity is not important, he is just another human being, faceless, he is you, he is my friend, he is me.

It was show time. We were led downstairs to the cafeteria, a small one of the institutional, stainless-steel variety. Bean soup was being served. Inmates were shepherded into the room in groups of two dozen, heads bent down in supplication, shuffling one after another, hunched over. They knew the drill. After getting their lunchtime soup and piece of bread—the only meal of the day— they shuffled to the few tables and spooned the muck into their mouths as quickly as possible. They had about a minute or two before one of the guards said a word and they jumped out of their chairs, shuffling to the exit and handing their bowls and spoons to the next group. There was none of the dawdling or yawning that you would see at normal prisons. There was only fear and power, awesome power.

We were allowed to meander around the room and ask questions. It was another act of humiliation for the prisoners and, this time, for the journalists, too. Perhaps that's why it was done. The guards were never more than a few feet away, and there was no outdoor breeze to carry a prisoner's words out of snooping range. It was the sort of room in which the scraping of a spoon against a bowl was heard by everyone. I bent over to a few prisoners and asked questions, but I never got a real response. They bowed their heads farther down, noses virtually in the bowls. This was a place where words, any words, could kill them. "Please, don't ask me questions," one of them begged in a whisper.

I was playing the game according to the rules of the jailers. The visit of journalists was just another form of torture. I tried to turn the tables a bit, to interview one of the guards. I settled on a massive oaf who, like the other guards, was in need of a shave. His height seemed somewhere between six and seven feet. Dressed in a dark combat outfit, he had the physique of a steroid-pumped linebacker and was packing enough weapons to arm a platoon: a pistol on either hip, a compact AK-47 assault rifle hanging by a strap from his right shoulder, and a foot-long bowie knife dangling from his belt. His hands were covered to the knuckles by black leather gloves. He wore reflector sunglasses. We were indoors.

I tipped my head toward the skies and tried to soften him up. The only thing we seemed to have in common is that we were sweating a lot. "Hot in here, isn't it?" I suggested. He peered down at me for a second or two. He didn't respond. I tried again. "How long have you worked here?" No response. The interview was going nowhere. Vlatka gave me a look that said, Forget about it. I gave it one last try. "Is it true that you torture the prisoners?"

I had gotten his attention. He glanced down at me, and his lips arched into the kind of thin smile that fails to make you smile in return. "Why would we want to beat them?" he said.

Coda: After the war ended, Simo Drljača was indicted on genocide charges by the International Criminal Tribunal for the Former Yugoslavia. Drljača was killed while resisting arrest by British troops in 1997.

Roy Gutman was a correspondent for *Newsweek* and *Newsday* before becoming foreign editor of McClatchy Newspapers in Washington. He won a Pulitzer Prize for his coverage of the 1993 war in Bosnia-Herzegovina, where he provided the first documented reports of concentration camps. His reporting led to his book *A Witness to Genocide* (Macmillan, 1993). This article appeared in *Newsday* on November 8, 1992.

Bosnia's Elite "Disappeared"

Omarska, Bosnia-Herzegovina

The Serb guards strode menacingly into the crowded basement room in the middle of the night and called out the names of seven men. It was a virtual who's who of leading Muslims and Croats from nearby Prijedor: Muhamed Čehajić, the elected lord mayor of the city of 112,000; two gynecologists at the Prijedor hospital; the owner of a café and art gallery; a state prosecutor; and two others. Aside from one Croat, all were Muslims. One by one, they arose from the corrugated cardboard and rags on which they slept in the administration building of the mine complex turned concentration camp. They were led away by the guards and never again seen alive.

Several eyewitnesses reported seeing and identifying the corpses of the seven men in a nearby field the next day. The witnesses, who are among the 10,000 or more former Omarska detainees waiting in Serb prisons for a Western country to offer refuge, spoke on condition of anonymity. Over two days, July 26 and 27, the Serbs called about 50 people, according to witnesses, and they included judges, businessmen, teachers, surgeons, and civil servants—"all the prominent people of Prijedor," in the words of one ex-detainee. With their disappearance, Prijedor's power structure was virtually eliminated, a graphic example of the deliberate destruction of the non-Serb elite that was an apparent war aim of the military juggernaut the Serbs rolled across Bosnia.

"It seems as if everything happening to me is as in an ugly dream, a nightmare," Čehajić had written his family from a Banja Luka jail six weeks earlier. "I keep wondering whom and how much I have offended so that I have to go through all of this. . . . It is inconceivable for me all of this that is happening to us. Is life so unpredictable and so brutal?"

It is a question asked repeatedly by the 2 million Muslims of Bosnia-Herzegovina as they witness the systematic destruction of their people, their land, their economy, and their 500-year-old culture. Methods differed from town to town, but the underlying pattern, according to extensive interviews with refugees and Bosnian police, was to round up the most educated, the wealthiest, the most successful, and the political and religious leadership from previously prepared lists. In mostly Muslim eastern Bosnia, Serb paramilitary forces reportedly executed them in their villages. In some conquered areas of northern Bosnia, they took them to camps, where they were executed without any judicial proceedings. But in northwestern Bosnia, a mainly Serb area including Prijedor, there are signs of a power struggle between the Serbs long entrenched in power, who favored judicial proceedings, and radicals, who preferred summary executions. The latter group apparently carried the day.

"They killed the judges, teachers, the president of the court, company directors, the wealthy—all the prominent people" at Omarska, said one former Omarska detainee, a 40-year-old professional man. Čehajić's daughter, Amira, compiled a list of 59 names of well-known Prijedor residents who reportedly had been taken to Omarska. After she fled to Zagreb, Croatia, in late July, she gave a copy to *Newsday* in hopes that publicity might lead to the release of all the prisoners, including her father. Unbeknownst to her, Čehajić apparently had died two days earlier. Prijedor's lord mayor was one of those caught in the power struggle over the detainees. Ousted by Serbs in a military coup on April 29 and arrested on May 23, Čehajić was transferred back and forth between concentration camps and jail, and the Serbs seemed unable to decide how to deal with him. On August 18, nearly three weeks after his reported death, a court in Prijedor formally announced that he had been charged with the criminal offense of resisting the armed forces, but said it had turned his case over to a military court.

Serb officials give vague and varying accounts of what happened to Čehajić and the other dozens of Prijedor men. In the first of two *Newsday* interviews in September, Simo Drljača, a law graduate who rose from obscurity to become police chief in Prijedor after the Serb coup, said Čehajić was among 49 inmates who "escaped" from the camp in northern Bosnia. "His followers organized his escape from Omarska," Drljača asserted in the presence of his superior, Stojan Župljanin, the Serb chief of security for the Banja Luka region. A week later, on his home turf in Prijedor, he put it more bluntly. Čehajić, who was 53 at the time, had "disappeared." "You know how it is. You find they disappeared," said Drljača. "There may be some who died in the process of disappearing." Drljača later escorted a *Newsday* reporter on a tour of Omarska and listened as Željko Mehajić, the former commander of the guards at the camp, recited the official explanation. "There was a power cut at 11:47 p.m. on July 26, and it lasted until 4:30 a.m. the next morning," said Mehajić. Čehajić "disappeared among seven who left at that time." Former detainees at Omarska have said without exception that no one, in fact, ever escaped the camp, which was at the edge of a Serbian mining village. Drljača had a ready answer to that contention. "People got out of Alcatraz," he said.

Čehajić, who spent his adult life as a high school teacher, had had no involvement in politics until 1990, when he decided to join the newly formed Muslim party, the Party of Democratic Action, and run for office. "I urged him not to join the party. I said there was no future for ethnic parties," recalled his wife, Minka, 54, a pediatrician and the former director of the Prijedor hospital, who is now living in Zagreb. But Čehajić would not be stopped. "He said this would be a civil party, a middle-class party. He told us, 'All my life I've done everything out of love for you. If you don't like it, you should make a sacrifice this time,'" she said. In the first elections of the postcommunist era, Muslims, composing 44 percent of the population of Prijedor, voted as a bloc for the party. Serbs, who composed 42 percent, were divided, with the radical, nationalist Serbian Democratic Party taking 28 percent, and a more moderate party associated with then-federal prime minister Ante Marković taking the rest of the vote.

Čehajić became mayor, and Milomir Stahić, a member of the Serbian party, became his deputy. Čehajić first ran up against Serb power in mid-1991, when the Serb-led Banja Luka corps of the Yugoslav army announced a general mobilization and began drafting men to join in the war against secessionist Croatia. "My father strongly opposed this and, as a pacifist, put himself on the side of all Croats, Muslims, and Serbs who did not want to take part in that war," recalled Amira, 27, who, like her mother, is a pediatrician. Čehajić's son, Amir, 20, is a medical student in Zagreb. Čehajić's stand won him sympathy among Croats, but the Serbs never forgave him. In February this year, after the United States and Western Europe recognized Croatia, the predominantly Muslim government of Bosnia-Herzegovina held a referendum on independence from Yugoslavia. Muslims and Croats, who together compose 61 percent of the republic's population, voted in favor, but Serb leader Radovan Karadžić declared an independent Serb state within Bosnia.

Backed by material aid and manpower from Serbia and the enormous arms and ammunition stockpile, military bases and command structure taken over from the Yugoslav army, Bosnian Serb forces launched a massive military offensive. In Prijedor, the Serb police and armed forces took over the city hall and police station and ousted the Muslims. "We took power by force," Drljača said matter-of-factly. "We took power with guns." He was especially pleased to note that Serbs from the left, who voted against the Serbian party in the elections, "have now joined us."

Čehajić was first taken for interrogation to the police station, then to two detention camps the Serbs had set up in industrial sites, one at the Kereterm tile factory within the Prijedor city limits, the other at Omarska, a vast iron-ore mining complex. He was jailed, pending charges in Banja Luka, from June 6 to June 20, and assigned a lawyer. Then he was returned to Omarska, where he was held for five weeks, until July 26. Few of the other men called out with Čehajić on those two fateful nights were politically active or even members of the Muslim party. Most were leaders in commerce, medicine or law.

One of the seven, Mehmetalija Kapitanović, 48, a brother-in-law of Čehajić who headed a catering company, was arrested on June 19. "I can't find any real connection between Meho and these other people who were arrested," his wife,

Sena, told *Newsday*. The only possible connection, she said, was wealth or social prominence. "It seems they tortured the more eminent ones, whereas the ordinary, everyday people they would just kill," she said. Osman Mahmuljan, a doctor specializing in internal medicine and about 47 years old, was also arrested in June, on charges he had attempted to kill an ethnic Serb doctor by prescribing the wrong treatment after a heart attack. Željko Sikora, a gynecologist, was arrested in mid-June and accused in the Serb-dominated media of sterilizing infant Serb boys at birth. Asaf Kapitanović, a cousin of Čehajić, was Prijedor's most prominent restaurateur and one of its wealthiest people. He had just gotten married and opened a new café–art gallery and was building a new house when he was arrested in June. The complete list of those called out with Čehajić is not known, but family members believe it also included Esad Mehmedagić, a public prosecutor about 55 years old, and Esad Sadiković, the head of the ear, nose and throat department at Prijedor hospital. Sadiković had been indirectly involved in politics, having written a satirical political column in the newspaper in nearby Kozarac. But he had organized a peace demonstration in mid-1991 against the war in Croatia, and he was charged, by the Serbs who arrested him, with being a "false peace activist," according to Sena Kapitanović.

The Serbs who run Prijedor today seem indifferent to the fate of the man they ousted from the job of mayor. When asked what happened to his predecessor, Stahić replied, "I don't know. He escaped." Later he added, "I would prefer to have him in jail so that tomorrow we could put him before the court in a proper trial or release him." Milan Kovačević, the city manager, joked that "there is even the chance he will call us from Paris. Or we can go to the other extreme, and he is among the dead. No one can say. There is more chance that he will phone from Paris or London than that you will exhume him dead." Confronted with the assertion of eyewitnesses who saw Čehajić's corpse, Drljača did not try to dispute it. "They have their version. We have ours. You have the complete right to choose between them," he said.

Of the 59 names on Amira Čehajić's list, Serb authorities confirmed to *Newsday* that 13 had "escaped" or "died in the process of disappearing." No eyewitness has confirmed to their faces that their father and husband is dead, and the Čehajić women, who are both intelligent and self-assured, cling to the hope that he is still alive. His wife continues to hope he may have been taken elsewhere, citing the case of a Croatian friend whose husband, the president of the Prijedor court, was called out from Omarska and taken to another camp. "We know that everyone else who 'disappeared' is dead," said Čehajić's daughter. "They were killed inside the camp. People saw their corpses."

Serb authorities closed the Omarska camp around August 6, four days after *Newsday* first reported that massive atrocities had occurred there, and moved the surviving detainees to Trnopolje, which the Serbs describe as a transit camp, and Manjača, which they call a prisoner-of-war camp.

A few days after Omarska prisoners arrived at Trnopolje, a middle-aged woman garbed in a scarf and old clothes boarded one of the rare trains from Prijedor to Trnopolje. It was Minka Čehajić. For an hour and a half, she talked to prisoners who had seen her husband at Omarska, but they could give her no firm word of his fate. She walked the eight miles home, using an umbrella to conceal her face from Serb guards. Shortly before she escaped from Prijedor, Minka Čehajić received from a newly released prisoner a letter her husband had written in early June. It is an intense and personal document, in which he expressed his love for the family, his hope that he would be freed and his gratitude that a friend had brought him cigarettes. "Thank him for eternity," he said. "If it hadn't been for that, I would have thought I was completely alone in the world." He appealed to her to find him a new lawyer and send some cigarettes, more changes of underwear, a shaving set, a track suit and ground coffee. The letter arrived weeks after Čehajić was last seen alive. Despite all the indications to the contrary, his wife and daughter hope that Čehajić is still alive. They want him to be vindicated. "I would like my father to live for the day when the truth comes out," said Amira. "He was unjustly accused. But not just to live for this truth, but for the whole truth, because there were so many innocent people."

Letter from Muhamed Čehajić, June 9, 1992

My dear Minka: I am writing you this letter though I am not at all certain that you will get it. But still I feel the irrepressible need to talk with you in this way. Since that 23 May when they came to our house for me, I have been living in another world. It seems as if everything happening to me is an ugly dream, a nightmare. And I simply cannot understand how something like this is possible, dear Minka, Amira, and my son.

You know how much I love you, and because of this love I have never done anything, nor could I do anything, that could cause you pain. I know you know what they are trying to put on me hasn't even a single part in the thousand of connection with me. I keep wondering whom and how much I have offended so that I have to go through all of this. Nevertheless, I believe in justice and the truth, and this will all be cleared up.

Otherwise, I think of you constantly, of your faces, which are always before my eyes. I have to admit that Amir's image emerges before my eyes, and then an occasional tear flows. I know how hard this will be for him, because I know how much he loves me. I especially ask you, Minka, that you try to console him if you manage to get in touch.

Time is passing with dismal slowness, and I can hardly wait for the day when I will be with you again. And you will be sufficient for me for the whole of another world. I would be happiest of all if we could go together so far away, where there is nobody else.

Dear Minka, I am terribly worried about Sejdo, Naso, Biho, and the others. I have heard some very terrible things, so please let me know what happened to them. Mustafa S. brought me cigarettes, underwear and the essentials. Thank him for eternity. If it hadn't been for that, I would have thought I was completely alone in the world. I keep wondering where are those good friends now. But so be it. How is my Beno? Does he ask for his grandfather? I miss him terribly. Today's the 18th day since I was deprived of my freedom. But to me it seems like a whole eternity.

I don't even know how many times I've been interrogated, and now the investigation is being conducted by a Judge Živko Dragosavljević. I also asked the lawyer Bereta to attend the interrogations, and I beg you also to engage Shefik P. or Emir Kulenović, whoever wants to. I don't know how much longer they're going to keep me here.

If you can, buy me some cigarettes somewhere, soap, toothpaste, two to three pairs of underpants, and undershirts, a track suit, shaving set and shaving cream. Don't send me any food because I can't eat anyway. If you have any, send me some ground coffee. Tell Amir to stay at Orhan's and if, God willing, all of this settles down, then you go to him. Tell him to just keep studying, and for the 100th time, tell him that Daddy loves him much much more than he loves himself.

I don't even think about myself any more, but he must be an honest and honorable man. It is inconceivable for me all of this that is happening to us. Is life so unpredictable and so brutal? I remember how this time last year we were rejoicing over building a house, and now see where we are. I feel so as if I'd never been alive.

I try to fight it by remembering everything that was beautiful with you and the children and all those I love. That's all for this time, because I don't have any strength any more.

Give my greetings to all who ask about me, and to you and the children I love very, very much.

Muhamed

Calvin Sims is a program officer for the Ford Foundation, where he adminis-
ters grants that support public television and radio, investigative and foreign reporting, ethnic and online media, and press freedoms. Before joining Ford, he was a foreign correspondent for the *New York Times*, with
postings in South America, Japan, Korea, and Indonesia. His work has appeared across multimedia platforms as well as in print, podcasts, documentaries, and web videos. These articles appeared in the *New York
Times* on March 11 and July 5, 2001.

Stone Age Ways Surviving, Barely

Anemaugi, Indonesia

When the first Western explorers came to the lush Baliem Valley of Irian Jaya,
Indonesia's most remote province, in the late 1930s, Mayok Mabel was just a
young boy at play in this ancient farming village. Back then, his tribe, the Dani,
the largest ethnic group in Irian Jaya, lived in circular thatched huts and bathed
in the river. Dani men wore only penis gourds and women, grass skirts. Their
tools were the stone ax, bow and arrow, and spear. Six decades later, life in
Anemaugi remains much as it always has been. Dani women still do most of
the work, tending the fields, raising the children and watching over the tribe's
most prized possession—the pig, a symbol of wealth. The Dani men have remained polygamous. And Mr. Mabel, who is now blind and retired as chief
of this village, boasts that his clan continues to live as their ancestors did for
countless generations in one of the world's last vestiges of the Stone Age.

But change is on the horizon. Tribal leaders and anthropologists express concern that a growing number of Dani young people are abandoning the tribe's
traditions and animist beliefs for modern conveniences and Christianity. They
blame mounting pressure from the government and missionaries, who have
tried hard to bring the Dani into the modern world, as well as a recent influx
of migrants from other parts of Indonesia and foreign tourists. If the trend
continues, some anthropologists fear that within a generation, Dani customs
could become a relic of the past, practiced only for tourists, except in a few
far-flung villages that have little or no contact with the outside world. "Once
the Dani convert to Christianity or go to school and become educated, most of
them want nothing to do with the old ways," said Mince Rumbiak, chairman
of the anthropology department at the University of Cenderawasih in Jayapura,
the provincial capital. "The Dani are being taught that these customs are sinful
or that they are uncivilized and an embarrassment." She fears that many oral
traditions, including village histories, songs and dances that have been passed
down for generations, could be lost.

Already, many Dani, ill equipped to operate in their changing environment, feel trapped between two worlds. In the valley's capital, Wamena, where the Dani go to sell their pigs and vegetables, it is not uncommon to see Dani men wearing a traditional penis gourd, called a *koteka*, listening to a Sony walkman and begging from visitors, who take their pictures for a few rupiah. Even Anemaugi has not been immune to outside influences. Although most villagers here dress in traditional clothing, Mr. Mabel's toddler grandchildren run around the village wearing matching red and blue Pokémon outfits. Clad in a burgundy polo shirt and khaki shorts, Mr. Mabel's 21-year-old grandson, Natalis, who may one day be chief, said he liked both traditional and modern clothing. But his friends said they could not remember the last time he donned a koteka, and on this recent day he looked more Abercrombie & Fitch. Some Anemaugi women said that while they preferred Western clothing, they could not afford it. Other village women said it was more comfortable to go bare-breasted and wear fiber or grass skirts, which require little maintenance, especially for work in the fields. Whatever their choice of clothing, most Dani women carry string bags, called *noken*, across their foreheads. The bags, which hang down the back, are filled with vegetables, wood, a child, a piglet or anything that needs carrying.

As for Mr. Mabel, he bathed in a nearby river this day, with the help of his son Jalee, both wearing nothing but long orange penis sheaths, and returned to the village compound chanting, "*Wa! Wa! Wa!*"—which means "thanks" in Dani and is often repeated to make foreign visitors feel welcome. They excused themselves, briefly retired to a hut, and emerged minutes later wearing feather headdresses, their mostly naked bodies glistening with pig fat used for warmth and styling hair. "Who needs a coat when this pig grease has worked just fine for centuries?" said the elder Mr. Mabel, who does not know his exact age but estimates that he is about 75 years old. "Some people think it's strange that we continue to dress this way and live in these huts," said Jalee, 46, who recently succeeded Mr. Mabel as village chief. "But these traditions are who we are, and we plan to maintain them for as long as we can. I'm a Christian, but I wear my koteka to church."

For decades, the Indonesian government and missionaries have had only limited success in their aggressive efforts to change the beliefs and styles of the Dani. In the 1970s, the government came under heavy criticism for a military-style campaign to eradicate the koteka, but the effort failed miserably, as did an attempt to get the Dani to move from their smoked-filled huts into concrete-block houses. The modern housing proved too hot during the day and too cold at night, and the Dani said they preferred their thatched-roof huts, which retain an optimum temperature. Some Dani have built huts near their new government-supplied concrete-block houses, which are now used to harbor their pigs. The government has also built numerous schools, community health centers and hospitals and introduced new crop technology and livestock, but the valley remains mostly undeveloped.

The first missionaries came to the Baliem Valley in the middle 1950s. The early evangelical work was slow going and focused mainly on gaining the trust of the Dani, literacy and building missions and airstrips. "The early years were difficult ones, and we came under attack more than a few times, sometimes even during Sunday church services," said Betty Wilson, who came to Irian Jaya with the Christian and Missionary Alliance in 1959. Mrs. Wilson said that over time many Dani accepted the Christian religion but others refused. Many Dani who leave the valley for the modern life in the provincial capital, Jayapura, never return.

While there are more than 100 distinct tribes scattered around Irian Jaya, situated on the western half of New Guinea, the Dani is perhaps the best known. Native Papuans are Melanesians; their skin is dark and their hair like lamb's wool. Using the fat of pigs, they fashion their hair into a variety of styles, many resembling cornrows, dreadlocks and twists. For all the exposure to the outside world, many Dani traditions show little sign of dying out. Within the village compound, Dani men and women continue to sleep apart, the men in one hut and women and children in another. After a child is born, Dani couples abstain from sex for as long as five years, allowing the woman to concentrate her efforts on raising the child, a practice that contributes to polygamy. Although not as common as in the past, some Dani women still breast-feed hungry piglets if the sow is nowhere to be found.

And, although it is outlawed by the government, many Dani women continue to follow an ancient ritual of amputating one or two joints of a finger when a relative dies. The joint is removed to placate the ancestral ghosts. Some women in Dani villages have only four stubs and a thumb on each hand. In tribute to her dead mother and brothers, Soroba, 38, has had the tops of six of her fingers amputated. "The first time was the worst," she said. "The pain was so bad, I thought I would die. But it's worth it to honor my family."

Oshima Journal: After 90 Years, Small Gestures of Joy for Lepers

On a dreary afternoon, as heavy rain drenched this remote island in the Inland Sea, the sounds of unbridled merriment resonated through the scrubbed halls of the Oshima National Sanitarium, where leprosy patients were conducting their annual karaoke contest. One by one, the patients, many blinded and disfigured by the disease, were led to a microphone onstage, where they belted out traditional *enka* songs, much to the cheers and delight of their comrades, many of whom had had more than a few beers and glasses of sake.

For the 4,500 people with leprosy who survive in Japan, forced to live in isolation for decades, long after effective treatments had been found, there has been much to celebrate. In May, the government, in a sharp departure from its usual stance, said it would not contest a court ruling that ordered it to pay $15 million to 127 plaintiffs who had challenged the law that kept patients confined to sanitariums on distant mountains and small islands like Oshima. The government also issued a formal apology, its first, for the pain and suffering the patients had endured during their confinement, and it promised to provide all patients, whose average age is 74, with compensation and to help them, if they wanted, to return to society. "We plan to take a trip overseas, maybe go to New York or to Europe," said Yasue Tojyo, 68 and blind, who sang a duet with her husband of 50 years, Takashi Takechi, 70. "I think Japanese people are more sympathetic to us now than in the past. We had a difficult life in here, but we feel fulfilled because we were blessed to have each other."

While on this rainy day there was much merrymaking in Oshima, a dazzling island of white-sand beaches, rolling green hills and pine forests, residents of this lepers' colony, accessible only by boat, have not forgotten the great sorrow and indignity they have suffered. Men and women told tragic tales of family separation and abandonment, forced abortions and sterilization, inadequate food and medical care, and hard labor.

The Leprosy Prevention Law, enacted in 1907, was enforced for almost 90 years, until it was finally abolished in 1996. Under the law, people found to have leprosy, or Hansen's disease, were rounded up and forced to live in sanitariums. When Yoshio Yakushiji, 71, arrived in Oshima in 1951, he had an eerie feeling that he would never leave what he described as an amazingly beautiful but forbidding place. He was immediately put to work nursing seriously ill lepers. "It was disaster, people were dying all over the place," he said. "There were about 700 patients and only 2 doctors and 10 nurses. Even I was giving injections." Separated from his family and friends, Mr. Yakushiji said he nearly died of loneliness until, at 25, he met and married another patient.

A few years later, Mr. Yakushiji said he suffered the greatest tragedy of his life. His wife, who was seven months pregnant, was summoned to the medical office and forced to have an abortion. "After the procedure, the nurse handed me a plastic bag with the fetus and placenta, and she told me to get rid of it," Mr. Yakushiji said. "I dug a hole and buried it. This was our punishment for having a child." Although leprosy is not hereditary, Mr. Yakushiji's case is not unusual; many people with leprosy were sterilized, and many women forced to undergo abortions. Lawyers for plaintiffs who sued the government estimated that 3,500 abortions were carried out.

Despite popular belief, it is not possible to contract leprosy simply by touching someone who has the disease, which is spread by a bacterium. Once contracted, leprosy attacks the nervous system; untreated, it causes severe deformities. Hands and feet curl inward, hair disappears, the nose collapses and flattens, the lips droop. The face often resembles that of a lion. Many of the deformities are the result of loss of feeling from nerve damage. Patients without a sense of pain or pressure do not notice burns, cuts or bruises, or attend to the pressure sores caused by the disease.

Because of the severe social stigma of leprosy, many Japanese families not only committed their relatives to sanitariums, but also deleted their names from social records and had no further contact with them. Some families maintained contact through letters and telephone calls, but kept their leper relatives a closely guarded secret. Although he had occasional contact with his family in Kochi prefecture by telephone, Kazumi Sogano, 74, who arrived in Oshima in 1948, said his family had made it clear he was not to return home, even when his father became gravely ill eight years ago. "My sister called to tell me he was sick but she never said, 'Brother, please come back and see Father before he dies,'" he said. "It was evident that they didn't want me there." He later learned his father had died, and he has not spoken with his family since.

For many of the 229 people with leprosy still living on Oshima, the court ruling ordering compensation and the government's apology are expected to have little or no impact, apart from the symbolism. Many patients are too weak to travel or to make use of the compensation money they have coming. Others said that while the government policy of segregating leprosy patients was a violation of their rights, they had come to accept their lives here because of the cruel discrimination they encountered—and continue to encounter—beyond the island, elsewhere in Japan. "I'm old and handicapped and couldn't leave this place even if I wanted to," said Masao Tane, 78, who is blind and has lost the use of his hands and feet. "I wouldn't say I've had a happy life," he said, "but I've got my television and radio, a few friends and the nurses, who are really sympathetic."

Even some relatively healthy patients, fearing discrimination in the outside world, said they had no desire to leave. "The patients here have been isolated and mistreated in the past and that was wrong and very sad," said Dr. Shinzo Inoue, the current president of the sanitarium. "Now, as they are living out their last days, I want them to feel like their lives were not a waste of time and that they had been fulfilled and meaningful," he said.

One patient, Mikio Tomita, 58, who was committed to Oshima when he was 13 but remained in good health because of new treatments, tried many times to live in the outside world. But he always returned to the island because, he said, he faced constant discrimination and lacked the skills and resources to sustain himself. Mr. Tomita said he once tried to obtain a driver's license, but when the driving school discovered his home address was Oshima, he was dismissed. He had to hide his past constantly. When he hurt his leg while working in construction, he said, he pretended to feel the doctor pinching his leg, although he really felt nothing. "I was lucky that I had a place to come back to," he said, "a place where I felt at home and normal."

Margo Jefferson is a cultural critic for the *New York Times* and winner of the 1995 Pulitzer Prize for Criticism. She is the author of *On Michael Jackson* (Pantheon, 2005) and of essays and reviews in many publications. These articles appeared in the *New York Times* on December 29, 1996, and January 19, 2003.

Ella in Wonderland

Ever since I found out about the horrors of Ella Fitzgerald's youth, I've wanted to protect her from the scrutiny of critics and fans like myself, who have always inflected the pleasure we took in her singing with patronization. Sweet Ella, we said when she was alive, she's wonderful, but she has no emotional depth. Poor Ella, we say now: she did suffer but she denied it—banished it from her life so she could dwell in a pristine musical wonderland.

That voice never did give us intimations of the stepfather who abused her when her mother was dead; of the aunt who rescued her, then had no time or money to care for her; of Ella herself as a teenage truant who did time in a New York reformatory for girls, where discipline was instilled through beatings and solitary confinement. When she ran away, she went from wayward girl to urchin, shuffling alone through the streets of Harlem, singing and dancing for small change, sleeping wherever she could find a night's bed and board.

It was this grimy little urchin who got herself onto the stages of the Apollo Theater and the Harlem Opera House, won their amateur singing contests, then almost stumbled back into oblivion because she lacked glamour or sex appeal. Big-band girl singers were fresh bait in those days, dangled in front of audiences to soothe their souls and stir their hormones. Fletcher Henderson wouldn't hire her. Chick Webb's band rose to new heights of popularity after she joined, but at first he didn't want her either. Too ugly, said the bandleader with the tubercular spine that had made him a hunchback. Was he afraid that the sight of two plain people on stage, one malformed, the other dowdy and gawky, presumed too much on the goodwill of his audience?

But he did hire the brown-skinned girl in the raggedy clothes, and Ella Fitzgerald rewarded him three years later with "A-Tisket, A-Tasket," her own version of a little-girl-lost nursery rhyme, meant to make you swing joyously, not sleep peacefully. She was beginning to spin autobiographical straw into musical gold.

Thank God for the radio and the phonograph: they gave a singer like Ella Fitzgerald the same advantage—invisibility—that letters gave Cyrano de Bergerac. And thank God for jazz. It gave black women what film and theater gave white women: a well-lighted space where they could play with roles and styles, conduct esthetic experiments and win money and praise. Ella Fitzgerald had a voice any romantic-comedy heroine would kill for: can you imagine her trying to fit her persona into one of those bossy, sassy or doggedly stoic movie-maid's roles patented for hefty women of color? Can you see her in *Imitation of Life* or *I'm No Angel*, in *Alice Adams* or *Gone with the Wind*?

Actually, her looks and manner always reminded me of certain quiet, well-spoken librarians and music teachers in the Negro neighborhoods of my youth. She had been a good student, but she didn't want to tend books or teach scales. She wanted to sing, dance and be famous.

Ella Fitzgerald fit no available or desirable cultural type. She wasn't a lusty, tragic blues diva, and she wasn't a sultry, melancholy torch singer. People didn't fantasize about her love life; they didn't want to be her or have her. And so she turned herself into a force of music: music as it releases us from the dramas of our lives and lets us experience something airier and more other-worldly. She became Ella in Wonderland, where rhythm, harmony and melody ruled.

Ah, but a singer must make the lyrics matter, you say. Well, she found ways to make the lyrics sing, and that matters just as much. Anyway, this was a question of strategy as well as temperament. If you're stuck with the 32-bar banalities she was so often handed, especially in the early years, you would be a fool to take them to heart or ask your listeners to. Ella eluded banalities with her buoyant phrasing and supple time sense, her melodic revisions and inter-polations. Her scatting is a jazz form of nonsense poetry. And there's her love of mimicry too: an infusion of Louis Armstrong here and of Connee Boswell there; some serious Dizzy Gillespie pyrotechnics and line readings fit for Shirley Temple or Marilyn Monroe.

By the 1960s, she was singing wonderful songs. But she was never a dramatist. She doesn't really interpret songs; she distills them. She gives us pure gaiety and clarity. Pure rue and longing too: listen to her sing Gershwin ballads, especially accompanied by Ellis Larkins; listen to her sing "You Turned the Tables on Me," "Something to Live For," "Can't We Be Friends?" or "Angel Eyes," especially that wistful final line: "Excuse me while I disappear."

Sadness is an emotion recollected in tranquility. Despair is absent from the work and (so it seems) from the life: how else could she have invented herself, then sustained the invention for so long? There was a core of fierceness, though, which her invincible musicality let her deploy with cunning. Popular music is one endless love song that, I suspect, the basically solitary Ella Fitzgerald approached much as the basically solitary Marianne Moore approached poetry: reading it with a certain contempt for it, Moore said, you could find a place in it for the genuine. Think of contempt as a self-protective code word here: we are talking about the refusal to write or sing in any voice but the one you know to be your own.

On Writers and Writing: D. H. Lawrence Frees the Slaves

"Listen to the States asserting: 'The hour has struck! . . . The U.S.A. is now grown up artistically. It is time we ceased to hang on to the skirts of Europe, or to behave like schoolboys let loose from European schoolmasters.'" That's D. H. Lawrence in his 1923 *Studies in Classic American Literature*. "We like to think of the old-fashioned American classics as children's books. Just childishness, on our part . . . It is hard to hear a new voice, as hard as it is to listen to an unknown language." He was writing about Poe, Hawthorne and Melville— canonical now, but radical then. And "studies" is too mild: these are blasts, rants, taunts and thunderbolt revelations hurled every which way. The old American artists were "hopeless liars. But they were artists, in spite of themselves." Then comes the line that could be the password to all postmodern literary theory: "Never trust the artist. Trust the tale."

Brilliant or rampantly bigoted, Lawrence wrote as "a soul at the White Heat." The words are Emily Dickinson's, a writer Lawrence doesn't discuss. For Lawrence, classic American writers were escaped slaves from Europe, whose first (self-serving) commandment was, "Thou shalt not presume to be a master." And they were all men. (Which is just as well, given such pronouncements as: "If a woman doesn't believe in a man she believes, essentially, in nothing. She becomes, willy-nilly, a destructive force.") But what women could and should have been included on his list, at least for starters?

Lawrence begins with Benjamin Franklin. We would start with Susanna Rowson, whose best-selling novel *Charlotte Temple* was published in 1791, the same year as the first part of Franklin's mythmaking *Autobiography*. "For the perusal of the young and thoughtless of the fair sex this Tale of Truth is designed," she wrote, and what follows is a spirited, cannily high-minded story of seduction, betrayal and retribution.

Rowson lectures on duty, goodness and perfect humility, on the "propriety inherent in the female bosom." (She would soon open a young ladies' academy in Boston.) And she revels in dramatizing folly and wickedness (she was already a successful actress and playwright), airily mocking snobbish or stiffly virtuous readers. Like Franklin, she understands that her readers crave education and advancement; like his, her piety is based on pragmatism. Good morals go to waste if you are gullible and naive.

Lawrence talks about how Americans need to hide their true motives, cloaking passion in religion and violence in ethics. American women had to justify their intellectual ambitions too, finding the right disguises for sexuality and speaking to and for an audience whose lives were being formed—and deformed—by the demands of marriage and motherhood or of life outside that sanctioned sphere. Their writing was proud and desperate, veering from defiance to abjection; explosive confessions or rhetoric here, oblique self-protection there.

The two 19th-century women who, even by 1923, had a just claim on Lawrence's attention were Dickinson and Harriet Beecher Stowe. Dickinson has long since gotten her due. Stowe is still disdained and patronized. But *Uncle Tom's Cabin* is the closest thing we have to a national epic, and epics always reveal both the lies and the truths of a civilization: its prejudices, its vanities, the visions that still move us and those that shame or disgust us. "Never trust the artist. Trust the tale." Trust this tale and you will find all kinds of revelations: great storytelling, and prose that is philosophical, born-again religious, robust and slangy, genteel and overwrought. You will also find the revelation of every hypocrisy America preached or practiced when it came to slavery. And you will find characters who are unforgettable. You can find the improbably good and tubercular Eva in Milly Theale in James's *Wings of the Dove*. And when D. W. Griffith traps the free, blond and besieged Lillian Gish on an ice floe in *Way Down East*, that's his answer to the slave mother Eliza's flight across the ice.

Religion—a feminized Christianity—was Stowe's hope. But it was her cover story too. It's not Uncle Tom's actions that are embarrassing and insufferable; it's his aura. He's an impossible dream, built to assuage Stowe's rage at masculine power, her fear of black violence and her guilt over her own will to power and her failure to be the selfless Christian she makes Tom.

Lawrence wrote, "You have got to pull the democratic and idealistic clothes off American utterance, and see what you can of the dusky body of it underneath." The slave narrative did this. It led the way to what we might call Gothic realism, or the documentary Gothic. Harriet Jacobs's 1861 *Incidents in the Life of a Slave Girl* is one of the most fascinating. Jacobs's was the dusky body beneath all the talk of morality, justice and virtue. A house slave in North Carolina who was lucky enough to be strong-willed and literate, and unlucky enough to be pretty, she improvised her way out of the usual female plot of seduction, betrayal and marriage. She punished the master who wanted to force himself upon her by choosing a "lover" who, she hoped, would free her children.

She hid in her grandmother's attic for seven years and became a guerrilla tactician instead of a madwoman. Once she and her children were free, she wrote herself into the female literary tradition with this challenge and homage to *Jane Eyre*: "Reader, my story ends with freedom; not in the usual way, with marriage."

Was there ever a girl who read *Little Women* without mixed feelings when each daughter's story ended with marriage? Louisa May Alcott gave us the freedom to know them as we knew our sisters, friends and rivals before boys become part of our manifest destiny. It's a treacherous book too. Alcott deals out punishments and rewards with a justice and symmetry that life rarely manages.

And that one-size-fits-all garment of gentle, pious womanhood that each girl must be encased in! Alcott never broke entirely from what her biographer Martha Saxton calls "the moral world" to which "she was indentured growing up." She put the flesh and blood of that world into *Little Women*. Into *Moods* (her passionate adult novel) and her female revenge thrillers, she put every alternative she had ever seen or imagined.

A. Scott Berg is the author of *Max Perkins: Editor of Genius* (Dutton, 1978), *Goldwyn: A Biography* (Knopf, 1989), and *Lindbergh* (Putnam, 1998)—for which he received the National Book Award, a Guggenheim Fellowship, and the Pulitzer Prize respectively. In 2003, he published *Kate Remembered* (Putnam)—a biographical memoir of his longtime friend Katharine Hepburn. This is the opening chapter of *Max Perkins: Editor of Genius*, which originated as a senior thesis submitted to the Department of English at Princeton University in 1971.

Max Perkins: Editor of Genius

Shortly after six o'clock on a rainy March evening in 1946, a slender, gray-haired man sat in his favorite bar, the Ritz, finishing the last of several martinis. Finding himself adequately fortified for the ordeal ahead, he paid the check, got up, and pulled on his coat and hat. A well-stuffed briefcase in one hand and an umbrella in the other, he left the bar and ventured into the downpour drenching mid-Manhattan. He headed west toward a small storefront on Forty-third Street, several blocks away.

Inside the storefront, thirty young men and women were awaiting him. They were students in an extension course on book publishing which New York University had asked Kenneth D. McCormick, editor-in-chief of Doubleday & Company, to conduct. All were eager to find a foothold in publishing and were attending the weekly seminars to increase their chances. On most evenings there were a few latecomers, but tonight, McCormick noted, every student was on hand and seated by the stroke of six. McCormick knew why. This evening's lecture was on book editing, and he had persuaded the most respected, most influential book editor in America to "give a few words on the subject."

Maxwell Evarts Perkins was unknown to the general public, but to people in the world of books he was a major figure, a kind of hero. For he was the consummate editor. As a young man, he had discovered great new talents such as F. Scott Fitzgerald, Ernest Hemingway, and Thomas Wolfe and had staked his career on them, defying the established tastes of the earlier generation and revolutionizing American literature. He had been associated with one firm, Charles Scribner's Sons, for thirty-six years, and during this time, no editor at any house even approached his record for finding gifted authors and getting them into print. Several of McCormick's students had confessed to him that it was the brilliant example of Perkins that had attracted them to publishing.

McCormick called the class to order, thumping the collapsible card table in front of him with the palm of his hand, and began the session by describing the job of editor. It was not, he said, as it once had been, confined mainly to correcting spelling and punctuation. Rather, it was to know what to publish, how to get it, and what to do to help it achieve the largest readership. At all this, said McCormick, Max Perkins was unsurpassed. His literary judgment was original and exceedingly astute, and he was famous for his ability to inspire an author to produce the best that was in him or her. More a friend to his authors than a taskmaster, he aided them in every way. He helped them structure their books, if help was needed; thought up titles, invented plots; he served as psychoanalyst, lovelorn adviser, marriage counselor, career manager, moneylender. Few editors before him had done so much work on manuscripts, yet he was always faithful to his credo, "The book belongs to the author."

In some ways, McCormick suggested, Perkins was unlikely for his profession: he was a terrible speller, his punctuation was idiosyncratic, and when it came to reading, he was by his own admission "slow as an ox." But he treated literature as a matter of life and death. He once wrote Thomas Wolfe: "There could be nothing so important as a book can be."

Partly because Perkins was the preeminent editor of his day, partly because many of his authors were celebrities, and partly because Perkins himself was somewhat eccentric, innumerable legends had sprung up about him, most of them rooted in truth. Everyone in Kenneth McCormick's class had heard at least one breathless version of how Perkins had discovered F. Scott Fitzgerald; or of how Scott's wife, Zelda, at the wheel of Scott's automobile, had once driven the editor into Long Island Sound; or of how Perkins had made Scribner's lend Fitzgerald many thousands of dollars and had rescued him from his breakdown. It was said that Perkins had agreed to publish Ernest Hemingway's first novel, *The Sun Also Rises*, sight unseen, then had to fight to keep his job when the manuscript arrived, because it contained off-color language. Another favorite Perkins story concerned his confrontation with his ultraconservative publisher, Charles Scribner, over the four-letter words in Hemingway's second novel, *A Farewell to Arms*. Perkins was said to have jotted the troublesome words he wanted to discuss—shit, fuck, and piss—on his desk calendar, without regard to the calendar's heading: "Things to Do Today." Old Scribner purportedly noticed the list and remarked to Perkins that he was in great trouble if he needed to remind himself to do those things.

Many stories about Perkins dealt with the untamed writing and temperament of Thomas Wolfe. It was said that as Wolfe wrote *Of Time and the River*, he leaned his six-and-a-half-foot frame against his refrigerator and used the appliance's top for a desk, casting each completed page into a wooden crate without even rereading it. Eventually, it was said, three husky men carted the heavily laden box to Perkins, who somehow shaped the outpouring into books. Everyone in McCormick's class had also heard about Maxwell Perkins's hat, a battered fedora, which he was reputed to wear all day long, indoors and out, removing it from his head only before going to bed.

As McCormick talked, the legend himself approached the shop on Forty-third Street and quietly entered. McCormick looked up, and seeing a stooped figure in the door at the rear, cut himself off in mid-sentence to welcome the visitor. The class turned to get their first glimpse of America's greatest editor.

He was sixty-one years old, stood five feet ten inches, and weighed 150 pounds. The umbrella he carried seemed to have offered him little protection—he was dripping wet, and his hat drooped over his ears. A pinkish glow suffused Perkins's long, narrow face, softening the prominences. The face was aligned upon a strong, rubicund nose, straight almost to the end, where it curved down like a beak. His eyes were a blue pastel. Wolfe had once written that they were "full of a strange misty light, a kind of far weather of the sea in them, eyes of a New England sailor long months outbound for China on a clipper ship, with something drowned, sea-sunken in them."

Perkins took off his sopping raincoat and revealed an unpressed, pepper-and-salt, three-piece suit. Then his eyes shot upward and he removed his hat, under which a full head of metallic-gray hair was combed straight back from a V in the center of his forehead. Max Perkins did not care much about the impression he gave, which was just as well, for the first one he made on this particular evening was of some Vermont feed-and-grain merchant who had come to the city in his Sunday clothes and got caught in the rain. As he walked to the front of the room, he seemed slightly bewildered, and more so as Kenneth McCormick introduced him as "the dean of American editors."

Perkins had never spoken to a group like this before. Every year he received dozens of invitations, but he turned them all down. For one thing, he had become somewhat deaf and tended to avoid groups. For another, he believed that book editors should remain invisible; public recognition of them, he felt, might undermine readers' faith in writers, and writers' confidence in themselves. Moreover, Perkins had never seen any point in discussing his career—until McCormick's invitation. Kenneth McCormick, one of the most able and best-liked people in publishing, who himself practiced Perkins's philosophy of editorial self-effacement, was a hard man to refuse. Or perhaps Perkins sensed how much fatigue and sorrow had subtracted from his own longevity and felt he had better pass along what he knew before it was too late.

Hooking his thumbs comfortably into the armholes of his waistcoat, speaking in his slightly rasping, well-bred voice, Perkins began. "The first thing you must remember," he said, without quite facing his audience: "An editor does not add to a book. At best he serves as a handmaiden to an author. Don't ever get to feeling important about yourself, because an editor at most releases energy. He creates nothing." Perkins admitted that he had suggested books to authors who had no ideas of their own at the moment, but he maintained that such works were usually below their best, though they were sometimes financially and even critically successful. "A writer's best work," he said, "comes entirely from himself." He warned the students against any effort by an editor to inject his own point of view into a writer's work or to try to make him something other than what he is. "The process is so simple," he said. "If you have a Mark Twain, don't try to make him into a Shakespeare or make a Shakespeare into a Mark Twain. Because in the end an editor can get only as much out of an author as the author has in him."

Perkins spoke carefully, with that hollow timbre of the hard-of-hearing, as if he were surprised at the sound of his own voice. At first the audience had to strain to hear him, but within minutes they had become so still that his every syllable was quite audible. They sat listening intently to the diffident editor talking about the electrifying challenges of his work—the search for what he kept calling "the real thing."

Once Perkins had concluded his prepared remarks, Kenneth McCormick asked the class for questions. "What was it like to work with F. Scott Fitzgerald?" was the first.

A fragile smile floated across Perkins's face as he thought for a moment. Then he replied, "Scott was always the gentleman. Sometimes he needed extra support—and sobering up—but the writing was so rich it was worth it." Perkins went on to say that Fitzgerald was comparatively simple to edit because he was a perfectionist about his work and wanted it to be right. However, Perkins added, "Scott was especially sensitive to criticism. He could accept it, but as his editor you had to be sure of everything you suggested."

The discussion turned to Ernest Hemingway. Perkins said Hemingway needed backing in the beginning of his career, and even more later, "because he wrote as daringly as he lived." Perkins believed Hemingway's writing displayed that virtue of his heroes, "grace under pressure." Hemingway, he said, was susceptible to overcorrecting himself. "He once told me that he had written parts of *A Farewell to Arms* fifty times," Perkins said. "Before an author destroys the natural qualities of his writing—that's when an editor has to step in. But not a moment sooner."

Perkins shared stories about working with Erskine Caldwell, then commented on several of his best-selling women novelists, including Taylor Caldwell, Marcia Davenport, and Marjorie Kinnan Rawlings. At last, as though the class had been reluctant to raise a tender subject, came questions about the late Thomas Wolfe, from whom Perkins had become estranged. Most of the inquiries for the rest of the evening concerned Perkins's intense involvement with Wolfe, the most arduous endeavor of his career. For years it had been widely rumored that Wolfe and Perkins had been equal partners in producing Wolfe's sprawling novels. "Tom," he said, "was a man of enormous talent, genius. That talent, like his view of America, was so vast that neither one book nor a single lifetime could contain all that he had to say." As Wolfe transposed his world into fiction, Perkins had felt it was his responsibility to create certain boundaries—of length and form. He said, "These were practical conventions that Wolfe couldn't stop to think about for himself."

"But did Wolfe take your suggestions gracefully?" someone asked.

Perkins laughed for the first time that evening. He told of the time, at the midpoint of their relationship, when he had tried to get Wolfe to delete a big section of *Of Time and the River*. "It was late on a hot night, and we were working at the office. I put my case to him and then sat in silence, reading on in the manuscript." Perkins had known Wolfe would eventually agree to the deletion because the reasons for it were artistically sound. But Wolfe would not give in easily. He tossed his head about and swayed in his chair while has eyes roved over Perkins's sparsely furnished office. "I went on reading in the manuscript for not less than fifteen minutes," Max continued, "but I was aware of Tom's movements—aware at last that he was looking fixedly at one corner of the office. In that corner hung my hat and overcoat, and down from under the hat, along the coat, hung a sinister rattlesnake skin with seven rattles. It was a present from Marjorie Kinnan Rawlings." Max looked at Tom, who was glaring at the hat, coat, and serpent. Wolfe exclaimed. "The portrait of an editor!" Having had his little joke, Wolfe then agreed to the deletion.

A few of the questions from the would-be publishers that evening had to be repeated so that Perkins could hear them. There were long, puzzling silences in his speech. He answered the questions eloquently, but in between them his mind seemed to wander among a thousand different remembrances. "Max seemed to be going into a private world of his own thoughts," McCormick said years later, "making interior, private associations, as though he had entered a little room and closed the door behind him." All in all it was a memorable performance, and the class sat mesmerized. The rural Yankee who had stumbled in out of the rain hours earlier had transformed himself before them into the very legend of their imaginings.

Shortly after nine o'clock, McCormick notified Perkins of the time so that Max could catch his train. It seemed a shame to stop. He had not even mentioned his experiences with novelists Sherwood Anderson, J. P. Marquand, Morley Callaghan, Hamilton Basso; he had not spoken of biographer Douglas Southall Freeman, or Edmund Wilson, or Allen Tate, or Alice Roosevelt Longworth or Nancy Hale. It was too late to talk about Joseph Stanley Pennell, whose *Rome Hanks* Perkins considered the most exciting novel he had edited in recent years. There was no time to talk about new writers—Alan Paton and James Jones, for example, two authors whose promising manuscripts he was presently editing. Perkins, however, undoubtedly felt he had said more than enough. He picked up his hat and tugged it down over his head, put on his raincoat, turned his back on the standing ovation of his audience, and slipped out as unobtrusively as he had entered. It was still raining hard. Under his black umbrella he trudged to Grand Central Station. He had never talked so much about himself so publicly in his life.

When he arrived at his home in New Canaan, Connecticut, late that night, Perkins found that the eldest of his five daughters had come over for the evening and was waiting up for him. She noticed that her father seemed melancholy, and she asked why.

"I gave a speech tonight and they called me 'the dean of American editors,'" he explained. "When they call you the dean, that means you're through."

"Oh, Daddy, that doesn't mean you're through," she objected. "It just means you've reached the top."

"No," Perkins said flatly. "It means you're through."

Claudia Roth Pierpont is a staff writer at the *New Yorker*, where she has written about subjects ranging from Nietzsche to Mae West. A collection of her essays, *Passionate Minds* (Knopf, 2000), was nominated for a National Book Critics Circle Award. She holds a doctorate in Italian Renaissance art history from New York University. This is an excerpt from a longer article about Machiavelli, published on the occasion of a new translation of *The Prince*. It appeared in the *New Yorker* on September 15, 2008.

The Prince

The Prince, Machiavelli's how-to guide for sovereigns, turned out to be "a scandal that Western political thought and practice has been gazing at in horror and in fascination since its first publication," to quote from Albert Russell Ascoli's introduction to Peter Constantine's new translation. Circulated in manuscript for years, the book was not published until 1532—nearly five years after Machiavelli's death—and received its first significant critique within the decade, from an English cardinal who pronounced the author "an enemy of the human race." Machiavelli stood accused of having inspired Henry VIII to defy papal authority and seize ecclesiastical power for the crown. Some thirty years later, in France, the book was blamed for inciting Queen Catherine de' Medici to order the massacre of two thousand rebel Protestants. (There seems to have been little besides her family connection to warrant the Machiavellian association.) His notoriety grew, less through knowledge of the offending book than through the many lurid and often skewed attacks it prompted, with titles on the order of *Stratagems of Satan.* Wherever a sovereign usurped power from the church or the nobility, whenever ostentatious deceit or murderous force was used, Machiavelli was spied in the shadows, scribbling at his desk amid the olive groves, his quill dipped in a poison so potent that it threatened the power structures of Europe.

What caused the furor? Here, out of context and placed end to end (a method not unfamiliar to his attackers), are some of Machiavelli's most salient and satanic points: "A prince, particularly a new prince, cannot afford to cultivate attributes for which men are considered good. In order to maintain the state, a prince will often be compelled to work against what is merciful, loyal, humane, upright, and scrupulous"; "A wise ruler cannot and should not keep his word when it would be to his disadvantage"; "Men must be either flattered or eliminated, because a man will readily avenge a slight grievance, but not one that is truly severe"; "A man is quicker to forget the death of his father than the loss of his patrimony." And, the distilled spirit of this dark brew: "How one lives and how one ought to live are so far apart that he who spurns what is actually done for what ought to be done will achieve ruin rather than his own preservation."

To underscore how shocking such notions were, they should be compared with other examples from the genre in which Machiavelli was consciously working: the "Mirrors of Princes," a type of professional primer offered by advisers to young or recently elevated monarchs, meant to shape their judgment and, with it, the future of the state. A philosopher could not hope for a more direct influence on the fate of mankind than by writing such a book; or, practically speaking, for a better advertisement for a royal job. Erasmus, whose *Education of a Christian Prince* was written two years after Machiavelli's work—he presented his treatise first to Charles of Aragon and, after it failed to elicit the desired financial result, to Henry VIII—spun his pious counsel around the central thesis "What must be implanted deeply and before all else in the mind of the prince is the best possible understanding of Christ." Machiavelli, on the other hand, proposed the best possible understanding of the methods of Cesare Borgia.

There is a context, however, that, if not ameliorating, is richly complicating and easily overlooked in the light of Machiavelli's aphoristic skill. One doesn't wish to fall back on the excuse that this is the way that rulers (or other people) often behave, although it is true that Machiavelli no more invented political evil by describing it than Kinsey invented sex. Like all the celebrated artists of his time and place—and statecraft was one of the Renaissance arts—Machiavelli was in thrall to ancient pagan models. But there is a crucial difference: a painter could situate a Madonna within a classical portico without disturbing the figure's Christian meaning. Works that delve beneath the surface of classical forms to get at classical thinking—works of literature, philosophy, politics—require a recognition, at least, of the conflict between pagan and Christian ideals: strength versus humility, earthly life versus the hereafter, the hero versus the saint. For Machiavelli, the choice was not difficult. The Roman republic was for him the undisputed golden age; even before writing *The Prince*, he had begun a commentary on Livy's *History of Rome*, closely analyzing the Roman system of liberty and leaving no doubt that he was a republican at heart. ("It is not the particular good but the common good that makes cities great. And without doubt this common good is observed nowhere but in a republic.") But Christian piety had sapped the strength needed to bring this heroic form of government back to life. The great republic of his own era had failed because the men entrusted with its liberties did not know how to fight for them. He had seen his friend Soderini forfeit Florence by refusing to limit the freedoms ultimately employed against him by his enemies; that is, by trusting that goodness and decency could triumph over the implacable vices and envious designs of men.

This was not Borgia's defect. Yet he was not a monster, if one considered the question of morals honestly, in terms of the good actually accomplished rather than the reputation created for oneself. Unafraid of being known for cruelty, Borgia had deposed a number of petty rulers who were so weak that robbery and murder had been rampant in their lands, until—"with a few exemplary executions"—he established peace and order. Machiavelli asserts that Borgia had thus proved more genuinely merciful than the Florentines, who, guarding their reputation, had allowed the town of Pistoia to be destroyed by factional fighting rather than intervene with their own arms. "A prince, therefore, must not fear being reproached for cruelty," he concludes, issuing one of the memorably black-hearted maxims that do not mean exactly what they say. (On the question of murdering a few to save a greater number, Thomas More took a similar position in *Utopia*, which followed *The Prince* by just three years and, giving its name to the very notion of political idealism, has stood in moral counterpoint ever since.) For Machiavelli, cruel and unusual measures were to be used only out of necessity, to be ended quickly, and to be converted into benefits (safety, security, wealth) for the prince's subjects. Rulers who perpetrated needless or excessive cruelties—such as King Ferdinand of Spain, who had robbed his country's Christianized Jews and Moors, and then expelled them—are rebuked, no matter what their achievements may have been. "These means can lead to power," Machiavelli confirms, and then departs from his famous counsel of Realpolitik to add, "but not glory."

So is he in fact a moralist? Or, heaven forbid, a saint? Machiavelli was a very precise writer, continually reworking his manuscripts to achieve a style that is as clear as daylight. Writing in his native Tuscan-inflected Italian (rather than in the scholarly Latin commonly used for significant works), he relied on simple words and expressions, proud of his freedom from the "unnecessary artifice with which so many writers gild their work." One of the conundrums that Machiavelli poses for his readers is that this verbal clarity lends itself to such uncertain meaning. Peter Constantine, who has won many awards for his staggeringly multilingual work in translating Chekhov, Thomas Mann, Voltaire, and Sophocles (among others), has translated *The Prince* with the stated intention of winning its author the status of "a major stylist, a writer of beautiful prose." True, "major stylist" is rarely one's first thought when Machiavelli comes up in conversation. And when a book has been translated as often as *The Prince*— there are more than half a dozen English translations currently in print—some new claim is expected. Yet, on careful comparison, the most stylistically elegant version of *The Prince* remains George Bull's nearly fifty-year-old translation, a taut and almost Hemingwayesque account of Machiavelli's strong republican prose. (Sample evidence: Constantine renders one of Machiavelli's famous sentences, "Since a prince must know how to use the nature of the beast to his advantage, he must emulate both the fox and the lion, because a lion cannot defy a snare, while a fox cannot defy a pack of wolves." Defy a snare? Bull's less wordy version is smoother English and also better mimics the punch of Machiavelli's Italian: "So, as a prince is forced to know how to act like a beast, he must learn from the fox and the lion; because the lion is defenceless against traps and a fox is defenceless against wolves.")

A translator's work is meant to be transparent, providing access to a text without agenda or interpretation. But the choice even of a word can amplify a thought in a significant way. Constantine may not provide the most nimbly literary Machiavelli, but he pushes us in the right political direction when, early in *The Prince*, he offers: "Even with the most powerful army, if you want to invade a state, you need the support of the people." No other version of this line is quite as democratically ringing, not even Machiavelli's, which states that the success of an invasion depends on the *favore de' provinciali*, a phrase rendered by Bull as "the goodwill of the inhabitants" and by other translators in more or less the same comparatively pedestrian way. The support of the people: this idea or a near variant—"*el popolo amico*," "*la benivolenzia populare*"—occurs throughout Machiavelli's little book and slowly gathers weight as the one possession that the prince cannot afford to be without. Constantine is right to underscore it.

The following observations—which could never pass as "Machiavellian"—should be viewed against the author's more famously glittering advice: "A prince must have the people on his side, otherwise he will not have support in adverse times"; "A prince need not worry unduly about conspiracies when the people are well disposed toward him. But if they are his enemies and hate him, he must fear everything and everybody." And the forthright climax of this theme: "The best fortress for the prince is to be loved by his people." Presented as no more than another component of the book's message of self-serving Realpolitik, Machiavelli's steady drumming of the lesson that the prince must treat his subjects well has an almost subliminal force. Whether the prince turns out to be a lion or a fox, *The Prince* sets a trap to render him, in relation to his people, a lamb.

Machiavelli is often credited with the phrase "The end justifies the means." Although he never used exactly these words, and the notion appears to date from Greek tragedy, the implied moral relativism is essential to his work. Insofar as *The Prince* was intended as a means to an end, however, it was a failure: there is no evidence that Giuliano de' Medici ever read it, and the Florentine successor to whom Machiavelli eventually dedicated the book, Giuliano's despotic nephew Lorenzo, was said to have preferred the gift of a pair of hounds. In any case, neither prince saw fit to offer the author a job. Within the plan of the book itself, the final chapter envisions an end so important—the unification of the Italian states—that it justifies not only whatever means must be used to attain it but whatever language must be used to describe it. The prose suddenly becomes effusive, lyrical, and determinedly rousing: the verbal equivalent of pennants flying, trumpets sounding. For Machiavelli is no longer justifying or advising but actively urging the prince toward a goal, and it is a goal much larger than personal power. "Italy, after so many years, must welcome its liberator," he declares. "The love with which these lands that have suffered a flood of foreign armies will receive him will be boundless, as will be their thirst for vengeance, iron loyalty, their devotion and tears. All doors will be flung open. What populace would not embrace such a leader?" Judged as a means to this end, too, *The Prince* was a failure: it was three hundred and fifty years before Machiavelli's nationalist hopes prevailed. Still, he understood that many of his ideas, being so radically new, would meet resistance. Living in the age of great explorers—his assistant in the Florentine Chancery was Agostino Vespucci, cousin of Amerigo—Machiavelli saw himself as one of their company, with a mission "no less dangerous" than seeking "unknown seas and continents."

To the culture at large, the danger was real. *The Prince* offered the first major secular shock to the Christianized state in which we still live. Long before Darwin, Machiavelli showed us a credible world without Heaven or Hell, a world of "is" rather than "should be," in which men were coolly viewed as related to beasts and earthly government was the only hope of bettering our natural plight. Although his ideas have drawn sporadic support throughout history— among seventeenth-century English anti-monarchists, among nineteenth-century German nationalists—it was not until the present age that scholars began to separate the man from his cursed reputation. Roberto Ridolfi's landmark biography, of 1954, made a passionate case for its subject's Italian warmth of spirit. Leo Strauss, a few years later, claimed that Machiavelli intended his most outrageous statements merely to startle and amuse. And, in full redemption, Sebastian de Grazia's Pulitzer Prize–winning *Machiavelli in Hell*, of 1989, argued for the quondam devil's stature as a profoundly Christian thinker. There is today an entire school of political philosophers who see Machiavelli as an intellectual freedom fighter, a transmitter of models of liberty from the ancient to the modern world. Yet what is most astonishing about our age is not the experts' desire to correct our view of a maligned historical figure but what we have made of that figure in his most titillatingly debased form. *The Mafia Manager: A Guide to the Corporate Machiavelli*; *The Princessa: Machiavelli for Women*; and the deliciously titled *What Would Machiavelli Do? The Ends Justify the Meanness* represent just a fraction of a contemporary, best-selling literary genre. Machiavelli may not have been, in fact, a Machiavellian. But in American business and social circles, he has come to stand for the principle that winning—no matter how—is all. And for this alone, for the first time in history, he is a cultural hero.

Richard Eder was for twenty years a foreign correspondent, drama critic, and film reviewer for the *New York Times*. As book critic for the *Los Angeles Times*, he received a Pulitzer Prize and a National Book Critics Circle citation. He writes frequent book reviews for the *New York Times* and the *Boston Globe*. These reviews appeared in the *Times* on January 1, 2008, and February 22, 2000.

Diary of a Bad Year, by J. M. Coetzee
Penguin Books, 2007

J. M. Coetzee's novel *Diary of a Bad Year* is something of a self-managed funeral, but a lavish one: mordant, funny and wise. Mr. Coetzee writes circles around any attempt to pin him down. You imagine him sardonically outthinking the Nobel Prize he won in 2003. To review him is to play *Alice in Wonderland*–style croquet, with the flamingo mallets curving around to stare at the player.

And so the aging, internationally celebrated novelist who is *Diary*'s protagonist, sitting in his Sydney apartment to expatiate upon the world, both is and is not Mr. Coetzee, who did in fact move to Australia a couple of years ago. (A tiny silhouette on the book cover manages to look something like him and something like Calvin's Hobbes.)

He is identified as C., and he, like Mr. Coetzee, is from South Africa, which has been his fictional subject. His views are undoubtedly the author's, reflecting fierce ideals estranged from a contemporary relativism where "is, like" dilutes "is." And yet Mr. Coetzee has always resisted expounding. His thoughts and their counterthoughts are bent and curled, snail-like, inside the whorls of fiction. He has been criticized for not using a public platform to denounce and espouse.

So here you are, the author seems to say, "I can do platforms too." His C. occupies one for a while (a German publisher has commissioned him to write his thoughts about the world) before crawling underneath to subvert it. His critical expositions range from American exceptionalism to the use of torture, the war on terror and the devil's bargain by which the state offers safety by eroding liberties; and from there to number theory, the personal afterlife and much else.

But platforms isolate as they elevate. And while C. expounds on the top half of each page, Anya, one of Mr. Coetzee's best fictional inventions, inserts herself at the bottom, setting up a typographical counterpoint that is successively comic and biting, and, by the end, curiously moving.

A blend of Marilyn Monroe and the Wife of Bath, she saws away at the platform and ends up, through a kind of seduction that finally becomes instruction—her own as well—with C.'s taking a hand at the saw. Under her influence, what has changed is not his opinions but "my opinion of my opinions." Mr. Coetzee moves through the country of old age as if it were a fresh journey, this one traveling second class. As C. explores the place, he shifts from arrogance to anger to humility and finally to something like mystical acceptance.

All this indicates what *Diary* does, and quite misses what it is: Mr. Coetzee somewhere close to his most serious, and having—and giving—lovely fun. I think of the childlike simplicity of late Beethoven on a profound return trip from profundity. C., already entombed writing his "Strong Opinions" (the title of the first section) for the Germans, is doing his laundry in his apartment basement when an old man's fantasy—short red skirt, glossy black hair, undulant lushness—arrives with her own wash load. Anya snubs his initial attempt at conversation. Later she confides her situation: between jobs, and living upstairs with a prosperous young investor.

C. offers her a job typing his book. He pays triple the going rate; the real bait is his plea that he needs an intuitive mind to help him. No woman can resist that, he calculates. She doesn't; she comes to work, yet almost from the start she shows that if sexy is one part of her nature, critical independence is another.

And from here on, the pages divide: the top third, C.'s philosophical opinions; the middle third, his account of Anya, as well as his feelings; the bottom third, her account of C., as well as hers. Gradually the last two parts grow more vivid, while the opinions grow dustier. Anya expands into her reality; C. deflates, magnificently, into his.

He goes from seeing her as sexual illusion to seeing her as human. Being desired is part of her identity. She will prize even an old man's fantasies—they are his last, best effort, after all—but she demands to be recognized for her life of struggle and her untrammeled mind. And bit by bit she untrammels his. After quitting briefly because of his arrogance, she returns, responding to his admission that she has begun to soften his opinions.

The book's second half is a teeming counterpoint. There are the softer opinions, with C.'s private artist evicting his public intellectual, among other things, with haunting tributes to Bach and Dostoyevsky. (This is who I am, Mr. Coetzee tells us; that funeral referred to at the start is in fact a resurrection.)

There is a biting subplot about Anya's crass lover upstairs, soon to be discarded. And there is an ever richer recognition of each other's humanity, by Anya as well as C.

"Why should not old men be mad?" Yeats wrote. In his comic, witty and compassionate novel Mr. Coetzee tells us why not.

Beowulf and Fate Meet in a Modern Poet's Lens

Beowulf: A New Verse Translation, by Seamus Heaney
Farrar, Straus and Giroux, 2000

Seamus Heaney's *Beowulf* rises from the dead.

Except for the minutely few who mastered Anglo-Saxon in graduate school (of the merely very few who struggled with it), our first English classic, read in translation, has been a museum piece. We patrolled it dutifully with a sense of importance, a flash or two of insight and sore feet.

Now, as he did in his great archaeological poems, "The Tollund Man," for instance, Mr. Heaney drops a ladder deep into the literary Cenozoic. It is not excavation but a dialogue in situ. Addressing the same mummified figure we once addressed—with whatever interest but little love—he breaks our hearts.

Mr. Heaney's verse rendition of the epic's 3,182 lines has percolated for 15 years. The excavation became a double one: into the poet's own national, poetic and linguistic roots as well as the poem's. His Beowulf is no Geat in modern get-up (the monster-slayer belonged to a Scandinavian people of that name). This translation does something other than bring him up into our time. It transports us to his and lets us wander there; after which home will never seem entirely the same.

Take the notion of fate. Yes, we had learned that this is what those murky figures with consonant-clotted names—Ecgtheow, Hygd—are about as they splash through northern meres and mists, hacking at ogres or each other with iron swords and wooden shields. Dark and strange, it seems; and we are not likely to recall that the lucid light and language of Greek tragedy rested upon, though it did not rest in, a sense of fate. Mr. Heaney brings the light and the lucidity. His Beowulf circles with fate as humanly and naturally as a woodcutter maneuvers around his falling trees.

As Beowulf goes into the three battles of the epic—his victories against the cannibal monsters Grendel and Grendel's mother and, after a prosperous 50-year reign, his fatal combat with the "wyrm" (dragon)—we get lines like:

> Whichever one death fells
> must deem it a just judgment by God.
> If Grendel wins, it will be a gruesome day. . . .
> Then my face won't be there
> to be covered in death: he will carry me away
> as he goes to ground, gorged and bloodied. . . .
> No need then
> to lament for long or lay out my body. . . .
> Fate goes ever as fate must.

And as an old man, going out to rid his land of the wyrm, while knowing he will perish:

> He was sad at heart,
> unsettled yet ready, sensing his death.
> And, after receiving his mortal wound:
> For the son of Ecgtheow, it was no easy thing
> To have to give ground like that and go
> Unwillingly to inhabit another home

In a place beyond; so every man must yield
The leasehold of his days.

As belief in salvation allowed the religious martyrs to undergo all kinds of painful handling, belief in fate does something similar for the figures in the Beowulf epic. Each is a means of stepping out of your own self so you can dispatch it, respectively, toward the stake or an ogre's supper. Before Hamlet's "to be or not to be" was the "not to be so as to be" of the martyr and the pagan warrior. Has this abstract notion ever come so alive? Mr. Heaney's translation beats with a recurring pulse, from homely and concrete to elevated and back again.

The great battle scenes are rendered with a power and grisly horror both increased and made oddly transparent by a freshness and innocence of diction. Beowulf tells of a battle with sea monsters:

. . . in the morning, mangled and sleeping
the sleep of the sword, they slopped and floated
like the ocean's leavings.

After the fearsome struggle in which Beowulf rips off Grendel's arm and shoulder, the monster flees, "hasped and hooped and hirpling with pain." He retreats to his fen

exhausted in spirit
and beaten in battle, bloodying the path,
hauling his doom to the demons' mere.
The bloodshot water wallowed and surged,
There were loathsome upthrows and overturnings
Of waves and gore and wound-slurry.

In sustaining contrast is the lyricism, quiet yet immediate, of the small passages. "I . . . have wintered into wisdom," the aging Danish king tells Beowulf, his deliverer, discoursing on the vanity of power. Morning comes, "a hurry of brightness / overran the shadows." A sense of evening pervades the most rousing actions. Mr. Heaney renders the sunset light, sadly or wryly or even with gaiety.

Anticipating, performing or recalling his great deeds, Beowulf remains intently human. Not by substituting a present colloquial for the old strangenesses: "word-hoard" for language, "wave-vat" for sea, "ring-giver" for king and once, at least, "battle-torch" for sword. However, Mr. Heaney writes—in a preface that is part biography, part a testament of faith in language and all shining essay—"I have tended to follow modern usage and in the main have called a sword a sword."

We chew vertically; we read horizontally. Much of the Old English chewiness—the rigorous alliterations, the craggy epithets, the caesuras in the middle of each four-beat line—has been retained, but some has been softened. An epic must flow to remain alive. Mr. Heaney's flow of language, action and character is poetry's fight against dying.

There are those who will mind. Professor Alfred Davis, an Old English scholar, was detailed to keep an eye on Heaney by Norton, whose editors commissioned the translation back in the mid-1980's for its *Anthology of English Literature*. (Later it arranged to share publication with Farrar, Straus & Giroux). "Nevertheless, I was often reluctant to follow his advice and persisted many times in what we both knew were erroneous ways," Mr. Heaney writes.

It was at least as fortunate, and of course less bloody, than Nelson's clapping his blind eye to his spyglass so as not to see the signal to retreat. Translation is not mainly the work of preserving the hearth—a necessary task performed by scholarship— but of letting a fire burn in it.

Robert Christgau, a *Village Voice* senior editor for thirty-two years, is currently a monthly columnist at the *Barnes & Noble Review* and a regular contributor to NPR's *All Things Considered*. His "Consumer Guide" column ceased publication in July, 2010, after forty-one years at the *Voice, Creem,* and MSN Music. He is vice chairman of the National Arts Journalism Program and a regular contributor to its *ARTicles* blog.

John Leonard

When the Kissing Had to Stop: Cult Studs, Khmer Newts, Langley Spooks, Techno-Geeks, Video Drones, Author Gods, Serial Killers, Vampire Media, Alien Sperm Suckers, Satanic Therapists, and Those of Us Who Hold a Left-Wing Grudge in the Post-Toasties New World Hip-Hop,
by John Leonard
New Press, 1999

Begin by rereading—or reading, because you couldn't be bothered the first time—that gaudy subtitle. Think about it a little. Do those adjective-noun combos interest you? Do they interest you more than the long, defensive final clause puts you off? I ask because, even if it was deceptive of this Serious Fiction maven to bury "Author Gods" in the middle, he's summed up his latest collection pretty accurately. "I read this stuff so you don't have to," he declares, and although he's referring to the novels of the "Poisoned Twinkies" (Bret Easton Ellis et al.), that could be his credo. In the same essay, Leonard, who is 60, recalls "the monastic cell in which I read all night" as a teenager. When he's on, he writes like he's still that teenager—inhaling a raft of spy books, or several decades' speculation on Atlantis, or the whole vast oeuvre of Doris Lessing (obliged to review each new one because none of his colleagues had the heart to keep up), then coming downstairs with all-new info. In addition to outlandish noun-adjective combos fueling arcane series, his discourse bristles with weird theories bouncing off one another, with words and names you never heard of. *Paranomasia, sacajou, fatidic, tiger op, parlamente, torii.* Gaviotas, Yuratum, Akroteri, Rawalpindi, Hermapolis, Ascona, Matteo Ricci, Sabbatai Zevi, Aristarchus, Aby Warburg, Christa Winsloe, Johann Valentin Andreae.

Leonard worked for the *Times* from 1967 to 1982—reviewing books, profiling culturati, even editing the *Book Review* during the brief period when radical connections had cachet on 43rd Street—and by age 40 had published three novels and three essay collections. He's also written TV criticism for *Life, Newsweek,* and eventually *New York,* his money gig since 1983, and held down broadcast spots with NPR and CBS; from 1995 to 1998, he ran an excellent book section with his wife, Sue, at the *Nation,* where most of the gratifyingly full-bodied essays that dominate *When the Kissing Had to Stop* first appeared. This is a prodigious amount of writing for a guy who watches so much television on top of reading everything in creation. But without both inputs, Leonard couldn't have turned himself into a 20th-century generalist. It's clear from 1997's *Smoke and Mirrors* that TV is his main way of staying in touch with the world beyond books. Far from having no personal life, he is unusually forthcoming with autobiographical marginalia—about his marriages, his friendships, his career, his alcoholism—that put flesh and crotchet on his ideas. But the normal guy in him is hooked on the tube, which he believes has its mitts on some crude version of the American zeitgeist—plus it's good for more info.

Cultural journalists are paid to care mightily about how they write, which leaves a book man like Leonard in a state of ongoing postpartum anxiety—all his tiny babies, interred in microfiche. He's so productive you assume he doesn't sweat blood over every sentence, but he's such a showoff you know he loves his own prose. So he must have suffered in the 14-year stretch between his hot youth and his gray eminence, when he published no books. Having read one of his novels once, I'm entitled to hope there'll be no more; he has better uses for his creative juices, like transforming journalism into bound volumes with his name on them. This isn't as easy as is believed. His *Times*-dominated 1973 collection, *This Pen for Hire*, which opened with a longer essay (written for *Cultural Affairs*) dissecting the limitations of the book reviewer's "800-word mind," ended up exemplifying them—however entertaining and insightful, it also seemed arbitrary, undeveloped, a bit herky-jerk. Humbler now, he's edited hard and worked for flow with his three '90s titles—which include the 1993 anthology *The Last Innocent White Man in America* as well as *Smoke and Mirrors*, a full-length polemic that folds plot descriptions and analyses from his *New York* and CBS work into the thesis that TV is our most socially responsible popular medium.

When the Kissing Had to Stop is the best-realized of these, in part because it avoids the left-liberal point-scoring that was right on in the context of *New York* and *New York Newsday* but seems too predictable from the nonprofit New Press (although it's nice to imagine high school students happening upon his class warfare stats in the library, a possibility that would be enhanced were the books indexed). Freed of any obligation to preach to the heathens, Leonard reserves the *Nation* for more recondite projects. There's the Atlantis essay, which climaxes in two utopian communities, the fictional Botswanan one of the glorious Norman Rush novel *Mating* and the actually existing Colombian one of Gaviotas. There's a measured appreciation of Edward Said opening onto the surprising vista of the obscure Ahmadou Kourouma masterwork *Monnew*. There's a mordant overview of the moral lives of the philosophers—against the mean-spirited likes of Hypatia, Wittgenstein, Simone Weil, Foucault, and other more curtly dismissed notables, he'll take the "boozehound, pillhead, and womanizer" Jean-Paul Sartre and his 20 pages a day. There's an invidious Willie

Morris–Paul Krassner comparison, a surreal history of the CIA, a defense of Luddism, a piece that calls complaints about public television's "Byzantine complexity" "unfair to Constantinople." There's more.

For any partisan of intellectual journalism, Leonard is a small treasure. Combined with his sheer fecundity, his double specialty in television and literature leaves such fellow progs as Barbara Ehrenreich and Ellen Willis (although not the Alexander Cockburn of the wild and woolly *The Golden Age Is in Us*) looking rather austere. But while his intimacy with Serious Fiction— the subject of nearly half the book—adds flair and texture to his arguments, which break into literally novelistic detail at the oddest moments, it's also his weakness. Like many left-wing aesthetes before him, Leonard wants to believe that his pet pleasure is the key to human progress. But if indeed "good writers are better citizens than most of the rest of us," constituting "a parliament of hungry dreamers," then they're trickle-down legislators at best. When television's feel-good humanity fails to dent America's real-life social brutality, how are mandarins writing for other mandarins supposed to make themselves felt?

Though Leonard is no snob, he's enough of a climber to forgive elitism in the unforgiving likes of William Gass and Joan Didion (about whom he at least has the perspective to cite Randall Jarrell on T. S. Eliot: "he'd have written *The Waste Land* about the Garden of Eden"). As a corollary, he's a brazen old fart. Novel lovers of every birthdate share his disdain for the Poisoned Twinkies. But when his essay on the cyberpunks, whom he's sci-fi enough to enjoy, ends by suggesting they read Toni Morrison, fight Viacom, and help the homeless, the burnt-rubber smell of '60s self-righteousness spinning its wheels leaves one to conclude that his sniping at sitcoms in general and *Seinfeld* in particular has nothing to do with art. And hey, he's not to be trusted on popular music either. But without him I would never have gotten the dirt on James Jesus Angleton, discovered *Mating*, or had the chance to opine that *Monnew* is twice the formal achievement *Beloved* is. Really, who has the time? Somehow John Leonard does. Then he comes downstairs and tells us about it.

Growing by Degrees

Kanye West adds new subtlety, complexity, and Jon Brion to the idea of sophomoric.

Kanye West did not arrive unheralded. Between his production credits and his Jay-Z connection, *The College Dropout* was winter 2004's presold hip-hop debut the way Game's *The Documentary* was winter 2005's. Relative to Jayceon Taylor's bullet holes and career in sales, however, West was pretty anonymous—he lacked that realness thing. But when *The College Dropout* blew up, the preppy-looking double threat became E! material. Did he worship Christ or Mammon? RZA or Puff Daddy? Backpack or bling? Was he respectful or, oh no, arrogant? Was he put on earth to save hip-hop from whatever? West's jewelry was appraised. It was learned that his sainted mother was an English prof and his absent father a Black Panther turned Christian marriage counselor. He scandalized the scandalmongers by announcing that he damn right had more jam than Gretchen Wilson, then wrote a quasi apology that had diamonds in it. When he tacked on a verse about Sierra Leone, he was chided for his failure to earn a degree in geopolitics first.

All this celebrity profiling preceded the August 30 release of West's heralded-to-the-nth sophomore *Late Registration*. Though a few journos obtained clandestine preliminary copies, most got the jump editors demand in the instant-information age via one-shot listening sessions. Old fart me, I just biked over to Virgin at 10:15 August 29—*Late Registration* was on the sound system, isn't that illegal?—and bought a copy with a knot of collegiate-looking African Americans at the stroke of 11:58. Since then I've immersed—the realistic way, with breaks to let my mind and ears adjust. But I still couldn't tell you whether it's better or worse than *The College Dropout*, and neither could West. He's too close to have any perspective, he wouldn't tell the truth if he did, and his judgment is so skewed he's crazy about *The Documentary* and that Common joint he produced.

Statistically, chances are it's worse. Few albums meet the measure of *The College Dropout*, a winsome thing that performed the rare feat of deepening with overexposure—the samples, the jokes, the skits, all that shallow stuff. While *Late Registration* may harbor something as brilliant as "All Falls Down," "Slow Jamz," or "We Don't Care"—the wickedest opener since Eminem's "My Name Is," flipping pop morality the bird in a laff riot of racial solidarity and sociological fact—it can't harbor anything as startling, because *The College Dropout* set the surprise bar too high. Nor can it harbor anything as funny, because if it did we'd already know—like Eminem, West has cut down on the comedy now that he's taken seriously, and let's hope he gets over it. Nevertheless, no reviewer's deadline is long enough to plumb this music. Even the one-dimensional "Hey Mama" tosses off an oxymoronic "I promise you I'm going back to school" before milking West's oft dissed flow to rhyme "chocolates," "doctorate" "profit with," and "opposite," and the epic grandma eulogy "Roses" lauds the extended family and interrogates the hospital system while plucking heartstrings you thought were tougher than that.

In both cases, as is the rule on this record, the rhymes are real good and the music is better—not the samples per se, from the obscure black folkie Donal Leace and a newly unearthed Bill Withers demo, but their contextualization and deployment. "Roses"'s Ervin Pope–Keenan Holloway keyboard-and-bass combo is more effective than Withers, but West's prize catch, audibly enriching at least half his new songs, is coproducer Jon Brion. It's silly to marvel over the rap–Fiona Apple hookup—we expect guts and imagination of our saviors, and modern pop's canniest orchestrator acts as West's own personal Bernard Herrmann. Unlike Herrmann, Brion doesn't have to be tweaked or seized to solve a musical problem, because he'll do the job himself, adding an unprecedented third element to West's proven meld of hit-bound soul hooks and rhythm tracks made or played. There's never been hip-hop so complex and subtle musically, and no matter how much you prefer simple and direct, some of these songs will absolutely sneak up over the long haul—via the folded-in orchestra of "Bring Me Down," the treated John Barry of "Diamonds From Sierra Leone," the Otis-with-strings of "Gone," the Chinese bells and berimbau that finish "Heard 'Em Say."

Each of these songs offers more exquisite details than I could earmark in twice this space, many of them literary, which the English prof's dropout son rightly claims as his calling. But secret brilliance is more likely to emerge from the sops to his hip-hop base, including several added late. The star-as-shorty reminiscence "Drive Slow" winds down into a dire fog. "Gold Digger," marked by cognitively dissonant Jamie Foxx–as–Ray Charles backup, lays on misogynistic clichés until all of a sudden the oppressed black male West is defending leaves a non–gold digger for a white girl. "Crack Music" enlists Game (dis Kanye's flow, he dares you) in an unpackable gangsta tribute-critique. The seven-minute starboast "We Major" drags collaborator Nas down into West's self-criticism. And when you think on it, the champagne-party come-on "Celebration" is the most ambivalent big-dick lie ever. I suspect the penis in question belongs to R. Kelly—the narrator is one conniving dude.

Mammon in practice, Christ in spirit—that's neat. RZA over Puffy because RZA subsumes Puffy as West subsumes them both. Arrogant for sure, only that's not why he always samples. Anyway, he's as good as he thinks he is—a backpacker at heart who, like many brilliant nerds before him, has accrued precious metal by following his dream. He wants everybody to buy this record. So do I.

Martin Gottlieb, global editions editor of the *New York Times* and *International Herald Tribune*, is a longtime investigative editor and reporter, a former editor in chief of the *Village Voice*, and a former managing editor of the *New York Daily News*. Journalists' best sources are often people who simply see what is in front of them. The late Vernon Boggs, a gifted and wry sociologist at the City University of New York, was such a person. These articles appeared in the *New York Times* on January 17 and February 14, 1993.

Pop Music: The Durability of Doo-Wop

In a country where Bill Clinton rustled votes by doing Elvis imitations, it may well be time to pay homage to doo-wop. Elvis and doo-wop started out at the same time to a like mixture of teen idolatry and adult approbation. Doo-wop's most resonant star, Frankie Lymon, of the Bronx, sang with the passion of his tenement streets as much as Elvis embodied Memphis. And Lymon led a life even more drug-filled and tormented than the King's and, not incidentally, died every bit as prematurely. But Elvis achieved sainthood, while Frankie Lymon's grave remained unmarked for years. Big surprise.

Doo-wop is so submerged in caricature and deprecation that shadings of Rodney Dangerfield color its very name. Beyond associations with dorky proms and some of pop music's most insipid lyrics, however, is a lost world, lush, raw and, in the words of more than one of its habitués, "a little bit weird." In its richest artistic period, from about 1951 to 1956, it often possessed an unaffected beauty created with the simplest ingredients—a straightforward chord structure, spare instrumentation, a strong lead singer and baroque background harmonies replete with "yips," "werps" and the occasional "poppa-ooh-mow-mow." Embedded in this era is a trove of powerful, self-taught tenors whose names are all but forgotten, as well as silky, ethereal harmonies offered up by groups that fans can distinguish instantly—the Moonglows, the Flamingos, the Cadillacs, fronted by the famous Earl (Speedo) Carroll.

With some frequency, particularly in the New York metropolitan area, where doo-wop became a teenage cottage industry that supplied Tin Pan Alley, this world periodically surfaces in concerts that draw thousands to hear groups reconstituted with fill-ins and whatever original members can be found. Most consistently, however, the doo-wop world exists in a string of specialty record shops, small club dates and gatherings of devotees sprinkled through blue-collar byways. This network, in fact, approximates the poles of Mr. Clinton's winning coalition: an audience made up heavily of classic Reagan Democrats—white, middle-aged, working-class men—and the black performers most fans venerate.

The dichotomy is vivid at monthly meetings of the United in Group Harmony Association, a 2,000-member organization headed by a Clifton, N.J. record store owner named Ronnie Italiano. Other record shops have albums in their windows. Mr. Italiano has a 2,000-pound granite tombstone for Lymon. (With the unmarked grave, at St. Raymond's Cemetery in the Bronx, as their call to arms, association members chipped in for the headstone, but Lymon's widow eventually said she would place a marker there.)

The association gathers in an old German restaurant complex called Schuetzen Park in North Bergen, N.J. Against a background of black walls and mirrored ceilings with gold trim, the mood is casbah-like, with rows of fans transfixed by activities on stage and a moving parade of others cruising from tables of souvenirs and collector's records to the bar to knots of friends.

The crowd is mostly 45 to 60 years old, outer borough or suburban. In it are folks who were infected by the music circa 1954, when Alan Freed and other disk jockeys electrified the first postwar generation of teenagers, mostly white, with the authenticity, passion and sexuality of music that was then entirely black. White doo-wop groups eventually proliferated, most heavily in Brooklyn, but as Bob Diskin, manager of several of them, says: "All the white groups themselves only like black groups. When they started, they didn't want to sound white, but in most cases they couldn't help it."

To have been in a black group, no matter how insignificant, is to be royalty at Schuetzen Park. Ask Eugene Tompkins, a retired captain for the New York City Corrections Department. When he was a sophomore at Morris High School in the South Bronx in 1956, he was a member of the Limelighters, who cut a single record featuring a quickly forgotten flop, "Cabin Hideaway."

Twenty-one years later, he found himself at an association festival, and when word passed of his presence, he was called to the stage, where he received an ovation. Association members recited to him the lyrics of "Cabin Hideaway."

"The scene is spontaneous and it's friendly," said Vernon Boggs, a sociologist at York College and the City University Graduate Center who is immersed in this world. "It reminds you of the gospel church—people moving back and forth and exchanging greetings. The dynamics of this crowd are so different from those of jazz or rock crowds." As a measure of racial bifurcation between audience and performer, Mr. Boggs, who is black, was once greeted at the men's room door at Schuetzen Park by a white fan who looked at him quizzically before brightening. "Hey, you sung good," he said.

Nostalgia, of course, played a huge part in bringing most people back to doo-wop, but for many it is respect for the music that holds them. "I think the nostalgia stage was over for these people in the early '70s," said Donn Fileti, co-owner of Relic Records of Hackensack, N.J., which has reissued scores of doo-wop albums. "I think they've developed a genuine appreciation for the music."

Association members greet esteemed groups like the Harptones with warm cheers. In a recent appearance, the group members dressed in red blazers with narrow lapels, much as they did in the mid-'50s when they used to ignite the Apollo with daring dance routines, and ran through their hits—"Life Is But a

Dream," "A Sunday Kind of Love," "Since I Fell for You" and more. The adula-
tion that followed came from more than tinted memories. Harptone harmony
glows, and the group's lead singer, a genre icon named Willie Winfield, has a
voice marked by gentleness and clarity. Even in his 60s, his unlined face seems
to capture the music's innocence and good will.

He is the friendliest of people, who, for all the veneration, lives in the Gowa-
nus public housing project in Boerum Hill, Brooklyn, and delivers prayer cards
to funeral homes for a living. But at Schuetzen Park he is numinous. It often
takes association members months to find the courage to approach him. "It took
me a year," said Phil Groia, a Long Island teacher who wrote and published *They
All Sang on the Corner*, a book about New York's black harmony groups.

Doo-Wop's simplicity was its strength and undoing. It was easy for teenagers to
emulate, but it also led to broad parody, mediocrity and a creative cul de sac
that caused pop music to move on without it. Most parameters were established in the early '50s by groups like the Ravens and Sonny Til and the Ori-
oles, who while idolizing the fabled Ink Spots, developed a prismatic sound
featuring bigger beats and more distinct basses and cresting falsettos. Instrumentation was minimal, the songs carried by lilting harmonies. The leads were
most frequently high, pleading tenors.

By the mid-'50s, teens by the thousands had taken to street corners and
school bathrooms. The prime purveyors were "relatively innocent bad boys,"
Anthony J. Gribin and Matthew M. Schiff wrote in their exhaustive and droll
book *Doo-Wop*. Girls were supposed to swoon and buy records.

Gilbert Valentin, whose Valentinos still perform, remembers a South Bronx
overrun by singers, with earnest social workers scheduling battles of the groups
as an alternative to juvenile delinquency. Mr. Groia wrote of one Harlem epicenter: "It would have been possible to walk along 115th Street in 1955 and
pass groups singing on the corners of Fifth, Lenox, Seventh, St. Nicholas and
Eighth Avenues."

There were levels of excellence, and one of the highest evolved at 55 West
119th Street, known simply as "55." It was here that the Harptones' Raoul Cita,
a self-taught keyboard maestro, rehearsed numerous ensembles, including the
first white group with a hit, the Neons, from Brooklyn. At his most far-reaching,
he merged the Harptones with two other groups into a 13-voice extravaganza
known as the Royale Cita Chorus. Teens from the neighborhood listened at a
respectful distance. "You couldn't help but wonder, 'Are they singing the same
stuff we're singing?'" recalled Bobby Jay, a disk jockey for the oldies station
WCBS-FM, who was a member of a group called the Laddins.

Last year, George Lavatelli and Bruce Grossberg of the Relic Records Shop
(across the street from but unaffiliated with the Relic Records label) polled
several dozen cognoscenti and produced a ranking of the 50 greatest groups.
The white group that ranked highest was the Skyliners, who recorded the

blockbuster "Since I Don't Have You" in 1959. They came in 52nd. "There was only one white singer who could ever truly sing like a black person," Mr. Lavatelli said. "Paul Himmelstein."

Mr. Himmelstein, who lives in the Bronx, fronted an otherwise black group, the Heartbreakers, that won four talent shows at the Apollo. "I come up in a black neighborhood, you know what I'm saying?" he explained. "We'd go to one another's houses to rehearse. In the background, there would be gospel singing or church music, you understand? Evidently I incorporated it into my singing style."

The only group on the survey with a female lead was Lillian Leach and the Mellows, who placed 49th. The Platters, the smooth pop-oriented group that outsold all the others, came in 25th. Ranking higher were Earl Lewis and the Channels, the Drifters, with the quintessential Clyde McPhatter, and Frankie Lymon and the Teen-Agers. They all were propelled by the synchronized, riveting feel of sleek diesels streaming through the night, their lead vocalists lighting the way.

At the top of the list, propulsion gave way to more mysterious, murky sounds, the tenors softer and idiosyncratic. Each group has its partisans: the Five Keys with Rudy West (finishing 1st), the Harptones (6th), the Spaniels with Pookie Hudson (10th) and the Heartbeats with James (Shep) Sheppard (12th). Discriminating among them, says Mr. Groia, is like "developing a taste in wine."

Legendary is the story of how most groups were robbed blind of royalties and writing credits. On top of this, other ensembles, most often white, were hired to re-create—some would say steal—the originals' songs in antiseptic versions that were less competent, better distributed and more successful. To this day, Ernie Sierra, a police officer in the Bronx, remembers what he earned—$165— when his still-active group, the Eternals, scored with the hit "Babalu's Wedding Day," which reached number 14 on the charts in 1959.

By the '60s, the British Invasion shoved doo-wop off the radio and the Vietnam War sent performers and fans alike to the battlefield. Heroin finished Frankie Lymon and many others.

Fame was where you could find it. Returning home from his clerical job at the Methodist Church headquarters in Manhattan one day, Mr. Cita got on a subway at 116th Street and heard the conductor announce, "Now entering our train, Mr. Raoul Cita of the world-famous Harptones!" Mr. Cita raced through the cars until he found the voice responsible. It belonged to William Dempsey, the group's longtime second tenor. He had to quit, Mr. Dempsey said recently, for a transit job "mostly to support my family."

Doo-wop's survival strikes some as miraculous. It can be traced to a revival stimulated in the early '70s by a charismatic New York disk jockey, Gus Gossert, and an outburst of live oldies shows. Vintage records sell for thousands of dollars. According to Lou Silvani, who wrote the encyclopedic *Collecting Rare Records*, the rarest Harptones recordings can command $2,000.

More than a touch of bitterness colors Mr. Cita's voice when he reviews a lifetime of musical promise and legitimate success that never yielded a break-through or financial security. He still arranges music in the brownstone at 55 West 119th Street, which he manages for the city. His family lost the build-ing in a tax foreclosure 20 years ago.

Mr. Cita works with a synthesizer purchased with his biggest performance paycheck, $1,100, received when the Harptones appeared at a concert head-lined by Bowser of the oldies goof group Sha-Na-Na. He still practices twice a week with the Harptones.

Mr. Winfield, his star singer, also thinks of might-have-beens that, at times, leave him with what he called "an envy thing." But he has a balm: "I fall in love with my audience, and I can feel very happy."

In Schuetzen Park, that feeling can be infectious. There, two blocks from a boulevard filled with Korean, Arab and Cuban shops, a crowd made up mostly of Italians and Jews of a certain age will spill into the parking lot after a long night of song, carrying a love of the black music of the city of their youths. Late into the night, many break into groups and offer up "Gloria," "Hello" and "A Sunday Kind of Love." The echoes bounce off the red brick of a nearby senior citizens' housing project and into the New Jersey night.

On the White Side of Crossover Dreams

Black History Month is celebrated in a big way by the United in Group Har-mony Association, whose 2,000 members are overwhelmingly white. It is sponsoring two concerts of the '50s rock genre now called doo-wop, which found its finest expression in the harmonies of black street-corner singers.

The difference in racial makeup between the organization and most of the groups it idolizes is striking: the largest number of the U.G.H.A.'s members are blue-collar suburban men between 45 and 60 years old, many of whom can be characterized as Reagan Democrats who don't share, and often are hostile to, broad social agendas endorsed overwhelmingly by the black community.

The paradox, however, is but a small, benign reflection of a larger American phenomenon, one that Orlando Patterson, the Harvard University sociologist who wrote the book *Freedom in the Making of Western Culture*, describes as "the paradox of the black experience in America." He explains it this way: "The larger popular culture has been disproportionately influenced by blacks, but the society at large has allowed only very limited social contact for blacks. A lot of conservative whites look at *The Bill Cosby Show*, but wouldn't dream of inviting any of the characters home."

In Spike Lee's movie *Do The Right Thing*, the paradox is joined amid expressions of overt racism. In Sal's Famous Pizzeria, Mr. Lee's character, Mookie, quickly establishes that Sal's racist son Pino idolizes Magic Johnson, Eddie Murphy and probably Prince. "Sounds funny to me," Mookie says, pointing to the slur Pino often uses even though "all your favorite people" are black. The best a fumbling Pino can come up with in reply is, "It's different."

Cultural historians find American life laced with such seeming contradictions. When the Fisk Jubilee Singers, an all-black group, performed spiritual music in concert after the Civil War, the response from white audiences as well as black ones "was electric," according to Bernice Reagon, a musician and curator at the National Museum of American History. And from ragtime to rap, music that has grown out of the black community has often found a larger white audience that, aside from being drawn by the music's inherent appeal, has often attached values to it—authenticity, hipness, exoticism, danger—that come from its status as the product of a deeply marginalized community.

That this musical appreciation fails to lead to social acceptance or integration does not surprise many experts. "I think it is possible to respond to cultural outpourings in a consumer society without responding to the status of the community that created those cultural expressions," said Ms. Reagon. "The expressions become products separated from the community that created them."

To longtime doo-woppers like Jimmy Keyes, whose still-active group, the Chords, crashed the Top 10 in 1954 with the seminal rock 'n' roll song "Sh-boom," the contradictions and confusions abound. As teenagers, the Chords traveled from the South Bronx to perform before wildly appreciative southern audiences—divided racially by ropes that split dance halls and school gyms. Competing record companies employed white groups like the Crewcuts to re-record their songs. Yet when the Chords perform today, it is usually before heavily white audiences. "There isn't a week that goes by that I don't think about that," Mr. Keyes said.

Some fans, like Norman Siegel, executive director of the New York Civil Liberties Union, count the hours waiting on the integrated ticket lines for the '50s holiday extravaganzas hosted by the first rock 'n' roll DJ, Alan Freed, as formative experiences. But most others remained fans of the music without having their political or cultural beliefs shaken. "For a lot of the U.G.H.A. members, it's entertainment and that's it," said Ronnie Italiano, the Harmony Association's leader. Richard Carter, who is black and is writing the biography of one of the great groups, the Spaniels, said there is nothing particularly wrong with this. "The sad part, though, is that so few blacks go to these shows," he said. "The main reason I hear is that for black people there's very little nostalgia for the 1950s." Vernon Boggs, a City University sociologist, offers another: as middle-aged black people have left poorer neighborhoods for better surroundings, they have left behind the raw street music as well.

Mr. Italiano spends a good deal of time searching for members of the old groups. The reunions, before crowds of admirers they didn't know were still around, can sometimes be tearful. Largely because of the efforts of Mr. Italiano and other white suburbanites, an organization of '50s group members who are mostly black formed within the Group Harmony Association.

Russell Adams, the chair of the Afro-American Studies Department at Howard University, doesn't find this link between white and black, urban and suburban terribly surprising. "When it comes to aspects of pop culture," he said, "I often say America is culturally as mulatto a nation as they say Brazil is physically one."

Marc Fisher is enterprise editor of the *Washington Post*, where he leads a group of reporters working to create new forms of storytelling online and in print. Previously, he was a columnist at the *Post*; wrote a blog, "Raw Fisher;" and hosted a podcast and online chat show on washingtonpost .com. He is the author of *Something in the Air: Radio, Rock, and the Revolution That Shaped a Generation* (Random House, 2007), a history of radio from the advent of TV to the present, and *After the Wall: Germany, the Germans, and the Burdens of History* (Simon and Schuster, 1995), an account of the fall of the Berlin Wall and the struggle of East German families to blend into Western life. This excerpt from *Something in the Air* profiles Bob Fass, a 1960s pop-culture revolutionary who has spent five decades on the radio trying to find connections that can bring lonely people together in the night.

Something in the Air

Any night but Thursday, Bob Fass likes to wait until after twelve o'clock, after his wife, Lynnie, has gone to sleep, and then drive his banged-up old Chrysler from his ramshackle bungalow in Staten Island, across from a chocolate factory, to Manhattan, where he bombs up and down the avenues, imagining the radio show he might be doing. For nearly five decades, the hours before dawn have been Fass's prime time. He's an all-night radio man, a shy hulking fellow, round-shouldered and fleshy, with a few remaining strands of hair pulled back in a thin ponytail.

When Fass, who is 73, arrives downtown at the WBAI studios, he stops in to see one of the few old friends who still manage to keep his hours. Or he picks up his mail, or he just drives and listens for the connections. In his mind, he hears the juxtapositions of speech and song that, long before cable TV, the Internet, or satellite radio, made Fass's show on the listener-sponsored station a place where musicians tried out new material, political rebels plotted, and the young and the outsiders gathered to convince themselves that they were not alone. Fass's *Radio Unnameable* used to be on five nights a week. No more: most nights now, Fass tunes the radio to 99.5 FM and listens to his midnight successors: Moorish Orthodox anarchists, a bisexual pagan feminist, ravers, and an African American comedy troupe—a lineup that reflects the factionalism that has come to consume WBAI. While much of the station's white, liberal audience drifted away, managers and program hosts went at one another with lawsuits, personnel purges, and fights over race and ideology. As a result of those internecine struggles, Fass, the station's last link to its role as narrator and organizer of New York's 1960s protest movement, has been relegated to one night a week, Thursday.

For twenty years, Fass has been almost a ghost at WBAI. Some staffers know how he found a way, even at the pinnacle of the Top Forty era of shouting DJs and dance crazes, to put the counterculture on the radio. Some have a vague notion that he started free-form radio, each night creating a program with no format, an improvised mélange of live music, speeches, and random phone calls. *Radio Unnameable* was a radio party line on which Fass piled one caller atop another and said, "Speak among yourselves." It was a forum for eyewitness reports from war zones and urban conflicts, recitations of poetry and prose, solicitations for political causes, testimonials for illegal drugs, and experiments with noise and silence.

Now, as his Chrysler glides over the empty Bayonne Bridge, Fass's mind is already in the radio studio, cuing up a Hare Krishna chant to accompany a speech by Adolf Hitler; or playing the first version of Arlo Guthrie's "Alice's Restaurant," which Fass liked so much that he once played it repeatedly for the better part of five hours; or inviting Marshall Efron to recite "The Poetry of Donald H. Rumsfeld," in which snippets from the erstwhile secretary of defense's news briefings are rejiggered to make him sound like a steely version of a Beat poet.

The Fass show is like the inside of his house, a thicket of memories and adventures. The house on Staten Island is a jumble of old clothes, towers of videocassettes, and hundreds of boxes containing tape reels, the primary archive of *Radio Unnameable*. The tapes form teetering piles in the living room, down the halls, and into the bedrooms—boxes and boxes of them, thousands of hours of recordings featuring Bob Dylan and Abbie Hoffman, Timothy Leary and Wavy Gravy, Allen Ginsberg and Kinky Friedman. Many of the tapes are not labeled. Fass fumbles through a pile and finds a show to play. From the writing on the box, it's not clear whether the show originally aired in 1969 or 1999. Whatever the year, the program begins the same way, a bed of quiet and then, very softly, "This is *Radio Unnameable*. My name's Bob Fass. Good morning, cabal."

In his bunk at Fort Bragg, North Carolina, just after the Korean War, Robert Morton Fass, a draftee from Brooklyn, starved for a bit more irony than the United States Army's training programs provided, tucked his transistor radio under the pillow and tuned to WOR's powerhouse signal from New York City. Fass stayed up, listening to the stories spun by Jean Shepherd, the all-night talker who might deliver a play-by-play account of the Christians' battle against the lions or tell of the mysterious man whose taste buds were so finely developed that he could identify the year and model of refrigerator that produced a given ice cube.

Growing up in the 1940s, Fass built a pretend radio with his Erector set and practiced speaking into the microphone. On his stoop, on East Twenty-sixth Street and Avenue K, Bob introduced friends to folk music. At Midwood High School, where he was selected to make the announcements over the intercom each morning, "Bob found that he could change himself and the people around him with his voice," his brother Dick said. After stints at Syracuse University and a paper-cup factory in Queens, Fass acted Off-Broadway. At the same time, he volunteered to read stories and novels on WBAI, an odd little FM station that aired radio drama, jazz, and a program entitled *Existentialism for Young People*.

When a job opened up for a staff announcer, Fass's voice and speaking style—mellifluous and strong yet unusually relaxed, like a classical-music announcer without the intellectual superiority—seemed perfect. WBAI offered $80 a week, a good bit more than the theatre paid. The station, one of the first FM outlets in New York, was accustomed to taking chances.

The basics of announcing quickly bored Fass, but he craved a chance to use radio to bring his nightly observations of and adventures in Greenwich Village to his listeners. He thought he'd spin some of the music he heard from Phil Ochs and other emerging folkies who played the coffeehouses, throw in bits of theatre, share some of the novelty records he picked up at secondhand shops. Fass got permission to keep WBAI on the air past 1 a.m., its usual sign-off time. "I tried to make it as unlike anything else as I could," he said. "I wanted to put my culture on the air—the Greenwich Village 'cul-chah'—politics and exotic people."

No one at the station much cared what Fass did—after midnight, who was listening? So if Fass played a record called *How to Teach Your Parakeet to Talk* just because he thought it was funny, or if he featured a strange, falsetto-voiced singer who called himself Tiny Tim and sang songs that paid tribute to the a cappella groups of the 1930s, that was fine. The all-night show emerged from the sounds of the streets and from three turntables, two tape machines, and Fass's burgeoning library of tape—boxes stacked randomly in his apartment on Cornelia Street in the Village and around the WBAI studios. Fass recruited regular guests from the Village scene who became part of a free-flowing collage of music and speech as messy and wild as his apartment. "When two pieces of information bump up against each other, something else occurs," Fass said. "Dylan sings 'While riding on a train goin' west,' and I juxtapose sounds of war and battle, and it creates a third thing, one commenting on the other."

Marijuana was a constant on *Radio Unnameable*. (The title had come from a novel Fass was reading, *The Unnameable*, by Samuel Beckett.) Larry Josephson, WBAI's manager in the seventies, said, "Drugs were as much a part of Fass's show as coffee was for Arthur Godfrey"—the genial morning man of forties radio. Fass, by being open about drugs, built credibility. Listeners would phone for guidance on the quality of acid being sold in the Village. When a caller needed to be talked down from a bad trip, Fass would ring up a young psychiatrist he knew, and she'd calm the frightened listener.

Fass had no idea what to call this relationship he had created with his audience. He asked listeners to name themselves. The best suggestion was a word that could describe people who meet secretly, mostly at night, their identities unknown even to one another. From then on, Fass opened each program with the same greeting: "Good morning, cabal."

As word spread about *Radio Unnameable*, people just walked into the station to watch, listen, smoke a joint, push their cause. Over time, Fass spoke less on the air; it was as if the show conducted itself. As Miles Davis said of his own embrace of silence, Fass chose "not to play all the notes you could play, but to wait, hesitate, let space become a part of the configuration." After midnight—free from the drive-time tyranny of time and temperature, news and ads—a voice on the radio reaches listeners in cars and bars, isolated in empty offices and darkened bedrooms. "If we sit and talk in a dark room, words suddenly acquire new meanings and different textures," Marshall McLuhan said of late-night radio.

Fass took advantage of the night to make his show calm where AM radio was frenetic. "Something cracked, and America said, 'Wow, I don't have to be like that anymore,'" Fass said, mimicking the loud, overenunciated AM-DJ style. "I can be"—he slipped into his buttery FM voice—"like this."

Listeners went to sleep with Fass on the radio and would wake to find him still there at dawn. But he did get out, and one evening in 1966 he visited some friends from an artists' collective that staged a multimedia show in a hangar at John F. Kennedy International Airport. A week later, Fass stumbled upon a group of stoned hippies staring at the huge Alexander Calder mobile installed in the International Arrivals Building. "What a great place for a party," Fass recalled thinking. He went on the air and invited his audience to show itself at a fly-in.

On February 11, 1967, thousands of people showed up at the JFK arrivals building to dance and sing, hand one another flowers and candy, smoke pot, and watch one another. The *Village Voice* declared the event a "tribal" phenomenon, and Fass celebrated it on the air as "a colossal amount of human connection. . . . We're planning another one at your house."

By the end of 1967, Fass's listeners were a street force, celebrated by Abbie Hoffman, who spoke on *Radio Unnameable* about the magic that might result if acidheads and political activists joined together. On New Year's Eve, in 1967, at Hoffman's apartment, with everyone smoking marijuana and listening to Fass, the conversation focused on how to radicalize the hippies. By the end of the night, Hoffman called Fass on the air and said, "Hey, we're yippies now." The Youth International Party needed a coming-out bash, and Fass joined Hoffman and friends to promote the Yip-In at Grand Central Station, a rehearsal for the demonstration the following summer that the yippies were planning for the Democratic National Convention, in Chicago. "Why Grand Central?" a reporter asked at the press conference announcing the event.

"It's central, man," a yippie replied.

During the Vietnam and Watergate years, membership numbers at WBAI soared, as did listener donations. But as the nation's political street battles

receded, the station came to sound like an artifact of another era. Listener donations declined. In 1977, with audience numbers down by almost half from
the peak of some 200,000 during the antiwar protests, WBAI planned a format
with more music and talk aimed at Hispanics and blacks. Appalled, a small band
of WBAI staffers invaded the station's transmitter room, atop the Empire State
Building, locked themselves in, and took control of the airwaves, playing Dylan
and Pete Seeger songs between denunciations of the unilateral and drastic
changes in programming. Management cut off the power, and WBAI remained
silent for fifty days.

For weeks, Fass and other staffers, often joined by listeners, occupied
WBAI's studio, in the former church on East Sixty-second Street. How could it
be that Fass and other WBAI veterans were now being called reactionaries, accused of standing in the way of the same blacks and Hispanics for whom they
thought they'd been fighting? The answer, Fass was told, was simple: the sixties
were over.

Fass was banned from the station. For the next five years, his nights
stretched before him, empty and quiet. Most of his friends at the station had
moved on. Many chose a more middle-class existence, signing on at National
Public Radio.

Fass collected unemployment, and then he didn't. He acted in a couple of
Off-Broadway shows, and then he didn't. He made voice-overs for commercials, and then he decided that that wasn't quite right. He had a public-access
cable show for a while, called *If I Can't Dance, You Can Keep Your Revolution*.
He worked in telephone solicitation, selling tickets to productions at Lincoln
Center. For a long time, he didn't do much of anything. He was, he said, very
depressed.

In 1982, new managers at WBAI let Fass back on the air, but his show
would never again be on five nights a week. WBAI has never paid Fass more
than $175 a week. For many years, he lived on Social Security and the salary
his wife made as a research librarian at a Manhattan law firm. The couple
moved to Staten Island.

It is finally Thursday night. WBAI, once headquartered in a converted
church near the Queensboro Bridge, is now, incongruously, on the tenth floor
of an office building on Wall Street. Fass arrives a few minutes before midnight,
weighed down by bulging canvas bags stuffed with news clippings, CDs, tapes,
and a vinyl record or two. He settles in behind the microphone. He waits
through five seconds of silence, a quiet long enough to induce mortal panic in
any broadcast professional. But at exactly the moment when it seems as if the
station had fallen off the air, Fass leans in, inhales deeply and loudly, waits
another long second, and, in a soft tone, says, "This is WBAI in New York City.
Preceding program brought to you on recording. This is *Radio Unnameable*. My
name's Bob Fass." Then he closes his eyes for a moment and, in barely more
than a whisper, says, "Good morning, cabal."

And then, at 12:34, Fass interrupts the musicians in midtune. "There's a caller who says something important is happening," he says. He punches up line 1 with repeated jabs of his thick fingers; technical grace was never his strong point.

"I'm in the Fort Greene housing project in Brooklyn," the caller says, "and there's a riot situation. They have the block blocked off. They murdered a young man in the back."

"What's happening now?" Fass asks, and the caller describes police officers pointing guns and helicopters circling overhead.

"I didn't know who else to call," the caller says.

"Is there someone who can call us from the street?" he asks. Within a couple of minutes, four phone lines light up. Over the next hour, Fass teases out the story, about how a plainclothes detective shot a man whom he'd seen shoot another man on the street, and about the rage in the escalating confrontations between residents and police.

"You want a presence, people to witness what's going on?" Fass asks one caller, and now six lines light up, and listeners volunteer to go watch what the police are doing. Callers from all over the city talk about how it's hard to afford an apartment even in the ghetto. Other callers relay eyewitness accounts of the original shooting, and now eight lines are flashing, and a caller, Maria, reads from real-estate listings in the *Times*, noting that addresses in Fort Greene are now being called Brooklyn Heights—after the affluent, mostly white neighborhood nearby.

The callers are Caribbean and Hispanic and African American, and they thank Fass for being there. He says nothing but "You're on the air," and punches more buttons, putting callers on the radio alone and in pairs and in small groups. They debate the future of the city and talk about organizing a march. Their conversation shifts to how jobs are being sent to Bangladesh and India, and when you call American Express or America Online, the customer-service person is often halfway around the world.

The next morning, when Fass wakes up, there are a few inches in the *Times* about the incident, under the headline "POLICE KILL MAN THEY SAY HAD JUST KILLED ANOTHER." In the *Post*, the headline is "NARCS GUN DOWN MURDERER." Fass later says that if he could have stayed on the air only another few hours, he might have been able to help the Fort Greene residents organize themselves into a credible protest force. But there will be no more hours until next Thursday at midnight, when the mike goes live. "I like now," Fass said. "Nostalgia means sickness for the past. Past, future—these are things that cannot be altered. But the moment—the immediate moment—that's what it's about."

Alex Ross has been the classical-music critic of the *New Yorker* since 1996. His first book, *The Rest Is Noise: Listening to the Twentieth Century* (Farrar, Straus and Giroux, 2007), won a National Book Critics Circle Award and the Guardian First Book Award. His second book, *Listen to This*, appeared in 2010. This article appeared in the *New Yorker* on April 19, 2004.

The Sonata Seminar

"There are so few notes," the pianist Leon Fleisher said, "but so many implications." The setting was a master class at Carnegie Hall, in 2004. Fleisher, the master in question, was leading four young musicians through the mystical landscapes of the late sonatas of Schubert. He was speaking about the Andante movement of Schubert's B-flat-major Sonata, but he might as well have been describing Bach's *Well-Tempered Clavier*, or Brahms's intermezzos, or any other music in which a smattering of notes conveys a world of feeling. "There are so few notes, but the implications go back billions of years," Fleisher went on. "You have to be like the Hubble Space Telescope, which sees stars as old as the universe. The stars are dead, but their light is reaching us just now."

Fleisher is seventy-five, but he looks an eternal, grizzled, professorial sixty. He is one of the incorruptible legends of his profession; some time ago, students took to calling him the "Obi-Wan Kenobi of the piano." Working with him on the Schubert sonata was Inon Barnatan, a twenty-five-year-old Israeli pianist with a clean-cut look. Barnatan smiled nervously and looked at the keyboard. How do you make notes sound like ten-billion-year-old stars? He tried again. He had been playing with exceptional stylishness; he obtained a hypnotic tone from the piano. But in his hands the Andante felt a little too finished, too smooth; the main theme didn't sing out enough against the accompaniment, which consists only of C-sharps slowly rising by octaves.

Fleisher changed his tack. "O.K., try playing these C-sharps as if you were a conductor giving a beat. You are making a grid underneath the music. It has to stay exactly the same. The melody can sway this way and that, it can come in a little before the beat or a little after it, but the C-sharps must be unbending."

Barnatan resumed playing. The C-sharps chimed in clockwork patterns. Suddenly, the melodic line was freer, more sensual; its shape was framed by the grid. "Good," Fleisher said. Barnatan added a few accents of passion and began swaying from side to side. "Not so good," Fleisher said. "When you get louder, the character changes. Your plaintive, yearning creature, your nymph or naiad, is turning into some horrible, saliva-dripping alien."

The two dozen or so people who were attending the class laughed at the image—an alien clinging to the Hubble telescope. The rapt mood was broken. Barnatan's shoulders drooped, but he kept smiling, and tried once more. This time, Fleisher was satisfied. "Lovely," he said. The next day, Barnatan did it again, and Fleisher said nothing for a minute or two. "I'm enormously moved by your growth," he said. "Now all you have to do is play it a hundred and fifty times."

Playing the same sonata hundreds of times in public is something that Leon Fleisher never got to do. In the 1950s, he was hailed, along with William Ka-pell, as one of the most brilliant American pianists of his generation; he made near-definitive recordings of the Brahms concertos with George Szell and the Cleveland Orchestra. Then, in 1964, while preparing for a tour of the Soviet Union, he found that the fourth and fifth fingers of his right hand were invol-untarily curling up. He gritted his teeth and practiced harder. Within a few months, his right hand was almost useless. He was suffering, although he did not know it at the time, from a neurological condition known as dystonia, which is a kind of short circuit between the fingers and the brain. Only in the past few years, after receiving Botox injections in his hand, which relaxed his muscles, has he been able to play again at full strength.

Fleisher recently told his life story at a presentation sponsored by the Dysto-nia Medical Research Foundation, in New York. Not one to sentimentalize, he began by saying, "It's a pretty good soap opera." Nonetheless, he confessed that the loss of his right hand had nearly broken his spirit. What saved him was the realization that he loved music more than he loved the piano. He took up pieces written for the left hand alone, he learned conducting, and, above all, he taught. His reputation as a sage of the piano crystallized at this time. By his own account, he could no longer push his students off the bench in order to demonstrate how a passage should go; instead, he had to use words. He had the advantage of hav-ing studied in the 1940s with Artur Schnabel, who was perhaps the sagest pia-nist of the century—a poet of the instrument, a scholar of the repertory, a master of language. Many of Fleisher's ideas about articulating rhythm, melody, and harmony come straight from his memories of Schnabel's classes, which took place in a famously overupholstered apartment on Central Park West.

Listening to Fleisher talk about music is delightfully dizzying. The meta-phors come in an endless flow. Play like a cat, he might say, but with sheathed claws. Play it like a Bavarian milkmaid, not like Britney Spears. Fingers shouldn't be hammers, they should be dolphin flippers. This chord change could be from a Marlene Dietrich song; croak over it. Don't slow down like a bad Italian tenor. More Talmudic. Play it as if with the tip of a bow. Make it motionless, prayerful: a penitent lifts his eyes toward heaven. Clothe the bass line in summer linen, not heavy wool. Syncopations should land like counter-punches: "Float like a butterfly, sting like a bee." (Schnabel was the Muham-mad Ali of pianists, Fleisher says: he didn't have a big sound, but he always knocked out the orchestra.)

Fleisher's references were sometimes arcane, as when he alluded to the *Toonerville Trolley* comic strip, which stopped running in 1955, or when he asked one student playing a meditative passage for "a chakra point below the navel." Even his most fanciful images, however, had a precise application. Yuja Wang, a dynamic player who was tackling Schubert's C-minor Sonata, was too brutal in her attack. The piece has violence in it, Fleisher told her, but not of a modern kind. "Back in 1828, when this was written, people fought duels, and before they took out their swords they looked each other in the eye," he said. "Now our killing is long-distance. Bombs travel hundreds of miles. They explode. So what? I want a different intensity." Fleisher grabbed Wang's arm and showed how she was "dive-bombing" the keyboard from above. He asked for a more lateral motion. "Play forward and upward," he said, echoing a favorite phrase of Schnabel's. The transformation was instantaneous: in place of chords that crunch on impact, Wang got sounds that sang out after the initial zing.

The real Obi-Wan moments arrived when Fleisher told the pianists to "beat time" with their bodies, even when they were holding a chord, or to "want expression without trying to get it." And he had unnerving news for those who were listening in on the class, eagerly recording his every word: "I'm flattered that you're sitting here with pencils and scores, but if you were playing I might say the opposite."

Fleisher's demands can be grueling, but the results in this case were dramatic. In a collective concert at Carnegie's Weill Hall, four pianists—Barnatan, Wang, Hiroko Sasaki, and Mana Tokuno—demonstrated what they had learned from some fifty hours of instruction. Wang's performance was the most immediately gripping. She had total command of the sometimes sadistically difficult C-minor Sonata, and she conveyed a kind of joy in the challenge of it. Early on in the piece, she had trouble negotiating simpler, more songful passages, and by the end she still had not fully grasped the slow movement: the central, heart-stopping modulation from A minor to A-flat major went by as if nothing special had happened. But the second theme of the first movement, which she had initially pronounced "plain," glowed with life.

Barnatan was the most naturally poetic of the four pianists; he has an instinctive understanding of Schubert's fragile, deep world. Sometimes he got lost in the sounds he was creating; in the first movement, he kept losing track of the pulse and speeding up when he got loud. But in the Andante he made sounds that might have won the approval of Schnabel himself. Several times, he let his eyes drift penitentially toward the rafters, so that if you had been looking straight at him, you would have seen only the whites of his eyes.

Mark Feeney, the author of *Nixon at the Movies: A Book about Belief* (Chicago, 2004), is an arts writer at the *Boston Globe*, where he has worked in various editorial capacities since 1979. He won the 2008 Pulitzer Prize for Criticism. This piece ran in the *Globe* on April 13, 2003, three weeks after U.S.-led coalition forces invaded Iraq.

Shooting War

Homer must have had counterparts in the visual arts. That we don't know who they were suggests just how much words have prevailed over images from the very start of the reimagining of battle. The few exceptions (think of Uccello's *Battle of San Romano* or, supremely, Goya's *Disasters of War*) simply underscore the disparity. The invention of photography radically changed the equation. Roger Fenton's photographs of the Crimean War or Mathew Brady's of the Civil War showed the battlefield with a particularity, an immediacy, previously inconceivable. Never again would—or could—war be imagined in the same way. The camera, no less than the repeating rifle or machine gun, transformed warfare—or, rather, it transformed the relationship of the general populace to warfare. The camera took the democratization of battle that had begun with the conscript armies of the French Revolution and extended it to the home front. Professional armies had given way to citizen armies, and now an ability to visualize war was extended to the entire citizenry.

A century and a half later, we are back to professional armies, and in demonstrating how warfare looks, the photograph—not moving images, but the single, discrete photograph—may be more important than at any time since Fenton and Brady.

For proof of this, simply look at the massive amounts of space newspapers are devoting to photographs from the war in Iraq. Partly, their doing so is attributable to technology (the high-quality reproduction of color, the ease of digital transmission). Even more, though, it's attributable to the very inundation of images that had seemed to make photography, and war photography especially, passé, if not obsolete, in this age of real-time everything. It's true that the moving image long ago supplanted the still image as chief witness on the battlefield. Even as such war photographers as Robert Capa, during World War II, or David Douglas Duncan, during Korea, became legendary, newsreels and then television were supplanting them.

Photographers flourished during the Vietnam War. Some of them became famous: Larry Burrows, Sean Flynn, Horst Faas, Tim Page. But try to summon up their work, as one so readily can Capa's from the Normandy beaches or Duncan's from the Chosin Reservoir. It's impossible, not because of any lack of skill on their part but because their work gets lost amid the memory of all the muddy browns and lush greens that filled the nightly news. The two images that do stand out—Eddie Adams's of a South Vietnamese general about to execute a suspected spy, holding a pistol to his head; and Nick Ut's of a naked Vietnamese girl fleeing a napalm attack—are so horrific they could never be mistaken for anything seen on television.

Four decades later, the television camerawork considered so astonishing in Vietnam seems closer to Fenton or Brady than to the technological marvels that made Baghdad besieged seem as accessible as the next street. Yet those very marvels are their own undoing. In a market economy, the miraculous inevitably becomes the ubiquitous. The wonders proffered round the clock on CNN, Fox News, and MSNBC increase exponentially the image glut that has turned visual perception into a kind of perpetual aerobics class: fatiguing, relentless, loud. (Can images be loud? They can if Wolf Blitzer's talking over them.) What once seemed overwhelming now verges on the meaningless.

The photograph, though, consists of nothing if not meaning. "Nonstop imagery (television, streaming video, movies) is our surround," Susan Sontag writes in her book *Regarding the Pain of Others*, "but when it comes to remembering, the photograph has the deeper bite. . . . The photograph is like a quotation, or a maxim or proverb." Poetry, it has been said, aspires to the condition of music. Television aspires to the condition of air: all everywhere, all the time. A wide-angle lens that could take in 360 degrees is the ultimate and ideal TV technology. (What could be fairer, more balanced, as the folks at Fox News would say?) No need for cutaways—other than commercials, of course—no talking heads, just endless, ongoing footage . . . except footage indicates the past, and this would be constant real time, an all-encompassing now.

Television, at its most potent, says, "You are there." But to be there while still here is to be a 21st-century version of Stendhal's Fabrizio, dazedly wandering the battlefield at Waterloo. The televised battlefield is made that much more incomprehensible by its simultaneous distance in space and immediacy in time.

Photography is a starkly different proposition. It is always about the past (however recent that past might be), always about mediation, always about discrimination. It's the difference between "This has happened" and "This is happening," between narrative and flux. Where television assimilates, photography edits. "The central act of photography," John Szarkowski, the longtime curator of photography at the Museum of Modern Art, has argued, is "the act of choosing and eliminating." In an age of inundation, no visual act is more necessary—or, perhaps, more striking. Television is a stream, a presence, a climate—and climate we can control. Turn on the air conditioner, reach for the remote: all is well. But a photograph is an instant arrested and made concrete, an object, a fact—and as Ronald Reagan liked to say, "Facts are stubborn things." The words about the war run together. Three weeks later, who remembers "shock and awe" (or was it "awe and shock")? The television feeds run together, even the broadcasts tinged in memory with that kryptonite green produced by night-sight imaging.

The photographs do not run together. That stubbornness is their beauty, their utility, their indispensability. Consider just two examples. A Royal Marine fires a wire-guided missile in southern Iraq. This image taken by the Associated Press's Jon Mills is one of startling beauty: gases and flame erupt from the missile, their white-hot trail dominating the pale blue of sky and delicate beige of sand and camouflage gear. Another Royal Marine stares off in profile, a fellow viewer, our surrogate, though his gaze is directed at target rather than projectile. Accurate and even evocative as such words may be, they cannot begin to do justice to the image, cannot capture it—indeed, cannot comprehend it without the stop-time assistance of the photograph. Television would do the firing a different sort of justice, rendering it as whomp and whoosh and trajectory: a process, not an event. Certainly, it wouldn't be able to show the actual missile. Just as certainly, it would quickly turn away from the man who fired it and move on to something somewhere else. Most important, it would give us no leave to reflect, if we so chose, on those the missile is intended to kill. Mills's photo is an archetypal image of war: a faceless soldier fires a weapon at an unseen target. The merest glance identifies its genre.

Such is not the case with the photograph by Stephen Crowley of Donald Rumsfeld shaking hands with Robert McNamara at a Pentagon luncheon a week after the war started. It's old men we see, unarmed and in suits, not young men carrying weapons and in uniform. The scene is 6,000 miles from Baghdad, good cheer and congratulation the order of the day. Ostensibly, it's all about consensus. Two Republicans (Rumsfeld, reaching down, and Frank Carlucci, seated on the left) meet with two Democrats (McNamara, seated in the middle, and Zbigniew Brzezinski, standing on the right). An opponent of the war could interpret the scene one way, as the triumph of Rumsfeld's hope over McNamara's experience. A supporter might see it as the triumph of Rumsfeld's experience over McNamara's hope.

Either way, it's all so undramatic, so sedate, pacific even—yet as an example of the unique power photographs possess to condense narrative and amplify it, this image might be the most extraordinary of this war. Really, it's nothing if not narrative, a narrative of American history that runs uninterrupted from today to the '60s, indeed, all the way to Jefferson, that evangelist of democracy, and Washington, who warned against "foreign entanglements." More than that, it's a narrative that stretches the full length of military conflict, a reminder that ever and always it has been old men who send young men into battle. Amid glasses of ice water, a modern-day Agamemnon, aged and grinning, shakes hands with an even more aged Nestor. What wouldn't blind Homer have given to record such a sight?

Barton Gellman, contributing editor-at-large at *Time* magazine, is author of *Angler: The Cheney Vice Presidency* and *Contending with Kennan*. He previously covered law, national security, and the Middle East for the *Washington Post*, where he shared Pulitzer Prizes in 2002 and 2008. This piece is adapted from the *Washington Post Magazine*, July 24, 1994.

A Battalion of One's Own

Implausibly agile at 63 tons, the Abrams tank wheeled through a sharp right turn and accelerated into the bush, looking for something to kill. It sounded almost like an animal, transmission growling, turbine keening, treads squealing and rattling on their tracks. Inside, in the gunner's seat and having his first fun of the day, was a 41-year-old lieutenant colonel named Scott R. Feil.

The occasion was a test of sorts, but Feil felt confident enough. Rusty or not, he was back in the saddle. After years behind a desk, he could smell kerosene again, and soon the tanks around him would be his own. Feil had reached a lifelong goal: command of an armored battalion. The new assignment would begin in a week. Today he planned to refresh his tank-fighting skills. Feil was heading for Texas, but he had stopped on the way at Fort Knox, Kentucky, the Army's hub for armored warfare. He wanted to subject himself to a practical exam that all his enlisted tank crewmen had to pass. Feil's men would be suspicious, he knew, when he arrived from a tour as head speechwriter for the Army chief of staff. "The typical thing coming from a high-level staff job is, 'Who is this feather merchant and what does he know?'" he said, standing on a hot tarmac between tests.

In fact, Feil was a seasoned armor officer, blooded in combat against Iraq. But two years of driving a word processor had done nothing for his proficiency in the tank. Already this day he had dropped a screwdriver in a crevice and fouled up assembly of a breechblock. He was passing every test, but not exactly acing them. Loading the tank's main gun between shots, for instance, is still done by hand: you kick a knee switch, yank a 43-pound shell from behind a sliding door, flip it nose over base on its way to the breech, slam it home, raise the safety lever and say, "Up!" Feil did that in six seconds, one second faster than he had to, but a really good loader can do it in four.

Now he was prowling the Kentucky bush, face pressed to the gunner's daylight sight for the hunt. His task was to locate and destroy a series of wooden silhouette targets. Staff Sgt. Brian Fretschel, stopwatch in hand, would serve as Feil's tank commander and time the test. Since this was a dry run, with empty guns, there was room for me to tag along in the loader's seat.

First to appear, some 700 meters away, was a squad of enemy troops. Tankers like to mock the infantry. They call foot soldiers "crunchies," for the sound they suppose the soldiers would make under their treads. But tankers know they also have reason to fear. Shoulder-fired missiles, especially from behind, can disable even an Abrams tank, and grenades are hell on the fuel trucks that follow all that gas-guzzling armor across the battlefield. You don't just drive past a crunchy on your way to more important targets.

"Gunner! Co-ax! Troops!" Fretschel barked. With that economical order, Fretschel identified which crewman he was addressing, selected a weapon and announced whom he wanted to kill. Feil swept crosshairs over the wooden cut-out soldiers, magnified the image, and switched his fire controls from the main cannon to a 7.62 mm coaxial machine gun. He did not fire, yet. He would have failed the test if he had. Instead he used a single word to say the quarry was in his sights. "Identified!" he said. "Fire!" Fretschel ordered. "On the way!" Feil replied, thumbing down the red fire button. Every word of that exchange went by the book, concise and unambiguous. The book, *Field Manual 17-12*, even specifies when to fire: at the word "way" in the phrase "on the way." But now Feil did something that left the book behind. It was startling in its frivolity, as unexpected as if he had broken into song. After 20 years in uniform, Feil sat there in an actual tank playing tanker. Holding down the button for two short bursts, he began chanting the staccato sound effects. "Da-duh-da-duh-da-duh-da-duh-da-duh," he said, under his breath. "Da-duh-da-duh-da-duh-da-duh-da-duh." On the next engagement, when he let fly with the unloaded main gun, he muttered, "BOOM!"

He did not smile. He had that look of solemn concentration 8-year-olds get when they duel. He looked like the "little bit of a pyromaniac" he was as a kid, "lighting stuff up because it just seemed neat," except now he had the ultimate cap gun in his holster. He looked like a man who made tanks his life's work because they filled him with awe. "There's two big thrills," he said. "One is being in the tank and squeezing the trigger and seeing—FOOM!—and shooting stuff. The other is standing outside on a road march and you can feel the ground shaking. It's a real feeling of power."

On a warm day last October, Feil came to Fort Hood, Texas, to take charge of the 3rd Battalion, 66th Armored Regiment, 2nd Armored Division. Seldom subtle in propaganda, the Army nicknames Fort Hood "The Great Place." You learn this at the main gate and from signs all over the post. The Great Place is a dusty installation of 56,000 souls, with 330 square miles of tumbleweed hills sprawled across two counties north of Austin. Feil's new battalion—known as 3/66 Armor, or "Burt's Knights," after a World War II alumnus—was not what the Army calls a "high speed" assignment: not a flash-and-dash cavalry squadron, not the 82nd Airborne, not an elite contingency unit that gets extra money and better equipment to be first off the blocks when war begins. To be blunt, it was rather an average tank battalion.

The change of command conformed to a ritual that would be recognized by the Romans. The battalion formed up on a dull green parade ground. The 2nd

Armored Division's "Hell on Wheels" band played patriotic songs. Feil marched stiffly alongside the outgoing commander, Lt. Col. Travis Hooper, and trooped the line—one circuit around the field, inspecting, and making his first impression on, the men he would lead. A young enlisted baritone, trained to speak in the inspirational tones of a newsreel announcer, took to the loudspeaker. He recited the regimental history: formed in 1918 for World War I; assigned during World War II to the 2nd Armored Division; fought in North Africa, Sicily and the Battle of the Bulge; destroyed a dug-in brigade of the Republican Guard in a six-hour battle during the 1991 Gulf War.

In truth, Feil's new unit had an uncertain claim on that proud legacy. With budgets shrinking and whole divisions standing down, the Army has been breaking up and disbanding less famous units, then "reflagging" their parts in colors of greater glory. Most of the men and equipment in Feil's battalion had just finished moving to Texas from Fort Polk, Louisiana, where they were known as the 4th Battalion, 35th Armored Regiment, and belonged to the 5th Infantry Division. The change left some soldiers unsettled, as if the National Football League took the Eagles defense and Falcons offense, moved them to Galveston and told them they were the Redskins.

The Army leaves no ambiguity when command shifts from one man to another. At the designated moment, Command Sgt. Maj. Kan Tong, the senior enlisted man, took the yellow embroidered battalion flag and passed it for the last time to Hooper, the departing commander. Hooper returned it to his own boss, Col. James Grazioplene. Grazioplene, in turn, extended the colors to Feil. For one moment, both men held the nine-foot staff in two-fisted grips. Then Grazioplene withdrew his hands, and the battalion was Feil's.

November brought the new commander's first big training exercise, four nights of tank duels across a cold expanse of desert. Each platoon had to assault a dug-in enemy outpost before dawn. The outpost had a single tank, and the idea was to destroy it before it could warn the main enemy force. "You must kill that tank. That's your number one priority," Feil told a group of platoon leaders gathered inside a canvas tent. A little field stove threw off smoky heat inside the dirt-floored enclosure. The tent smelled of charred wood and coffee. Three young lieutenants perched on battered metal folding chairs, listening to their company commander and taking notes.

Someone had built a 12-foot sandbox, filled it with dirt and shaped it roughly to match the battlefield. For all its high-tech Gulf War image, the Army still does plenty of business with crude tools like that. Grease pens on sheets of acetate still make the overlays on tactical maps. Soldiers still dig trenches and hang canvas and take simple machines apart to clean and oil them. The "terrain board," made of dirt and pocket scraps, remains the standard tool to describe a patch of ground. Capt. Jeffrey Nelson, the company commander, squatted over this one and talked his lieutenants through the planned assault. Little twigs stood for trees; scraps of toilet paper represented a riverbed. Red yarn marked the objective. It looked like a grade-school diorama.

In the battlefield that Nelson described, the enemy tank had dug into a "reverse slope defense," a protected position behind a low hill with only its turret poking over the top. "The threat tank can shoot to 2,800 meters but can only see 1,200 meters at night," Nelson said. "There's not a lot of concern for crunchies, but in the assembly area you want to keep good security just in case there's hostile civilians." When Nelson had finished, each lieutenant had plenty left to sort out. Should he maneuver in a column (for ease of control), on line (for maximum firepower), or in a wedge (a bit of a compromise)? Should his four tanks bound into the fight in pairs, with one pair standing to cover the other's advance, or should they rush their foe together to speed the kill? Should he move in frontally, keeping his thickest armor pointed at the enemy, or sneak in from the flank?

All those decisions, all the tradeoffs, were the lieutenant's to make. He knew what results he had to achieve—kill the tank, take the hill—but he had to solve the tactical problem himself. Feil stood and left the tent for a short drive to the low bluff from which he would watch. Just as he reached his Humvee, the radio crackled. Feil's operations officer, Maj. Gary Whitehead, was calling ahead with a warning that the boss was not meant to hear. "Golf 56 is on his way," he said, using Feil's radio call sign. "So clean up what you've got screwed up there." Feil did a double take at the radio, deciding how to react. Then he laughed. "I'm glad they think that way," he said.

Lt. Andrew Skinner's platoon was the first into the assault. Feil climbed down a rocky slope for a better view through the trees. Miles from Killeen's city lights, night had fallen thick and black. Skinner's four tanks were invisible to the naked eye. They made murky dark shapes in the wash of electric green produced by Feil's night-vision goggles. Feil did not much like what he saw. "Dispersion is poor," he said. Intent on keeping formation in the dark, Skinner's tanks were too close together, vulnerable to wholesale destruction under artillery fire. Worse, they were moving too slowly, apparently worried about hitting an obstruction or a ditch. "Definitely too long," Feil muttered.

Tanks are weapons of shock and momentum, the role they inherited from the horse cavalry. Aggressive movement is the name of the game. More and more in recent years, seconds count. The popular view of the tank is of something invulnerable, but anything on the modern battlefield can be killed. One tank can usually destroy another, and the big change is that it often can do so now on the first shot. In World War II, a tank would have to fire 13 rounds at 1,500 meters to have a good chance of hitting a target once. With computer-controlled ballistics, today's tanks can easily hit with their first shot from twice that far, or nearly two miles away. Some U.S. tank crews recorded one-shot kills from 4,000 meters in the Gulf War. There are plenty of reasons why a crew might miss—adrenaline, fear, equipment failure—but a wise tank commander assumes his enemy knows what he is doing. Most of the time, the rule applies: who shoots first, wins.

In this case, the enemy seized the initiative. As Skinner's platoon crawled into range, the bad guy fired a parachute flare. Eerie shadows darted across the terrain as the flare drifted down. Skinner's tanks froze like cockroaches, and the enemy got off six shots before the good guys fired at all.

In the Pentagon office where Feil used to work, the Army still dispenses a book called *America's First Battles*. A collection of historical monographs, the volume puts forth a thesis that goes roughly like this: Americans grow bored with their Army between wars, demobilize too fast and forget how to fight. When the next war comes, they get creamed for a while, then build back up eventually and win. (Let's leave Vietnam out of this.) The cost in lives, in the early going, is gruesome.

Today's Army leaders, and those in the Defense Department across the board, are obsessed with breaking that cycle. When I was assigned to the defense beat in 1990, they sounded confident that they knew how to manage the trick. These officers had lived through the hollow 1970s and spoke of those times with contempt. Today, four years later, they seem less sure of themselves, the choices of their predecessors less clearly wrong. Somehow, they find themselves making compromises they used to abhor.

Sen. Sam Nunn, chairman of the Armed Services Committee, proposed a plan in 1990 for "flexible readiness," with some units kept readier than others. The Pentagon deplored it. In the Army today, flexible readiness is an accomplished fact. What changed was that the bottom dropped out of the budget, and still is dropping. The Army grieves that it must slim down from 18 active-duty divisions to 10, convinced that Americans are repeating their historic error. But the fact is that the Army cannot support even 10 divisions in the style to which divisions have grown accustomed.

On the grand scale of national priorities, the country may be making the right choice. More money would certainly buy more readiness, but there are other things Americans might rather buy. What cannot be overlooked, though, and what has not been squarely faced, is that the world's most competent military force is beginning to fray.

It is left to mid-grade leaders like Feil to try to hold their units together. They fight the tides and swallow their frustrations every day. For the rank and file, life is simpler. In the weeks I spent with Feil's battalion, soldiers did what soldiers do. They spent their days turning wrenches in the motor pool, hoisting differentials and replacing wedge bolts. They read the official Army comic book on preventive maintenance, starring the voluptuous Connie Rod and Sergeant Halfmast. (Sample dialogue: "Wow!" exclaims Halfmast, gawking at

Connie Rod and her magnificent M-916 armored tractor. "Sure it's awesome!" replies Connie Rod, nimbly returning conversation to the topic at hand, preventive maintenance. "But good PM will tame it!!!")

When Feil assembled his men in formation, before dismissing them for a long weekend's leave, he sounded like any commander in any year. Driving wind whipped a cold rain, and the whine of tank turbines across the road drowned out anything like a conversational voice. No matter. Feil seemed a man transformed. Earthy, bellowing, rigid, profane, he snapped salutes and played his role to the hilt. The formation divided into five neat squares: four line companies and a headquarters. The soldiers hunched as best they could against the chill. "Companies, attteeeeeeeeeeeen-HUT!" screamed Sgt. Maj. Tong, beginning the ritual. One by one, the companies bellowed their refrains. Each man snapped to attention as his company shouted in unison its fighting motto.

"Strike fast, kick ass!" began Alpha Company, on Feil's left.

"Steel on steel!"

"War dogs!"

"Dragons!"

"Hard and heavy!"

Feil leaned forward, face contorted and chest puffed out. "Burt's Knights, you're down here in the motor pool, the place you love to live in! We gotta be able to do our job day and night, in any kind of weather," he sang out. He told them to drive carefully so he wouldn't have to send their bloody carcasses home to their mothers. He told them they were good soldiers—no, great ones, and doing a superb job. No one knew where they might be sent, but they'd just keep doing what they were paid to do until someone told them to do it somewhere else.

"I'm not concerned about all the other non-tanking [people] on this post," Feil concluded, using lots of words unfit for a family audience. "Tell 'em you're one of 500 elite tanking killer [ahem, ahem] ready to do the job." Feil stood and watched his men depart, platoon by platoon. In the distance, he could hear them sing out their jodies, marching in time to the ribald, rhythmic words. "Here we go again . . . same old [stuff] again . . . marching down the avenue . . ." If he had any doubts about what he had said, they did not show.

Deborah Sontag is a member of the investigative team at the *New York Times*, where this feature story appeared on April 5, 2007. Reported and written in a week, it provides an intimate snapshot of a wounded combat veteran whose life gradually disintegrated after he returned from Iraq. It also prompted the *New York Times* to examine cases of other war veterans who ended up in trouble with the law, culminating in a series of stories entitled "War Torn," published in 2008.

Injured in Iraq, a Soldier Is Shattered at Home
Dunbar, Pennsylvania

Blinded and disabled on the 54th day of the war in Iraq, Sam Ross returned home to a rousing parade that outdid anything this small, depressed Appalachian town had ever seen. "Sam's parade put Dunbar on the map," his grandfather said. That was then.

Now Mr. Ross, 24, faces charges of attempted homicide, assault and arson in the burning of a family trailer in February. Nobody in the trailer was hurt, but Mr. Ross fought the assistant fire chief who reported to the scene, and later threatened a state trooper with his prosthetic leg, which was taken away from him, according to the police. The police locked up Mr. Ross in the Fayette County prison. In his cell, he tried to hang himself with a sheet. After he was cut down, Mr. Ross was committed to a state psychiatric hospital, where, he said in a recent interview there, he is finally getting—and accepting—the help he needs, having spiraled downward in the years since the welcoming fanfare faded. "I came home a hero, and now I'm a bum," said Mr. Ross, whose full name is Salvatore Ross Jr.

The story of Sam Ross has the makings of a ballad, with its heart-rending arc from hardscrabble childhood to decorated war hero to hardscrabble adulthood. His effort to create a future for himself by enlisting in the Army exploded in the desert during a munitions-disposal operation in Baghdad. He was 20. He was also on his own. Mr. Ross, who is estranged from his mother and whose father is serving a life sentence for murdering his stepmother, does not have the family support that many other severely wounded veterans depend on. Various relatives have stepped in at various times, but Mr. Ross, embittered by a difficult childhood and by what the war cost him, has had a push-pull relationship with those who sought to assist him.

Several people have taken a keen interest in Mr. Ross, among them Representative John P. Murtha, the once-hawkish Democrat from Pennsylvania. When Mr. Murtha publicly turned against the war in Iraq in 2005, he cited the shattered life of Mr. Ross, one of his first constituents to be seriously wounded, as a pivotal influence. Mr. Murtha's office assisted Mr. Ross in negotiating the military health-care bureaucracy. Homes for Our Troops, a nonprofit group based in Massachusetts, built him a beautiful log cabin. Military doctors carefully tended Mr. Ross's physical wounds: the loss of his eyesight, of his left leg below the knee and of his hearing in one ear, among other problems.

But that help was not enough to save Mr. Ross from the loneliness and despair that engulfed him. Overwhelmed by severe symptoms of post-traumatic stress disorder, including routine nightmares of floating over Iraq that ended with a blinding boom, he "self-medicated" with alcohol and illegal drugs. He finally hit rock bottom when he landed in the state psychiatric hospital, where he is, sadly, thrilled to be. "Seventeen times of trying to commit suicide, I think it's time to give up," Mr. Ross said, speaking in the forensic unit of the Mayview State Hospital in Bridgeville. "Lots of them were screaming out cries for help, and nobody paid attention. But finally somebody has."

Fayette County in southwestern Pennsylvania, once a prosperous coal-mining center, is now one of the poorest counties in the state. The bucolic but ramshackle town of Dunbar sits off State Route 119 near the intersection marked by the Butchko Brothers junkyard.

Past the railroad tracks and not far up Hardy Hill Road, the blackened remains of Mr. Ross's hillside trailer are testament to his disintegration. The Support our Troops ribbon is charred, the No Trespassing sign unfazed. Mr. Ross lived in that trailer, where his father shot his stepmother, at several points in his life, including alone after he returned from Iraq. Its most recent tenant, his younger brother, Thomas, was in jail when the fire occurred. Many in Mr. Ross's large, quarreling family are on one side of the law or the other, prison guards or prisoners, police officers or probationers. Their internal feuds are so commonplace that family reunions have to be carefully plotted with an eye to who has a protective order out against whom, joked Mr. Ross's 25-year-old cousin, Joseph Lee Ross.

Sam Ross's childhood was not easy. "Sam's had a rough life from the time he was born," his grandfather, Joseph Frank Ross, said. His parents fought, sometimes with guns, until they separated and his mother moved out of state. Mr. Ross bore some of the brunt of the turmoil. "When that kid was little, the way he got beat around, it was awful," said his uncle, Joseph Frank Ross Jr., a prison guard. When he was just shy of 12, Mr. Ross moved in with his father's father, who for a time was married to his mother's mother. The grandfather-grandson relationship was and continues to be tumultuous. "I idolized my grandpaps, but he's an alcoholic and he mentally abuses people," Mr. Ross said.

His grandfather, 72, a former coal miner who sells used cars, said, "I'm not an alcoholic. I can quit. I just love the taste of it." The grandfather, who still keeps an A-plus English test by Mr. Ross on his refrigerator, said his grandson did well in school, even though he cared most about his wrestling team, baseball, hunting and fishing. Mr. Ross graduated in June 2001. "Sammy wanted me to pay his way to college, but I'm not financially fixed to do that," his grandfather said.

Feeling that Fayette County was a dead end, Mr. Ross said he had wanted to find a way out after he graduated. One night in late 2001, he said, he saw "one of those 'Be all you can be' ads" on television. The next day, he went to the mall and enlisted, getting a $3,000 bonus for signing up to be a combat engineer. From his first days of basic training, Mr. Ross embraced the military as his salvation. "It was like, 'Wow, man, I was born for the Army,'" he said. "I was an adrenaline junkie. I was super, super fit. I craved discipline. I wanted adventure. I was patriotic. I loved the bonding. And there was nothing that I was feared of. I mean, man, I was made for war."

In early 2003, Private Ross, who earned his jump wings as a parachutist, shipped off to Kuwait with the 82nd Airborne Division, which pushed into Iraq with the invasion in March. The early days of the war were heady for many soldiers like Private Ross, who reveled in the appreciation of Iraqis. He was assigned to an engineer squad given the task of rounding up munitions. On May 18, Private Ross and his squad set out to de-mine an area in south Baghdad. Moving quickly, as they did on such operations, he collected about 15 UXOs, or unexploded ordnances, in a pit. Somehow, something—he never learned what—caused them to detonate. "The initial blast hit me and I went numb and everything went totally silent," he said. "Then I hear people start hollering, 'Ross! Ross! Ross!' It started getting louder, louder, louder. My whole body was mangled. I was spitting up blood. I faded in and out. I was bawling my eyes out, saying, 'Please don't let me go; don't let me go.'"

When his relatives first saw Mr. Ross at Walter Reed Army Hospital in Washington, he was in a coma. "That boy was dead," his grandfather said. "We was looking at a corpse lying in that bed." As he lay unconscious, the Army discharged him—one year, four months and 18 days after he enlisted, by his calculation. After 31 days, Mr. Ross came off the respirator. Groggily but insistently, he pointed to his eyes and then to his leg. An aunt gingerly told him he was blind and an amputee. He cried for days, he said.

It was during Mr. Ross's stay at Walter Reed that Representative Murtha, a former Marine colonel, first met his young constituent and presented him with a Purple Heart. From the start of the war, Mr. Murtha said in an interview, he made regular, painful excursions to visit wounded soldiers. Gradually, those visits, combined with his disillusionment about the Bush administration's management of the war, led him to call in late 2005 for the troops to be brought home in six months. "Sam Ross had an impact on me," Mr. Murtha said. "Eventually, I just felt that we had gotten to a point where we were talking so much about winning the war itself—and it couldn't be won militarily—that we were forgetting about the results of the war on individuals like Sam."

Over the next three years, Mr. Ross underwent more than 20 surgical procedures, including: "Five on my right eye, one on my left eye, two or three when they cut my left leg off, three or four on my right leg, a couple on my throat, skin grafts, chest tubes and, you know, one where they gutted me from belly button to groin" to remove metal fragments from his intestines. But although he was prescribed psychiatric medication, he never received in-patient treatment for the post-traumatic stress disorder that was diagnosed at Walter Reed. And, in retrospect he, like his relatives, believes he should have been put in an intensive program soon after his urgent physical injuries were addressed. "They should have given him treatment before they let him come back into civilization," said his grandfather.

The parade, on a sunny day in late summer 2003, was spectacular. Hundreds of flag-waving locals lined the streets. Mr. Ross had just turned 21. Wearing his green uniform and burgundy beret, he rode in a Jeep, accompanied by other veterans and the Connellsville Area Senior High School marching band. The festivities included bagpipers, Civil War re-enactors and a dunking pool. "It wasn't the medals on former Army Pfc. Sam Ross's uniform that reflected his courage yesterday," the *Pittsburgh Post-Gazette* wrote. "It was the Dunbar native's poise as he greeted well-wishers and insisted on sharing attention with other soldiers that proved the grit he'll need to recover from extensive injuries he suffered in Iraq."

For a little while, "it was joy joy, happiness happiness," Mr. Ross said. He felt the glimmerings of a new kind of potential within himself, and saw no reason why he could not go on to college, even law school. Then the black moods, the panic attacks, the irritability set in. He was dogged by chronic pain; fragments of metal littered his body. Mr. Ross said he was "stuck in denial" about his disabilities. The day he tried to resume a favorite pastime, fishing, hit him hard. Off-balance on the water, it came as a revelation that, without eyesight, he did not know where to cast his rod. He threw his equipment in the water and sold his boat. "I just gave up," he said. "I give up on everything."

About a year after he was injured, Mr. Ross enrolled in an in-patient program for blind veterans in Chicago. He learned the Braille alphabet, but his fingers were too numb from embedded shrapnel to read, he said. He figured that he did not have much else to learn since he had been functioning blind for a year. He left the program early. Similarly, Mr. Ross repeatedly declined outpatient psychiatric treatment at the veterans' hospital in Pittsburgh, according to the Department of Veterans Affairs. He said he felt that people at the hospital had disrespected him.

After living with relatives, Mr. Ross withdrew from the world into the trailer on the hill in 2004. That year, he got into a dispute with his grandfather over old vehicles on the property, resolving it by setting them on fire. His run-ins with local law enforcement, which did not occur before he went to Iraq, the Fayette County sheriff said, had begun.

But his image locally had not yet been tarnished. In early 2005, Mr. Murtha held a second Purple Heart ceremony for Mr. Ross at a Fayette County hospital "to try to show him how much affection we had for him and his sacrifice," Mr. Murtha said. A local newspaper article about Mr. Ross's desire to build himself a house came to the attention of Homes for Our Troops. "He's a great kid; he really is," said Kirt Rebello, the group's director of projects and veterans affairs. "Early on, even before he was injured, the kid had this humongous deck stacked against him in life. That's one of the reasons we wanted to help him." Mr. Ross, who had received a $100,000 government payment for his catastrophic injury, bought land adjacent to his grandfather's. Mr. Rebello asked Mr. Ross whether he might prefer to move to somewhere with more services and opportunities. But Mr. Ross said that Dunbar's winding roads were implanted in his psyche, "that he could see the place in his mind," Mr. Rebello said.

In May 2005, Mr. Ross broke up with a girlfriend and grew increasingly depressed. He felt oppressively idle, he said. One day, he tacked a suicide note to the door of his trailer and hitched a ride to a trailhead, disappearing into the woods. A daylong manhunt ensued. Mr. Ross fell asleep in the woods that night, waking up with the sun on his face, which he took to be a sign that God wanted him to live. When he was found, he was taken to a psychiatric ward and released after a few weeks.

The construction of his house proved a distraction from his misery. Mr. Ross enjoyed the camaraderie of the volunteers who fashioned him a cabin from white pine logs. But when the house, which he named Second Heaven, was finished in early 2006, "they all left, I moved in and I was all alone," he said. "That's when the drugs really started." At first, Mr. Ross said, he used drugs— pills, heroin, crack and methadone—"basically to mellow myself out and to have people around." Local ne'er-do-wells enjoyed themselves on Mr. Ross's tab for quite some time, his relatives said. "These kids were loading him into a car, taking him to strip clubs, letting him foot the bills," his uncle, Joseph Ross Jr., said. "They were dopies and druggies."

Mr. Ross's girlfriend, Barbara Hall, moved in with him. But relationships with many of his relatives had deteriorated. "If that boy would have come home and accepted what happened to him, that boy never would have wanted for anything in Dunbar," his grandfather said. "If he had accepted that he's wounded and he's blinded, you know? He's not the only one that happened to. There's hundreds of boys like him." Some sympathy began to erode in the town, too. "There's pro and con on him," a local official said. "Some people don't even believe he's totally blind."

After overdosing first on heroin and then on methadone last fall, Mr. Ross said, he quit consuming illegal drugs, replacing them with drinking until he blacked out. Mr. Ross relied on his brother, Thomas, when he suffered panic attacks. When Thomas was jailed earlier this year, Mr. Ross reached out to older members of his family. In early February, his uncle, Joseph Ross Jr., persuaded him to be driven several hours to the veterans' hospital in Coatesville to apply for its in-patient program for post-traumatic stress disorder. "Due to the severity of his case, they accepted him on the spot and gave him a bed date for right after Valentine's Day," his uncle said. "Then he wigged out five days before he was supposed to go there."

It started when his brother's girlfriend, Monica Kuhns, overheard a phone call in which he was arranging to buy antidepressants. She thought it was a transaction to buy cocaine, he said, and he feared that she would tell his sister and brother. After downing several beers, Mr. Ross, in a deranged rage, went to his old trailer, where Ms. Kuhns was living with her young son, he said. "He started pounding on the door," said Ms. Hall, who accompanied him. "He went in and threatened to burn the place down. Me and Monica didn't actually think he was going to do it. But then he pulled out the lighter." Having convinced himself that the trailer—a source of so much family misery—needed to be destroyed, Mr. Ross set a pile of clothing on fire. The women and the child fled. When a volunteer firefighter showed up, Mr. Ross attacked and choked him, according to a police complaint.

A judge set bail at $250,000. In the Fayette County prison, Mr. Ross got "totally out of hand," the sheriff, Gary Brownfield, said. Mr. Ross's lawyer, James Geibig, said the situation was a chaotic mess. "It was just a nightmare," Mr. Geibig said. "First the underlying charges—attempted homicide, come on—were blown out of proportion. Then bail is set sky high, straight cash. They put him in a little cell, in isolation, and barely let him shower. Things went from bad to worse until they found him hanging." Now Mr. Geibig's goal is to get Mr. Ross sentenced into the post-traumatic stress disorder program he was supposed to attend. "He does not need to be in jail," Mr. Geibig said. "He has suffered enough. I'm not a bleeding heart, but his is a pretty gut-wrenching tale. And at the end, right before this incident, he sought out help. It didn't arrive in time. But it's not too late, I hope, for Sam Ross to have some kind of future."

David Maraniss is an associate editor at the *Washington Post*. He won the 1993 Pulitzer Prize for National Reporting and was part of a team of *Post* reporters who won the 2008 Pulitzer for coverage of the Virginia Tech tragedy. He has written books about Bill Clinton, Vince Lombardi, and Roberto Clemente. This text is excerpted from *They Marched into Sunlight*: *War and Peace, Vietnam and America, October 1967* (Simon and Shuster, 2003).

Connections

When Cathay Pacific flight 765 from Hong Kong touched down at Ho Chi Minh City on the morning of January 27, 2002, here I was, finally, decades late, the FNG—fucking new guy. This was my first visit to a country that I had only imagined, for better and worse. With my wife at my side, I looked out the window from seat 45C as the airplane rolled toward the terminal. Everything seems exotic the first time: guard towers, machine guns, uniforms of deep olive green and dark red; motorbikes racing our jet on a parallel dirt road, three-packs of teenaged boys clinging to each seat; a hive of gray hangars, giant, culvertlike cement half-moons that once provided cover for U.S. helicopters; patient queues of travelers at the checkpoints inside; more soldiers, stone-cold serious, born after the war was over; a clattering, expectant sea of people waiting outside, fingers gripping the chain-link fence, heads straining for the first glimpse of arriving relatives bringing appliances and cardboard boxes full of other material wonders from the world beyond. Then into the sunlight and a surprising jolt of exhilaration in the steamy Saigon heat.

Connections are what fascinate me, the connections of history and of individual lives, the accidents, incidents, and intentions that rip people apart and sew them back together. These interest me more than ideological formulations that pretend to be certain of the meaning of it all. I came to Vietnam looking for more connections. And I brought some connections with me.

I grew up in Madison, Wisconsin, where half the events recorded in *They Marched into Sunlight* would take place. During the days in October 1967, when the Black Lions were fighting and dying in the jungle of the Long Nguyen Secret Zone and antiwar protesters were staging a sit-in at the Commerce Building on the University of Wisconsin campus, I was a naïve freshman at the school. I observed the protest against Dow Chemical, maker of napalm, from the edge of the crowd, and felt the sting of tear gas, and saw a few things that I mostly forgot. Three years later I received a low number in the draft lottery and rode the bus to Milwaukee for an induction physical but was declared 4-F because of chronic asthma that I'd had since childhood. Campus demonstrations were still going on, and I began covering them in newspaper and radio reports. None of this was enough to warrant making myself a character in a book of history. I had no intention of including myself in any case, beyond the extent to which all authors of nonfiction or fiction are hidden characters in anything they write. But I was of Madison. I was steeped in its progressive tradition, honoring the right to dissent; I carried that with me wherever I went, and in that sense I was making a connection as soon as I landed in Ho Chi Minh City, bringing the Wisconsin side of the story to the Vietnam side.

In the lobby of the Hotel Continental a few hours later, there stood Clark Welch, the great soldier of Delta Company, at age sixty-two his stomach filled out and his crewcut turned gray, but still with that characteristic forward lean and disarmingly sheepish smile. He was back in Vietnam for the first time in three decades, and he looked exactly like what he was: American veteran and tourist, wearing a short-sleeved striped shirt and fanny pack, his keen blue eyes occasionally darting around the room, always scouting the territory. Next to him was Consuelo Allen, the oldest daughter of Lieutenant Colonel Terry Allen Jr., the battalion commander who was killed thirty-five years earlier on that bloody autumn day. People had always commented that Consuelo was the spitting image of her father, and the resemblance was now stronger than ever.

For more than three decades after the battle, Clark Welch burned with hostile feelings about Commander Allen and the flawed leadership decisions that sent the 2/28 Black Lions battalion into the jungle that morning of October 17, 1967, on a search-and-destroy mission that ended up destroying them, with sixty men killed and an equal number wounded in an ambush that the U.S. government lied about and described as a victory. Welch had questioned the decision to march into the jungle that day, suspicious of a trap, and had fought valiantly as so many of his "boys" had died. He had thought about that battle every day since, and as he rose through the ranks to captain, major, and colonel, he committed himself to the promise that no one who trained under him would get caught in a similar situation. He knew that Allen had three daughters but was wary of meeting them. He was afraid that they would not like him and that seeing them would bring him pain. But in the final few years of the twentieth century, after he had retired, he was tracked down by an old comrade, Jim Shelton, who had been Terry Allen's closest friend in Vietnam. Shelton had told him about the Allen girls and how bright and curious they were, and it started Welch on the path of wondering.

"I'm going to ask you something: where are Terry Allen's daughters and what do they think of me?" Welch asked me at the end of our first long interview, conducted in the lobby of a Denver hotel. I told him the daughters were in Texas—El Paso and Austin—and that they did not know enough about Welch to think much about him at all, except that he was a soldier with their father and that he had lived and their father had died.

"I dream about them," Welch confided. "I want them to be wonderful people."

Now here they were, together, Clark Welch and Consuelo Allen, connected for this mission in Vietnam. Consuelo came with questions. Where did her father die? What did it look like? What must it have felt like? How has it changed? Welch had fewer questions; he thought he knew the answers. He anticipated that the experience would be difficult, that his mind would ricochet endlessly from present to past to present to past.

Once, long ago, on an early summer evening in 1967, after he had flown over his little section of Vietnam in a helicopter, Lieutenant Welch wrote to his wife: "This place can be beautiful! The winding rivers, the little hamlets, the neat rice paddies and little gardens are very tranquil looking. And the rivers are either bright blue or brown, the fields and forests are deep green, and the shallow water on the rice looks silver from up there. Riding in the chopper with the doors off—there's a nice cool breeze, too. Maybe we could come back here some day when it's as peaceful and beautiful on the ground as it looks from the sky."

Nothing is that peaceful, ever, and certainly not the Democratic Republic of Vietnam, but now the war was long over and Clark Welch was back. He was eager to see the beauty of the country again; and to reflect on what happened in 1967 and how things might have gone differently, in the battle and the war; and to be there when and if I found soldiers who had fought that day for the other side, the VC First Regiment. He and Consuelo would come with me to walk the battlefield in the Long Nguyen Secret Zone south of the Ong Thanh stream. Big Rock, as his young soldiers once called him, was ready. He had his old army pictograph map with the coordinates of the battle and a little global-positioning-system location finder that dangled from his neck like a good luck pendant.

Here we sat, across from each other at a long conference table in a quiet room inside the offices of the foreign ministry in Ho Chi Minh City: Clark Welch and I on one side, Vo Minh Triet and two interpreters on the other. Two days earlier, I had given the Vietnamese press office Triet's name, which I had seen on U.S. military documents: intelligence reports from the late 1960s and more recent reports regarding MIA searches in Vietnam. Now Clark and I were looking at Triet in the flesh, the officer who had commanded the First Regiment in 1967. I was afraid that he might not remember anything about the battle, and I wanted to learn as much as I could from him for the first few hours that had nothing to do with October 17. Clark thought this was a waste of time, though he was polite enough to tolerate it.

Then, finally, after a lunch break, we pulled out our maps of the area north of Lai Khe in the Long Nguyen Secret Zone and I started to say a few things about the Black Lions battalion and what they were doing on so-called search-and-destroy missions in the weeks leading up to the battle. Triet rose from his chair, examined the maps for a few minutes, which seemed like forever, and at last put his finger right on the coordinates of the battlefield and said something in Vietnamese, which was translated by my interpreter, Kyle Horst. The words gave me chills. "Of course I remember," Triet said. "We weren't supposed to be there. Let me tell you how it happened."

For the next two hours he talked about the battle and the days before and after: how his regiment was starving, in desperate search for rice. They had been subsisting on bamboo shoots and boiled stink grass for days, and had entered the Long Nguyen Secret Zone because they knew there was a rear service supply group for the Viet Cong there, not far from the Ong Thanh stream. But when they reached Rear Service Group 83 headquarters, there was no rice there, either, and they decided to wait there for the next shipment. They were supposed to make their way north and west for the start of an offensive in War Zone D. But as he waited, he received news that an American battalion was in the jungle, rumbling around looking for action. His reports said it was a battalion, a few hundred men. He had a regiment, more than twelve hundred soldiers. He decided to set up a three-sided ambush and lure the Americans into an ambush.

The more Triet talked, the more it seemed that Clark Welch's comprehension of Vietnamese, which he had studied briefly before being sent to Vietnam in 1967, came back to him. The two old soldiers were talking the same language, communicating, even when they did not understand everything the other was saying. At the end of the interview, I asked whether Colonel Triet would be willing to ride with us the next day to the battlefield. He said why not, he had nothing better to do. He was seventy-two years old and retired; he spent his days now as a functionary in Ho Chi Minh City's Ward 14, promoting population control.

At eight the next morning, our entourage piled into a van for the bumpy ride north up Thunder Road. Triet was there, and Clark Welch, and Consuelo Allen, and her friend Rob Keefe, and Kyle Horst, my guide and interpreter. Also my wife and I, a driver and our Vietnamese minder, Madam Ha. Before the van pulled away from the Hotel Continental, Triet turned to Welch, soldier to soldier, and said of that long ago battle on the ground we were visiting, "No one won that day." It was a statement with several levels of meaning, but above all, it was a grace note, a way of connecting men who had once tried to kill each other. Triet later made the same comment to Consuelo Allen.

Executing a few turns at intersections that were not apparent on every map, we made it to an unmarked road closer to the battlefield. We drove down that road until it became impassable, then got out and walked. Our destination was the bamboo-and-tin house of Nguyen Van Lam, another local farmer. He had served as a company commander in Rear Service Group 83 and fought in the October 17 battle. When we arrived at Lam's, he was out. A son said he was attending a wedding, but Lam showed up shortly thereafter, the word having spread quickly about the appearance of the bearded American (Kyle) and some other strangers with big noses.

Nguyen Van Lam had ten sons, the youngest ten years old. At the entrance to his house, they kept squirrels in a cage. In a muddy little enclosed pond in the side yard, they raised eels. There were several framed portraits and certificates on the walls of his living area, some honoring Lam for his war service, others honoring his wife's brother, who was considered a martyr, killed "opposing the Americans to save the country."

When Lam arrived from the wedding, Triet immediately recognized him, even though they had been together for a few days thirty-five years earlier. "Oh, my God," Lam said. "You are still alive?" They hugged and sat down in the shaded opening to the house, clasping hands much of the time as they talked. When Triet heard that Lam had ten children, he chastised him. "You give birth like chickens," he said, and asked whether Lam and his wife had ever heard of population control.

Are you sick at all? Triet asked.

No, Lam said. He had some hearing loss from air strikes and a cluster-bomb pellet in his lung, but other than that he was fine.

Do you have AIDS? Triet asked.

Lam laughed. Triet was still ribbing him for his prodigious family.

Soon we were off, walking tentatively across a creaking bamboo monkey bridge over the Ong Thanh stream, following a narrow path through the manioc fields, passing a herd of water buffalo, and moving south toward the battlefield. Our first stop was where the Black Lions had set up their night defensive perimeter on October 16. There were still a few holes in the field, remnants of American bunkers. The open land we walked through next had been dense jungle in 1967. Clark Welch, checking his GPS, said we were right on target, but he kept repeating, "It looks so different. Everything has changed."

Lam said that after the battle, the area was heavily bombed and then defoliated until there were no trees left. Years later everyone in the area started getting headaches, he said. Not long ago, a few local people in their forties and fifties had terrible headaches for three days and then died. The villagers thought it was because of Agent Orange.

As we moved closer to the battlefield, Triet and Welch seemed like they were in their own world again, the two proficient soldiers reliving the battle. They would walk off together and point and say a few things, describing the line of march of the American companies and the positioning of Triet's three battalions. At one point Nguyen Van Lam stopped and pointed to a depression in the ground and said this was where he and his men, on the morning after the battle, had found the torso of an American soldier that had been ripped apart by wild pigs. A hundred meters further, Clark checked his GPS and his maps and said we were nearing the ground of the battle. We had to move to our right, or east, a few hundred meters, he said, so we turned and walked in that direction.

In 1967 this had been dense jungle; now it was a government rubber plantation, a grove of medium-height trees planted in neat rows. It was refreshingly cool, away from the ninety-degree heat, and sunlight dappled gently through the grove. The ground was covered with dry brown leaves that crunched softly as we walked. It felt as though we were walking into a cathedral. And then Clark pointed to a spot that matched the coordinates of where Terry Allen and the battalion command were killed.

An anthill happened to be there, just as there had been during the battle. A different anthill, obviously, but it served as a fitting memorial nonetheless. I asked our Vietnamese companions to keep quiet so we could pay our respects. Clark Welch bit his lip and winced, memories of that day cascading through his mind. Tears streamed down Consuelo Allen's face as she studied the lonely spot where her father died. The moment he was killed and this moment, as she stood on the same ground, separated by thirty-five years, now seemed as one.

A few days later, Clark Welch and I returned to talk to Nguyen Van Lam. There had been too much going on that first day walking the battlefield for me to interview him in depth, but on the return visit we sat down and talked at leisure. When the interview was done, Lam introduced us to his family—all of the boys, his wife, a daughter-in-law, and a grandchild. His seventh son was maimed, one hand cut off at the wrist. He had been weeding around the family rubber trees in their garden across the road, he said, and an old grenade from an American M-79 came out of the ground and exploded, shattering his right hand. There was still a lot of ammo around, Lam said. He pointed to a pile near the squirrel cage. "My, my, my," Clark said, looking at a collection of bullets and pieces of shrapnel hidden under a banana tree. Lam reached down and picked up some shrapnel. "You left these behind," he said.

Pippa Green a writer and journalist based in Pretoria, South Africa, has worked as a reporter and editor on South African newspapers and radio news since 1982. In *Choice, Not Fate: The Life and Times of Trevor Manuel* (Penguin, 2008), she tells this story of Nelson Mandela's release from prison.

Trevor Manuel and the Liberation of Nelson Mandela

Trevor Manuel's working-class family embodied the fate that befell thousands of people classified as colored under apartheid: a mother who struggled to bring up her children on a garment worker's wages; homes lived in and lost under the cruel Group Areas Act; clashes with gangsters who roamed the streets; a truncated education. Manuel stared down fate to become one of the most prominent anti-apartheid leaders in the internal resistance movement of the 1980s. He confronted apartheid's police and prisons with a reckless boldness. In 1996, Mandela appointed him to be South Africa's first black finance minister. Under Manuel's stewardship, South Africa entered its longest growth period ever.

In December 1989, an anti-apartheid conference that Trevor Manuel had been arrested for trying to organize the previous year, took place. This time it was called the Conference for a Democratic Future. It was held at the University of the Witwatersrand in Johannesburg.

More than 4,000 people from about 2,000 organizations attended. Its purpose was to discuss whether there should be negotiations between the liberation movement and the apartheid government. Using the language of the revolution, the African National Congress aimed to persuade its constituency to change tack. Negotiations were now "a terrain and method of struggle." Walter Sisulu, Nelson Mandela's prison mate and closest friend, now free after 26 years in jail, gave the keynote address, endorsing negotiations as a way forward.

By the following month, at a lower profile but more strategy-driven meeting, Trevor Manuel spoke an entirely different language from the discourse of opposition and defiance of the 1980s. In the political climate of the day, it took considerable courage to risk breaking with a people who could easily have been swayed by more militant arguments.

F. W. de Klerk, the new president of the country, faced the same challenge with his constituency. At the time the Conference for a Democratic Future took place in December, he was meeting with his cabinet in a remote private game reserve in the northwest of the country. But he spent most of the South African summer holidays alone, contemplating his speech, and had drafted the final part at midnight on February 1. He told only his few closest advisors the main points. "I didn't even tell my wife what I was going to announce," he said.

(Probably wisely: Marike de Klerk, his first wife, was renowned for her conservative views and unreconstructed racial prejudices).

Expectations were never higher than they were on February 2. Foreign correspondents from around the world descended on South Africa. Western TV networks brought out their expensive news anchors. Newspapers, small and large, sent reporters. And the ANC waited on tenterhooks outside the country.

As de Klerk began speaking, it was clear that the tone was different from that of any previous government speech. He spoke about a "negotiated understanding" among "representative leaders of the entire population . . . The alternative is growing violence, tension and conflict. That is unacceptable and in nobody's interest. The well-being of all in this country is linked inextricably to the ability of the leaders to come to terms with one another on a new dispensation. No one can escape this simple truth."

He spoke of 1989 as a year of "change" and "major upheaval" for South Africa and the whole world; about the collapse of the Soviet Union, the clampdown at Tiananmen Square, about the new relations in southern Africa that the demise of the Soviet Union would bring. "The season for violence is over. The time for reconstruction and reconciliation has arrived."

And then he did what the world waited for: he lifted the prohibition on the ANC, the South African Communist Party, and the Pan African Congress; he rescinded the restrictions against 33 opposition organizations. He said that political prisoners jailed only because they were members of banned political parties would be released; and he lifted restrictions on all 374 of the former detainees, including Manuel. He announced that the government had taken a "firm decision to release Nelson Mandela unconditionally."

Everyone expected it, yet everyone was surprised. The dream so distant just a few months ago was today, here, now. The narrative of freedom that echoed around the world began in Cape Town.

Eight days after de Klerk's speech, Manuel got a phone call from the office of General Johan Willemse, the commissioner of prisons. Would he be at the H. F. Verwoerd building in the parliamentary complex (the Cape Town offices of cabinet ministers) at 2:30 p.m.?

"General Willemse told us that the President was making the announcement now. Nelson Mandela was going to be released tomorrow, here in Cape Town. We must prepare to receive him."

That afternoon, Manuel was among the anti-apartheid leaders who drove to Victor Verster prison outside the little town of Paarl, about 40 miles from Cape Town, to meet Mandela for the first time. Other activists met at the black University of the Western Cape to plan Mandela's release rally. Willie Hofmeyr, a young Afrikaner who had turned against apartheid, was one of them. He had just emerged from several months of imprisonment without trial. He had been on a hunger strike that shrank his already slim fame to just 65 pounds.

The meeting on the eve of Mandela's release alternated between wild excitement and frustration because, while there was so much to do, there was so little that could be done—24-hours' notice for an event that the country had been awaiting for years. "By that time," recalled Hofmeyr, "we were fairly experienced rally-putter-togethers because we'd been doing it through most of the emergency, but this was a real last-minute thing." They had to organize posters, pamphlets, buses, sound systems, and all on a Saturday afternoon.

Mandela wanted to be released in Cape Town, where he had been jailed for the past 27 years. His homecoming rally would take place on the Grand Parade, a large public space in front of the City Hall in downtown Cape Town.

The rally was advertised for 3:00 p.m., the time Mandela was due to walk out of jail—he'd opted to walk rather than be driven out. The roads to the city centre were already thick with traffic by 11:00 that Sunday morning. "That's the first time I realized we may be in trouble," said Hofmeyr.

A crowd of at least 50,000 gathered on the Grand Parade soon after midday. It was a sweltering day. People wilted, tempers frayed. Some collapsed in the heat. And soon a group known in the black townships as "com-tsotsis"— gangsters who used political protest as a cover for thuggery—took over. They looted a liquor store and several shops in a nearby mall. Riot police at the corners of the crowd opened fire. Crack! Crack! Nobody in the crowd knew whether the police were firing live ammunition, rubber bullets or tear gas. Later reports said four people died that day. The reek of tear gas drifted in from the edges of the Parade. Mandela's supporters, who volunteered as marshals, battled valiantly to maintain order. One of the problems, said Hofmeyr afterward, was that they had not managed to get walkie-talkies. "Our marshals were just overcome, and we were not used to having to deal with people who came in with knives and fists to get to the front of the crowd."

A platform erected for photographers and TV crews was overrun by impatient youngsters hoping to get a glimpse of Mandela. Cameramen are known to be a brave breed. When the last of them jumped off, so did the marshals. Even more people scrambled up the structure, which withstood their weight for another ten minutes or so before buckling and spilling its usurpers into the dense crowds below.

It was now well past 3:00 p.m. Still Mandela didn't arrive. An angry murmur went through the crowd that this was all a trick by de Klerk. The crowd swelled. Then the sound system broke down. There were now more than 60,000 people in front of the City Hall, and the "most aggressive were right in front," recalled Hofmeyr. "We were seriously contemplating using firehoses just to spray them down. People were fainting in the masses, in the crush and the heat, which just dragged on and on."

At 4:15 p.m., Nelson Mandela finally walked out of Victor Verster Prison, an hour and quarter behind schedule, 27 years after he was arrested. He was both triumphant and dazzled by the attention, especially by the aptly named rifle-mikes that camera crews pushed toward him. "Every time I moved away, they would come closer," he told me shortly before his 80th birthday.

Manuel helped him pack his belongings into one of the waiting vehicles, and got into a car behind his. Then they drove the back roads to Cape Town. Hofmeyr heard over a two-way radio on a traffic officer's bike that Mandela's convoy was on its way to Cape Town from the prison, some 40 miles away. But now there was mayhem outside the City Hall, as the crowd grew and became more chaotic. Hofmeyr rushed to the freeway exit ramp to warn them not to come into the city centre. His T-shirt was ripped to shreds and hung in strips around his emaciated figure. "We'd all been involved in physical combat for hours!"

"Comrades, stop! They're killing people in the city," he shouted to Manuel.

Manuel ordered Mandela's driver to skirt the volatile crowds outside the City Hall. He found a safe council building about a mile away and told the driver to wait there. He, meanwhile, went to scout out a safe back route for the ANC leader into the City Hall. But as Manuel departed, an officious traffic officer blocked Mandela's way, telling him he was in the wrong venue, and redirected his driver into the heart of the impatient and angry crowd. Scores of people swamped his car. A local newspaper reported afterward that Mandela's cavalcade had "roared" into the city just after 5:20 p.m. "A huge crowd ran wildly alongside his car as it wound through the city, beating on the windows and chanting. A group of women jostled and pushed, desperate to see their leader. They wept and laughed simultaneously. The press of the crowd slowed the motorcade to jogging pace and Mandela, in the back seat with his wife Winnie, looked out at the mad crush of faces. He was impassive, with his fist raised stiffly in salute."

Mandela may have looked impassive but his driver panicked, edged out of the crowd, and took the first turn out of town. He sped south along the freeway, ending in Rosebank, a suburb near the University of Cape Town. There they pulled up outside a house and knocked on the door. A woman who had been watching the release on TV looked out in astonishment. The man she had just seen walking out of jail was now here outside her house. Her name was Vanessa Watson. Coincidentally, she happened to be an urban-planning researcher who had written extensively on the parlous state of black housing in the Cape, information that had been used by Manuel's community organization in the early '80s. Instead of watching the rest of the chaos on the Grand Parade on TV, she chatted to the freed leader while he played with her newborn twins.

The diversion may have given Mandela's minders breathing space, but it didn't help the organizers. The sun faded and still there was no sign of their leader. They were terrified about what might happen.

When Mandela disappeared, Manuel was "beside himself. "How could we lose Madiba [Mandela's clan name] on the day of his release? How would you write that thing in history?"

At around 6:00 p.m., a traffic cop near the City Hall beckoned Manuel and said there was "someone who wanted to talk to him" on his two-way radio. It was a colonel in the security police whom Manuel knew from his frequent spells in jail. He said: "Trevor, you must go fetch Mandela. If you don't bring him here, the city will burn down and hundreds of people are going to be killed. Go fetch him!"

By this time, Mandela was having tea in another outlying Cape Town suburb with the family of a local Cape Town activist, whom his driver knew. The colonel directed Manuel, who raced to fetch him, and brought him back to the city along the less congested De Waal Drive, which winds along the mountainside, and through the back streets of the city. This time, they got him into the City Hall through its back entrance. With the late-summer evening fast fading to darkness, Mandela addressed the crowd on the Parade and millions more around the world who had been waiting for years for this moment.

"I stand here before you today not as a prophet but as a humble servant of the people. Your tireless and heroic sacrifices have made it possible for me to be here today. I therefore place the remaining years of my life in your hands."

The following day, the 200 or so journalists who clambered over the flowerbeds at Bishopscourt, the home of Archbishop Desmond Tutu, ranged from representatives of the world's most important and powerful newspapers and TV networks to those from local "struggle" publications, eager to impress him with left-wing questions. Mandela was asked about his views on redistribution of wealth.

"The question of the nationalization of the mines and similar sectors of the community is a fundamental policy of the ANC," he replied. He elaborated on a remark in his speech that the economy of the country lay in "ruins": "There are three important aspects we must consider when we are discussing the economy of a country. The question of full employment, the question of productivity, and the question of social responsibility. Once we can guarantee that there is progress in these three aspects, then the economy of the country is performing very well. But it is my impression that it is not performing well."

Manuel was at the press conference. He didn't know then how heavily Mandela's words on the economy would weigh on him.

At the time, he had more literal weights on his mind. After nearly 48 hours without sleep, he had collapsed into bed at around midnight after the rally, only to be awakened at 4:00 a.m. by a phone call from Mandela. "Trevor, where are my weights?" asked the old man.

They had been packed into one of the vehicles that had left Victor Verster Prison the day before. Manuel tracked them down before driving Mandela to the airport that afternoon to see him off on his homeward journey to Johannesburg. "Goodbye, Comrade Chief," he said. He hugged him and handed over his weights.

Michael Duffy has been a correspondent and editor at *Time* magazine since 1985. This story appeared in *Time* on May 21, 2006. In March 2010, Brown announced that he would seek the office of governor of California, a position he held from 1975 to 1983.

Jerry Brown Still Wants Your Vote

California's Jerry Brown, age 68 and ageless, is running for statewide office this year, 36 years after he did it the first time, and the question you have to ask is, why doesn't he give it up? It's Thursday morning, and Brown, mayor of Oakland, is standing in incandescent sunshine outside the renovated Sears store he calls home. Not much is going smoothly this morning: the city had its 50th murder the night before, adding to a huge spike above 2005; his opponent in the race for California attorney general has just called him soft on crime; one of the two charter schools he helped start is in need of cash; and now Fox television wants him to go on camera as a commentator and defend a new text-messaging service being marketed to teens that offers information on sex. "I am a little stressed today," he says.

But asking Edmund Brown Jr. to give up politics is a little like asking the Rolling Stones to quit rock 'n' roll. It's just what they do. Brown is a rock star himself. The son of a storied California governor and a veteran of nearly four years in a Jesuit seminary, he ran for California secretary of state at 32, was on the cover of *Time* by 36, served two terms as California governor, ran unsuccessfully for the Senate once and for president three times, moved to Japan, studied Buddhism, worked with Mother Teresa and was a radio talk-show host—all before diving into the unforgiving cauldron of Oakland politics a decade ago. He is at an age when overachievers in nearly every other profession would start to pack it in. But no man who wakes up at 5 a.m. to read and has been known to keep an eye on Fox News after midnight should be considered a candidate for retirement anytime soon.

Brown is in an aide's car, talking nonstop, jabbing and gesturing, impervious to interruption, pointing out potholes and telling the aide where to stop and when to turn. Brown is fun to watch. He is trim, constantly in motion, his brown eyes still piercing and just a touch sad. Compared with almost any other politician, he's a riot to talk to, a one-man romp through everyone from St. Paul to Albert Camus. Jane Brunner, a city councilwoman who didn't vote for the mayor but thinks he has done a good job, says that when she goes into his office, she is never certain whether she is going to be in there for two minutes or two hours.

It's an old joke that Oakland has been a city of the future since forever, but that is finally coming true in ways that are good and bad. The city of 412,000 is roughly 35 percent black, 31 percent white, 21 percent Hispanic and 15 percent

Asian. Refugees from more expensive ZIP codes across the bay have fled to Oakland in the past decade, seeking cheaper housing. But the city has long been slow to seize its opportunities, and Brown's time as mayor has been a test of whether even that can be changed. When he was elected in 1998, he successfully led an effort to restructure Oakland's government and give the mayor new powers to break through a stolid municipal bureaucracy. Since then, he fired his city manager and two city planners, replacing them with people who worked harder to lure private investment. As he tours through a booming residential area south of downtown, he sounds a little dismayed by how resistant some Oakland residents remain to change.

The neighborhood known as Jack London Square, a district of noodle factories and produce warehouses on Oakland Inner Harbor, is giving way to dozens of new loft-apartment and condo buildings. That explosion in private investment—although limited to only a few pockets of the city—is the centerpiece of Brown's tenure as mayor, the fulfillment of a promise he made eight years ago to bring 10,000 residents to downtown Oakland. Brown points to building after building, each financed with private capital, opening their doors to tenants or just completing construction. "That is new. That is new. That one is finished. This one will be finished soon," he says as we drive around. "For 40 years, there was nothing here. Now there are going to be 10,000 people living in downtown Oakland." All that concrete and mortar may be a special source of pride for a man who picked up the nickname Moonbeam in the 1970s for being a little too theoretical. "This is the most visible achievement that I've ever done," Brown says. "This is a tangible. It wasn't there before."

This being the Bay Area, not everyone is thrilled. Longtime residents say Brown is driving up rents and tax assessments. Hard-boiled leftists say Brown has sold off the city's commercial heritage to profiteers. And affordable-housing advocates want builders to provide various givebacks and mitigations before putting up high-end condos—a demand Brown, sounding more like an Orange County conservative, can't fathom. "The problem with that is that this is just one of 100 possible markets where private developers can put their money. If we make it even a little harder to come here, they won't come. We need to be more attractive than those places, which is why some progressives don't like me."

But the main reason many liberals don't love him has to do with his battle to contain the city's crime rate. The number of murders this year has nearly doubled last year's count for the same period. There are problems with street robberies and what the cops call rat packers, gangs of kids who beat up people on buses and then head back to school to brag about it. The local jails are sometimes too full to permit arrests for certain crimes. A local television report recently quoted an Oakland police estimate that one-fourth of the city's prostitutes were underage. Crime has dropped since Brown became mayor, but it's rising again, fast.

All that is one reason Brown is spending part of the afternoon with 40-odd police supervisors, talking about crime trends. Another is that his main opponent in the race for the Democratic nomination in the state's attorney-general race, Los Angeles city attorney Rocky Delgadillo, aired an ad in mid-May accusing Brown of proposing to slash funding for Oakland cops. Although Brown did propose cuts in 2003, the police budget has grown more than 50 percent since 1999. Brown has pushed the force to transfer officers from desk jobs to street patrols, and he backed a 10 p.m. curfew on some parolees and probationers. The city is trying to raise bails to keep suspects in jail, and cameras have been installed in high-crime areas. Recently the city tested "shot spotter" technology to isolate gunshots using acoustic technology.

Brown has come under withering criticism from African Americans and civil libertarians who say he has turned Oakland into a police state, and the cops are under a court order to mend their more abusive habits. Some Brown critics have said he has adopted a tough-on-crime stance to help him elsewhere in the state in his race for attorney general. But as Brown questions the cops at headquarters, he doesn't sound like their friend. How many cops are on the street right now? How many of them are on patrol, and how many are responding to calls? Why don't we know that? Are they all paid the same? Is there special pay for the more effective officers? What time does crime pick up in the day? When does it slack off? It goes on like that for nearly 90 minutes, until it becomes clear that everyone needs a break. Walking out, Brown says his job is to keep the pressure on police. "I was trying to get them to think differently. We have a lot of dedicated criminals here."

Brown sits down the next morning to talk over a cappuccino at a downtown coffee shop. You don't really interview Jerry Brown. He does that for you. You just try to keep up. He talks about California and whether it is becoming more conservative. (He's not sure.) He is worried about the growing number of workers who can find jobs only in the underground economy. (It's not the taxes employers are avoiding, he says. It's the health benefits and safety regulations.) He complains that to reach undecided voters, candidates have to buy ads on *American Idol* and *Desperate Housewives*—an absurd context for messages about governing. (But he adds, "You gotta take 'em where they are.") He insists that journalists are clueless captives of the narrow-minded worlds they come from—a number he has been running on reporters for more than 30 years, but it's still pretty effective. "You are a prisoner of the Time-Life world that sent you," he says. When I'm not immediately sure how to respond to that, he goes in for the kill: "Well, is it true, or is it not?"

Even when he is rolling, Brown will engage only briefly about national politics. Brown describes Hillary Clinton as "iconic" and disagrees with those who say she can't win. "Sure, she can win," he says. "Anything is possible." Al Gore "would be powerful" as an antiwar candidate if, Brown says, "he loses some weight." The mayor has no patience for George W. Bush. Brown calls him a "cowboy." Republicans are under fire for so many things, Brown observes, that even "Fox News is exhibiting signs of anxiety."

He can't run for mayor again. He made sure the job was term limited when he took it in 1998, he says, "in case I got tempted to stay." How come? "You lose your edge. You need new challenges. You start thinking you own the place." Why does he want to be attorney general when he has already been governor? Brown says the jobs are completely different. A governor plays defense across a broad front, he says, whereas an attorney general can play offense in a more targeted way—on workers' rights, the environment and consumer protection, all at a time when the "rule of law has been undermined" by the Bush administration. "The balance between change and continuity has always been a part of my life. Continuity looms a lot right now." He thinks about that for a moment and then adds, "In a society of rootlessness and rapid change, I'm running as the traditionalist."

Brown did the most traditional thing of all last year. He married Anne Gust, a former Gap executive he had been seeing steadily for 15 years. Friends say she has calmed down the frenetic Brown and given his sense of humor a beta boost. Brown, a Catholic, organized the ceremony, chose the medieval chants, cleared the whole thing with Rome and held the private service in the same San Francisco parish in which his parents were married. When I ask the obvious question—"So, how's married life?"—his reply is pure, distilled, 100-proof Brown: "It's a good thing. There is a certainty, a finality about it. I was very conscious that it was a vow, and I liked that. It's part of a higher order. In a frivolous age, it has a depth that is very welcome."

And, he might have added, so does Jerry Brown himself.

Jeff Gerth was an investigative reporter at the *New York Times* for thirty years, during which he won one Pulitzer Prize, shared another, and won a George Polk Award. After retiring from the newspaper in 2006, he co-wrote, with Don Van Natta, Jr., a biography of Hillary Clinton and joined ProPublica, a nonprofit news organization, as a senior reporter. This text is drawn from *Her Way: The Hopes and Ambitions of Hillary Rodham Clinton* (Little, Brown, 2007).

"I Don't Feel No Ways Tired"

In the autumn of 2003, Greg Craig, a classmate of Hillary and Bill Clinton at Yale Law School, received a phone call from Vernon Jordan. During Bill Clinton's presidency, Jordan was regarded as the ultimate Washington insider; later he opened an office in New York to facilitate his corporate networking. This time, Jordan was rounding up "the regular establishment types" for a fund-raising event at his home in Washington, D.C., for a then little-known state senator from Illinois named Barack Obama. Obama, then forty-two years old, was pursuing the Democratic nomination in the race for a United States Senate seat from Illinois.

"I didn't know who he was," Craig said, though he accepted the invitation and wrote a $500 check to Obama's campaign.

Several dozen people gathered at Jordan's house, about a block away from the Clintons' Washington home, on a late October evening to meet the young candidate. It was the first Washington fund-raiser for Obama. After hearing Obama speak that night from the staircase in Jordan's spacious home, Craig came away "very, very impressed with him."

As Hillary was privately considering embarking on a historic bid for the presidency, she probably never imagined that her law school classmate would not only leave her side but also end up helping to persuade her most formidable adversary to run against her.

What Hillary and her top advisers did not know at the time was that one of Hillary's old friends was urging Obama to run. "I'm brand new here in Washington," Obama told Craig, "and it would be presumptuous of me to arrive so soon and run for president."

"Yes, it would be presumptuous," Craig replied, telling Obama his newness in Washington was an asset, not a liability, and that he should reconsider his reluctance. Craig felt the longer Obama stayed in Washington, the more he would be afflicted by Senatitis," where he would have to face difficult votes "every other day and where individual senators have to distinguish themselves from each other."

Obama spent the Christmas break in Hawaii, talking over his future with his wife and two daughters. When he returned to Washington after the New Year, he decided to run.

Obama began his quest to become the nation's first black president on February 10, 2007 in Springfield, Illinois, at the Old State House, where, in 1858, Abraham Lincoln had delivered his famous condemnation of slavery in which he declared, "A house divided against itself cannot stand." Wearing an overcoat but no gloves on an unseasonably frigid morning, Obama portrayed his quixotic candidacy less as a campaign and more as a generational movement, just as Bill Clinton and Al Gore had done in 1992. Craig, watching the speech back in Washington on television, was gratified to hear Obama had also adapted his argument that his lack of experience should be considered a potent political asset.

"I recognize there is a certain presumptuousness—a certain audacity—to this announcement," Obama said. "I know I haven't spent a lot of time learning the ways of Washington. But I've been there long enough to know that the ways of Washington must change." Obama's comments about Washington elicited some of the loudest and most sustained applause of his two-minute speech.

A few weeks earlier, Greg Craig had written a short note to Hillary, explaining his decision to support Obama for president. She did not reply.

Every seat in every pew of the New Birth Missionary Baptist Church was filled on a chilly Tuesday in February 2006. The crowd had come to the big church outside Atlanta to pay their last respects to Coretta Scott King. In the church's center well, a flower-draped mahogany casket contained the body of the first lady of America's civil rights movement. It was surrounded by her three grown children, four American presidents, and more than 10,000 other loved ones, friends, and admirers.

Bishop Eddie L. Long raised the microphone to his lips and said, "I now present, the honorable William J. Clinton and . . ." A roaring ovation thundered down from the congregation, drowning out the rest of the bishop's introduction. Long went on to say "and the honorable Hillary R. Clinton, Senator," but by then no one could hear him. As Bill and Hillary walked toward the pulpit with their hands clasped, everyone in the predominantly black congregation stood up, cheering and waving; men whistled and hollered and women of all ages screamed and called Bill's name. Mrs. King's memorial service had suddenly become a pep rally.

As the waves of cheers kept rolling, Bill stood behind the podium and raised his hands, once, then twice, signaling the crowd for quiet. Hillary stood to her husband's left, beaming at him and nodding and mouthing "thank you's" to the crowd, though there was no mistaking that the giant gush of love and affection was not for her but her husband.

Finally, the applause waned and the mourners retook their seats. "I thank you for that wonderful reception," Bill said, adding with a sly grin, "You may not feel like repeatin' it after you hear what I've got to say." Everyone laughed. Turning over his right shoulder and leaning into the podium, the former president then nodded his head at the church's pastor and drawled, "Rev." Again, everyone laughed.

"We are honored to be here," Bill said. "I'm honored to be here with my president . . . and my former presidents . . . and . . . and, uh . . ." It was quiet only a moment until Bill moved his left hand slightly toward Hillary, as if his next few words might just be "and my next president." The crowd certainly interpreted the gesture that way, responding with another ovation. Bill quickly said, "Nooooooo, nooooooo," and then Hillary shook her head no, no, no. But the cheering did not stop until Hillary put up both her hands and then moved them down repeatedly in front of her. The motion seemed to say: no, this is neither the time nor the place for any talk of that, but her husband's perfect set up had served its purpose of talking without saying, right here and right now.

Bill paused a moment and, gesturing toward the casket, said, "This is a woman, as well as a symbol, as well as an embodiment of her husband's legacy, as well as the developer of her own."

Of course, the former president was speaking about Coretta Scott King. But Bill Clinton could have easily been referring to the woman standing by his side.

He had promised to keep his remarks brief, but Bill Clinton is incapable of keeping that kind of pledge. As his speech stretched on, Hillary began sighing; at first, her exhales were barely noticeable. But as she sighed again and again, her deep breaths were impossible to miss.

At last, after ten minutes, it was her turn. Her hand found her husband's, and she held it atop the podium. Whether that handclasp was about affection or need, it was indisputable that Hillary, in front of a throng of people and a national television audience, was about to follow the toughest act in American politics.

"As we are called," she began, reading from her prepared text, "each of us must decide whether to answer that call by saying, 'Send me.' And when I think of Coretta Scott King, I think of a woman who lived out her calling."

Hillary's flat delivery sounded even more monotone after the folksy lullaby of Bill Clinton's southern purr. If his eulogy was a casual hymn to Mrs. King, Hillary's was a scripted monologue she delivered with her eyes cast mostly downward.

This was not her crowd. The fact that Hillary had a speaking role in the memorial service in the first place was as conspicuous as it was surprising. No other presidential spouse joined her husband at the podium. The only other senator to speak that day was Edward M. Kennedy of Massachusetts, who had a decades-long friendship with Mrs. King. A person close to the King family said that Hillary was included in the program only at the insistence of Bill Clinton's representatives. "She was not even on the family's radar screen—they wanted Bill Clinton," the King family confidant said. "They love him, but when they heard that he wanted her to speak, too, they said, 'OK, that's fine.'"

At the memorial service, Hillary told the congregation that Mrs. King "had lived her life as an extension of her faith and conviction." The senator paused, and her tone took on a folksy lilt: "Now, when she met this young divinity student, and he told her what Bill has just reminded us, and proclaimed that he was looking for a woman like her to be his wife, I can imagine that she thought for a minute, What am I getting myself into? And, in fact, she waited six months to give him an answer. Because she had to have known in her heart that she wasn't just marrying a young man, but she was bringing her calling to be joined with his. As they began their marriage, and their partnership, it could not have been easy." Like her husband's words before her, Hillary's speech could have applied to the Clintons themselves.

Even after Obama's announcement, several members of Hillaryland continued to view his candidacy as a non-threat. There was one notable exception among these enthusiastic Hillary supporters: Bill Clinton, who had recognized early on that Obama was the candidate among the current crop with the best chance of derailing his wife's chances of cruising to the nomination.

Obama's early momentum was only one reason why the money race was even more important. The other was the front-loaded primary schedule. Because, for the first time in history, as many as twenty states were slated to hold primaries by February 5, 2008, locking up fund-raisers, money, and momentum became more critical in this presidential campaign than in any previous one.

Obama had shown sudden adeptness at recruiting some of Bill and Hillary's old moneyed friends from Hollywood—something that deeply worried several of Hillary's finance people. The scrum made national headlines after the billionaire David Geffen signed on with Obama. Geffen, a cofounder and partner in the film studio Dreamworks, had been one of Bill's most unabashed financial supporters, raising a total of $18 million for the Clintons and the Democrats across the 1990s.

In mid-February, a week prior to the Academy Awards, Geffen held a fund-raising dinner for forty of his friends to honor Obama at his sumptuous mansion in Beverly Hills, built by studio magnate Jack Warner. The take: $1.3 million. One fund-raiser pronounced Hillary "flipping out" about the unabashed enthusiasm for Obama in Hollywood—territory that had been nearly unanimously devoted to the Clintons since 1992.

"Whoever is the [Democratic] nominee is going to win," Geffen told the New York Times' Maureen Dowd, "and I don't think that another incredibly polarizing figure, no matter how smart she is and no matter how ambitious she is—and God knows, is there anybody more ambitious than Hillary Clinton?—can bring the country together." Geffen added that Obama was "inspirational, and he's not from the Bush royal family or the Clinton royal family."

When Howard Wolfson, Hillary's communications director, read Dowd's column early in the morning of February 21, 2007, he was furious. Wolfson was especially angry about this remark by Geffen: "Everybody in politics lies but [the Clintons] do it with such ease, it's troubling."

After consulting Hillary, Wolfson quickly put out a statement that criticized Geffen for "viciously and personally attacking Senator Clinton and her husband."

He added that there was no place in the campaign for "the politics of personal destruction," pinned the blame for Geffen's outspokenness on Obama and somewhat preposterously called on the senator to return Geffen's money. Obama decided to take the high road, insisting that he did not want to "get in the middle of a disagreement between the Clintons and someone who was once one of their biggest supporters."

"They infuriated the African Americans," said a Democratic strategist who is a close friend of Hillary's. "They mishandled it . . . They gave [Obama] standing, and they made him an African American martyr. It looked like an attack. This is right out of Southern Politics 101—you don't give blacks the opportunity to be martyred, which is what they did."

One person close to both Clintons said Bill thought the contretemps over the Geffen fund-raiser was a serious misstep on the part of Hillary's campaign: "Bill was livid about it. He was very upset at the attack. He thought it was dumb." The former president had "to be more involved" in Hillary's campaign, concluded one longtime strategist, complaining that the attack on Obama "would never have happened" if Bill had been consulted. But there was only so much Bill could do. In the end, it was Hillary's race, and she'd run it her way.

Within days of Hillary's clash with Obama, the two found themselves, for the first time, on the same patch of the campaign trail, in Selma, Alabama, to commemorate the forty-second anniversary of the famous "Bloody Sunday" march against racial segregation on March 7, 1965.

Obama had been invited to commemorate the "Bloody Sunday" anniversary weeks earlier, and Hillary was invited a week or so before the event. Her presence was perhaps the most dramatic evidence that she was no longer taking Obama lightly. As one longtime Hillary friend noted about her campaign, "They were not taking him that seriously and now they are. They are concerned about him. He's a legitimate threat."

From the pulpit during Sunday services, Hillary and Obama spoke at churches on the same street separated by three short blocks. Both credited the march in Selma with paving the way for their own historic bids for the presidency.

Obama spoke first that Sunday, from the pulpit of the Brown Chapel AME Church, the launching pad for the historic demonstration. He was joined in the church by John Lewis. Obama saluted the brave men and women who had marched, including Lewis. Obama compared himself, and others who were small children or not yet born in 1965, to Joshua, who, the Bible says, followed Moses and completed the job of leading his people to the Promised Land. "The question, I guess, that I have today is, what's called of us in this Joshua generation?" Obama asked. "What do we do in order to fulfill that legacy?" His speech was interrupted often by ecstatic shouts from worshippers and long gusts of applause.

Four minutes after Obama completed his speech, Hillary took the pulpit at the First Baptist Church of Selma. To the audience watching live at home on cable news channels and C-SPAN, the difference in the two candidates' oratorical style was evident. Obama had an easy, conversational manner, while Hillary sounded more scripted.

Hillary said the march made it possible for her to run for president, and she also gave credit to the march for making Obama's bid possible. But the civil rights struggle in America, Hillary declared, was far from over. She told the congregation, "We've got to stay awake. We've got to stay awake because we have a march to finish, a march toward one America." With her voice rising, as the congregation roared, she said, "Poverty and growing inequality matter. Health care matters. The people of the Gulf Coast matter. Our soldiers matter. Our future matters."

Both Hillary and Obama used their personal histories to build a bridge to the civil rights movement. This was an easier task for the Illinois senator, who had talked passionately about the struggle of his father, a Kenyan man, who worked as a "house boy" to wealthy British families. For her part, Hillary spoke about going to hear the Reverend Martin Luther King Jr. speak in Chicago in 1963, but compared to Obama's story, her link with the civil rights movement seemed more remote.

Hillary was further hampered by a perception that she had pandered when, at one point, she shifted suddenly to a thick southern drawl as she recited a popular hymn by black clergyman James Cleveland: "I don't feel no ways tired, / I've come too far from where I started from. / Nobody told me that the road would be easy, / I don't believe He brought me this far to leave me." Members of the congregation whooped and cheered, but Hillary's recitation of the lyrics was almost instantly mocked on the Internet and, later, predictably, on Fox News. Her supporters pointed out she lived nearly two decades in Arkansas, but a strategist for Hillary later acknowledged that "in a panic about Obama," she had turned to the southern drawl, only to find herself, in the end, in "trouble."

After the pulpit speeches, Obama and Hillary prepared to re-enact the march. While they were waiting, they were joined by Bill, who joked, "All the good speaking has been done by Hillary and Senator Obama already. I'm just sort of bringing up the rear."

Bill and Hillary shook hands with Obama, and they chatted briefly. As the cameras clicked, the former president smiled at his wife's challenger. Then the candidates joined arms with John Lewis and other local congressmen and officials for the walk across the bridge. As the long, straight line of people marched, their arms joined and their hands clasped, Hillary and Obama were separated by just two people. Everyone sang "We Shall Overcome."

When Bill returned later that week to New York, he spoke admiringly with a friend about Obama's political and oratorical skills. "He's the real thing," Bill said.

Kay Mills, the author of five nonfiction books, worked for the *Los Angeles Times* from 1978 to 1991 as an editorial writer and an assistant Opinion section editor. The following profile is drawn from *This Little Light of Mine: The Life of Fannie Lou Hamer* (University Press of Kentucky, 2007).

Fannie Lou Hamer

Time was when the flat and endless horizon of the Mississippi Delta was broken only by rows of slow-moving people turning the earth with mules in the early spring, chopping cotton through the staggering summer heat, and stooping to pick that cotton from September through November. It was weary work that bent the back, calloused the hands, cut the fingers, and numbed the soul. It also had no reward in this world because the white landowner got what profit there was. The black people trudging through the fields could only sing out to God to carry them along until they could rest on some distant shore.

It was a world of harsh contradictions: there was absolutely nothing romantic about the life, but at the same time there were moments of sublime beauty as a flock of birds flew over a field in a perfect V formation at sunset or a child smiled as a fish caught the hook in the quiet down by the river. It was, at least, a life out of doors, not confined to concrete and crowds. It was a world many black people refused to leave even as their brothers and sisters filled the trains north.

Today cultivators and giant mechanical pickers cross the fields. They have driven the black workers off the land, into small, fading towns or out of the state entirely. Tufts of cotton that float wispily off trucks headed for the gins still cling to the shoulder of the road, and the landscape looks much the same. But now the people are gone.

Fannie Lou Hamer was born into that old Mississippi but died in the new. She began life humbly and ended it the same, like countless other poor Mississippians. But some alchemy of inborn intelligence, strong parents, love of country, and a sharecropper's gutty instincts for survival made her different. Make no mistake about it: "There were many strong leaders in Mississippi," says Rims Barber, who worked with them all in the Mississippi movement, "but she was a cut above."

Over the years since her death, the issues that Fannie Lou Hamer addressed throughout her life—racism, poverty, war, and political powerlessness—have remained the issues at the core of American political debate. Was Fannie Lou Hamer's history, was her struggle, in vain? Given the disparity in the lives of black and white that one can still see in Ruleville and in Mississippi, had it mattered that she lived there and worked there? Yes, of course.

On the practical level, Mrs. Hamer led the way for hundreds of thousands of black Mississippians to register to vote, to participate in the political life of their communities. "Her greatest victory," Ed Brown of the Voter Education Project told me, "was that ultimately she did in [Senator James] Eastland. He decided not to run again because he would not win again. . . . He was the arch symbol of what we were against. And she had registered people and gotten things to the point that he could not win again."

Nine years after the Hamer funeral services at Williams Chapel Church in Ruleville, there was a second funeral—at the Ruleville Methodist Church one mile away—that drew dignitaries from around the nation. James O. Eastland died February 19, 1986. Who will be better remembered?

There are those who will tell you that Jim Eastland was the most consummate politician Mississippi ever had. That may be. In the end, though, Fannie Lou Hamer did overcome James O. Eastland. She and Victoria Gray and Annie Devine and Unita Blackwell and the other civil rights workers campaigned for the vote and for jobs and food and housing for people who had had little before they began their efforts. Many still have little. But "people became aware, most for the first time, that they had a right to enjoy whatever the society, the country, has to offer," said Victoria Gray Adams years later in looking back on their work. Mississippi had truly been a closed society, for white as well as black, a society that killed the possibilities for everyone. To have altered that situation— and the movement did alter that situation—was a lasting accomplishment.

Smaller-scale accomplishments occurred as well, things the ear could hear, the heart could sense. These were "the little intangibles—the races regarding each other as people, whites learning that blacks loved their families, wanted to work, wanted to educate their kids, cry when a baby dies," said Mrs. Hamer's Indianola ally, Carver Randle. Mrs. Hamer helped win daily courtesies, like being called Mrs. Hamer or Mr. Randle. "White people had a tendency to think of blacks as less than human. She did a lot to improve that."

Sunflower County produced two giants of twentieth-century Mississippi history. Both Fannie Lou Hamer and James O. Eastland showed that one person can make a difference. Mrs. Hamer resisted being beaten down, literally and figuratively, by a political system that refused to give poor people like her, white or black, a voice in running their lives. Eastland simply resisted.

Through time, there has been a touch of organizational claim jumping over who "found" Fannie Lou Hamer. She had worked with all the groups that shared her aims—signing up people for the NAACP, working for SCLC [the Southern Christian Leadership Conference] and attending some of its citizenship education sessions, and working for SNCC [the Student Nonviolent Coordinating Committee], to which she gave the most credit for turning Mississippi around. After her death, Julian Bond addressed the question: "Some people thought they'd 'discovered' Fannie Lou Hamer, the way entertainers are discovered by talent scouts looking for something new. But she discovered herself, celebrated herself, lived for herself and her people, and died because she could not stop trying."

Fannie Lou Hamer also inspired younger women like Dorie Ladner, who had gone with her the day she first tried to register to vote; Euvester Simpson Morris and June Johnson, jailed with her in Winona; Marian Wright Edelman, a civil rights attorney who handled many cases in Mississippi and is now president of the Children's Defense Fund; and Mary Hightower, who still works as an organizer for the Freedom Democratic Party in its remaining outpost in Holmes County, a rural area near the center of the state. Whenever she would call on Mrs. Hamer in the troubled days of the 1960s, "she would always be there. She would always speak out; she wasn't afraid," Hightower told me. "Having people like Mrs. Hamer and Mrs. Devine and Mrs. Gray encouraged us and gave us more confidence. Knowing that they were doing it and sacrificing made us think it's all right, we can join in. The commitment overrode the fear."

Hollis Watkins also worked closely with Mrs. Hamer as a young man. Graying now, he recalled that she challenged those around her to give their talents. She defined those talents as a light, he said, and "she challenged all of us to use those talents against injustice and evil wherever we were."

Fannie Lou Hamer held her light over some of the dark places in the American soul. She recognized that a web of power had been woven to keep some people up and some people down. She worked to make people recognize that web, and she tried to sweep it away, to create a fairer balance in society so that people for whom and among whom she worked might be able to say that they were no longer "sick and tired of being sick and tired." That was her lament in life, and those are the words on her tombstone in a dusty, weedy field in Ruleville. They remind us of her history and her mission, the latter as yet unfulfilled. Someday, we must believe, commitment will again override fear.

Greil Marcus, a music writer and cultural critic, is coeditor of *A New Literary History of America* (Harvard, 2009). The author of many books, he has been a columnist for the *New York Times, The Believer*, and other publications. He delivered this commencement address at the University of California at Berkeley on May 19, 2006. It was published in *Salon* on July 4, 2006.

The Fourth of July

It's Sunday night, April 16—the sixth episode of the sixth season of *The Sopranos* is on. Vito Spatafore—the most reliable and loyal captain in the New Jersey crime family run by Tony Soprano—is on the run. The story is out—Vito has a wife, two kids, the requisite mistress, but he's been seen in a gay bar, dressed like the biker in the Village People. The other mobsters want him dead; he's dishonored them all.

Heading north, Vito's been on the road for hours. His cell phone rings; he throws it out the window. He has no idea where he is. His car breaks down. He makes it into the next town, finds an inn, puts his gun under his pillow.

The next day he wakes up in a little New Hampshire village where gay people walk the streets without fear. In a diner, looks pass between Vito and the counterman. A male couple comes in, sits down, and begins speaking a language Vito has never before heard in the light of day, only in the dark. He's confused: what does it mean to be in a place where, for the first time in your life, you might feel at home in your own skin? Could that even be right?

He goes into an antique shop. He picks up a vase, and the gay owner compliments him on his taste: "That's the most expensive item in the store." But then Vito sees something else, probably the cheapest thing in the store: an old New Hampshire license plate. "LIVE FREE OR DIE" reads the slogan across the top.

The phrase burns into Vito's mind. You can see his face change. The words were written in 1809 by General John Stark, a New Hampshire hero of the Revolutionary War, on the occasion of the thirty-second reunion of veterans of the 1777 Battle of Bennington, Vermont; too ill to attend, General Stark sent a toast. "Live free or die," another man read for him: "Death is not the worst of evils." The words echoed across the nation, down through the decades; in 1945, with the end of the Second World War, New Hampshire took the first four words and put them all over the state.

Vito stares. "LIVE FREE OR DIE"—it's as if the metal can talk. It's just a license plate; for him it might as well be the Declaration of Independence, ringing its bell. "We hold these truths to be self-evident, that all men are created equal, that they are endowed by their Creator with certain inalienable Rights, that among these are Life, Liberty, and the pursuit of Happiness," Jefferson wrote—and suddenly, as it has for so many for so long, through that license plate the Declaration is speaking to Vito as if it were addressed to him. "Live free or die"—what if all this, the shock in his face says, was meant for him as much as anyone?

It's one of those signal moments when the whole weight of the national story, its promises and its betrayals, hits home, leaving the citizen at once part of a community and completely alone. It doesn't matter that, well, yes, of course, on the fourth of July 1776, when the Declaration of Independence was presented, everyone understood that "all men" meant men, not women; whites, not blacks; Christians, not Jews or Hindus or heathen; decent people, not Sodomites. The idea that "all men are created equal" was not a "self-evident truth," Senator John Pettit said on the floor of the Senate in 1853: it was "a self-evident lie." It was in the midst of the debates over the Kansas-Nebraska Act; Pettit was arguing for the voiding the Missouri Compromise of 1820 and opening the territories to slavery. It *was* a debate: "The great declaration cost our forefathers too dear," Senator Benjamin Franklin Wade of Ohio replied to Pettit, "to be so lightly thrown away by their children."

Abraham Lincoln read these debates from his oblivion in Springfield, Illinois; he was a forty-four-year-old lawyer who had served one term in Congress before being turned out of office. Pettit's words and the words against him brought Lincoln back to the world. Soon he was speaking as if the Declaration of Independence contained all the words the nation ever needed to hear—and in a certain sense, it didn't matter that Lincoln did not believe that once men and women left the hand of their creator, they were equal on earth. "Pettit called the Declaration of Independence a lie," Lincoln said in Peoria in 1854, answering a speech by Stephen Douglas. "If it had been said in old Independence Hall seventy-eight years ago, the doorkeeper would have thrown him into the street." That might have been a fairy tale; the Declaration of Independence itself might be a fairy tale, but not one that can be given an ending, happy or not. The charge in the Declaration was boundless; no limits placed upon it hold.

"Life, liberty, and the pursuit of happiness"—it's what the rest of the world understands by America when America isn't forcing the rest of the world to understand America as something else. "We are caught in a world of limits where there's no such thing as the self-made man," said a graduate student in France last week; Claire de la Vigne was speaking to a *New York Times* reporter about the French university system, where doors are made to be closed, not opened. "We are never taught the idea of the American dream, where everything is possible," she said. It's what Americans understand by America, when the facts of everyday American life somehow recede and an idea of America takes their place.

Here's a passage from *The Enthusiast*, a novel written by a friend of mine, Charlie Haas. A man—a scientist, a businessman—is trying to recover from brain damage. His father is trying to reintroduce him to time, place, names, faces.

Dad and Barney sat at the desk with the datebook open in front of them. "Okay," Dad said, "what's something you might have to do this afternoon?"

"Go to a meeting," Barney said.

"Okay. So you write that in there."

Barney scrawled MEETING over half the afternoon grid. "We're going to have a country," he said. "We have some farmers coming, and some horse-shoe guys."

"Like blacksmiths?" Dad said.

"Yes," Barney said. "So we get liberty. And we wear wigs in the room."

This doesn't even have the weight of a fairy tale, or of a dream you can just barely remember, and yet it's inescapable, and unbreakable.

There's a way in which you can see every American story as a version of the Declaration of Independence: every story an attempt to make it true or prove it a lie. In 1941, Henry Luce called the twentieth century "the American century"; he meant this was the century when America became a colossus from which the rest of the world would have to step back, trembling with awe. But if that American century was truly American, you can almost see Lincoln reminding us—or, if not Lincoln, the doorkeeper at Independence Hall—then the story of the American century is the story of all sorts of previously excluded, marginalized, scorned, despised, ignored, or enslaved people—laborers, women, African Americans, Asian Americans, Jews, Latinos, gay men and women—entering into full citizenship and full participation in national life. If not full citizenship, a more complete citizenship than even Lincoln or the doorkeeper could in fact have imagined, as, again and again, decade after decade, those echoing words of the Declaration of Independence sounded as if for the first time.

It can be easy to forget this, when people on both the left and the right tell the story of the country as if it were a story of power, not speech, a story of the movements of money and armies, not the acts of men and women, acting alone or together.

This came home to me last week at a meeting in Cambridge, Massachusetts. A group of sixteen people—distinguished historians, critics, poets, novelists, professors—sat around a table determining what would and what would not be included in an ambitious new book: a thousand-page, two-hundred-chapter *New Literary History of America. All God's Dangers: The Life of Nate Shaw*, one person said—and there was silence. Few people there had heard of the book; only two had read it.

The book appeared in 1975, and then it disappeared. Why? It won a National Book Award; it received reviews that were like trumpets. But somehow the tale told by Nate Shaw—the name the historian Theodore Rosengarten gave to one Ned Cobb, born in Alabama in 1885, dead there in 1973, who, over hundreds of hours, spun Rosengarten the story of his life—did not fit the American story as it was being reconstructed once again. This was a man whose parents were slaves, and who reveled in his superiority—in mind, body, will, desire, courage, and wit—over other men, be they black or white. "All men are created equal," but what men and women become is not equal, and proving himself in that arena was America to Nate Shaw.

"I was climbin up in the world just like a boy climbin a tree. And I fell just as easy, too." It's 1931, in the heart of the Depression, and a banker is squeezing him:

> "Bring me the cotton this fall, bring me the cotton." When he told me that I got disheartened. I didn't want him messin with me—still, I didn't let him take a mortgage on anything I owned. I was my own man, had been for many years, and God knows I weren't goin to turn the calendar back on myself.

You can hear it in the cadence, in the uniqueness of the speech: "I weren't goin to turn the calendar back on myself." This is someone for whom liberty is real—as real in its absence as when he can all but hold it in his hands. At twenty-one, in 1906, Nate Shaw set out to raise his first cotton crop; in 1932 he stood for the Alabama Sharecroppers Union against a gang of sheriffs sent to take over a friend's property, and paid for his stand with twelve years in prison; he found God. He walked out of prison. He lived a new life.

From his first day on his own, he was not someone who could be reduced to a type, a symbol, or made to stand for a cause. Against all odds he had in fact achieved what the country promised him: "life," on his own terms; "liberty," seized, acted out, taken from him; "the pursuit of happiness"—which, at the end of his life, meant firing a revolver in the air. "I shoots it some times just to see if it will yet answer me," he said. "I throw it to the air and ask for all six shots: YAW YAW YAW YAW YAW YAW." The story came off the pages with suspense, order, clarity, and drama, as if Shaw had long before determined not to quit this life without leaving a piece of his own behind.

His own—all he had, to pass on to whoever might stumble upon the now-forgotten book made of his particular pursuit of happiness. But if the historians gathered to choose the books of our history had not heard of Nate Shaw—and, hearing his story, they finally chose to fold it into the story they themselves were trying to tell—if they hadn't heard of Nate Shaw, in a certain way, Vito, standing in that New Hampshire antique story, was hearing Nate Shaw speak as he read the words on the license plate.

As Vito read "LIVE FREE OR DIE," a song began to come up on the soundtrack: a song called "4th of July," recorded in 1987 by the Los Angeles punk band X. It's thrilling, and it's heartbreaking; a couple's marriage is falling apart, but it's the Fourth of July. The feeling is that by failing their marriage they are betraying the country: "We gave up trying so long ago."

Can Jefferson save their marriage? Can they save the country? Like *The Sopranos*, the song doesn't say yes or no—it makes the question real, makes it yours.

ACKNOWLEDGMENTS _____

The editors and the publisher would like to thank the following copyright holders for permission to reprint the pieces in this book.

Jill Abramson. "Finding Respite from Worries," from *The New York Times* 9/21/2008. © 2008 *The New York Times*. Reprinted by permission.

Joel Achenbach. Excerpt from *Captured by Aliens: The Search for Life and Truth in a Very Large Universe*, published by Simon and Schuster, 1999. © 1999 Joel Achenbach. Reprinted by permission.

Peter Applebome. "Atlanta Journal; A Sign: It's Jesus, or a Lunch Bargain," from *The New York Times* 5/25/1991; "A Pit Bull Who Provided Lessons in Loyalty and Unfailing Love," from *The New York Times* 3/28/2007. © 1991, 2007 *The New York Times*. Reprinted by permission.

Ken Armstrong and Nick Perry. "Curtis Williams—Victory and Ruins," from *The Seattle Times* 1/29/2008. © 2008 *The Seattle Times*. Reprinted by permission.

Felicity Barringer. "Chernobyl: Five Years Later the Danger Persists," from *The New York Times* 4/14/1991. © 1991 *The New York Times*. Reprinted by permission.

Jeff Bartholet. "Alaska: Oil's Ground Zero," from *Newsweek* 8/13/2001. © 2001 Jeff Bartholet. Reprinted by permission.

Ralph J. Begleiter. "Whose Media Are We?" from the *Brown Journal of World Affairs*, Winter 2002. © BJWA 2002. Reprinted by permission.

A. Scott Berg. Excerpt from *Max Perkins: Editor of Genius*, published by Berkley Books, 2008. © 1978 A. Scott Berg. Used by permission of Dutton, a division of Penguin Group (USA), Inc. and by permission of Russell & Volkening as agents for the author.

Walt Bogdanich. "The Everyman Who Exposed Tainted Toothpaste," from *The New York Times* 10/1/2007. © 2007 *The New York Times*. Reprinted by permission.

Filip Bondy. "Sports: The Glue For Lost Kids," from the *New York Daily News* 8/24/2008. © 2008 New York Daily News, L.P. Used with permission.

Ethan Bronner. "The Promise," from *The New York Times* 11/5/2008; "Gaza Notebook: The Bullets in My In-Box," from *The New York Times* 1/25/2009 © 2008, 2009 *The New York Times*. Reprinted by permission.

Thanassis Cambanis. "Transformation Bypasses the Heartland," from *The Boston Globe* 3/21/2005; "Hezbollah Fighter Strove to Be a Martyr," from *The Boston Globe* 12/20/2006. © 2005, 2006 *The Boston Globe*. Reprinted by permission.

Robert Christgau. "The Informer" [John Leonard], from the *Village Voice* 7/20/1999; "Growing by Degrees" [Kanye West], from the *Village Voice* 9/13/2005. © 1999, 2005 *Village Voice*. Reprinted by permission.

Lisa Cohen. Excerpt from *After Etan*. © 2009 Grand Central Publishing. Reprinted by permission.

Roger Cohen. Excerpt from "The End of the End of the Revolution," from *The New York Times* 12/5/2008. © 2008 *The New York Times*. Reprinted by permission.

Juanita Darling. "A Hostage Crisis Hits Latin America," from the *Los Angeles Times* 4/19/1998. © 1998 *Los Angeles Times*. Reprinted by permission.

Barbara Demick. "In Albania, a Girl Who Became a Man," from *The Philadelphia Inquirer* 7/1/1996. © 1996 *The Philadelphia Inquirer*. Reprinted by permission. "No Stars, No Swag, but What a Crowd!" from the *Los Angeles Times* 10/11/2008. © 2008 *Los Angeles Times*. Reprinted by permission.

Michael Dobbs. Excerpt from *Saboteurs: The Nazi Raid on America*, published by Alfred A. Knopf, 2004. © 2004 Michael Dobbs. Used by permission of Alfred A. Knopf, a division of Random House, Inc.

Craig Duff. Excerpt from the script for the documentary *Arctic Rush*, aired in 2005 and 2006 by the Discovery Times Channel and the Canadian Broadcasting Corporation. Produced, directed, and written by Craig Duff, with *New York Times* reporters Andrew C. Revkin, Steven Lee Myers, Simon Romero and Clifford Krauss. Editor: Tom Swartwout; Executive Producer: Ann Derry; Executive Director of Radio and Television: Laurie Miffin; Executive in Charge: Michael Oreskes. For the CBC Documentary Unit: Research by Griffin Ondaatje and Robert Scott; Executive Producer: Susan Dando; Area Executive Producers: Diana Sperrazza and Mark Starowicz; Associate Producer: Stacy Atlas; Vice President of Production and Development: Bill Smee; Executive in Charge of Production: Vivian Schiller. Produced by Discovery Productions Services, LLC for Discovery Times Channel and CBC. Used by permission.

Michael Duffy. "Jerry Brown Still Wants Your Vote," from *Time* 5/21/2006. © 2006 Time Inc. Reprinted by permission.

Jim Dwyer. "A Nation Challenged: Objects; Fighting for Life 50 Floors Up, with One Tool and Ingenuity," from *The New York Times* 10/9/2001; "Old Hands on the River Didn't Have to Be Told What to Do," from *The New York Times* 1/16/2009. © 2001 *The New York Times*. Reprinted by permission.

Richard Eder. "Books of the Times; a Writer, a Muse, their Laundry," [review of *Diary of a Bad Year*, by J. M. Coetzee] from *The New York Times* 1/1/2008; "Books of the Times; Beowulf and Fate meet in a Modern Poet's Lens" [review of *Beowulf*, translated by Seamus Heaney], from *The New York Times* 2/22/2000. © 2000, 2008 *The New York Times*. Reprinted by permission.

Juliet Eilperin. Excerpt from "Ice Accommodations," *The Washington Post* 2/24/2008. © 2008 *The Washington Post*. Reprinted by permission.

Mark Feeney. "Shooting War," from *The Boston Globe* 4/13/2003. © 2003 *The Boston Globe*. Reprinted by permission.

Marc Fisher. Edited excerpt of *Something in the Air: Radio, Rock, and the Revolution That Shaped a Generation*, published by Random House, 2007. © 2007 Marc Fisher. Reprinted by permission.

Gilbert Gaul. "Players Gamble on Honesty, Security of Internet Betting," from *The Washington Post* 11/30/2008. © 2008 *The Washington Post*. Reprinted by permission.

Barton Gellman. Excerpt from "A Battalion of One's Own," *The Washington Post* 7/24/1994. © 1994 *The Washington Post*. Reprinted by permission.

Jeff Gerth, with coauthor Don Van Natta Jr. Edited excerpt of *Her Way: The Hopes and Ambitions of Hillary Rodham Clinton*, published by Little, Brown & Company, 2007. © 2007 Jeff Gerth and Don Van Natta Jr. Reprinted by permission.

Nancy Gibbs. "If You Want to Humble an Empire," from *Time* 9/14/2001. © 2001 Time Inc. Reprinted by permission.

Peter Godwin. Excerpt from *When a Crocodile Eats the Sun*, published by Little, Brown & Company, 2007. © 2007 Peter Godwin. Reprinted with permission of Little, Brown and Company and Pan MacMillan, London.

Martin Gottlieb. "Pop Music; the Durability of Doo-Wop," from *The New York Times* 1/17/1993; "Ideas and Trends; On the White Side of Crossover Dreams," from *The New York Times* 2/14/1993. © 1993 *The New York Times*. Reprinted by permission.

Daniel A. Grech. "Believing Principal Leads Battle to Save a School," from *Miami Herald* 2/23/2003; "Edison's Big Loss," from *Miami Herald* 3/10/2003. © 2003 Miami Herald Media Company. Reprinted by permission.

Pippa Green. Edited excerpt from *Choice, not Fate: The Life and Times of Trevor Manuel*, published by Penguin, 2008. © 2008 Pippa Green. Reprinted by permission.

James Grimaldi. "Baby's First Helmet. As More Infants Get Misshapen Heads, Parents Grapple With Questions, Headgear," from *The Washington Post* 3/8/2005. © 2005 *The Washington Post*. Reprinted by permission.

Roy Gutman. "Bosnia's Elite 'Disappeared,'" from *Newsweek* 11/8/1992. © 1992 *Newsweek*. Reprinted by permission.

Chris Hedges. Excerpts from "A Gaza Diary," from *Harper's Magazine*. © 2001 *Harper's Magazine*. Reproduced from the October issue by special permission.

Margo Jefferson. "Ella in Wonderland," from *The New York Times* 12/29/1996; "On Writers and Writing; D. H. Lawrence Frees the Slaves," from *The New York Times* 1/19/2003. © 1996, 2003 *The New York Times*. Reprinted by permission.

Julia Keller. "The Lure of the Frozen Lake," from the *Chicago Tribune* 3/13/2003. © 2003 *Chicago Tribune*. Reprinted by permission.

Elizabeth Kendall. "A Backward Glance," originally published in *Vogue* April 2008. © 2008 Elizabeth Kendall. Reprinted by permission.

Kathy Kiely. "Children Caught in the Immigration Crossfire," from *USA Today* 10/8/2007. © 2007 *USA Today*. Reprinted by permission.

Athelia Knight. "Environment Fosters Mediocrity" [McKinley High School], from *The Washington Post* 9/13/1987. © 1987 *The Washington Post*. Reprinted by permission.

Daoud Kuttab. "The West and the Arab World: The Case of Media," from *Al Hayat* 11/21/2004. © 2004 *Al Hayat* Newspaper. Reprinted by permission.

Charles Lane. "A View to a Kill," from *Foreign Policy* #148, May/June 2005. © 2005 *Foreign Policy*. Reprinted in entirety with permission.

Mitchel Levitas. "The Renaissance of the Marais," from *The New York Times* 11/26/1995. © 1995 *The New York Times*. Reprinted by permission.

Charles Lewis. "Seeking Ways to Nurture the Capacity to Report," from *Nieman Reports*. © 2008 *Nieman Reports*. Courtesy of *Nieman Reports*.

Emilie Lounsberry. "Arson Science—To Their Rescue?" from *The Philadelphia Inquirer* 1/14/2007. © 2007 *The Philadelphia Inquirer*. Reprinted by permission.

Peter Maass. Excerpt from *Love Thy Neighbor*, published by Alfred A. Knopf, 1996. © 1996 Peter Maass. Used by permission of Alfred A. Knopf, a division of Random House, Inc.

David Maraniss. Excerpt from *They Marched into Sunlight: War and Peace, Vietnam and America, October 1967*, published by Simon and Schuster, 2003. © David Maraniss. Reprinted by permission.

Greil Marcus. "The Fourth of July," from *Salon* 7/4/2006. Originally the commencement address for American Studies, Religious Studies, Cognitive Science, Mass Communications, and Interdisciplinary Studies at the University of California at Berkeley on May 19, 2006. Reprinted by permission.

Jane Mayer. Excerpt from *The Dark Side: The Inside Story of How the War on Terror Turned into a War on American Ideals*, published by Doubleday, 2008. © 2008 Jane Mayer. Reprinted by permission.

Melvin McCray. "The Two Lives of John Favors," from *Princeton Alumni Weekly* 2/3/1983. © 1983 Melvin McCray. Reprinted by permission.

John McPhee. Title piece of *Silk Parachute*, Farrar, Straus, and Giroux, 2010. Reprinted by permission.

Martha Mendoza. "Between a Woman and Her Doctor," from *Ms. Magazine*, Summer 2004. © 2004 *Ms. Magazine*. Reprinted by permission.

Kay Mills. Excerpt from *This Little Light of Mine: The Life of Fannie Lou Hamer*, published by the University of Kentucky Press, 2007. © 2007 Kay Mills. Reprinted by permission.

Bob Mondello. "Title Inflation: How Hollywood Watches Our Wallets," aired on NPR's *All Things Considered* 1/16/2009. © 2009 NPR. Used with permission.

Geraldine Moriba Meadows. Edited transcript of the documentary *A Father's Promise*, premiered on NBC News *Dateline* 2/8/2009. © 2009 NBC News. Used with permission.

Claudia Roth Pierpont. Excerpt from the "The Prince," published in the *New Yorker* 9/15/2008. © 2008 Claudia Pierpont. Reprinted by permission.

T. R. Reid. Excerpt from *Confucius Lives Next Door*, published by Vintage Books, 2000. © 2000 T. R. Reid. Used with permission.

Elizabeth Rosenthal. "Stinging Tentacles Offer Hint of Oceans' Decline," from *The New York Times* 8/3/2008. © 2008 *The New York Times*. Reprinted by permission.

Alex Ross. "The Sonata Seminar," from *The New Yorker* 4/19/2004. © 2004 Alex Ross. Reprinted by permission.

Roberta Oster Sachs. "Role Model: Sarah McLendon," from the *Columbia Journalism Review* May/June 2003. © 2003 CJR. Reprinted by permission. "Remembering a Friend: Ed Bradley Was a Gift to Journalism," from the *Richmond Times-Dispatch* 11/11/2006. © 2006 *Richmond Times-Dispatch*. Reprinted by permission.

Paul Salopek. "In Horses, a Personal Refuge," Letter from Pec, Kosovo, 6/25/1999; "Hints of Lives are All that Remains," Letter from the Shomali Plain, Afghanistan, 12/4/2001; "Now They Execute Polite Shuffles: There's a Strange Sameness in the Stories of Baath Party Members in Iraq," Letter from Mosul, Iraq, 4/15/2003; "In Land of Ruin, a House of Stone Shelters Delight," Letter from Luanda, Angola, 3/26/2004. All from the *Chicago Tribune*. © 1999, 2001, 2003, 2004 *Chicago Tribune*. Reprinted by permission.

Serge Schmemann. Excerpt from *When the Wall Came Down: The Berlin Wall and the Fall of Soviet Communism*, published as a New York Times book by Kingfisher, 2006. © 2006 *The New York Times*. Used by permission.

John Seabrook. "My Father's Closet," from *The New Yorker* 3/16/1998. © 1998 John Seabrook. Reprinted by permission.

Calvin Sims. "Oshima Journal; After 90 Years, Small Gestures of Joy for Lepers," from *The New York Times* 7/5/2001; "Stone Age Ways Barely Surviving," from *The New York Times* 3/11/2001. © 2001 *The New York Times*. Reprinted by permission.

Deborah Sontag. "Injured in Iraq, A Soldier Is Shattered at Home," from *The New York Times* 4/5/2007. © 2007 *The New York Times*. Reprinted by permission.

Paula Span. "A Moving Experience," from *The Washington Post* 9/25/2005. © 2005 *The Washington Post*. Reprinted by permission.

Joel Stein. "The Lessons of Cain," from *Time* 7/10/2000; "Millions of Women Weep," from *Time* 8/6/2001. © 2000, 2001 Time Inc. Reprinted by permission. "Don't E-mail Me," from the *Los Angeles Times* 1/2/2007. © 2007 *Los Angeles Times*. Reprinted by permission.

Rose Tang. Excerpt from a memoir manuscript *Tiananmen Massacre*. Published by permission of the author.

Evan Thomas. "Baby Jessica Grows Up," from *Newsweek* 10//27/1997; "History: How American Myths Are Made," from *Newsweek* 8/7/2006. © 1997, 2006 *Newsweek*. Reprinted by permission.

Marilyn Thompson. Excerpt from *The Killer Strain: Anthrax and a Government Exposed*, published by HarperCollins, 2003. © 2003 Marilyn Thompson. Reprinted by permission.

Michael Vitez. "True Love is Made of This," from *The Philadelphia Inquirer* 2/13/1998; "The Greatest Penn Success Story," from *The Philadelphia Inquirer* 3/19/2000. © 1998, 2000 *The Philadelphia Inquirer*. Reprinted by permission.

Thomas E. Weber. "The X-Files: For Those Who Scoff at Internet Commerce, Here's a Hot Market," from *The Wall Street Journal* 5/20/1997. © 1997 Dow Jones and Company, Inc. Reprinted by permission.

Alexander Wolff. "When the Terror Began," from *Sports Illustrated* 8/26/2002. © 2002 *Sports Illustrated*. Reprinted by permission.

Christopher Wren. Excerpt from *Walking to Vermont,* published by Simon and Schuster, 2004. © 2004 Christopher Wren. Used by permission.

INDEX